VOYAGES

IN ENGLISH

Writing and Grammar

Elaine de Chantal Brookes

Patricia Healey

Irene Kervick

Catherine Irene Masino

Anne B. McGuire

Adrienne Saybolt

LOYOLAPRESS.

Grateful acknowledgment is given to authors, publishers, photographers, museums, and agents for permission to reprint the following copyrighted material. Every effort has been made to determine copyright owners. In the case of any omissions, the publisher will be pleased to make suitable acknowledgments in future editions. Continued on page 536.

Cover Design/Production: Loyola Press, Steve Curtis Design, Inc.
Cover Illustration: Jeff Parks
Interior Design/Production: Think Design Group, Loyola Press

ISBN: 0-8294-2100-9

Manufactured in the United States of America.

LOYOLAPRESS.
3441 N. ASHLAND AVENUE
CHICAGO, ILLINOIS 60657
(800) 621-1008
www.LoyolaPress.org

05 06 07 08 09 10 11 12 13 14 VH 10 9 8 7 6 5 4 3 2 1

CONTENTS

PART 1

Written and Oral Communication

CHAPTER 1 **Personal Narratives**   **6**

Lesson 1   What Makes a Good Personal Narrative?   8
Lesson 2   Introduction, Body, and Conclusion   12
Lesson 3   *Writing Skills:* Sentence Variety   16
Lesson 4   *Study Skills:* Thesaurus   20
Lesson 5   *Word Study:* Exact Words   24
Lesson 6   *Speaking and Listening Skills:*   28
            Oral Personal Narratives
            Personal Narrative Writer's Workshop   **32**

CHAPTER 2 **How-to Articles**   **44**

Lesson 1   What Makes a Good How-to Article?   46
Lesson 2   Order, Accuracy, and Completeness   50
Lesson 3   *Writing Skills:* Transition Words   54
Lesson 4   *Word Study:* Synonyms   58
Lesson 5   *Study Skills:* Using the Internet   62
Lesson 6   *Speaking and Listening Skills:* How-to Talks   66
            How-to Article Writer's Workshop   **70**

CHAPTER 3   **Business Letters**   **82**

Lesson 1	What Makes a Good Business Letter?	84
Lesson 2	Purpose	88
Lesson 3	*Word Study:* Roots	92
Lesson 4	*Writing Skills:* Combining Sentences and Sentence Parts	96
Lesson 5	*Life Skills:* Filling Out Forms	100
Lesson 6	*Speaking and Listening Skills:* Business Telephone Calls	104
	Business Letter Writer's Workshop	**108**

CHAPTER 4   **Descriptions**   **120**

Lesson 1	What Makes a Good Description?	122
Lesson 2	Ordering a Description	126
Lesson 3	*Writing Skills:* Graphic Organizers	130
Lesson 4	*Word Study:* Suffixes	134
Lesson 5	*Study Skills:* Dictionary	138
Lesson 6	*Speaking and Listening Skills:* Oral Descriptions	142
	Description Writer's Workshop	**146**

CHAPTER 5   **Book Reports**   **158**

Lesson 1	What Makes a Good Book Report?	160
Lesson 2	Writing a Book Report	164
Lesson 3	*Writing Skills:* Revising Sentences	168
Lesson 4	*Word Study:* Prefixes	172
Lesson 5	*Study Skills:* Fact and Opinion	176
Lesson 6	*Speaking and Listening Skills:* Oral Book Reports	180
	Book Report Writer's Workshop	**184**

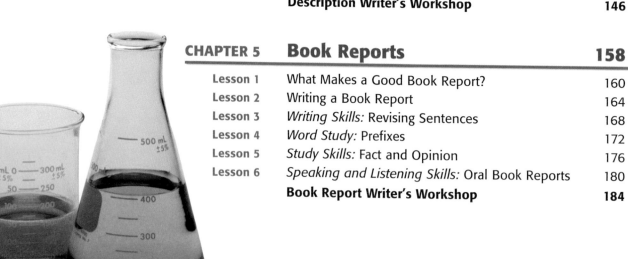

CHAPTER 6   **Creative Writing**   **196**

Lesson 1   What Makes a Good Tall Tale?   198
Lesson 2   Writing a Tall Tale   202
Lesson 3   *Writing Skills:* Figurative Language   206
Lesson 4   *Word Study:* Homophones   210
Lesson 5   *Poetry:* Nonsense Verse   214
Lesson 6   *Speaking and Listening Skills:* Storytellers' Contests   218
             Tall Tale Writer's Workshop   **222**

CHAPTER 7   **Persuasive Writing**   **234**

Lesson 1   What Makes Good Persuasive Writing?   236
Lesson 2   Writing a Persuasive Article   240
Lesson 3   *Writing Skills:* Expanding Sentences   244
Lesson 4   *Word Study:* Antonyms   248
Lesson 5   *Study Skills:* Library   252
Lesson 6   *Speaking and Listening Skills:* Persuasive Speaking   256
             Persuasive Writing Writer's Workshop   **260**

CHAPTER 8   **Research Reports**   **272**

Lesson 1   What Makes a Good Research Report?   274
Lesson 2   Gathering and Organizing Information   278
Lesson 3   *Writing Skills:* Outlines   282
Lesson 4   *Word Study:* Compound Words   286
Lesson 5   *Study Skills:* Library Reference Materials   290
Lesson 6   *Speaking and Listening Skills:*   294
             Oral Research Reports
             Research Report Writer's Workshop   **298**

PART

Grammar

SECTION 1	**Nouns**	**313**
1.1	Common Nouns and Proper Nouns	314
1.2	Singular Nouns and Plural Nouns	316
1.3	More Singular Nouns and Plural Nouns	318
1.4	Possessive Nouns	320
1.5	Collective Nouns, Count and Noncount Nouns	322
1.6	Nouns as Subjects and Subject Complements	324
1.7	Nouns as Objects	326
1.8	Nouns as Indirect Objects	328
1.9	Nouns in Direct Address	330
1.10	Words Used as Nouns or as Verbs	332
1.11	Words Used as Nouns or as Adjectives	334
	Noun Challenge	**336**

SECTION 2	**Pronouns**	**337**
2.1	Singular Pronouns and Plural Pronouns	338
2.2	Personal Pronouns	340
2.3	Subject Pronouns	342
2.4	Object Pronouns	344
2.5	Indirect Objects	346
2.6	Uses of Pronouns	348
2.7	Possessives	350
2.8	Intensive Pronouns, Reflexive Pronouns	352
2.9	Antecedents	354
2.10	Pronouns and Contractions	356
2.11	Demonstrative Pronouns, Interrogative Pronouns	358
	Pronoun Challenge	**360**

SECTION 3	**Adjectives**	**361**
3.1	Descriptive Adjectives	362
3.2	Proper Adjectives	364
3.3	Articles	366
3.4	Repetition of Articles	368
3.5	Demonstrative Adjectives	370
3.6	Adjectives That Tell How Many	372
3.7	Subject Complements	374
3.8	Adjectives That Compare	376
3.9	*More, Most* and *Less, Least*	378
3.10	*Fewer, Fewest* and *Less, Least*	380
3.11	Interrogative Adjectives	382
	Adjective Challenge	**384**

SECTION 4	**Verbs**	**385**
4.1	Action Verbs and Being Verbs	386
4.2	Verb Phrases	388
4.3	Principal Parts of Verbs	390
4.4	Irregular Verbs	392
4.5	More Irregular Verbs	394
4.6	Simple Tenses	396
4.7	Progressive Tenses	398
4.8	Present Perfect Tense	400
4.9	Past Perfect Tense	402
4.10	Future Perfect Tense	404
4.11	Linking Verbs	406
	Verb Challenge	**408**

SECTION 5   **Adverbs**   **409**

5.1   Adverbs of Time, Place, and Manner   410
5.2   Adverbs That Compare   412
5.3   Troublesome Words, Negative Words   414
5.4   *There Is* and *There Are*   416
5.5   Adverb Clauses   418
       Adverb Challenge   **420**

SECTION 6   **Prepositions, Conjunctions,**
                 and Interjections   **421**

6.1   Prepositions and Their Objects   422
6.2   Prepositional Phrases as Adjectives   424
6.3   Prepositional Phrases as Adverbs   426
6.4   Coordinating Conjunctions   428
6.5   Subordinate Conjunctions   430
6.6   Interjections   432
       Section 6 Challenge   **434**

SECTION 7   **Sentences**   **435**

7.1   Kinds of Sentences   436
7.2   Simple Subjects and Simple Predicates   438
7.3   Complete Subjects and Complete Predicates   440
7.4   Direct Objects and Indirect Objects   442
7.5   Subject Complements   444
7.6   Sentence Order   446
7.7   Compound Subjects and Compound Predicates   448
7.8   Compound Direct Objects   450
7.9   Compound Subject Complements   452
7.10   Compound Sentences   454
7.11   Complex Sentences   456
       Sentence Challenge   **458**

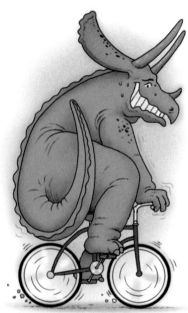

SECTION 8	**Punctuation and Capitalization**	**459**
8.1	End Punctuation	460
8.2	Commas in Series	462
8.3	Commas with Conjunctions	464
8.4	Direct Address and *Yes* and *No*	466
8.5	Apostrophes	468
8.6	Capital Letters	470
8.7	Titles	472
8.8	Other Uses of Capital Letters	474
8.9	Abbreviations	476
8.10	Direct Quotations	478
8.11	Addresses and Letters	480
	Section 8 Challenge	**482**

SECTION 9	**Diagramming**	**483**
9.1	Subjects, Predicates, Direct Objects, Modifiers	484
9.2	Indirect Objects	486
9.3	Subject Complements	488
9.4	Prepositional Phrases	490
9.5	Interjections	492
9.6	Compound Subjects and Compound Predicates	494
9.7	Compound Direct Objects and Indirect Objects	496
9.8	Compound Subject Complements	498
9.9	Compound Sentences	500
9.10	Adverb Clauses	502
9.11	Diagramming Review	504
	Diagramming Challenge	**506**

	Grammar Handbook	**507**

	Index	**529**

What do all of these

people have in common?

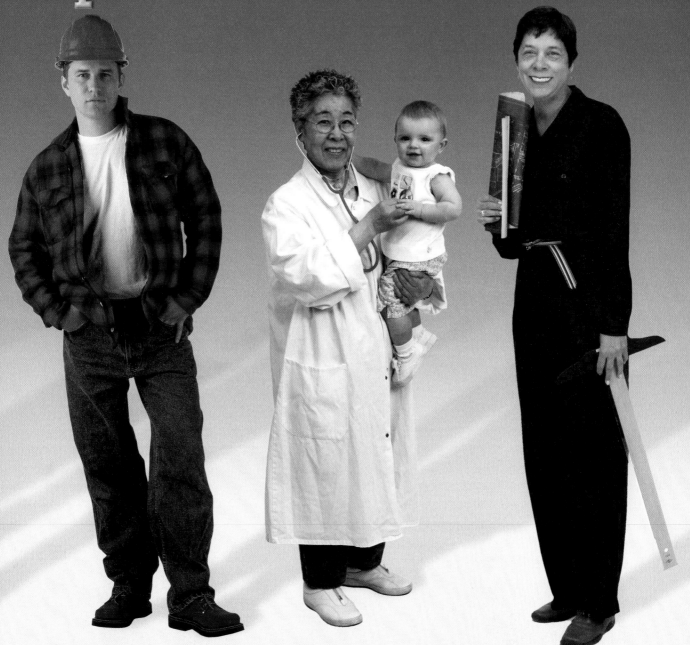

They all use writing in their jobs.

How do you think that writing helps them in their everyday lives?

Written and Oral Communication

CHAPTER 1

Christopher Columbus set sail from Palos, Spain, on August 3, 1492, and a few months later landed in the Caribbean. He believed that he had found a new trade route to the Far East. Columbus was probably not the first European visitor to the Americas. However, his voyage is considered important because it led to trade between the old world and the new. Do you know what valuable goods the Americas had to trade with Europe at that time?

Personal Narratives

Knight of the Road

Last year my family took a trip to the Grand Canyon, but we never reached it. What we saw instead was a lot of water. And while our van didn't survive the trip, we did make a new friend along the way.

The trip started smoothly. It wasn't until we reached the Mississippi River that we ran into trouble. I could see thunderheads gathering over the horizon and heard the low rumbling of thunder in the distance. Rain began to fall. At first the drops hit the van unevenly, then all at once we were in a raging storm. It was like driving through Niagara Falls.

Suddenly we came to a place in the highway where water had gathered in a pool. Dad couldn't see how deep it was, but it quickly became very deep. The van fishtailed and spun around. I grabbed the handle above the side door. My sister Jenny saw something outside her window, and her eyes grew as big as saucers. I looked in her direction and saw it too. It was an 18-wheel truck, and it looked like it was bearing down on us. Luckily the truck had stopped at the edge of the pool of water. I could see the driver climb out of the cab.

He ran to our van, carrying a flashlight. When he reached us, he told us to come with him. Dad told us to pick up our stuff, and we quickly got out. Just as we cleared the van, it started moving. We stood in the rain and watched it float away. The driver said he was sorry about our van. Then he offered to let us sit in the cab of his trailer while we waited for the state police to arrive.

Mom and Dad looked sad because we lost our van, but when they saw how much fun Jenny and I were having talking to other truckers on the driver's CB radio, broad smiles broke out on their faces. That's when I learned that real vacations are not about where you go, but how you get there and who you have along for the ride.

Personal Narratives

What Makes a Good Personal Narrative?

A personal narrative tells a story about something that happened to the writer. You can see personal narratives in many kinds of writing. It can be an e-mail from a friend or a personal letter to a relative.

Here are some ideas to remember when you write a personal narrative.

I walked through bushes to find my cat.

Point of View

Personal narratives are told from the writer's point of view. This is the first-person point of view. When you write a personal narrative, use words such as *I, me, my, our,* and *we* to tell the story.

Topic

The topic of a personal narrative is an experience that actually happened to you. When you select a topic, choose something that has some special meaning for you. Think of times that you have learned something important. Good personal narratives use the experience to show something that readers can think about.

Details

A good personal narrative has many details that paint in the reader's mind a clear picture of what happened. Descriptive details make events in personal narratives more real to the reader. However, not all details are needed. Unnecessary details can slow down a reader and become distracting.

Activity A

Which idea in each pair is a good idea for a personal narrative? Explain why you chose each one.

1. **a.** how scuba equipment works
   b. how I learned to swim

2. **a.** the turtle in my garden
   b. the life cycle of the giant sea turtle

3. **a.** the history of candy
   b. the first time I made fudge

4. **a.** why I always wear a hat
   b. hats from around the world

5. **a.** the rules of baseball
   b. my trip to the Baseball Hall of Fame

Activity B

The personal narrative below contains two sentences that are not necessary. Which sentences do not belong?

My clown act was funnier than I had planned. I had practiced for days until I could balance a red ball on my nose. I borrowed the ball from my cousin Jake. But when I began to perform, I sneezed and dropped the ball. I often catch colds in the summer. I picked it up quickly and balanced it. Afterward, my family said I was so good that I was almost ready to join the circus.

Writer's Corner

Brainstorm a list of five possible topics for a personal narrative. Some topics could be the time you first met a friend, an adventure while traveling, or an embarrassing moment. Save your list.

Audience

The kind of information and language you include in your writing will depend on your audience. For example, if you are writing a personal narrative about your family to be read by your teacher, you might tell who your brothers or sisters are.

The writer of the personal narrative on page 7 tells the reader in the third paragraph that his sister's name is Jenny. When Jenny's name is mentioned in the last paragraph, the reader knows who Jenny is.

Some details could be unnecessary if the reader knows the people in the personal narrative. For example, if the reader was the writer's grandmother, do you think the writer would need to tell that Jenny is his sister?

Voice

The voice, or tone, of a personal narrative tells the reader how the writer feels about what happened. The voice of a personal narrative also tells a little about the writer's personality. Just as when listening to a person speak, readers can often "hear" the writer's voice. A writer makes the voice clear by choosing certain adjectives and adverbs.

• Activity C •

The following sentence pairs are from personal narratives about a science fair. Each sentence in a pair is written for a different audience—a teacher or a friend. Tell which sentence was written for each audience.

1. **a.** You know how I am always trying to invent stuff?

   b. Because you encouraged my interest in science, I wanted to tell you what I invented.

2. **a.** I invented a machine that a dog can use to knock on a door.

   b. I figured out how to make a cool doggy doorknocker.

3. **a.** I entered it in the Palos Park science fair, and I won first prize!

   b. Your buddy's invention won first prize in our science fair.

4. **a.** You can buy me a pizza when I see you next weekend.

   b. Thanks again for all you taught me.

Activity D

Each example below describes the same event, but each uses a different voice. Read each example. Then answer the questions.

Example 1

Last night I saw the world's most popular rock band, Jelly, perform at the Horse Castle. Fans jammed the entrances and the aisles, but I managed to get a seat. For the first two hours, the performers delighted us with their classic songs. After intermission the high-spirited Jelly pulled out all the stops. Under the flashing lights, the performers stunned us with hits from their recent albums. We lingered long afterwards just to recover from hours of thrills and excitement.

Example 2

Last night's concert by Jelly was fantastic! There were thousands of people there. In fact there were so many that there were not enough seats for everyone. I could see people jammed in the aisles. I couldn't figure out why anybody needed a seat anyway. Jelly had everybody hopping along from the moment they started playing. For the first two hours of the concert, there was a light show that was beyond belief. Red and green laser lights waved over the crowd and pulsed in time with the beat. That concert was one of the coolest times I've ever had.

1. Which example uses a serious voice?

2. Which example uses an excited voice?

3. What words and phrases from the serious example lead you to think the voice is serious?

4. What words and phrases from the excited piece lead you to think the writer was excited about the concert?

Writer's Corner

Free write about what happened when you woke up this morning. Write the events in the first-person point of view and include necessary details.

Introduction, Body, and Conclusion

Our Wide Wide World

Spanish explorer Hernando de Soto explored what is now the southeastern United States in search of gold. His search took him as far west as the Mississippi River. De Soto and his men fought with many of the Native American tribes they met along the way.

Like most writing, personal narratives have parts that can be easily identified. The introduction, body, and conclusion are the parts of a personal narrative.

Introduction

The introduction of a personal narrative should grab the reader's attention. It should make the reader want more. The introduction should tell the reader the topic of the personal narrative. It should also lead the reader into the body of the narrative.

Body

The body is the main part of a personal narrative. It has details that let the reader see, smell, hear, feel, and taste what the writer experienced. It includes all the details that are important to the story. It does not include unnecessary details.

Every sentence in the body should keep the story going in time order from one event to the next.

Conclusion

The conclusion of a personal narrative is where the writer closes the story. The writer can use the conclusion to sum up ideas, comment on what the story means, or share what he or she may have learned.

• Activity A •

Which sentence in each pair makes a better introduction for a personal narrative? Explain why you think so.

1. **a.** My older sister painted my face.

   b. Having your face painted can turn your day around.

2. **a.** I'll never forget what happened at the Metropolitan Museum.

   b. One day my family went to the Metropolitan Museum.

3. **a.** I like to play computer games.

   b. Once, for a whole week, I was computer-game champion of my neighborhood.

4. **a.** My father and I often go fishing together.

   b. My father is usually a calm guy, but on one recent fishing trip I saw him get really excited.

5. **a.** The house next door burned down last night.

   b. I was almost asleep last night when the fire engines screamed around the corner.

• Activity B •

Write a conclusion for this personal narrative.

What a Fish Story!

I usually hate fishing because I never catch anything, but last Saturday was different.

I rowed out to the middle of the lake with my cousin, who loves fishing and who always catches a lot of fish. I baited my hook and cast it into the water. Almost immediately I felt a tug on the line. I reeled in the biggest fish I'd ever seen! Ten minutes later, I landed another huge fish! By the end of the day, I'd caught 17 beauties. And my cousin? Well, she didn't catch a thing.

Writer's Corner

Choose a topic from the list you brainstormed for the Writer's Corner on page 9. Write an introduction for it. Be sure to write each sentence so that your audience wants to read more about your topic.

Time Order

In a personal narrative, events should be in the order that they happened. When you remember an experience for a personal narrative, take time to think about everything that happened. Writing about an experience in time order can help the reader understand what happened and why things happened.

Sometimes it's helpful to free write about an experience so that you can remember all the details about it. When you free write about something, write down everything you can remember. Later you can put the events together in the order that they happened.

Writers use transition words, such as *then, yesterday, first, last,* and *next,* to show how events are connected.

Activity C

Read the personal narratives below. Find the transition words. Then choose the best introduction from the list that follows each personal narrative. Explain your choice.

1. _____ I had never ice skated before last weekend, but my sister insisted that I try. I put on a pair of her old skates and hobbled over to the rink. At first I held my sister's hand. Then I took a small step on my own. My ankles wobbled, my feet slid, and I fell flat on the cold, hard ice! I spent most of the afternoon "practicing" how to fall. But I finally made it all the way around the rink in an upright position. Next week I may try doing a spin!
 a. It was a very cold day.
 b. Learning a new skill often has its ups and downs.
 c. I love ice skating.

2. _____ Yesterday I noticed that my grandmother was wearing an unusual ring. It looked very old and had a large black stone. I couldn't help wondering what mysterious stories the ring might tell. First I thought it had been handed down to her by an ancestor. Then I imagined it had been part of a pirate's treasure. It might even grant a wish! My grandmother laughed when she told me she'd bought the ring on sale at the mall last week!
 a. I've always loved antique jewelry.
 b. I like spending time with my family.
 c. Sometimes I let my imagination run away with me.

Activity D

In the personal narrative below, the events are not in time order. Rewrite the narrative, putting the sentences in correct time order.

Underground Travel

Every day when I get out of school, I walk to the train station. My train rattles into the station and squeals to a halt. At the end of the line, I jump out of the train, go up the stairs into the daylight, and walk home. While waiting on the train platform, I hear the roar and feel the rumble of approaching trains. There are seven stops before mine, and I count each one as we pass. Moving with the crowd, I squeeze through the doors and sit down.

Activity E

Leeann wrote these notes about her first time babysitting her sister Rayna. Write the notes as a personal narrative, using transition words. Add an introduction and a conclusion to the story.

- Rayna started crying when Mom left.
- It took forever to get her into her high chair.
- I had to fight to put her bib on.
- She spilled her food on the floor.
- I gave up trying to feed her and decided to let her play.
- She started grabbing the cat's tail.
- She tried to eat the TV remote.
- She looked up at me and said, "I'm hungry."

Writer's Corner

Think about what you did last weekend. Write in paragraph form to describe what happened. Use time order. Save your work.

Writing Skills

Sentence Variety

Writing different kinds of sentences will make your writing more interesting. When all of the sentences are the same kind, readers might become bored. To add variety to your writing, you can do these things.

- Change a sentence to a question.
- Change a sentence to an exclamation.
- Change the order of the words in a sentence.

Read each set of sentences below. Think about how sentence A has been changed to make sentence B.

Set 1
A. I always wanted to go white-water rafting.
B. Have you ever wanted to go white-water rafting?

Set 2
A. Gliding swiftly down the river was exciting.
B. How exciting it was to glide swiftly down the river!

Set 3
A. We hit some rapids suddenly and the raft spun around.
B. Suddenly we hit some rapids and the raft spun around.

In Set 1, sentence A was changed to a question. Questions invite readers to think about what they're reading. By asking a question, writers can get readers to start thinking.

In Set 2, sentence A is changed to an exclamation. An occasional exclamation helps readers share the enthusiasm and excitement of the writer. But be careful with exclamations and questions. Too many exclamations and questions can lose their effect and make your writing repetitive.

In Set 3, the word order of the sentence was changed. The word *suddenly* was moved to the beginning of the sentence to add variety. Changing the order of words in a sentence can shift the emphasis of a sentence. The change in Set 3 makes the event seem more urgent.

Our Wide Wide World

While historians dispute the exact date of its founding, most agree that Santa Fe, New Mexico, is America's second oldest European settlement. The city has been a seat of government for Spain, Mexico, the American Confederacy, and the United States. A Spanish celebration, "La Toma," which took place near Santa Fe, is now cited by some as America's first Thanksgiving.

Activity A

Rewrite each sentence, first as a question and then as an exclamation. You may change or add any words to make the sentences more interesting.

1. I was surprised to see a pizza with corn flakes on it.
2. On Saturday I saw my first rodeo.
3. Visiting the Statue of Liberty was very cool.
3. Everything seemed to go wrong this morning.
4. It took me many tries to jump that distance.
5. It's a long drive to Emma's house.
6. Eric didn't believe me when I told him about my beanbag collection.
7. Training a dog can be very difficult.
8. The first time I babysat was a disaster.
9. I'd always wanted to learn to ride a horse.
10. Life on a farm can be fun.

Writer's Corner

Rewrite the narrative you wrote for the Writer's Corner on page 15. Add variety to the piece by using questions or exclamations. You might also change the order of the words in some sentences. Do your revisions improve your paragraph?

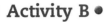

• Activity B •

Rewrite each sentence by moving the words in italics to a new position in the sentence. You may change or add any words to make the sentences more interesting.

1. I awoke *as the cuckoo clock began to strike.*

2. Black smoke poured out *when I opened the oven door.*

3. Everyone looked up *when I walked into the library with my squeaky shoes.*

4. We met Charlie and Doug *on the way to the costume party.*

5. Our backyard looked like an ice palace *after the winter storm.*

6. It was getting dark *when I realized I had taken the wrong road.*

7. I finally succeeded *after many attempts at twirling spaghetti on a fork.*

8. The telephone rang *just as we were going out the door.*

9. A big yellow snowplow rumbled down the street *just in time.*

10. We went to the Brooklyn Children's Museum *while we were in New York.*

• Activity C •

The sentences in each of the following paragraphs lack variety. Change the sentences to make the paragraphs more interesting. Try not to change the meanings of the paragraphs.

1. Jogging is not my idea of fun exercise. Running for the sake of running bores me to tears. Playing tennis is more exciting to me. Chasing after that fuzzy little ball wears me out, but at least I'm enjoying myself. Learning to play, however, was not as easy as I first thought it would be.

2. How kind she is, I thought, to share her umbrella with me! If only I had known what she had in mind! Collecting signatures for a petition is no fun! What a wasted afternoon! I would rather have gotten drenched! Imagine how you would feel if you spent your holiday like I spent mine!

3. Have you ever flown down a snowy hillside on a toboggan? Can you imagine screaming with three friends on a narrow wooden board as it skims downward at nearly 40 miles per hour? Who wouldn't feel her heart race as the wind lashes against her face? Would you like to know how I first got involved in this thrilling sport?

Activity D

This is the first paragraph of a personal narrative. It could be improved by varying the sentences. Rewrite the paragraph by following these directions.

1. Add a question to the beginning of the narrative.

2. Change the word order in two of the sentences.

3. End the paragraph with an exclamation.

You may change or add words to make the sentences more interesting.

Taking Off

My first plane trip was very exciting. The engines roared and the plane vibrated as it prepared for takeoff. The ground seemed to rush by as the plane sped down the runway. It was a thrilling moment when the plane rose from the ground.

Writer's Corner

Choose an article from a newspaper. Change some of the sentences in the article to add variety. How do your revisions affect the article?

Thesaurus

A dictionary can help you check that you use words correctly. But where do you turn if you think of a word, but it isn't the exact word you want? What tool can help you change a word that you have used too often? A thesaurus is the answer to these problems.

A thesaurus lists synonyms, or words with similar meanings. A thesaurus can help you find words that say exactly what you mean.

Jenna wrote a personal narrative about playing a game with her baby sister. She wanted to change *jumped* because she had already used that word three times in one paragraph. This was her original sentence.

Magda clapped her hands and jumped over a garden hose.

Her baby sister's jump over the garden hose was tiny. Look at these pages from a thesaurus. Which word would best describe Magda's jump as tiny?

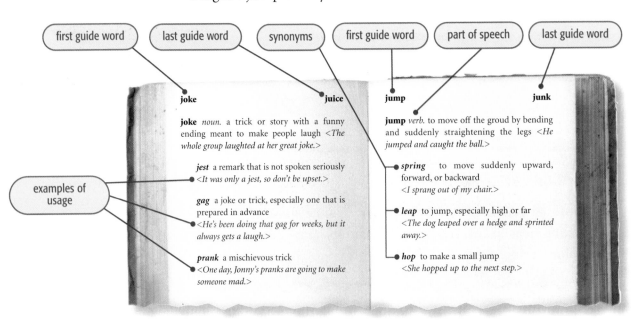

first guide word · last guide word · synonyms · first guide word · part of speech · last guide word

examples of usage

joke   **juice**   **jump**   **junk**

joke *noun.* a trick or story with a funny ending meant to make people laugh <*The whole group laughted at her great joke.*>

    jest a remark that is not spoken seriously <*It was only a jest, so don't be upset.*>

    gag a joke or trick, especially one that is prepared in advance <*He's been doing that gag for weeks, but it always gets a laugh.*>

    prank a mischievous trick <*One day, Jonny's pranks are going to make someone mad.*>

jump *verb.* to move off the groud by bending and suddenly straightening the legs <*He jumped and caught the ball.*>

    spring to move suddenly upward, forward, or backward <*I sprang out of my chair.*>

    leap to jump, especially high or far <*The dog leaped over a hedge and sprinted away.*>

    hop to make a small jump <*She hopped up to the next step.*>

Dictionary Thesaurus

Jenna's thesaurus is a dictionary thesaurus. It is organized like a dictionary. Words are listed in alphabetical order, and each section has words that start with the same letter.

At the top of each page of a dictionary thesaurus are the guide words. Guide words show you the first entry and the last entry that appear on those pages. If you were looking for the word *jump* in a thesaurus, you would know you had the right page if the guide words for that page were *joke* and *junk*. The word *jump* comes alphabetically between *joke* and *junk*.

Remember that synonyms may have slightly different meanings from one another. A hop is not exactly the same as a leap. Some dictionary thesauruses give definitions and example sentences for each synonym, but not all of them do. If you aren't sure about a synonym's exact meaning, look the word up in a dictionary.

Activity A

Tell which of the words in Column B might be found on a page with the guide words in Column A.

Column A	Column B
1. pace/pale	pack, paddle, parade
2. stall/stir	steep, sting, stock
3. bride/broken	bronze, bristle, brilliant
4. alike/angry	alert, alley, ancient

Writer's Corner

Find one of the words below in a dictionary thesaurus. Write a list of the synonyms you find. Then write one sentence that uses the word you chose and one sentence that uses one of the synonyms you wrote.

| go | break | smile | say |

Indexed Thesaurus

A dictionary thesaurus is organized by words in alphabetical order. An indexed thesaurus is organized by ideas or categories. In an indexed thesaurus, words that express the same idea are listed together in one entry.

An indexed thesaurus is divided into two sections. To find synonyms for a word, look up the word in the index. Words in the index are listed alphabetically, and guide words show the first and last word on each page. Most entry words are followed by a list of meanings. Next to each meaning is a number that tells you where to find synonyms with that meaning. Here is an example of an entry for *jump* from the index of an indexed thesaurus.

jump

noun:	step 177.11
	advantage 249.2
	increase 251.1
	leap 366.1
verb:	be startled 131.5
	parachute 184.47
	leap 366.5
	attack 459.15

The verb *leap* is closest to the meaning Jenna needed. The entry might look like this.

366 LEAP

    5 *verbs* leap, jump, hop, spring, skip

Activity B

Use the index entry for *jump* on page 22. Decide what numbers you would look under to find a synonym for *jump* in each of these sentences.

1. Petra had a jump on the competition because she had practiced her flute all summer.
2. When the monster pounced from a tree, everyone in the movie theater jumped.
3. Profits jumped when the company began to sell a new speedboat.
4. The team of soldiers jumped as their plane flew over the battlefield.
5. Anton jumped over the creek and kept on running.

Activity C

Use a thesaurus to rewrite these sentences. Replace each word in italics with a synonym.

1. When Peter goes to the ice-cream shop with his friends, they *talk* for hours.
2. Jessica Montray's first film as a director was a *success*.
3. Mark's bedroom is always so *clean* you could almost eat off the floor.
4. They are using their pickup truck to *carry* pipes and lumber across town.
5. The *outlaw* escaped the hound dogs by swimming upriver.

Writer's Corner

Use an indexed thesaurus to find three synonyms for the word *noise.* Write a sentence for each synonym you choose. Use a dictionary to check that you used each synonym correctly.

Word Study

Exact Words

Good writers choose exact words to give their readers the clearest picture with the fewest words. Often one well-chosen word can do the job of many overused words.

Exact Nouns

Read these two sentences.

A bird swooped down and knocked leaves from the tree.

A raven swooped down and knocked leaves from the oak.

When you read the first sentence, you might picture any kind of bird or tree. Exact nouns in the second sentence help you see more clearly what the writer is describing.

The writer might have changed "A bird" to "A big black bird" to create a clearer picture. But by choosing the word *raven,* the writer gave more information and painted a clearer picture in fewer words.

Exact Adjectives

Which of these two sentences creates a clearer picture by using exact adjectives?

The beautiful baton twirler wore a uniform with nice sequins.

The graceful baton twirler wore a uniform with glittering sequins.

The exact adjective *graceful* tells you that the baton twirler is beautiful because her movements are full of grace. The adjective *graceful* gives the reader more to imagine.

When someone says that something is "nice," what do you imagine? It's hard to picture what "nice" looks like. When someone says that something is "glittering," it is easier to imagine. The adjective *glittering* is exact. *Nice* is not.

When you write and revise, watch out for adjectives such as *pretty, nice, good, great, bad,* and *awful.* These adjectives do not give much information. Use exact adjectives that tell in what way something is nice, good, or awful.

Activity A

Rewrite these sentences by replacing the words in italics with exact words.

1. When Maria bit into her *piece of fruit,* the juice dribbled down her chin.

2. The weather yesterday was *bad.*

3. The mountains were *beautiful.*

4. We shared a *good* meal.

5. Have you seen his furry *pet*?

6. A *big* tree is growing in our yard.

7. The water around our boat was filled with *sea animals.*

8. Alfonso came running into the *room.*

9. Have you noticed the *pretty* picture hanging on the wall?

Writer's Corner

Imagine that you have discovered a buried treasure chest in your yard. Write a description of what you might find in it. Use exact words to help readers picture what is inside.

A constitution is a document that gives the citizens of a nation basic laws and rights. The Mayflower Compact, a document written by the Pilgrims, is considered the first written constitution of America. The Pilgrims had been given a charter, or contract, with an English company to settle the Hudson River area, but a wrong turn landed them in Massachusetts. Because the charter wouldn't apply to this new area, the Pilgrims created the Mayflower Compact to govern their new land.

Exact Verbs

Verbs such as *run, smile,* and *sing* are action words. Some verbs show an action more clearly than other verbs do. When you write and revise, use exact verbs to show readers what is happening in your writing.

> I walked through the haunted house.

> I strolled through the haunted house.

The second sentence tells readers that the writer walked leisurely through the haunted house. Readers get a clearer picture of how the writer walked. The second sentence also tells that the writer was not frightened in the haunted house. The word *strolled* gives more information than the word *walked.*

How does this revision change the meaning of the sentence?

> I raced through the haunted house.

When you revise, look for places where you can use exact verbs. Check the adverbs you used with the verbs. When you find one or more adverbs that describe a verb, think about whether a more exact verb might do the job. A thesaurus can help.

> I ran quickly and wildly through the scary forest.

> I scampered through the scary forest.

What other exact verbs might you use to replace the verb and adverbs in the first sentence?

Activity B

Replace each verb in italics with an exact verb. Use a thesaurus if you need help.

1. My horse *ran* across the swampy field.

2. A gray rabbit was *eating* a leaf of lettuce.

3. The campers *walked* along the crooked trail.

4. I caught the ball and *ran* toward the end zone.

5. Ned *took* the lollipop from the bully and gave it back to his friend.

6. "I'm going to get you!" *said* the wicked witch.

Activity C

Rewrite these sentences by replacing the words in italics with exact verbs.

1. The snake *went on its belly* across the basement floor.

2. A train *came loudly* into the station.

3. The bonfire *made loud noises* as we told our stories.

4. The mayor *went up* onstage and *spoke loudly* to the crowd.

5. The fox *looked for a long time* at the people *walking clumsily* through the bushes.

6. The clothes hanging on the line *moved slowly back and forth* in the wind.

Activity D

Rewrite this paragraph, using exact nouns, adjectives, and verbs.

In a faraway place, a group of animals were deciding what to do next. Their homes had been ruined by a very bad storm. They came together and started talking. "I don't know what to do," said an animal. A colored snake came to the middle of the circle. "We'd better decide soon," he said. He pointed to the clouds, which were looking bad. Finally one animal had a good idea. "Let's go into that cave for the night," he said. They were all happy with the idea, and they went into the cave.

Writer's Corner

Work with a partner to list three synonyms for each of the following verbs: *talk, walk, eat,* and *take.* Then choose one set of synonyms. Write three sentences, using a different synonym from your list in each sentence.

Speaking and Listening Skills

Oral Personal Narratives

Have you ever told someone about something funny or scary that happened to you? Telling an audience about something that happened to you is sharing an oral personal narrative.

Audience and Topic

To whom are you going to tell your story? You might tell your story one way for your teacher and another way for a classmate. Knowing your audience can help you decide which experience to tell about. What kind of story will your audience enjoy? Choose an a topic that you will enjoy sharing with your audience.

Introduction

Grab your listeners' attention in the introduction. You might let listeners know what kind of story you are going to tell. Will it be scary? Does it begin on a stormy night in a spooky forest?

Body

The body of your oral personal narrative tells what happened to you. Be sure to include only the most interesting details. Telling what happened in time order will help listeners follow your story. Use time words to make your narrative clearer.

Conclusion

In the conclusion of your oral personal narrative, you might tell listeners what you learned from the experience or how you felt about it.

Voice

How you tell your personal narrative will help you connect with your audience. Use a tone of voice that shows how you feel. You might speak quickly during the exciting parts of the story. If something scary is about to happen in the story, slow down and speak quietly to keep your audience on the edge of their seats. You might also make sound effects to go with your story, such as *crash, boom,* or *whoosh.*

• Activity A •

Read each sentence aloud to a partner, using a tone of voice that sounds as if you are angry, scared, excited, or happy. See if your partner can guess the feeling you are showing.

1. I ran to the corner as fast as I could.

2. It was the biggest toad I'd ever seen.

3. I knew my life would never be the same.

4. You'll never believe what happened next.

5. That's the last time I'll ever go there.

6. I didn't know what to say.

7. Finally I saw my balloon in the branches of a tree.

8. "Where did he go?" I wondered aloud.

Speaker's Corner

Write a list of three ideas for an oral personal narrative. Talk with a partner about which idea would be best for an oral personal narrative you might present to your classmates. Think about which narrative your classmates would most enjoy.

Personal Narratives • 29

Prepare and Practice

To prepare your oral personal narrative, write the important parts, or the parts you most want to remember, on note cards. You might write down a few good sentences that you want to include in your introduction or conclusion. Don't put every word on your note cards. Instead, use keywords and phrases that will help you remember what to say.

Practice your personal narrative in front of a mirror a few times. As you practice, try using different tones of voice to add feeling to your story. Try adding sound effects or body movements. The more you practice, the easier your oral personal narrative will be to present to your audience.

Present

Here are some tips for presenting your personal narrative.

- Before you begin, check that your note cards are in order.

- Look at the audience as you speak. The audience wants to know that you are speaking to them, not reading from your note cards. Move your eyes from person to person to let your audience know you want to include them all.

- Talk slowly. Taking a breath at the end of each sentence can help you remember to slow down.

- Speak so everyone can hear you, but do not shout.

- Use your tone of voice, your facial expressions, and your body movements to grab your listeners' attention.

Listening Tips

Listeners make a speaker feel comfortable when they show their interest. A speaker who is comfortable is more likely to tell a story you will enjoy. Here are some tips for being a good listener.

- Look at the speaker. Pay attention to what the speaker is saying.

- Picture the story in your mind. Imagine how the people and places in the story might look. Think about how the story might end.

- If you have questions, save them until the speaker is finished.

• Activity B •

Look at the three topics you wrote for the Speaker's Corner on page 29. Pick one you want to present. Write a set of note cards for that topic. Use keywords and phrases in your notes.

• Activity C •

Practice your oral personal narrative with a partner. Practice using your voice to show your feelings. Try using facial expressions, body movements, and sound effects to keep your partner's interest. When you have finished, talk with your partner about ways to improve your narrative.

Our Wide Wide World

Juan Ponce de León had been on Christopher Columbus's second voyage to the New World. It was his own search, however, for the "fountain of youth" that led him to what is now Florida. De León didn't find his fountain of youth. However, his return trip did locate the Gulf Stream, a fast-moving and reliable route for ships going from North America to Europe.

Speaker's Corner

Present your oral personal narrative to the class. Remember to make eye contact with your audience and to speak slowly and clearly. Use your voice to show your feelings. When your classmates present their narratives, use the Listening Tips to help you be a good listener.

Personal Narratives

Prewriting and Drafting

Writing a personal narrative is an opportunity to share an experience from your life with others. You might write about something that changed your life. You might also write about something funny, scary, or brave that you did. The choices are endless.

Prewriting

Elsa is a fifth grader who wanted to write a personal narrative to enter in the Pennsylvania It Happened to Me Contest. Elsa first took time to do some prewriting. During prewriting Elsa would choose her topic and plan what she wanted to write.

Choosing a Topic

Elsa had some ideas for what to write about, but she didn't know which one to pick. Elsa answered a list of questions from her teacher to help her narrow her possible topics. Here are some of the questions.

What is something that changed your life? when my family moved from the Army base in Germany, to Philadelphia when I was six

What is the most exciting thing that has ever happened to you? getting to play drums on the same stage as Bricks, the hip-hop artist

What is the funniest thing that ever happened to you? I ran into a tree while laughing at my friend for tripping.

What is the scariest thing that ever happened to you? playing drums onstage at Bricks concert

Elsa looked at her answers to the questions. She chose playing drums at the Bricks concert as her topic for a few reasons. She thought her amazing opportunity would interest her audience. She also thought that since the topic appeared more than once on the list of answers, she would have a lot to say about it.

Your Turn

Think of experiences that you have had that you would like to share with an audience. Use the following questions to help you think of ideas. Choose as your topic the idea that you would most enjoy writing about.

- What is something that changed your life?

- What is the most exciting thing that has ever happened to you?

- What is the funniest, scariest, bravest, or most embarrassing thing that you have ever done?

- What is the thing that you are most proud of doing?

Using a Storyboard to Plan

Now that Elsa had her topic, she wanted to plan what she would write about in her personal narrative. Elsa drew on sheets of paper simple pictures for each thing that happened to her. She left room at the top of each page to write what was going on in the picture. Then she organized the pictures in the order that the events happened. Here is a page from Elsa's storyboard.

Your Turn

Use a storyboard to plan your draft. Think about your topic. On the first pages draw the first thing that happened to you. Leave space at the top of the page to write about the picture. If people are speaking, write what they say in a bubble next to their mouth. If you were thinking something during that moment, write what you were thinking in a bubble next to your head. Draw each event of the story on a separate page. Make sure you include all of the important details of the experience. Then read the storyboard to see if it is organized in the order that your experience happened.

Drafting

Writing a draft is the first chance to write ideas for your personal narrative in paragraph form. Elsa used her storyboard to help her write her personal narrative. She made sure that her personal narrative was written in time order and that it had a clear introduction, body, and conclusion.

Elsa left extra space between the lines so that she would have room to make changes later. Here is Elsa's first draft.

Don't Lose the Beat

I won concert tickets to see Bricks, my favorite hip-hop artist! I also got a backstage pass to meet her two hours before the show started. I was so excited! I play drums for fun, and I loved playing the beat along with Bricks's CDs. I could hardly wait.

When the day of the concert came, I was so nervous. My stomack felt like it was doing gymnastics. My dad and I knocked on the back door of the Civic Center. The strongest-looking man I have ever seen opened the door. One of Bricks's managers took me and my dad down a dark hallway to the stage. The stage was cluttered with microphones, equipment for the DJ, and a silver and black drum set. The manager said that Bricks would be out in a minute.

I got more and more excited! I started tapping the beat to Bricks's hit song "My Street" on my leg. "My Street" was her newest song. I thought that it was her best too. Before "My Street" my favorite song by Bricks had been "Fool Me." Then I heard a voice behind me say, "You play that beat pretty well." It was Bricks! She asked if I would like to play the drums when she performed "My Street" that night. I couldn't believe it! We practiced the song in the empty Civic Center for the next hour. She told me that as long as I didn't lose the beat, I would do a good job.

The enormous crowd cheered! I started to play the beat of the song on the drum set. I concentrated hard on not losing the beat. All of a sudden, the DJ stopped scratching and Bricks stopped rapping. The song was over, but I was still playing the beat. I was so embarrassed I didn't know what to do. People in the audience saw Bricks smile and start to dance to the beat. Then Bricks starts rapping over my beat. We were making up a new part for "My Street" together. The crowd went wild. Bricks and I finally made eye contact and stopped at the same time. The crowd cheered and screamed for more!

After the show Bricks told me how well she thought I did. She said that she might even keep the new line we made together in her song. I felt famous. I couldn't believe what an amazing night I had had with my favorite hip-hop star.

Your Turn

Use your storyboard to help you write the first draft of your personal narrative. Remember to write from your point of view. Use words such as *I, me, my, our,* and *we.* Start with an introduction that catches your reader's attention.

Write the body of your personal narrative. Make sure the events in the body are told in time order. Add all the details necessary to make it seem as real as possible to the reader.

Finish by writing a conclusion. Try to sum up what happened in your personal narrative. You might also want to write a final line that will be remembered by the reader.

While you write your draft, keep in mind your audience. Who are you writing for? How much do they need to know to understand your experience? Remember to use a voice that tells your reader how you felt about what happened. Were you excited? Were you scared? Were you happy?

Personal Narratives

Content Editing

Now that Elsa had a draft of her personal narrative, she wanted to make it better. A content editor would improve the draft by checking that all the important ideas were included. A content editor would also make sure that the story was told in time order.

Elsa wanted to ask someone she trusted to content edit her personal narrative. She decided to ask Anton, her older brother. Anton wasn't at the Bricks concert, but he had heard his little sister telling the story of meeting Bricks and playing the drums. Anton used the Content Editor's Checklist below to content edit Elsa's personal narrative.

Content Editor's Checklist

✓ Does the writing stay on the topic?

✓ Is the personal narrative told from the writer's point of view?

✓ Are there an engaging introduction, a detailed body, and a satisfying conclusion?

✓ Are the details in the narrative necessary?

✓ Is the narrative told in correct time order?

Anton read Elsa's personal narrative. He told her that he liked how she used details to capture the excitement she felt when she met Bricks and performed onstage. He told her that although he had heard her tell the story many times, he thought that this was the best that she had ever told it. Then Anton told Elsa these ideas he had for her personal narrative.

- You get off the topic in the third paragraph when you mention your favorite song before "My Street."

- The introduction doesn't catch my attention. Maybe you shouldn't say what the topic is right away. You might start with a question or an interesting fact.

- The conclusion is satisfying, but you might add a line that will stick with the reader.

- The personal narrative is in the right time order, but something seems to be missing between the third and fourth paragraphs. It jumps from practicing the song with Bricks to being called up to play the song during the concert.

Elsa thanked Anton for his help. She was happy to have ideas on how to make her personal narrative better.

Your Turn

Exchange your personal narrative with a partner. Use the Content Editor's Checklist to check your partner's paper. Pay attention to one question in the checklist at a time. Take notes on changes you would like to suggest to your partner about his or her personal narrative.

When you have finished, take turns talking about each other's drafts with your partner. Start by saying something you like about your partner's personal narrative. Remember to write down your partner's ideas about your personal narrative. Think about each one. Ask your partner any questions that you might have.

Personal Narratives

Revising

This is how Elsa revised her draft, using the ideas from content editing.

I waited on the line as the phone **Don't Lose the Beat**
rang once, twice then three times. The voice that answered said that I was the winning caller!

V I ^ won concert tickets to see Bricks, my favorite hip-hop artist! I also got
            ^ had

a backstage pass to meet her two hours before the show started. I was so

excited! I play drums for fun, and I loved playing the beat along with Bricks's CDs.

I could hardly wait.

When the day of the concert came, I was so nervous. My stomack felt like it

was doing gymnastics. My dad and I knocked on the back door of the Civic Center.

The strongest-looking man I have ever seen opened the door. One of Bricks's

managers took me and my dad down a dark hallway to the stage. The stage was

cluttered with microphones, equipment for the DJ, and a silver and black drum set.

The manager said that Bricks would be out in a minute.

I got more and more excited! I started tapping the beat to Bricks's hit song

"My Street" on my leg. ~~"My Street" was her newest song. I thought that it was her~~

~~best too. Before "My Street" my favorite song by Bricks had been "Fool Me."~~ Then

I heard a voice behind me say, "You play that beat pretty well." It was Bricks! She

asked if I would like to play the drums when she performed "My Street" that night.

I couldn't believe it! We practiced the song in the empty Civic Center for the next

hour. She told me that as long as I didn't lose the beat, I would do a good job.

∧ The enormous crowd cheered! I started to play the beat of the song on the

When the time came for "My Street," Bricks invited me on stage.

drum set. I concentrated hard on not losing the beat. All of a sudden, the DJ

stopped scratching and Bricks stopped rapping. The song was over, but I was still

playing the beat. I was so embarrassed I didn't know what to do. ~~People in the~~

~~audience saw Bricks smile and start to dance to the beat.~~ Then Bricks starts

rapping over my beat. We were making up a new part for "My Street" together. The

crowd went wild. Bricks and I finally made eye contact and stopped at the same

time. The crowd cheered and screamed for more!

    After the show Bricks told me how well she thought I did. She said that she

might even keep the new line we made together in her song. I felt famous. I couldn't

As I left the Civic Center, Bricks yelled out, "You sure know how to follow advice, Elsa. You didn't

believe what an amazing night I had had with my favorite hip-hop star. lose the beat!"
                                                             ∧

Here are some of the things that Elsa did to improve her personal narrative.

- Elsa agreed that she got off the topic in the third paragraph. She deleted the sentences about her other favorite song by Bricks.

- Elsa agreed that the introduction didn't catch the reader's attention. But she didn't want to start her personal narrative with a fact or a question. She decided to write about the moment she won the tickets.

- Elsa had an idea for the perfect line to end her narrative. She thought people would like to know the last thing Bricks said to her.

- Elsa added a sentence at the start of the fourth paragraph to move readers from before the show to the moment she got onstage.

As Elsa looked over her personal narrative again, she noticed a part in the fourth paragraph that wasn't from her point of view. It was the sentence that described what Bricks was doing when Elsa kept playing the beat. It was not something Elsa had seen, so she could not include it.

Your Turn

Use your ideas and those of your content editor to revise your draft. Use only the ideas that you agree with.

    When you have finished revising, look at the Content Editor's Checklist again. Make sure that you can answer yes to each question.

Personal Narratives

Copyediting and Proofreading

Copyediting

Elsa had improved the ideas in her personal narrative by revising it. Now she wanted to check whether all of her sentences made sense and whether her words were used correctly. Elsa decided to copyedit by using this checklist.

Copyeditor's Checklist

✓ Are all the sentences complete sentences?

✓ Do the sentences follow each other in an order that makes sense?

✓ Are the sentences different lengths?

✓ Are questions and exclamations used correctly?

✓ Are exact words used?

Elsa realized that she had used too many exclamation points. She decided to keep the exclamation points only when she was really excited or surprised. She kept the second

exclamation point in the first paragraph because winning tickets to the concert was exciting. She kept the second exclamation point in the third paragraph because Bricks had startled her. What exclamation points in the final two paragraphs would you keep? Why would you choose the ones you did?

Elsa thought that she could use exact words to describe what she saw at the Civic Center. She used exact words to describe the door and the drum set.

Your Turn

Copyedit your personal narrative. Use the Copyeditor's Checklist. Check your questions and exclamations. If you overuse these, they will lose their effect. Be sure that exact words were used to describe your experience.

Proofreading

Elsa thought that a proofreader might catch mistakes that she had missed. Elsa's neighbor, Ms. Gabriel, often helped Elsa with her English homework. While proofreading, Ms. Gabriel would check the grammar, spelling, capitalization, and punctuation. This is the checklist Ms. Gabriel used.

Proofreader's Checklist

✓ Are the paragraphs indented?

✓ Are all the words spelled correctly?

✓ Are capitalization and punctuation correct?

✓ Is the grammar correct?

✓ Were any new mistakes added while editing?

Ms. Gabriel found a misspelled word in the second paragraph. The word *stomach* was spelled with a *k*.

Ms. Gabriel found one punctuation mistake. In the first sentence, Elsa put a comma after the word *once,* but she forgot to put a comma after *twice.*

In the fourth paragraph, Elsa had written *Then Bricks starts rapping over my beat.* Ms. Gabriel told Elsa that she needed to use the same tense throughout. Ms. Gabriel suggested replacing *starts* with *started*.

Your Turn

Ask a partner to use the Proofreader's Checklist to check your draft. Make sure that the changes from your partner are correct.

Common Proofreading Marks

Symbol	Meaning	Example
¶	begin new paragraph	over. ¶Begin a new
◠	close up space	close u͜p space
∧	insert	students ∧think (should)
ℐ	delete, omit	that the the̸ book
/	lowercase letter	/Mathematics
∩	letters are reversed	letters are reve∩rsed
≡	capitalize	washington ≡
⌄⌄	quotation	⌄I am,⌄ I said.

Personal Narratives

Publishing

Elsa made the changes Ms. Gabriel suggested. Then she wrote the final version of her personal narrative. She was ready to share her narrative with an audience. Her audience was her teacher, her classmates, and the judges of the Pennsylvania It Happened to Me Contest. Once she published her personal narrative, there would be no more chances to change her work. She knew her published copy had to be her best possible work.

Don't Lose the Beat

I waited on the line as the phone rang once, twice, then three times. The voice that answered said that I was the winning caller. I had won concert tickets to see Bricks, my favorite hip-hop artist! I also got a backstage pass to meet her two hours before the show started. I was so excited. I play drums for fun, and I loved playing the beat along with Bricks's albums. I could hardly wait.

When the day of the concert came, I was so nervous. My stomach felt like it was doing gymnastics. My dad and I knocked on the back door of the Civic Center. The strongest-looking man I have ever seen opened the heavy red door. One of Bricks's managers took me and my dad down a dark hallway to the stage. The stage was cluttered with microphones, equipment for the DJ, and a glittering silver and black drum set. The manager said that Bricks would be out in a minute.

I got more and more excited. I started tapping the beat to Bricks's hit song "My Street" on my leg. Then I heard a voice behind me say, "You play that beat pretty well." It was Bricks! She asked if I would like to play the drums when she performed "My Street" that night. I couldn't believe it. We practiced the song in the empty Civic Center for the next hour. She told me that as long as I didn't lose the beat, I would do a good job.

When the time came for "My Street," Bricks invited me on stage. The enormous crowd cheered. I started to play the beat of the song on the drum set. I concentrated hard on not losing the beat. All of a sudden, the DJ stopped scratching and Bricks stopped rapping. The song was over, but I was still playing the beat. I was so embarrassed I didn't know what to do. Then Bricks started rapping over my beat. We were making up a new part for "My Street" together. The crowd went wild. Bricks and I finally made eye contact and stopped at the same time. The crowd cheered and screamed for more!

After the show Bricks told me how well she thought I did. She said that she might even keep the new line we made together in her song. I felt famous. I couldn't believe what an amazing night I had had with my favorite hip-hop star. As I left the Civic Center, Bricks yelled out, "You sure know how to follow advice, Elsa. You didn't lose the beat!"

Your Turn

Make a final copy of your personal narrative. Add the changes from proofreading that you decided to use.

Be careful making this final copy. Once your personal narrative is published, you cannot make any more changes. Be sure that your writing is as clear and correct as possible.

Whenever you share something you write with an audience, you publish it. Just turning your personal narrative in to your teacher means that you have published it. You can also publish your personal narrative by hanging it on a bulletin board or by making copies to give to your friends and family. If you do this, you might draw a picture to display with your work.

Whatever you do, make sure you find a special way to share your personal narrative so that others can enjoy it.

The first states in the United States were the 13 British colonies in the New World that declared themselves free from British Rule by signing the Declaration of Independence (1776) and the Constitution of The United States (1787). The Declaration was written primarily by Thomas Jefferson, signed by representatives of each colony, and delivered to King George III of England. Do you know why the colonies wanted to be free of British Rule?

How-to Articles

Health and First Aid

As you know, Eric has diabetes. He knows how to check his blood sugar and take his medication. Just be sure that he does both at 8:00 p.m.

If you see that Eric is sweating or trembling—or notice him staggering, unusually hungry, or in a bad temper—his blood sugar is low. First have him drink a glass of juice, which will help to bring his blood sugar up. If he can't or won't drink, give him a piece of fruit or candy. Then wait a few minutes to see whether his symptoms stop. If they do, have him lie down for about 20 minutes before he resumes any activities. If the symptoms continue, call Dr. Welling. Her number is on the emergency list posted on the refrigerator.

For first aid, the first-aid kit is under the sink in the bathroom. It is fully stocked, and it contains a handbook of basic first-aid treatments. Use these for any minor injuries the kids might have. Just watch out—Melissa likes to wear bandages. If she is pestering you, let her have one to wear, but don't give her more than one. For any injury or emergency, call my cell phone or call 911.

TV Rules

The kids are allowed to watch TV until 8:00 p.m. Eric gets to choose shows on odd-numbered days, and Melissa gets to choose on even-numbered days. If either of the kids complain, give them a

What Makes a Good How-to Article?

Have you ever read directions for playing a new computer game? Have you followed directions to get to a party? Maybe you have used a recipe. How-to writing teaches a reader how to do something or how to make something. You can share your knowledge with others by writing a how-to article.

Topic

Write about what you know. Choose a topic that you can get excited about and can explain to others with confidence. Make sure you have a strong, clear topic. It might be hard to write a how-to article about cooking. A narrower topic, such as how to cook scrambled eggs, is much easier to explain.

Remember to stay on the topic. If you are writing about how to cook scrambled eggs, don't explain how to cook fried eggs or hard-boiled eggs. Too much information can confuse your audience.

Audience

Think about the people you are writing for. How old are they? Might they already know something about what you want to teach? What are the most important things your audience might need to know? Clear, simple steps written with your audience in mind will help readers follow your directions.

Point of View

When you write a how-to article, you are the expert and your readers are the learners. Use imperative sentences, such as "First heat the milk," to tell your reader how to do the steps.

Activity A

Tell which of the following would be good topics for how-to articles. Explain your choices.

1. the way to make a tasty sandwich
2. your day at a theme park
3. learning the rules for playing chess
4. watching a sunset at the beach
5. how to review for a math test

Activity B

The following are titles of how-to articles. Match each title in Column A to the intended audience in Column B. Some how-to articles may have more than one audience.

Column A	Column B
1. Applying Stage Makeup	**a.** high school students
2. Caring For Your Baseball Card Collection	**b.** actors
	c. card collectors
3. Study Skills for the SATs	**d.** fishers
4. How To Put Up a Tent	**e.** runners
5. Training for a Marathon	**f.** campers
6. A Guide to Trout Fishing	

Writer's Corner

Imagine that you need to teach a first grader how to make a peanut butter and jelly sandwich. Write step-by-step directions that you might share with the child. Then take turns with a partner to act out each other's steps.

Sometimes how-to articles are written as numbered or lettered lists. Sometimes they are written in paragraph form. When you write how-to articles in paragraph form, include an introduction, a body, and a conclusion.

Introduction

An effective introduction to a how-to article catches the readers' attention. A short description of what they will learn to make or to do is often a way to get readers interested. Using exact words will help readers imagine the end result of following your directions.

Body

The body of a how-to article in paragraph form has the steps needed to complete what you will teach. Using transition words such as *first, next, then,* and *finally* will help readers keep track of the steps. Make sure that the steps are in the correct order so that your audience does not become confused. The body of your how-to article may be one paragraph, or it may be many paragraphs.

Conclusion

The conclusion of your how-to article might explain the usefulness of what your audience just learned. You might also give tips or ideas for ways to adjust the directions for other situations. For example, in a how-to article about how to make homemade vanilla ice cream, you might conclude with ideas for other ice-cream flavors.

• Activity C •
Write introductions for how-to articles on two of the following topics.

A. how to train a dog

B. directions for getting to the new basketball court

C. how to do face painting

D. Grandma's secret apple pie recipe

Activity D

Read the three sentences below each how-to article topic. Tell which sentence would be a good sentence for an introduction, which would be a good conclusion, and which does not belong with the topic.

How to Make a Weather Vane

a. If you are puzzled about which way the wind is blowing, build your own weather vane.

b. Did you know that sailors used stars to guide them on long journeys?

c. Use your weather vane to solve the puzzle of the wind's direction.

How to Make a Delicious Smoothie

a. Once you've mastered this one, invent your own delicious combinations!

b. Nothing beats the summer heat like this simple fruit and juice smoothie.

c. Yogurt with fruit added is my friend's favorite snack.

How to Make a Soapbox Derby Car

a. One time a wheel came flying off my car!

b. Have you ever wanted to race in your own homemade car?

c. Be sure you always wear a helmet when you are racing, and always have lots of fun!

Writer's Corner

Work with a partner to write a list of snacks or crafts that can be made using popcorn. Then choose one item from the list. Write a numbered list of the steps needed to make that snack or craft.

Order, Accuracy, and Completeness

The purpose of a how-to article is to teach readers how to do or to make something. To help readers understand the body of your article, be sure that it is accurate, complete, and in logical order.

Logical Order

Imagine that you are reading an article about how to fix a hole in a bicycle tire. What would happen if the step for putting air in the tire came before patching the hole?

In a how-to article, the steps are presented in logical order, or the order in which the steps will be completed. Putting the steps in a numbered list before you write them in paragraph form can help you keep the steps in order.

● Activity A ●

The steps below are out of order. Write the steps in the correct order, using a numbered list.

How to Plant a Garden

   a. Plant the seeds.

   b. Turn over the soil with a rake.

   c. Water the seeds.

   d. Choose a spot for the garden.

   e. Clear weeds around the
   young sprouts.

• Activity B •

The directions below are for playing charades. Rewrite them in the correct order.

a. The team with the most correct guesses wins the game.

b. Stop when your team correctly guesses or when time runs out.

c. Begin with two teams and decide on a time limit for each round.

d. Use gestures to show what is on your paper and have your team try to guess the answer.

e. Have each team write on slips of paper the titles of books, TV shows, and movies; or the names of famous people. Then have each team place their slips in separate bowls.

f. Teams should take turns having players act out what the slips say.

g. When it's your turn, pick a slip from the other team's bowl. Read it to yourself.

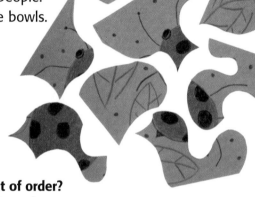

• Activity C •

Read the following how-to article. Which steps are out of order? Explain what would happen if the directions were followed as written. Then identify where you would put the misplaced sentences.

Make a Puzzle

Start with a sheet of heavy paper. Cut the picture into eight irregular shapes. Then draw a colorful picture on the paper. Trade envelopes with a partner and see whether he or she can put your puzzle together. Clip the pieces together and put them in an envelope.

Writer's Corner

Write a numbered list of directions from school to a place that your classmates know, keeping the place secret. Then use your numbered list to write the body of a how-to article. When you have finished, trade papers with a partner to guess each other's secret places.

Accuracy

Accuracy is important when you write a how-to article. Writing is accurate when it explains something exactly and without errors. For example, if you were writing a how-to article about putting a desk together, you might make sure that you told readers the right kind of screwdriver to use. If readers do not know what tools to use, or if they have been told to use the wrong tools, they might become discouraged. Giving readers accurate information will make what you are teaching easier for readers to complete.

Completeness

Completeness, which is including all of the necessary information, is important for a how-to article. When information is missing, readers can become confused. If you write about how to bake a pie, make sure that you include all of the ingredients. The pie could be a disaster if you don't tell readers to use flour.

• Activity D •

The list of ingredients below is for making blueberry muffins, but some of the information is not accurate. Identify the incorrect information. Explain your answers.

Ingredients for Blueberry Muffins

2 eggs	1 cup light brown salt
100 cups flour	1 cup raspberries
1 tbsp cinnamon	1/2 tsp baking soda

Activity E

The following steps explain how to make marbles. Some important information is missing. Write the information a reader would need to be able to make the marbles.

1. For regular marbles, begin with 1-inch cubes of air-dry clay. Use a piece of clay about 3 inches long to make a shooter.

2. Let the balls of clay harden overnight.

3. Allow time for the paint to dry.

4. Have fun playing marbles with your friends.

Activity F

The recipe below is missing some information. Imagine that you are making these pretzels with a grownup. What information would you need to make your pretzels?

Soft Pretzel Shapes

loaves of frozen bread dough   water

1 egg white   coarse salt to sprinkle

Separate thawed bread dough into 1-inch balls. Roll each ball into a long rope. Use the rope to make pretzel shapes, such as letters. Place the pretzels on a greased cookie sheet and let stand for 20 minutes. Then brush the pretzels with a mixture of egg white and water and sprinkle with salt. Place a shallow pan containing 1 inch of boiling water on the bottom rack of the oven. Bake the pretzels at 350°F on the rack above the water.

Writer's Corner

Choose a craft project you like to do. Make a list of the materials you will need and the steps to complete the project. Check your list for accuracy and completeness. Save your list.

Transition Words

You can help your readers follow the steps in a how-to article by using transition words. Transition words identify the order of the steps. They help to carry the reader from one step to the next. Read this list of common transition words.

after that	finally	one day
afterward	second	at first
last	soon	at last
later	next	then
first	now	third

Vary the transition words that you use when you write. Read the following examples and explain which is more interesting to read.

A. First, fill a 2-liter bottle 2/3 full of water and add a few drops of food coloring. Second, place a washer on the lip of the bottle. Third, tape a second 2-liter bottle to the first bottle, with the washer between them. Fourth, place the bottles on a flat surface with the water-filled bottle on top. Fifth, rotate the bottles to create a vortex as the water flows from the top bottle to the bottom bottle.

B. Begin by filling a 2-liter bottle 2/3 full of water and adding a few drops of food coloring. Then place a washer on the lip of the bottle. Next tape a second 2-liter bottle to the first bottle, with the washer between them. After that place the bottles on a flat surface with the water-filled bottle on top. Finally rotate the bottles to create a vortex as the water flows from the top bottle to the bottom bottle.

Activity A

The paragraph below comes from Laura Ingalls Wilder's book *Little House in the Big Woods.* It describes churning butter. Read the paragraph and identify the transition words.

She churned for a long time. . . . At first the splashes of cream showed thick and smooth around the little hole. After a long time, they began to look grainy. Then Ma churned more slowly, and on the dash there began to appear tiny grains of yellow butter. When Ma took off the churn-cover, there was butter in a golden lump . . . and she washed it many times in cold water, turning it over and over and working it with the paddle until the water ran clear. After that she salted it. Now came the best part of the churning.

Activity B

Read the how-to paragraph below. Choose a transition word for each blank. You may use transition words from the list on page 54 or use other transition words that you know.

Here's how to draft a writing assignment. _____ write your name and the date in the upper right-hand corner of a sheet of paper. _____ begin to write your ideas, skipping a line after each line that you write. Don't worry about spelling right now. _____ reread your work and make your corrections. _____ ask a classmate to edit your work. _____ copy your final draft in your best handwriting.

Writer's Corner

Look at the list you wrote for the Writer's Corner on page 53. Use the list to write the body of a how-to article. Remember to include transition words to help your readers move from step to step.

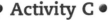
• Activity C •

The steps below belong in a how-to article about giving a dog a bath. The steps are out of order. Number the steps in the order in which they should be done. Then write the steps in paragraph form, using a transition word for each step.

a. Fill the tub with water.

b. Carry the dog to the tub.

c. Set up a tub in the yard.

d. Bathe the dog.

e. Stand out of the way while the dog shakes off the water.

• Activity D •

Write the steps for this peanut soup recipe in logical order. Use one of these transition words to begin each step: *first, finally, next, after that, then, now.*

a. Boil one quart of milk and add the mashed peanuts.

b. Slowly add the peanut milk to two tablespoons of flour, stirring the whole time. Don't add the flour to the peanut milk, or it will clump.

c. Mash the cooked peanuts until they are very fine.

d. Stir the two ingredients together over low heat, and cook for 20 minutes.

e. Add a little butter, salt, and pepper to the soup.

f. Cook one cup of shelled peanuts in a little water until they are soft.

g. Serve the soup hot.

• Activity E •

Where could you put transition words to make the how-to article below flow more smoothly? Rewrite the body paragraph to include transition words.

If you ever wished that you didn't forget facts so easily, a dose of this "memory potion" is the thing for you.

You will need a large bowl and a wooden spoon. Pour one cup of milk into the bowl. Add four tablespoons of powdered chocolate, one tablespoon of sugar, and four mashed worms. Stir until the worms are well mixed. Mix in one frog's eye and a mandarin orange slice. Add one shredded owl feather and stir until all of the ingredients are blended.

Drink the potion over ice in your best silver goblet. One drink will give you the best memory in your school!

• Activity F •

Write a numbered list of steps about one of the following topics.

A. how to build a snowman

B. how to become a rock star

C. how to capture a troll

D. how to make a paper airplane

E. how to play a musical instrument

F. how to invent something

Writer's Corner

Use the steps that you wrote for Activity F to write the body of a how-to article. Include transition words to help your readers. When you have finished, trade papers with a partner and identify the transition words in each other's work.

Synonyms

Synonyms are words that have the same or almost the same meaning. The words *gaze, glance, observe, peek,* and *watch* are all synonyms for the word *look.* Writers use synonyms to make their writing more interesting. Can you name a synonym for each of these words?

kind   easy   funny   say   special

Words often have more than one synonym. Each synonym has a slightly different meaning. Notice how synonyms for the word *surprise* are used in the following examples. How does each synonym fit the meaning of the sentence?

The dolphins *astounded* the audience with their grace and playfulness.

I was *startled* when I won first prize at the science fair.

The word *astounded* means "caused wonder." It gives the idea that the audience was surprised and impressed. The word *startled* means "jumped in surprise." It describes the action of the speaker or writer when the science fair winner was announced. Choosing the best synonym helps readers get the clearest meaning of what you are trying to explain.

Use a thesaurus to find other synonyms for the word *surprise.* How might the synonyms you find change the meanings of the sentences above?

Activity A •

Tell which synonym for the word in italics best fits each sentence. Use a dictionary or a thesaurus if you need help.

1. Because the detective was *alert,* he noticed the evidence at the crime scene. (wide-awake, observant)

2. The audience roared with laughter after hearing the comedian's *funny* joke. (amusing, hilarious)

3. Please *shut* the gate. (seal, close)

4. I just finished reading a really *good* book. (nice, excellent)

5. My sister was *glowing* on her wedding day. (radiant, shiny)

6. Lily's skateboard is her most prized possesion, so I was *puzzled* when she gave it to me. (baffled, confused)

7. Gunter thinks he is a great *writer.* He even rhymes when he talks. (scribe, poet)

Activity B •

Pick two of the four synonym groups below and write a sentence using each synonym in each group you choose. Write sentences that show how the words in each group have slightly different meanings.

A. scent	stink	fragrance
B. study	consider	ponder
C. worried	nervous	disturbed
D. comfortable	easy	relaxing

Writer's Corner

Awesome, happy, and *nice* are words that are often overused in speaking and in writing. List three synonyms for each of these overused words. Then use each synonym in a sentence to show the different meaning. Save your lists and sentences.

• Activity C •

Read the groups of words below. In each group, one word is not a synonym for the other words. Find the word that does not belong in each group.

1. nice, likable, unapproachable, agreeable

2. unusual, ordinary, normal, customary

3. devious, untruthful, trustworthy, dishonest

4. crowded, filled, stuffed, empty

5. many, multiple, few, numerous

6. divided, split, separated, unified

7. assist, prevent, help, aid

8. escape, elude, vanish, capture

9. perfect, flawed, accurate, excellent

10. healthy, sick, ill, unwell

• Activity D •

Match each word in Column A with its synonym in Column B.

Column A	Column B
1. succeed	a. pursue
2. firm	b. gloomy
3. examine	c. frisky
4. fall	d. serene
5. curious	e. achieve
6. follow	f. steady
7. playful	g. fix
8. dark	h. nosy
9. calm	i. descend
10. repair	j. inspect

Activity E

Replace each of the italicized words in the paragraph below with synonyms. Use a thesaurus or a dictionary to help you.

The roller coaster *shook* on its creaky foundation. It climbed the first hill *slowly.* I felt *sick* because I was so *scared.* A warm *wind* blew through my hair as the car reached the top of the hill. There was a *pause,* and then suddenly the car *went* down the hill at a *fast* pace. A *scream* burst out of my mouth as we zoomed toward the ground. I *like* roller coasters!

Activity F

Think of a synonym for the word in italics that will make each sentence clearer.

1. My older brother *walked* through Europe last summer.
2. The gardener had to *cut* down the sick elm tree.
3. When Marty heard the whistle, he *hurried* to the train.
4. The *noise* from my chinchilla's cage always startles people.
5. I saw a *wonderful* exhibit of Celtic art at the museum.
6. When we were hiking, we saw some *large,* mysterious tracks.
7. Maddy always gets the *correct* answer, even without a calculator.
8. There are a lot of school activities to *select* from this year.
9. Mom *said* that I could go camping if I got an A on the spelling test.
10. Andi makes *good* tandoori chicken.

Writer's Corner

Write a paragraph about a day that you did something special or exciting. Use the synonyms that you listed for the Writer's Corner on page 59 in your paragraph.

Study Skills

Using the Internet

Internet Research Checklist

✓ Who wrote the information?

✓ Is the author an expert on the topic? How do I know?

✓ What is the purpose of this site: to sell? to entertain? to inform?

✓ When was the site last updated?

✓ Does the site include facts, such as examples or quotations, that I can check in other sources?

✓ Does the information agree with other sources?

Some people call the Internet the world's biggest library. Writers use the Internet to find facts that they can use in almost any kind of writing.

Reliable Information

The main challenge for writers who conduct Internet research is to determine how reliable the information on a Web site really is. You need to be sure that the information is correct.

First check the three-letter extension at the end of a Web site address. The following are some common extensions:

.com	commercial sites	.mil	military sites
.edu	sites developed by schools	.org	sites developed by organizations
.gov	government sites		

Avoid using information from commercial Web sites. Because almost anyone can create a Web page with a .com extension, the information may not be reliable. Take care when using information from a site developed by a school. A Web article written by a university professor will probably be more reliable than a research report written by a student.

Check who the author of the information is and when the site was last updated. Check the facts that you want to use in a reference book or on at least two other Web sites.

The Internet Research Checklist can help you determine whether the information on a Web site is reliable.

Activity A

Find the Youth Service America Web site and answer the following questions.

1. What is the purpose of the Web site?

2. Does the Web site seem reliable to you? Explain why or why not.

3. What information does the Web site give?

4. Is the information up-to-date? Explain how you know.

Activity B

Choose two of the following topics. Go to a Web site that gives information on each topic. Use the Internet Research Checklist on page 62 to determine if each Web site is reliable.

1. global warming

2. volunteer programs for students

3. immunization

4. extreme sports

5. Walt Disney

Activity C

Imagine that you are writing a how-to handbook about first aid. Find a reliable Web site about the topic. List some of the first-aid skills you might explain in your handbook.

Writer's Corner

Choose one of the first-aid skills that you read about in Activity C. Research that skill, using at least three Web sites, or one Web site and one book. Then write a list of steps explaining how to do that skill.

Search Engines

Internet research usually starts with a search engine. A search engine locates Web sites about the topic that you are researching. Many search engines were made especially for kids. These search engines are helpful because they have many links to school topics.

Keywords

When you use a search engine to research a topic, you will type keywords into the search field. The keywords will help the search engine find Web sites about your topic.

Choose keywords carefully. Use words that are important to your topic. Which of the keywords below do you think will get the best results if you were researching blue jays?

A. Search the Web | birds, blue | **Go**

B. Search the Web | blue jays, habitat, recognizing | **Go**

Example A would probably get results for all blue birds, such as the blue heron or the blue-winged warbler. Example B will get better results because the search engine will know to look only for Web sites about blue jays. It will also search for specific information you might need, such as where blue jays live and how to recognize them.

Internet Safety

The Internet is used daily by millions of people for millions of different things. Just as in the real world, you need to be cautious online. Here are some tips for safely using the Internet.

- Do not give out any personal information, such as your name, age, address, phone number, or information about your family. If you register a screen name, use a catchy nickname instead of your real name.

- If you read or see something that makes you uncomfortable or suspicious, alert an adult right away.

- Do not download files without asking the person who owns the computer you are using. Some downloads can cause problems for a computer.

Activity D

For each topic below, choose the set of keywords that will get the best search results.

1. fifth-grade science fair projects
   A. science, easy
   B. science projects, science fair, fifth grade

2. nurses in the Civil War
   A. Civil War, nurses, training
   B. nurses

3. space exploration
   A. explorers, outer space
   B. astronauts, NASA

4. the best computer for your needs
   A. computers, price
   B. computer, software package, special deals

Activity E

Choose something that you would like to know about each topic below. List keywords that might get good results in an Internet search.

1. the Revolutionary War

2. ancient Rome

3. a famous author

4. the history of television

5. women in sports

Writer's Corner

Choose one of the topics from Activity E and use the keywords that you listed to search the Internet. Decide how well the first five Web sites fit the topic. Change your keywords if necessary to get better results.

How-to Talks

If you've ever given directions to your home or explained to a friend how to blow bubbles, then you have given a how-to talk. How-to talks teach an audience how to do or make something.

Topic

When you choose a topic for your how-to talk, think about what you know how to do. You could give a how-to talk about how to play your favorite sport or how to plan a birthday party. Choose a topic for your how-to article that can be done in a few steps that are easy to explain. Choose a topic you know a lot about.

Audience

Knowing who your audience is will help you think of how to give your talk. Your audience should be able to understand the steps you talk about. If you need to do so, define words or phrases that you think your audience will have trouble understanding.

Organization

Start your how-to talk with an introduction that grabs your audience's attention. You might want to start with a question such as "Have you ever wanted to learn how to . . . ?" Or you might want to begin with an exclamation such as "All right, everybody, let's learn how to . . . !" Be sure to organize your steps in the order they need to be done and to use transition words to help your audience understand the order.

End your talk with a sentence or two about why it's good to know how to do what you are teaching your audience. You might end your talk with some tips on the usefulness of what your audience has learned to do.

Activity A

Explain why each topic would or would not be interesting for fifth graders.

1. how to tie your shoe
2. how to play tick-tack-toe
3. how to get to your home from school
4. how to run the 50-yard dash
5. how to catch butterflies
6. how to find seashells on a beach
7. how to make a telephone call
8. how to play the harmonica
9. how to paint a picture
10. how to snap your fingers
11. how to build a birdhouse
12. how to go bird watching
13. how to play checkers
14. how to dress yourself in the morning
15. how to tie a bow tie

Activity B

Choose a topic from Activity A. Write an introduction to a how-to talk about that topic.

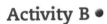

Speaker's Corner

Pretend you are giving a talk about how to clean a bedroom. Begin by making a list of all the things you must accomplish. Then write a step-by-step list of what you should do.

Prepare Your Talk

Writing the steps of your how-to talk on note cards can help you. Write each step on one note card and number the note cards. Then look over your cards and make sure that they are in order, that the information is complete, and that you remembered to include all of the steps.

You might want to prepare note cards for your introduction and conclusion too. If you think of something that will grab your audience's attention, write it on a note card. If you have ideas for other ways to do or use what you are teaching, write those on a note card. Label which card is for your introduction and which card is for your conclusion.

Prepare Your Visual Aid

Sometimes a how-to talk needs a visual aid. A poster that shows the steps of your topic can help make the steps easier for your audience to understand. Another kind of visual aid is a demonstration. For example, if you are doing a how-to talk on tying a tie, you can bring a tie to show your audience while you explain what to do for each step. If you are explaining how to make something, it might be a good idea to bring in an example of the finished product.

Practice

Practicing can help you discover and correct any problems in your presentation. As you practice, keep these questions in mind.

- Will my audience understand what I'm saying?
- Do I start my topic with an attention-grabbing introduction?
- Am I speaking loudly and clearly enough for my audience to hear and understand?
- Are all of my steps in the right order?
- Have I taken out steps that the audience doesn't need?
- Does my conclusion tell the audience why knowing my topic is good for them?

When you feel comfortable with your presentation, practice with a friend or family member. Ask your listener the above questions.

Listening Tips

Listening to a how-to talk can be just as important as giving one. Keep these points in mind while you listen to how-to talks.

- As you listen, imagine doing each step yourself.
- Carefully watch what the speaker does.
- Take notes of the steps if you can.
- When the speaker has finished, ask questions about any steps you didn't understand.

Our Wide Wide World

Because of its strategic location, New Jersey was a hotbed of activity during the American Revolution. The Battle of Trenton, the skirmish that inspired the well-known painting of General Washington crossing the Delaware River, took place there. New Jersey was the third state to ratify the U.S. Constitution. Shortly thereafter, it was the first to endorse the Bill of Rights.

Activity C

Select a topic for your how-to talk. You may choose your own or choose one of the topics from Activity A on page 67. Remember to select a topic that you know about and that can be done in a few easy-to-do steps.

Activity D

Use the topic you chose in Activity C and prepare and practice your how-to talk. Write your steps on note cards. Prepare a visual aid if you need one.

Activity E

Practice your how-to talk with a partner. Then listen to your partner's how-to talk. Give your partner suggestions on how to make the talk better.

Speaker's Corner

Present your how-to talk to your class. Remember to speak slowly, clearly, and with enthusiasm for your topic. Make sure everyone in your audience can see and hear you. When you have finished, invite your audience to ask questions.

Chapter 2 Writer's Workshop

How-to Articles
Prewriting and Drafting

You probably know how to do and make many things. This will be your chance to write an article that teaches how to do or make something.

Prewriting

Javier's class was writing how-to articles. Javier wanted to jump right in, but he knew he should get ready before he started writing. By prewriting, Javier could choose a topic and organize his directions.

Choosing a Topic
Javier began by making this chart to help him think of topics.

Things I do well

tell jokes
hit home runs

Things I do indoors

draw
magic tricks
collect comic books

Things I can make

clay figures
tuna surprise
a lasso

Things I do outdoors

swim
rollerblade

Javier looked at his chart and knew he had to shorten his list. First, he crossed off the topics that were too broad, such as drawing and swimming. He could have narrowed the topic of swimming to how to do the butterfly stroke, but he wanted a different topic. Some of his topics would be too hard to explain in writing, such as how to hit a home run or how to tell a joke. Of the topics left, he liked magic tricks the best. Javier thought his classmates would find it fun to learn how to do a magic trick.

Your Turn
Make a chart like Javier's to help you think of topics. When you finish, cross off any that would be hard to write about in a how-to article. If your topics are too broad, think of narrower ones. Pick a topic you are excited to write about. An enthusiastic writer can get a reader to become excited too.

Organizing Directions

Javier knew his magic trick pretty well. But he thought that explaining how to do his trick might be difficult. To make sure he kept the body of his article in logical order, he decided to organize his steps. Since a flowchart shows how one step flows to the next, he thought it might be a useful tool for organizing his article. Here is Javier's flowchart. Javier's flowchart helped him to see how each step leads to the next. He kept his flowchart to refer to when he started writing.

Your Turn

A flowchart can help you see whether your steps are in logical order. First, make a list of the steps in your how-to article. Then rewrite the steps as a flowchart. Do the steps lead from one to the next? Are there any steps missing? Should you delete any steps?

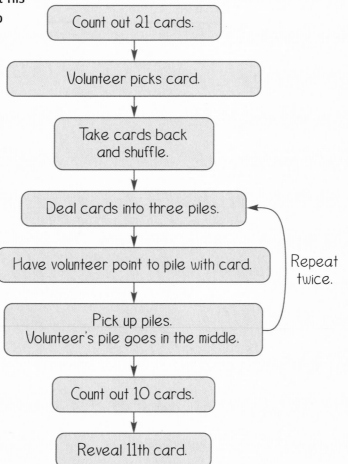

Count out 21 cards.

Volunteer picks card.

Take cards back and shuffle.

Deal cards into three piles.

Have volunteer point to pile with card.

Pick up piles.
Volunteer's pile goes in the middle.

Repeat twice.

Count out 10 cards.

Reveal 11th card.

Drafting

Javier was ready to begin. He had taken good notes, and he knew in what order to give his directions. Javier double-spaced his draft. He knew that his draft would be good, but he would want room to make changes later.

How to Do Magic

Everyone loves a magic trick. I know a magic trick that is based on math, not magic. If you follow these easy directions, you'll dazzle your friends every time! I love this trick so much that I just can't wait to tell you about it!

All you need are a deck of playing cards, a table, and a volunteer. First, count out 21 cards. Then ask the volunteer to pick a card and to look at it without showing it to you? Tell the volunteer to put it back. Then take the cards back and schuffle them.

Explain that you are going to deal out the cards face-up in three piles. Deal the cards in three piles. Deal left to right. Put one card in each pile. Do this until all the cards are in one of the three piles. Tell the volunteer to watch for his or her card without saying anything when it appears. When you finish, ask the volunteer to point to the pile that the card is in.

Now pick up the piles one at a time. The important part is to be sure that when you put the three piles together, the pile with the volunteer's card is in the middle. Then lay the cards on the table again in three piles, the same as before. Ask the volunteer to point to the pile that has the card. Then pick up the piles with that pile in the middle. Lay the cards on the table a third time.

After the volunteer has pointed to the pile, pick up the cards again the same way. Be sure that the cards never get shuffled or mixed up.

To finish the truck, count out the first 10 cards placing them face-down on the table. Then with a dramatic toss, drop the 11th card on the table face-up.

If you follow these directions exactly, the volunteer's card will always be the 11th card. Make sure you practice this trick alone a few times to get used to it. When you get used to it, you can think of ways to add dazzle to the trick.

Your Turn

Use your notes to help you organize the body of your how-to article. Be sure you also make notes about what you could write in your introduction and conclusion. As you write your first draft, keep your audience in mind. Try to get them interested in your topic and be sure that your directions are clear. Remember to double-space your draft so that you have room to make changes later.

How-to Articles

Content Editing

Javier knew his magic trick pretty well, but writing about it had been harder than he thought it would be. Still, he felt good about his first draft. He knew that if he edited his draft for content, he could make sure that readers would understand it. To content edit, he would check that his ideas were clear and that his article was complete. Here is the checklist Javier used to content edit his draft.

Content Editor's Checklist

✓ Does the introduction tell readers what they will make or do?

✓ Are the steps in logical order?

✓ Are the directions accurate and complete?

✓ Does the conclusion give readers a sense of completeness? Does it offer further tips?

✓ Does the article use imperative sentences?

Javier knew that asking someone else to read his draft might be a good idea. His pen pal Talisha lived in Chicago, and she was the best writer Javier knew. Javier decided to e-mail his first draft to Talisha. He also sent a copy of his Content Editor's Checklist.

Talisha replied to Javier's e-mail with several comments. She knew that she had to be extra careful writing her comments because Javier could not hear her tone of voice and might misunderstand something.

She started by telling Javier how much she liked his draft. She thought his topic was interesting and fun. Then Talisha made suggestions for how Javier might improve his draft.

- The introduction is good, but the title confused me. The title says it is a magic trick, but the introduction says the trick is based on math, not magic. Maybe you can fix the title.

- The last sentence of the introduction doesn't seem right. It's good to know that you are excited, but that sentence sounds like something you might say to your friends. It doesn't sound like a sentence that should be in a how-to article.

- Your directions are logical and accurate. I tried the trick on my mom, and it worked! I thought it might be more logical to tell the volunteer to look for the card before you deal the cards out. If you don't, he or she might not be looking for it when you deal.

- The second to the last paragraph doesn't seem complete. You tell the reader to drop the 11th card, but you don't say what the 11th card should be.

- I think you might want to add something to your conclusion. Maybe tell us how we can use this trick.

Javier was glad he'd e-mailed his how-to article to Talisha. She had some good ideas for how to make his draft better. Javier printed out Talisha's reply. He wanted to read it over later and decide which changes to make.

Your Turn

Read your draft and answer the questions on the Content Editor's Checklist one at a time. After you have made notes on how to improve the content of your draft, trade drafts with a partner. Use the Content Editor's Checklist as you read your partner's draft. Make notes on ways your partner's draft could be improved.

Then talk to your partner about your ideas. Remember to start by telling your partner what you liked.

Some of your partner's ideas may help you write a better article. Think about them carefully. Remember that you do not have to make all the changes your partner suggests.

How-to Articles

Revising

This is Javier's revised draft.

How to Do ^Magic
(Mathematical)

Everyone loves a magic trick. I know a magic trick that is based on math, not magic. If you follow these easy directions, you'll dazzle your friends every time! ~~I love this trick so much that I just can't wait to tell you about it!~~

All you need are a deck of playing cards, a table, and a volunteer. First, count out 21 cards. Then ask the volunteer to pick a card and to look at it without showing it to you? Tell the volunteer to put it back. Then take the cards back and schuffle them.

Explain that you are going to deal out the cards face-up in three piles. Deal the cards in three piles. Deal left to right. Put one card in each pile. Do this until all the cards are in one of the three piles. Tell the volunteer to watch for his or her card without saying anything when it appears. When you finish, ask the volunteer to point to the pile that the card is in.

Now pick up the piles one at a time. The important part is to be sure that when you put the three piles together, the pile with the volunteer's card is in the middle. Then lay the cards on the table again in three piles, the same as before. Ask the volunteer to point to the pile that has the card. Then pick up the piles with that pile in the middle. Lay the cards on the table a third time.

After the volunteer has pointed to the pile, pick up the cards again the same

way. Be sure that the cards never get shuffled or mixed up.

To finish the truck, count out the first 10 cards placing them face-down on
~~Your volunteer will be perplexed to see that the 11th card is his or her card.~~
the table. Then with a dramatic toss, drop the 11th card on the table face-up.∧

If you follow these directions exactly, the volunteer's card will always be

the 11th card. Make sure you practice this trick alone a few times to get used

to it. When you get used to it, you can think of ways to add dazzle to the trick.∧
Think about putting together a magic show for your friends. Save this
trick for last it is a real show stopper.

Look at the changes Javier made.

- Javier added the word *Mathematical* to the title. The new title told readers that the trick was based on math, but that it was also a magic trick.

- Javier realized that the last sentence of the introduction was a little too informal. He decided to delete it.

- He fixed the logical order of his third paragraph by moving a sentence.

- Javier wanted to tell the reader what to expect when he or she drops the 11th card. He wanted to write that the volunteer will be *surprised* to see his or her card, but *surprised* seemed like a dull word. He liked the word *perplexed,* so he used it instead.

- Javier thought his conclusion wasn't complete. He decided to give a suggestion on the way that readers could use the trick in a magic show.

Your Turn
Revise your how-to article. Use the ideas you and your partner had. When you have finished, go over the Content Editor's Checklist again.

How-to Articles

Copyediting and Proofreading

Copyediting

Javier knew he could improve his draft further by copyediting it. He checked that his sentences were clear and correct and that he'd used the words in his article correctly. Here is the Copyeditor's Checklist Javier used to check his draft.

Copyeditor's Checklist

✓ Are transition words used to help readers follow the steps?

✓ Are other kinds of sentences beside imperative sentences used to add variety?

✓ Are all of the sentences complete?

✓ Do all the words mean what I think they mean?

Javier had used plenty of transition words, but he checked to see if he could add more. He added *First* in the second paragraph to show that the trick was beginning. He also added *Finally* to the sentence that tells the reader to lay the cards out a third time. This transition word let the reader know that this is the last time to lay out the cards.

Most of the sentences in Javier's article were imperative sentences. He had also used other kinds of sentences for variety.

As Javier read his article, he noticed that the third paragraph sounded choppy. He decided to combine sentences to make it read more smoothly. He combined three sentences into the sentence "Deal left to right, one card in each pile, until all the cards are in one of the three piles." Do you see the three sentences he combined?

He also wondered if he used the word *perplexed* correctly. He liked the sound of the word, but he wasn't sure that he knew exactly what it meant. The dictionary said it meant "to confuse or puzzle." That wasn't really what he wanted to say. He replaced *perplexed* with *amazed,* which was closer in meaning to what he wanted to say.

Your Turn

Read your revised draft carefully. See if you can answer yes to the questions on the checklist. Look for ways to make your writing read smoothly. Remember to check for one kind of mistake at a time.

Proofreading

Javier wanted to check his article one more time so that he did not publish it with any mistakes. Proofreading his draft meant he would look for mistakes that he might have made in spelling, punctuation, capitalization, and grammar. Javier used this checklist to proofread his work.

Proofreader's Checklist

✓ Are the paragraphs indented?

✓ Are all the words spelled correctly?

✓ Are capitalization and punctuation correct?

✓ Is the grammar correct?

✓ Were any new errors added while editing?

Javier found two spelling errors in his draft. In the fifth paragraph, he'd written *truck* when he meant to write *trick.* Do you see the other misspelled word?

Javier asked his best friend, Earl, to proofread his draft. Javier knew that someone who hadn't already read his work would be more likely to see mistakes in it.

Earl found that the punctuation at the end of the third sentence of the second paragraph was incorrect. The sentence is not a question. What kind of punctuation should Javier use?

Earl pointed out that the last sentence should be written as two sentences. Javier saw that he had added that mistake when he was revising for content. He was especially glad that Earl had caught that mistake.

Your Turn

Read through your draft carefully. Use the Proofreader's Checklist to look for mistakes. Each time you read through your draft, check for only one kind of mistake.

When you have finished, trade drafts with a partner. Go over each other's drafts, using the Proofreader's Checklist. A dictionary can help you to spell words correctly. When you get your draft back from your partner, decide if the changes your partner suggested are correct before you make those changes in your draft.

How-to Articles

Publishing

Publishing happens the moment you finally share your finished work with your audience. Javier couldn't wait to publish his how-to article. He had worked hard, and he knew it was his best work. He was also excited because he knew his audience would enjoy reading about how to do a magic trick. He carefully typed his final copy on a computer and passed out copies of his article to his whole class.

How to Do Mathematical Magic

Everyone loves a magic trick. I know a magic trick that is based on math, not magic. If you follow these easy directions, you'll dazzle your friends every time!

All you need are a deck of playing cards, a table, and a volunteer. First count out 21 cards. Then ask the volunteer to pick a card and to look at it without showing it to you. Tell the volunteer to put it back. Then take the cards back and shuffle them.

Explain that you are going to deal out the cards face-up in three piles. Tell the volunteer to watch for his or her card without saying anything when it appears. Deal the cards in three piles. Deal left to right, one card in each pile, until all the cards are in one of the three piles. When you finish, ask the volunteer to point to the pile that the card is in.

Now pick up the piles one at a time. The important part is to be sure that when you put the three piles together, the pile with the volunteer's card is in the middle. Then lay the cards on the table again in three piles, the same as before. Ask the volunteer to point to the pile that has the card.

Then pick up the piles with that pile in the middle. Finally lay the cards on the table a third time. After the volunteer has pointed to the pile, pick up the cards again the same way. Be sure that the cards never get shuffled or mixed up.

To finish the trick, count out the first 10 cards placing them face-down on the table. Then with a dramatic toss, drop the 11th card on the table face-up. Your volunteer will be amazed to see that the 11th card is his or her card.

If you follow these directions exactly, the volunteer's card will always be the 11th card. Make sure you practice this trick alone a few times to get used to it. When you get used to it, you can think of ways to add dazzle to the trick. Think about putting together a magic show for your friends. Save this trick for last. It is a real show stopper.

Your Turn

Now it is time to make one last check of your work before you share it with your audience. To publish your work, follow these steps:

- Type your draft on a computer or rewrite it in neat handwriting.
- Make sure you did not leave out any words or punctuation as you made your final copy.
- Proofread one more time to make sure you caught all the mistakes.
- Add drawings or diagrams to your work. Some how-to articles can be made clearer with a visual aid.
- Share your work with your audience.

How will your class share your how-to articles? You might take turns reading your how-to article to the class.

You might decide to have a How-to Day at school. Each person could set up a station at which to share his or her information.

You might put together a classroom How-to Manual. Collect all the how-to articles in a binder. You could make the manual available in your classroom or school library.

CHAPTER 3

Our Wide Wide World

Martha Washington—
the wife of the first
President of the
United States, George
Washington—
reluctantly became the
first First Lady of the
United States. Martha
was content with a
private life on their
Mount Vernon estate.
She opposed George's
candidacy for
president and even
refused to attend his
inauguration. As First
Lady, however, Martha
became a gracious
hostess to the
president's many
visitors. Why do you
think that the role
of a First Lady is
important?

Business Letters

834 Gutherie Lane
Rooster River, MI 49103

March 3, 20—

Ms. Gertrude Bea
Coordinator of Youth Activities
Rooster River Park District
1002 North Case Drive
Rooster River, MI 49103

Dear Ms. Bea:

My family and I would like to encourage you to offer junior golf lessons or junior golf leagues at Quarry Greens this year. A visit to your excellent Web site did not indicate that you are offering either of these.

I am the father of two middle school students who are fast becoming golf enthusiasts. We are new to the area, and as spring approaches our thoughts turn to our favorite family sport. My children want to hone their golf skills, and I would like to give them that opportunity.

I have spoken about this with our school's physical education teacher and several parents. We would all be interested in working with you to encourage student participation. We feel that many parents will sign their children up if you offer club rentals and lesson fees at a reduced rate.

Please consider sponsoring golf activities for middle school boys and girls this spring or summer. I look forward to your response. Thank you for your consideration.

Sincerely yours,

Mike Hernandez

Mike Hernandez

What Makes a Good Business Letter?

Mr. Hernandez's letter on page 83 is a letter of inquiry, which is a type of business letter. Business letters are written to a company, an organization, or a person for a specific purpose. Unlike a personal letter that you might write to a friend, a business letter is formal in tone and sticks closely to a single topic. Mr. Hernandez does not know Ms. Bea, so he communicates his ideas to her in a formal way. Business letters all have the same parts to make the information easy to find. Look at Mr. Hernandez's letter below to see where the parts of the business letter are placed.

Heading

The writer's return address is in the top left corner of the letter. The date of the letter should be placed below the address. Notice the correct punctuation and capitalization of the address and date.

Inside Address

The receiver's name is first. It is followed by the receiver's job title if you know it, and the company or organization's address. Notice the correct punctuation and capitalization of the address.

Salutation

This is the greeting of the letter. It begins with "Dear" followed by the person's name and a colon. If the person's name is not known, "Dear Sir or Madam:" or "To Whom It May Concern:" is used.

Body

The body is the main part of the letter. It is single-spaced, with a line between paragraphs and an extra line after the last paragraph. The paragraphs are not indented.

Closing

This is the part of the letter in which the writer says goodbye to the receiver. Use a formal closing such as *Sincerely* or *Sincerely yours*, followed by a comma.

Signature

The writer's signature comes after the closing. It is followed by the writer's printed or typed name.

---

834 Gutherie Lane
Rooster River, MI 49103

March 3, 20—

Ms. Gertrude Bea
Coordinator of Youth Activities
Rooster River Park District
1002 North Case Drive
Rooster River, MI 49103

Dear Ms. Bea:

My family and I would like to encourage you to offer junior golf lessons or junior golf leagues at Quarry Greens this year. A visit to your excellent Web site did not indicate that you are offering either of these.

I am the father of two middle school students who are fast becoming golf enthusiasts. We are new to the area, and as spring approaches our thoughts turn to our favorite family sport. My children want to hone their golf skills, and I would like to give them that opportunity.

I have spoken about this with our school's physical education teacher and several parents. We would all be interested in working with you to encourage student participation. We feel that many parents would sign their children up if you offer club rentals and lesson fees at a reduced rate.

Please consider sponsoring golf activities for middle school boys and girls this spring or summer. I look forward to your response. Thank you for your consideration.

Sincerely yours,

Mike Hernandez

Mike Hernandez

Activity A

Identify which part of a business letter each item below is from.

1. Maria Ranier *Maria Ranier*

2. To Whom It May Concern:

3. I would like to know when the Apostle Island Park will open.

4. Mr. Wally Schiller
   Lead Writer
   Hanover Magazine

5. December 8, 2020

6. Sincerely,

Activity B

Rewrite the business letter so that all the parts are in the right order.

November 11, 2007
2434 Redwood Drive
Marin City, CA 94965

Dear Dr. Stein:
Dr. Mariel Stein
Oakland Community College
42 College Circle Drive
Oakland, CA 94606

I would like to bring my fifth-grade class to your botany lab. I feel that it would be worthwhile for them to see a botanist at work. Please let me know if you can make time for us.

Sincerely yours,

Gerald Fitzscott

Gerald Fitzscott

Writer's Corner

Write all of the parts of a business letter except the body. Make up a name and an address for the business or organization to which you are writing.

Language

The language of a business letter is more formal than the language of a personal letter. Choose words carefully. Keep descriptions and explanations brief and to the point. Don't include unnecessary details.

Formal Language

When you write a business letter, do not use slang, such as *cool* and *bummed*. Avoid casual language, such as contractions. Here are some other ways to make your writing more formal.

- Replace long phrases with single words.

  I <u>took a look</u> at the damaged shoe.

  I <u>inspected</u> the damaged shoe.

- Replace strong adjectives with more neutral adjectives.

  There was a <u>massive</u> hole in the bag.

  There was a <u>large</u> hole in the bag.

- Replace general verbs with more specific verbs.

  When I <u>got</u> the DVD, it was scratched.

  When the DVD <u>arrived</u>, it was scratched.

Polite Tone

Have you ever been told to be polite? Do you change your behavior when you are being polite?

Being polite means showing consideration and respect for other people. Saying things such as *when you have an opportunity,* and *thank you for your time,* are ways to show consideration for the receiver of your letter. You can show respect when you write a business letter by using words such as *please, thank you, sincerely,* and *I look forward to.*

Thank you.

Activity C

Read the body of the business letter below. Identify the parts of the letter that are informal.

I recently saw your cello concert at the Parkway Symphony. It was really cool! Boy, you're one great cello player. I would like to invite you to visit my fifth-grade orchestra class. Perhaps you could talk to us and play a short piece on your cello? We need to hear some good tunes from a real pro.

Our class meets every Monday, Wednesday, and alternate Fridays between 11:00 and 12:00. So whenever you want to cruise on by, then, go on ahead. If you are interested, please contact me at the address above.

Activity D

Change the language in each of these sentences to more formal language for a business letter.

1. The clerk was really crabby, and I got mad.

2. I want to get that game you have called Exploring the Amazon.

3. I'm writing a report about your state, and I need some stuff. You must have lots of information.

4. I think you're so cool! Want to speak to my English class?

5. Your Web site said delivery would take 6 to 8 days, but it took way longer!

Writer's Corner

Use one of these sentence starters in a body paragraph of a business letter. Use formal language and a polite tone.

A. Please send me . . .
B. I am enclosing . . .
C. I would like to inquire about . . .

Purpose

Business people have many things to do at their jobs. So when you write a business letter, it's important to state the purpose of your letter quickly and clearly. When you write a business letter, state briefly why you are writing the letter, and state what action you want the person to take.

Types of Business Letters

Business letters generally fall into three groups. Here are some common types of business letters.

Ordering a Product

Imagine you want to order a hollow log for your tarantula habitat. If you were to order the log from a magazine ad, you might write a business letter. You would include information such as the product number and where to ship your order.

Inquiry or Request

What if you wanted to invite a famous author to speak to your class? You might write a letter of inquiry. You would tell the author where your school is and times that the author could give a presentation. You might also write a letter to request information from an organization. The organization might answer questions in a response letter or might send you books or pamphlets with the information you requested.

Complaint

You might write a letter of complaint if a product you ordered was broken or took longer to arrive than you expected. When you write a letter of complaint, you should first explain what the problem is. Then you might suggest ways that the problem could be fixed, such as a refund or a replacement.

Our Wide Wide World

Abigail Smith Adams was the wife of the country's second president, John Adams, and the mother of the fifth president, John Quincy Adams. Abigail's letters to her husband while he served in the Continental Congress may be her most lasting legacy. The letters tell what life was like for her at the time, raising their children and tending to their farm alone.

Activity A

Read each situation below and identify the purpose of the business letter you might write about it.

1. Your parents said you could subscribe to a magazine that you like.

2. A server at a restaurant was rude to you.

3. You want information about rock formations for your report on the Carlsbad Caverns.

4. You received an order of invisible ink that turned out not to be invisible.

5. You want to know what the requirements are to become the manager of a basketball team.

Activity B

Match each sentence below to one of the following types of business letters: *ordering a product, inquiry or request, complaint*. You may use each type of letter more than once.

1. I have not yet received the tulip bulbs that I ordered 9 weeks ago.

2. Because you are Central's most accomplished graduate, we would like your permission to name a scholarship after you.

3. Please send three copies of the book, item #772859, to the address above.

4. I would like to know what the requirements are to become Drama Club treasurer.

5. I would like a one-year subscription to your excellent magazine, *Dog Fancy.*

Writer's Corner

Brainstorm three reasons you might have for writing a business letter. Identify the type of letter that you would write. Save your work.

The Body of a Business Letter

The body of a business letter is where you tell the person or company what you want. You might ask for a product or service, make a complaint, or offer a compliment.

No matter what you write about, it is important to be clear and to the point when you write a business letter. Stay on the topic and only write detailed information directly related to your problem or request.

The body of a business letter usually has three parts.

Beginning

In the beginning of a business letter, you state the purpose of the letter. In the letter on page 83, Mr. Hernandez wants to encourage the park district to offer golf activities for his children. That was his purpose for writing.

Middle

The middle of a business letter includes information that explains more about the letter's purpose. In Mr. Hernandez's letter, he supports his request by saying that his children enjoy playing golf and that the physical education teacher and other parents are in favor of his idea.

Ending

In the ending of a business letter, you invite the receiver to act on or respond to whatever you are asking. The ending of Mr. Hernandez's letter asks Ms. Bea to consider starting a golf program for young people. He also thanks her for considering his request.

Activity C

Identify whether each sentence below belongs in the beginning, the middle, or the ending of a business letter.

1. Thank you for your time.

2. I would like to know whether you have any information about rock formations in the Clovis area.

3. I am hoping you will talk about some of your new paintings.

4. I look forward to a quick resolution of this problem.

5. My class has already read *River Wolf*. What else might you suggest?

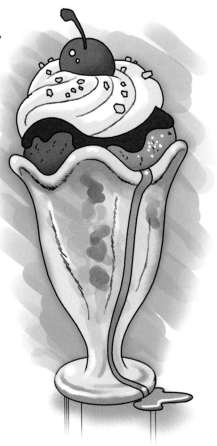

Activity D

Write the beginning of a business letter that relates to each of the following situations. Be sure that the receiver of each letter can easily figure out why the letter was written.

1. The clerk at a toy store laughed at your younger sister when she tried to buy a doll with the change in her piggy bank.

2. You bought an ice-cream maker that makes great ice cream. You want to tell the company how happy you are.

3. You bought a CD player that stopped working about a week later.

4. You read in the newspaper that the City Council wants to tear down your favorite historic building to build a shopping center.

Writer's Corner

Write the middle and ending of the letter you began in Activity D. Remember that the middle should support the purpose of the letter and that the ending should ask the receiver to act on or respond to what you are asking.

Roots

The legend of Molly Pitcher may have been based on Mary Hays McCauly, who supposedly carried pitchers of water to soldiers during the American Revolution. According to some accounts, when Mary's husband was critically injured during battle, Mary took over his cannon and continued to fight against the British. It is said that after the battle, General George Washington praised Mary for her bravery.

What do the words *bibliography, fortitude,* and *thermometer* have in common? All three words are formed from roots. A root is a building block for other words. Knowing the meaning of a root can often help you figure out the meaning of an unfamiliar word. The root *bibl* means "book." A bibliography is a list of books.

Often the root comes from an ancient language, such as Latin or Greek. Sometimes you add letters to the beginning (a prefix) of a root to form a new word. Sometimes you add letters to the end (a suffix) of a root to form a new word.

Root	Meaning	Examples
dict	to speak	pre<u>dict</u>, <u>dict</u>ionary

Another root is *cred*. It comes from the Latin word *credere*, meaning "to believe." Here are some words that share the same root. Read each word. Check the pronunciation and the meanings of unfamiliar words in a dictionary. How does each word relate to *believe?*

credence	miscreant	credibility
credit	credo	creed
discredit	incredible	incredulous

Notice that sometimes the spelling of the root changes. Which words are not spelled with *cred?* Which words have prefixes added to the root? Which words have suffixes added to the root?

Activity A

The Greek root *graph* means "to write or to draw." Read the words below and answer the questions that follow.

> graphic   epigraph   autograph   biography   paragraph

1. Which words have prefixes added to the root?
2. Which words have suffixes added to the root?
3. Which word has both a prefix and a suffix added to the root?
4. Which word means
   an inscription, motto, or quotation?
   a written or pictorial representation?
   a person's own signature?

Activity B

The Latin root *finis,* means "end or limit." Read the words below and answer the questions that follow.

> unfinished   finish   finally   finale   infinite   finalist

1. In which words does *-is* change to *-al?*
2. Which word means
   to bring to an end?
   a contestant in the finals of a competition?
   not complete?
   without limits or bounds, endless?

Writer's Corner

Identify the meaning of the common root in the words below. Then use the words in separate sentences that show the meaning of each word.

audible   audiovisual   audience   auditorium

Activity C

Read these roots and their meanings. Then read the sentences that follow. Combine two of the roots to make a word that completes each sentence. You may use a root more than once.

Root	Meaning	Root	Meaning
auto	self	*scope*	see
chrono	time	*graph*	write
tele	far	*meter*	measure
audio	hear	*phone*	sound
micro	small		

1. The nurse used an _____ to measure our ability to hear.

2. We used a _____ to see the tiny plant cells.

3. The author wrote her name in my book when I asked for her _____.

4. The _____ measured the time to the exact second.

5. My best friend lives far away, so I call him on the _____.

6. With my new _____, I can see the farthest stars clearly.

Activity D

Read the following paragraph. Make a list of words that have the root *port.* Give the meaning of the root. Then write the meaning of each word. Use a dictionary if you need help. Finally, list other words that contain the root *port.*

We were up early and ready for a day at the beach. Mom watched the weather report and told us that we would have a hot, sunny day. I brought my portable radio so that we could listen to music. Dad packed sandwiches and cold drinks for us to transport to our destination. With food, blankets, towels, and everything else, we almost needed a porter to help us carry everything.

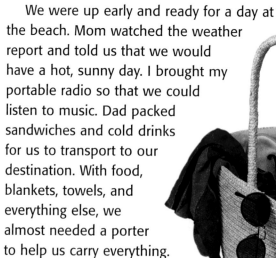

Activity E

Fill in the missing roots, examples, and meanings to complete the chart below. Use a dictionary for help.

	Root	Meaning	Example	Meaning
1.	cardi	_____	cardiac	of or near the heart
2.	therm	heat	thermal	_____
3.	_____	climb	ascend	go or move upwards
4.	act	do	_____	act in response
5.	vis	see	vision	_____
6.	_____	say	dictate	say or read aloud
7.	tract	pull	tractor	_____
8.	clar	_____	clarify	make or become clear
9.	scribe	write	_____	give an account of
10.	_____	sea, pool	marine	of the sea

Activity F

Identify and try to define the shared root of each of the following groups of words. Check your answers in a dictionary.

1. digress, progress, transgress
2. convert, divert, revert
3. eject, interject, project
4. depend, pendant, pendulum
5. coauthor, cochair, copilot
6. local, locate, location
7. benefit, benefactor, benevolent

Writer's Corner

Expand the chart in Activity E by adding three other examples of words with the same root. Define each word that you add. Use a dictionary for help.

Writing Skills

Combining Sentences and Sentence Parts

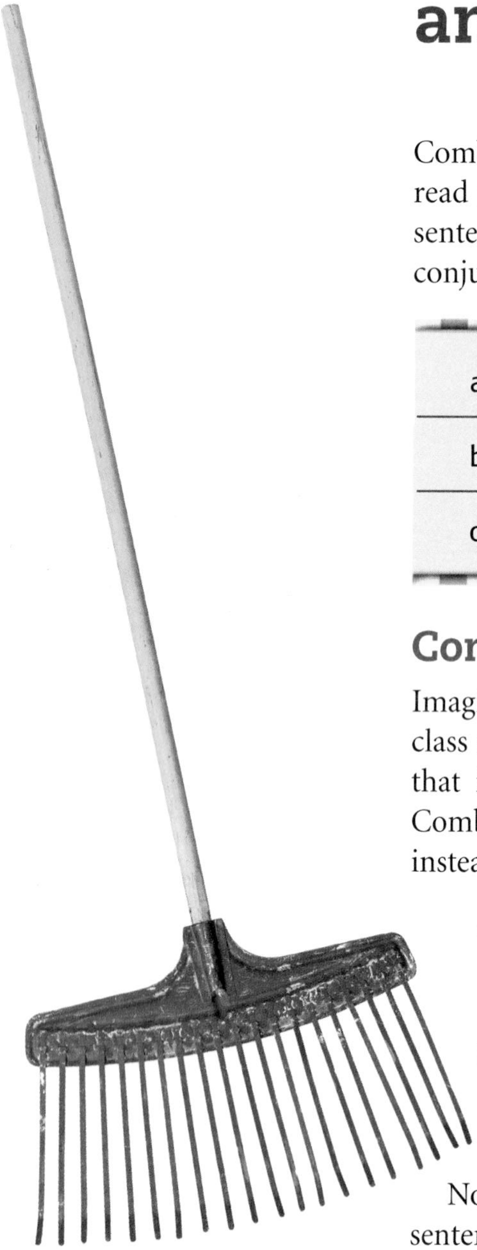

Combining sentences and sentence parts can help your writing read more smoothly. You use conjunctions when you combine sentences. Study the chart below to know when to use the conjunctions *and, but,* or *or.*

and	connects ideas that are alike in some way
but	connects ideas that are different
or	connects ideas that give a choice

Combining Simple Sentences

Imagine that your teacher asked you to deliver a note to another class and also to pick up a book in the library. You might decide that it is easier to do both tasks in one trip instead of two. Combining sentences is like that. You write one longer sentence instead of two short ones.

A. My father said I couldn't go to Brandon's house until I finished my chores. I still needed to take out the trash and rake the leaves.

B. My father said I couldn't go to Brandon's house until I finished my chores, and I still needed to take out the trash and rake the leaves.

Notice that in example B the conjunction *and* joins the two sentences from example A. Can you give examples of sentences that use the conjunctions *and, but,* and *or*? Where would you put a comma in those sentences?

Activity A

Combine each pair of sentences into one sentence. Use the conjunction in parentheses. Remember to use a comma before the conjunction.

1. Some animals have become extinct over time. Today many animals are dying out because of the actions of people. (but)

2. Many animals are already extinct. Many more are now on the list of endangered species. (and)

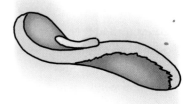

3. Illegal hunting and deforestation are changing our world. Few people worry about what the changes mean to wildlife. (but)

4. We must take care of our wildlife. We may lose many more animals. (or)

5. A lot of animals have become endangered. Wildlife organizations were formed to help save animals. (and)

Activity B

Add a second simple sentence to each of these sentences. Then use both sentences to make one sentence. Use the conjunctions *and, but,* or *or.*

1. I can make delicious pancakes.

2. It is a warm day today.

3. Would you like to see the new movie that just opened?

4. Talia's book report is due on Friday.

5. Should I wake Dustin now?

Writer's Corner

Imagine that you want to tell Wacky Wares Inc. about a defective dribble glass that you bought from them. Write the body of a letter of complaint that explains the problem. Write at least two sentences that use conjunctions to combine simple sentences.

Combining Sentence Parts

Sometimes two sentences are related, and the same words are repeated in both sentences. Often you can combine parts of sentences to make a compound subject, a compound predicate, or a compound direct object. You can use the conjunctions *and, but,* or *or.*

Compound Subjects

A compound subject is made up of more than one subject. Look at the examples below. The compound subject is underlined.

> **A.** Columbus Day is a fall holiday. Thanksgiving is a fall holiday.
>
> **B.** <u>Columbus Day and Thanksgiving</u> are fall holidays.

Compound Predicates

A compound predicate has more than one predicate connected by a conjunction. Look at the examples below. The compound predicate is underlined.

> **A.** On our camping trips, we sleep in a tent. We cook outside.
>
> **B.** On our camping trips, <u>we sleep in a tent and cook outside</u>.

Compound Direct Objects

A direct object answers the question *whom* or *what* after the verb. A compound direct object has more than one answer to the question. Look at the examples below. The compound direct object is underlined.

> **A.** We planted cherry tomatoes in our garden. We planted lettuce in our garden.
>
> **B.** We planted <u>cherry tomatoes and lettuce</u> in our garden.

Activity C

Combine each pair of sentences into one sentence by combining sentence parts. Identify whether each revised sentence has a compound subject or a compound predicate.

1. Hero sandwiches are large. Submarine sandwiches are large.

2. I picked the beautiful wildflowers. I put them in a large vase.

3. I ride my bike to school. I walk to school.

4. In the evening we roast marshmallows at the campfire. We sing songs at the campfire.

5. Bayani saw three movies in a row. Paul saw three movies in a row.

6. Frogs are amphibians. Newts are amphibians.

Activity D

Complete each sentence with a compound direct object. Remember that direct objects answer the questions *whom* or *what* after the verb.

1. For the next assignment, we will write a _____ or a _____.

2. My Aunt Steph bakes the best _____ and _____ in the world.

3. Ignacio invited _____ and _____ to his party.

4. Alexis and her friends like to play _____ or _____ on rainy days.

5. My favorite authors are _____ and _____.

Writer's Corner

Think of all the things that you have done since you got up this morning. Write in paragraph form to describe the events of your day. Include each of the compound sentence parts that you practiced in this lesson.

Filling Out Forms

A form contains information that you might also put in a business letter, such as your name and your address. When you order a product from a company, apply for a library card, or join a sports league, you might fill out a form.

A form has blank spaces for information. When you fill out a form, you should remember to do three things.

- Read the entire form first.
- Neatly fill in the blanks, using your best handwriting.
- Make sure that you have included all the necessary information.

When you have finished filling out a form, reread it carefully. Make sure that the form is completely and accurately filled out.

Internet Forms

It is common to fill out forms on the Internet, especially when ordering a product online.

Internet forms include boxes where you will type information such as your name and your address. Internet forms are often easier to fill out than paper forms. Internet forms will alert you to missing information, and they often have drop-down menus for information such as state abbreviations. Some Web sites let you create a user account so that basic information, such as your name and address, are saved. With a user account, you don't have to fill out the same form over and over again.

Below is an order form from Cheater Five, a surfing store in Hawaii. You want to order some items from their catalog. Copy the form and fill it out. Use your own information for the first part of the form, and make up the missing information for the second part.

Cheater Five   924 Kalauna Rd. • Honolulu, HI 96714

Name _____
       FIRST   LAST   MIDDLE INITIAL

Address _____
        NUMBER, STREET

_____
CITY   STATE   ZIP CODE

Telephone Number (_____)_____
             AREA CODE

E-mail Address _____

QUANTITY	ITEM NO.	DESCRIPTION	SIZE	COLOR	PRICE
1		Traveler Surf Bag	n/a		$40.00
	475981	2/2 Wetsuit	small		
3		Mini-Surf Paint Kit	n/a	n/a	
				Subtotal	
				Shipping	$22.95
				TOTAL	

Writer's Corner

Imagine that you are starting a new club in your school. List the information you might need from new members. Then use the information to create a form for your club.

Dolley Madison was the wife of James Madison, the fourth President of the United States. Dolley's social graces and kindheartedness helped her become one of the most well-liked women of her day. During the War of 1812, while her husband was president, the British burned the White House. Dolley's ability to soothe hostile guests and entertain in temporary housing helped assure her a place as one of history's most highly regarded first ladies.

● Activity B ●

Imagine that you are applying to join Tech Mentors, in which you would tutor students in various aspects of technology. Copy and fill out the application form below. Remember that neat handwriting and complete answers may influence the club sponsor who reads the application form.

TECH MENTOR APPLICATION

Please fill out the application form completely. You will be contacted for an interview after your application has been reviewed.

Name _____

Grade _____ Room _____ Teacher _____

Answer each of the following in a sentence or two.

Why do you want to become a Tech Mentor? _____

_____

_____

What are your favorite computer activities? _____

_____

_____

Is it possible for you to stay after school? If so, what days are good for you? _____

_____

Answer by putting an X in the proper box or boxes.

My lunchtime is ❏ early ❏ late

I can meet during lunchtime. ❏ yes ❏ no

I am most interested in these kinds of mentoring activities:

❏ teaching primary kids ❏ setting up equipment

❏ teaching kids my age ❏ troubleshooting

❏ other (please list below)

_____

_____

Your signature _____

Parent signature _____

Imagine that you are ordering a book from an online bookstore.
Below is the book that you have ordered. Fill in the blank fields.

books-R-us.com

SIGN IN   SHIPPING & PAYMENT   GIFT-WRAP   PLACE ORDER

Type	Item/Price	Quantity
	James and the Giant Peach - Roald Dahl	1
	$8.57 - Ships in 24 hours	
	Condition: new	

Full Name: _____

Address Line 1: _____
Number, Street

Address Line 2: _____
Apartment, Suite, Unit, Floor, etc.

City: _____

State/Province/Region: _____

ZIP/Postal Code: _____

Country: United States ⬍

Phone Number: _____

E-mail Address: _____

Writer's Corner

Imagine that you are applying to become a character
in a book that you like. What information might
you have to provide? Write a form that asks for
this information.

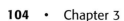

LESSON 6

Speaking and Listening Skills

Business Telephone Calls

Have you ever made a business telephone call? Business calls are different from personal calls, just as business letters are different from personal letters.

Imagine that you wanted to call Waterbrook Art Supplies to complain about an incomplete set of paints that they sent you. You might first look for the telephone number in a directory, on the Internet, or on the product packaging. After you have the correct telephone number, what would you do?

Speaking Professionally

It is important to speak in a professional, polite tone when you make a business call. Getting angry or forgetting what to say because you didn't plan your call wastes time and energy. Here are some tips to help you sound professional when you make a business call.

- Before you make your call, write notes about what you want to say. Use the notes to help you stay on the topic of your call. Notes can also help you leave an accurate message if you cannot reach the person you need to speak with.

- Identify yourself and explain why you are calling. If you are speaking to a receptionist or an operator, this information can help direct your call to the correct person. If you know the person you need to talk to, this information can help that person assist you.

- At the end of the call, sum up what was said during the conversation. This helps you make certain that you understand what was said and what action will be taken.

Leaving a Message

Sometimes the person that you are calling is unavailable. You might have to leave a short message on that person's voice mail. Here are some things to remember when leaving a message.

- Begin by giving your name and your telephone number. Speak slowly, especially when giving your telephone number. If you speak too fast, the person listening may not understand you or might miss important information.

- Briefly explain why you are calling. Remember to use a polite and professional tone of voice.

- End the message by giving your name and telephone number again. This will give the person a chance to check that he or she wrote down the information correctly.

Activity A

Read the following reasons for making a business call. Write notes about what you would say during a business call for each reason.

1. A statue that you ordered has a chip in it.
2. There is a fallen telephone line in your backyard.
3. You've been chosen to select and order your soccer team's new uniforms.
4. A magazine is sponsoring a short-story contest and you have questions about how to enter.
5. You want to invite the town historian to speak to your class.

Speaker's Corner

Choose one of the reasons for making a business call in Activity A. Work with a partner to role-play that business call. Take turns being the caller. Remember to use a professional and polite tone.

Listening Tips

It is important to listen actively when you make a business call. Here are some tips to help you listen actively.

- Keep a notebook and pencil nearby so that you can write down important information.
- Pay attention to the speaker's name.
  Write down the speaker's name so that you know whom to contact in the future.
- If the speaker explains anything complicated, repeat what was said to be sure that you understand completely. Ask questions about anything that you do not understand.
- Give verbal clues to let the speaker know that you are listening. Saying things such as *yes, OK,* or *I understand* will help the other person know that you are following the conversation.

Follow-up Calls

Occasionally you might have to make a follow-up call to a person or a company. It might be to check the results of your first call, to continue a previous conversation, or to thank someone for helping you. When you make a follow-up call, remember to identify yourself. Sum up what the purpose of your previous call was. Then explain why you are calling again.

Call Review Checklist

Use the following checklist when you make business telephone calls.

- Did I greet the person and give my name?
- Did I write down the name of the person I spoke with?
- Did I briefly explain why I called?
- Did I ask the person to take action or fix a problem?
- Did I give verbal clues that I was listening?
- Did I thank the person for taking time to talk with me?

Activity B

Choose one of the situations below. Write notes about what you would say during each of the following parts of the call: *greeting the person, identifying yourself, explaining your reason for calling, requesting help or action, thanking the person.*

A. Your new handheld video game has a defective battery, and you would like a replacement. You call Monstrous Games and speak with Tia, a customer service representative.

B. Famous filmmaker John Stedman has agreed to speak at your school's film club. You call him to arrange the details.

C. You call Matteo, the manager at Gia's Italian Restaurant, to thank him for the great service at your birthday dinner.

D. You call local librarian Gayle Burke with a proposal to set up a Saturday afternoon book club for kids.

Activity C

Work with a partner to role-play the business call you chose in Activity B. Take turns being the person making the call and the person receiving it. Use the Listening Tips from page 106. When you have finished, use the Call Review Checklist to decide how well you made your call.

Activity D

Choose a new situation from those listed in Activity B. Write notes about what you would say. Then imagine that you have reached the voice mail of the person with whom you wish to speak. Work with a partner to practice the message you would leave.

Speaker's Corner

Choose one of the business calls you practiced with a partner and present the call to the class. Use real telephones as props if you can. When you have finished, invite your audience to use the Call Review Checklist to give you feedback about your call.

Business Letters
Prewriting and Drafting

Writing a business letter is a great way to get the attention of a company or an organization. In a business letter you can make sure that everything you want to say is expressed clearly and in logical order.

Prewriting

Gabriella is a fifth grader who is interested in birds and bird watching. She wanted to find out more information about the types of birds that are in her area. She decided to write a letter of inquiry to the National Audubon Society. Gabriella first took the time to do some prewriting. She stated the purpose of her letter and then gathered and organized the information.

Stating the Purpose

Gabriella thought about the purpose of her letter, or what she wanted to accomplish. Gabriella knew that she wanted to inquire about the birds in her area. Did she just want to ask what types of birds could be found? Did she also want to ask where to look for the birds? Did she want to find out about other types of birds in other parts of Alabama? Gabriella wanted to actually go out and see the birds in her neighborhood, so she decided to ask for information on what types of birds to look for and where to look for them.

Your Turn

Think of something you would like more information about. Maybe you would like to know about volunteer opportunities in your community. Maybe you would like to learn how to start a business. You might ask for information about a product, a service, a place, an event, or how to do something. Whatever you decide will be the purpose of your letter of inquiry. Write down what you would specifically like to inquire about.

Gathering Information and Organizing Your Letter

After stating the purpose of her letter of inquiry, Gabriella gathered the information she needed to write the letter. She already knew that she was writing to the National Audubon Society. She looked at their Web site and found that there was a chapter of the society near her town. She wrote down that address. She also found the name of someone from that chapter.

Next Gabriella planned how to organize her letter by drawing a diagram of it. In each box she wrote something that would remind her of what to put in that part of the draft. She also filled in the information she had already gathered. Gabriella thought that by doing this she would have an easier time remembering what she wanted to write in her draft. Here is Gabriella's diagram.

Your Turn

Gather the information that you need to include in your letter of inquiry. First decide to whom you should send your letter. Then find the address. You may need to look online or in a phone book, or you may need to call the company directly.

Draw a diagram of a letter of inquiry, using Gabriella's as a model. In each box write something to help you remember what to include in your draft. Be sure to include the information that you gathered.

> My home address

> Robert Paulsen
> Mobile Bay Audubon Society
> P.O. Box 483
> Fairhope, AL 36532

> Dear Mr. Paulsen

> 1. Ask what types of birds in area.
> 2. Ask where to find them.
> 3. Thank for help.

> closing

Drafting

Gabriella wrote a draft of her letter of inquiry. She used her diagram from prewriting to guide her writing. Here is the first draft of Gabriella's letter.

2804 Poissonniere Road
Loyola Villa, AL 36532

July 14, 20–

Robert Paulsen
Mobile Bay Audubon Society
P.O. Box 483
Fairhope, AL 36532

Dear Mr. Paulsen:

My family and I have recently moved to the Mobile Bay area from New Orleans. I need some information before I go down to the bay with my binoculars. What types of birds should I be looking for in this area? I am used to looking for the types of birds that live in the city and on the Mississippi River, and I am not sure what will be living on and around Mobile Bay. In Louisiana my favorite birds to see were kingfishers.

Since I live so near the bay, the area I live in is swampy and wooded. Where would be a good place to start looking for birds? I would like to be able to find birds that live by the water and birds that I can see in the forest behind my house.

Could you please send me the information to get me started birdwatching? Thank you for your time.

Sincerely,
Gabriella Breton

In the body Gabriella tried to use formal language and a polite tone. The beginning of the body stated what she was inquiring about, the middle explained why she was interested in the information, and in the ending she asked for a response to her inquiry.

Your Turn

Use your diagram from prewriting to help you write the first draft of your letter of inquiry. Be sure to include a beginning that states the purpose of the letter, a middle that gives more information about the purpose, and an ending that requests an action from the receiver of the letter. Remember to use formal language and a polite tone.

Using Formal Language

Business letters should be written using formal language so the person you are writing to will take you seriously. Look for words in your letter that can be replaced by more formal ones. For example, <u>receiving</u> something in the mail sounds more formal then <u>getting</u> something in the mail. When making these changes, be sure to look up the words in a dictionary to make sure they mean what you think they do.

Chapter 3 Editor's Workshop

Business Letters

Content Editing

Now that Gabriella had a draft of her letter, she wanted to check the meaning, the order, and the tone.

Gabriella thought it might be a good idea to ask someone to first content edit her letter for her. She thought that another person might catch mistakes that she hadn't noticed. Gabriella asked her twin sister, Nadia, to content edit her letter. Since Nadia often went out on nature adventures with her sister, she was happy to help with the letter. This is the Content Editor's Checklist that Nadia used.

Content Editor's Checklist

✓ Does the beginning clearly state the purpose of the letter?

✓ Does the middle give detailed information about the purpose of the letter?

✓ Does the ending ask for a response or some kind of action?

✓ Does the order in which the information is presented make sense?

✓ Does the letter use a polite tone and formal language?

Nadia read Gabriella's letter of inquiry. She told Gabriella that she liked that the letter had a polite tone. Nadia said that words and phrases such as *please* and *thank you for your time* made the letter sound formal. Then Nadia told Gabriella these ideas she had for her letter of inquiry.

- The beginning doesn't state the purpose of the letter clearly enough. It seems as if the purpose is about what types of birds are in the area, but the next paragraph talks about where to look for birds.

- The middle seems to give information to support a different purpose. I thought the letter was about types of birds, not where to find them.

- I think the two questions you ask are out of order. You should ask where to find birds before you ask what types of birds are in the area.

Gabriella thanked Nadia for her help. She noticed that Nadia hadn't commented on the ending of her letter. In addition to asking for a response, Gabriella decided to ask for information on the society's events and meetings. She wanted the reader of her letter to know that she was serious about her requests.

Your Turn

Exchange your letter of inquiry with a partner. Use the Content Editor's Checklist to check your partner's paper. Pay attention to one question on the checklist at a time. Take notes on changes you would like to suggest to your partner about his or her letter of inquiry.

When you have finished, take turns talking with your partner about each other's draft. Start by saying something you like about your partner's letter. Think about each one of your partner's suggestions before you use them in your letter. Then content edit your own letter using the Content Editor's Checklist.

Revising

Gabriella carefully considered the content editing ideas that she and Nadia had. Here is her revised draft.

2804 Poissonniere Road
Loyola Villa, AL 36532

July 14, 20–

Robert Paulsen
Mobile Bay Audubon Society
P.O. Box 483
Fairhope, AL 36532

Dear Mr. Paulsen:

My family and I have recently moved to the Mobile Bay area from New Orleans. I loved birdwatching in Louisiana, and I would like to continue here. I need some information before I go down to the bay with my binoculars. What types of birds should I be looking for in this area? I am used to looking for the types of birds that live in the city and on the Mississippi River, and I am not sure what will be living on and around Mobile Bay. In Louisiana my favorite birds to see were kingfishers.

Since I live so near the bay, the area I live in is swampy and wooded. There are not a lot of people, houses or factories. Where would be a good place to start looking for birds? I would like to be able to find birds that live by the water and birds that I can see in the forest behind my house.

Could you please send me the information to get me started birdwatching? Thank you for your time. Please also send me any news about upcoming meetings and events held by the Mobile Bay Audubon Society.

Sincerely,

Gabriella Breton

Here are some of the things that Gabriella did to improve her letter of inquiry.

- Gabriella agreed that the purpose of her letter wasn't clearly stated. She added a sentence to the first paragraph about how she wanted to continue bird watching in her new home.

- Gabriella made the first paragraph into two paragraphs. Now the second and third paragraphs would both support the purpose of her letter, each in a different way. She also added a sentence to her third paragraph to support her purpose.

- Gabriella didn't agree with Nadia that the order should be changed. She felt that now that her purpose was clearer, it would be obvious to the reader that she needed to know what types of birds there were in the area before she went to look for them.

Gabriella also added a sentence at the end about attending Audubon Society events. She felt that all her changes made her letter stronger.

Your Turn

Use your ideas and those of your content editor to revise your letter of inquiry. Use only the ideas from your content editor that you think will make your draft better.

When you have finished revising, look at the Content Editor's Checklist again. Make sure that you can answer yes to each question.

Business Letters

Copyediting and Proofreading

Copyediting

When Gabriella was finished content editing her draft, she was happy that her ideas were in order and that they were written clearly. She wanted to copyedit her letter to make sure that each of her words and sentences were also clear and correct. She used this Copyeditor's Checklist to help her.

Gabriella thought that she really didn't need the last sentence of the second paragraph. Although she did see many kingfishers in Louisiana, this letter was about birds she would like to see in Alabama.

Copyeditor's Checklist

✓ Are any sentences awkward or confusing?

✓ Is every sentence in the letter needed?

✓ Is there a variety of sentence lengths?

✓ Are the parts of the business letter correct and in the right order?

Gabriella realized that two of the parts of her business letter were incorrect. Because this was a business letter, she would need to type her name below her signature. Can you find the other incorrect part of her business letter?

Your Turn

Use the Copyeditor's Checklist to check your letter for mistakes. Look for only one kind of mistake at a time. Make sure that all of your sentences are clear and necessary. Check that you have correctly included all of the parts of a business letter.

Proofreading

Gabriella was close to sending her letter. But first she wanted someone to proofread it. She knew that it was important that her letter did not have any spelling or grammatical mistakes.

Gabriella asked Ruby, her first new friend in town, to proofread her letter. Ruby used this Proofreader's Checklist to check Gabriella's letter for mistakes.

Proofreader's Checklist

✓ Have any words been misspelled?

✓ Are there capitalization or punctuation mistakes?

✓ Is the grammar correct?

✓ Were any new mistakes made during revising?

After she proofread the letter, Ruby shared with Gabriella the mistakes that she found. Ruby found two misspelled words. The word *birdwatching* should have been written as two words. Gabriella used this word twice, so she made sure to fix it in both places. Can you find the second misspelled word?

Ruby also found a punctuation error. A comma was missing in the series in the second sentence of the third paragraph. Gabriella thanked Ruby for her help and made this change. Gabriella then proofread her letter herself so that she would be sure that there were no mistakes.

Your Turn

Trade your letter with a partner. Use the Proofreader's Checklist to check your partner's draft. Check for only one kind of mistake at a time. When your partner returns your letter, make sure that the changes are correct. Ask someone to help you if you are not sure about any of the changes that your partner made. Then proofread your own letter.

Business Letters

Publishing

Here is the final copy of Gabriella's letter.

2804 Poissonniere Road
Loyola Villa, AL 36532

July 14, 20—

Robert Paulsen
Mobile Bay Audubon Society
P.O. Box 483
Fairhope, AL 36532

Dear Mr. Paulsen:

My family and I have recently moved to the Mobile Bay area from New Orleans. I loved bird watching in Louisiana, and I would like to continue here. I need some information before I go down to the bay with my binoculars.

What types of birds should I be looking for in this area? I am used to looking for the types of birds that live in the city and on the Mississippi River, and I am not sure what will be living on and around Mobile Bay.

Since I live so near the bay, the area I live in is swampy and wooded. There are not a lot of people, houses, or factories. Where would be a good place to start looking for birds? I would like to be able to find birds that live by the water and birds that I can see in the forest behind my house.

Could you please send me the information to get me started bird watching? Please also send me any news about upcoming meetings and events held by the Mobile Bay Audubon Society. Thank you for your time.

Sincerely,
Gabriella Breton
Gabriella Breton

Your Turn

Make your corrections from copyediting and proofreading, type your letter, print it out, and read it over one more time. Make sure all the parts of the letter are included. Check to see that you didn't add any new mistakes while typing. Don't forget to add your signature.

When you are sure that your letter is ready to be sent, fold it into thirds. Begin by folding the bottom third of the paper up. Next, fold the top third of the paper down. Last press the folds firmly so that the letter is flat.

Address a business-sized envelope to the recipient and put your return address in the upper left corner. Put your letter in the envelope.

You might share your letter with a classmate. You might also send your letter of inquiry. Before you send your letter, make sure your teacher has a chance to read it. If you do send it, share any response you receive with your teacher and classmates.

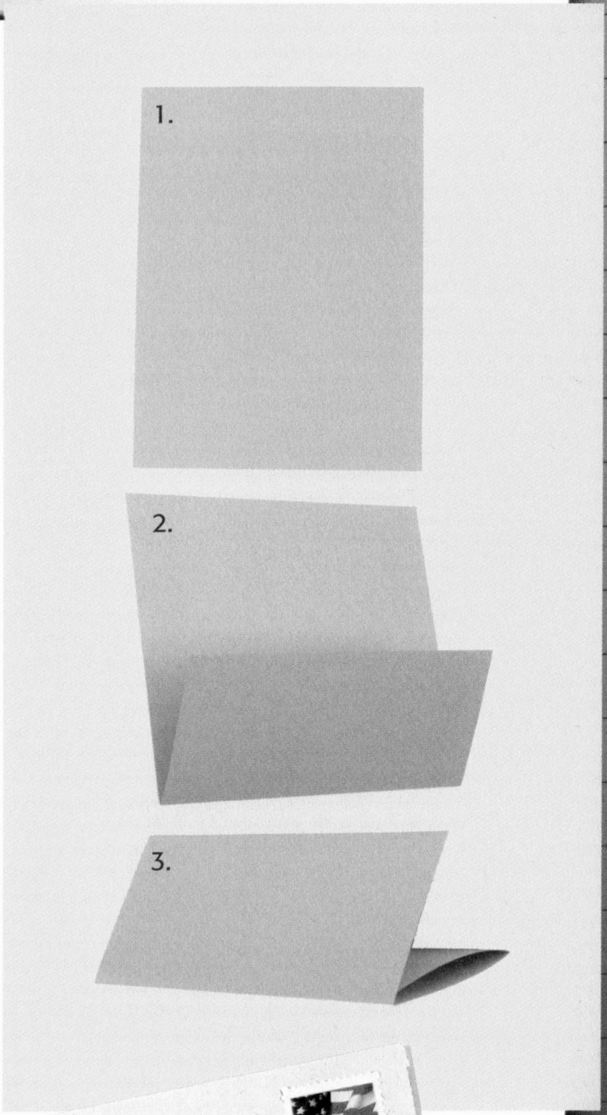

1.

2.

3.

Gabriella Breton
2804 Poissonniere Road
Loyola Villa, AL 36532

Robert Paulsen
Mobile Bay Audubon Society
P.O. Box 483
Fairhope, AL 36532

CHAPTER

4

In the late 19th and early 20th centuries more than 20 million people immigrated to the United States. They docked by the shipload at Ellis Island in New York Harbor to begin the screening process that would allow them to enter the country permanently. Immigrants were checked for disease, and their criminal records were researched. But only 2 percent of all those who attempted to enter were denied. Do you know what country or countries your own ancestors were from?

Descriptions

New Tricks from a Not So Old Dog

The best way to get tips about fire prevention is to listen to Coach, the well-loved mascot of the Glen Lake Fire Department. Before you question a dalmatian's ability to give advice, let me assure you that Coach is no ordinary mutt.

Coach's lanky six-foot frame is covered from head to toe in a costume of pure white fur sprinkled with jet-black spots. A bright red firefighter's hat perches between his floppy ears, and he sports a black protective vest and pants. Shiny yellow boots complete the picture and make him a handsome sight. As he extends his large right paw in a firm handshake, you know that this pooch is your pal!

Coach's presentations at school assemblies give insights into the caring nature of the man behind the dog. His boundless energy and amusing antics keep the students entranced. They love his history of dalmatians, especially when he runs around the gym to show how these swift runners sped alongside horse-drawn carriages and earned the name "coach dogs."

Coach's main message, however, is completely serious. He talks about the dangers of things such as matches, electricity, and fireplaces. He explains how to hold family fire drills. He demonstrates how to check smoke detectors and change the batteries. Everyone at the assembly follows his directions to "stop, drop, and roll" and practices speaking slowly and clearly to 911 operators.

You can see that Coach is more than just a goodwill ambassador. He is a teacher whose message students will always remember. Their homes will be safer places because of this caring canine.

Descriptions

What Makes a Good Description?

An effective description paints a picture with words. It makes the reader see and experience a particular person, place, thing, or event.

You can find descriptions in many places. A new video game might be described in an ad, or a park could be described in a travel brochure. A description can also be a part of a longer piece, such as a description of a character or of a setting in a novel.

When you write a description, choose a topic that is familiar or very important to you. The more you know about a topic, the easier it will be to remember a lot of details about it.

Here are some things to keep in mind when you write a description.

Visualizing

Before you write a description, try to visualize, or picture, the topic in your mind. Think about how the topic looks, but don't stop there. Imagine everything you hear, smell, taste, and touch. This will help you describe your topic completely and accurately.

Audience

Consider who will be reading your description. If you are writing for younger children, use words that they will understand. For adults, use language they will find interesting.

Think about how much your audience already knows about your topic. A sports fan doesn't need to be told what a soccer goalie wears. Someone who doesn't know anything about soccer, however, might need to be told that the goalie's uniform is different from that of the other players on the team.

Activity A

Read each of the following pairs of topics. Choose the one that is a better topic for a description. Explain your answers.

1. my sports hero   team sports
2. Grandmother's china cabinet   how to collect art
3. directions to my classroom   my school building
4. the history of hot dogs   my favorite lunch
5. birds of the desert   the Gila woodpecker

Activity B

Each of these sentences was written for an audience of older students and adults. Rewrite each sentence to make it suitable for young children. Use a dictionary or a thesaurus if necessary.

Example: The sky was an intense cerulean blue.

The sky was bright blue.

1. A dalmatian has a dense white coat randomly splashed with black spots.
2. His hands were gnarled and weatherbeaten with cracked, filthy fingernails.
3. A prairie dog is a small, burrowing rodent.
4. A serpentine path leads you past a thicket of juniper trees.
5. Suddenly an eerie wail pierced the air around the dilapidated barn.
6. The pungent aroma of the vinegar brought tears to my eyes.

Writer's Corner

Think of an object that you see or use every day. Write down five words you could use to describe that object to a young child and five different words you could use to describe it to an adult.

Sensory Details

You experience the world by using all of your five senses: sight, hearing, taste, smell, and touch. When you write a description, you should use words that appeal to all the senses. Using sensory details will help your reader visualize your topic and share your experience.

Read these two sentences. They both describe the same thing. Which one helps you feel more like you are actually there?

> The waves lapped against the beach.
>
> The waves gurgled against the rocky beach and filled the air with a cool, salty spray.

The first sentence tells only what the writer saw. In the second sentence, the writer used words to appeal also to the senses of hearing, touch, and taste. This helps readers visualize the experience.

• Activity C •

In the book *Sarah, Plain and Tall*, Sarah has moved from Maine to the prairie. The author, Patricia MacLachlan, includes many short passages in which Sarah describes her former home to those who have never seen the coast. Name the words and phrases in each description that appeal to different senses.

1. I've touched seals. Real seals. They are cool and slippery and they slide through the water like fish. They can cry and sing. And sometimes they bark, a little like dogs.

2. In Maine, there are rock cliffs that rise up at the edge of the sea. And there are hills covered with pine and spruce trees, green with needles. But William and I found a sand dune all our own. It was soft and sparkling with bits of mica, and when we were little we would slide down the dune into the water.

3. The sea is salt. It stretches out as far as you can see. It gleams like the sun on glass.

Activity D

Write a one-sentence description of each subject below. Use the sense given in parentheses.

1. an old clock (hearing)

2. stale pretzels (taste)

3. a sandy beach (touch)

4. a popcorn shop (smell)

5. a sunset (sight)

Activity E

Write at least three sentences to describe each topic below. Use details that appeal to two or more senses for each.

1. a fast-food restaurant at lunchtime

2. a marching band in a parade

3. a playground at recess

4. a garden on a summer afternoon

5. a sailboat race on a lake

Activity F

Choose a topic from Activity E. Write a paragraph describing that topic. Try to appeal to all five senses in your paragraph.

Our Wide Wide World

Mount Rushmore, a granite mountain with the likenesses of four U.S. presidents—George Washington, Thomas Jefferson, Theodore Roosevelt, and Abraham Lincoln— carved into its side, is located near Keystone, South Dakota. The project was conceived and begun by the American sculptor Gutzon Borglum in 1927. It wasn't completed, however, until 1941—seven months after his death.

Writer's Corner

Write a descriptive paragraph about a food you especially like. Use details that appeal to as many different senses as you can to make your readers' mouths water.

Ordering a Description

A good description is well organized. The reader is led from detail to detail in a way that makes sense. Irrelevant details, things that do not stick to the topic, are left out. The result is a vivid snapshot of a person, a thing, a place, or an event.

Spatial Order

The most common way to organize a description is spatial order. In spatial order you might describe something from side to side, from near to far, from top to bottom, or from inside to outside. If you are describing a person, you might work from head to toe or from toe to head. Whichever order you choose, be sure to stick to that order. Lead your readers along in a clear and logical way.

• Activity A •

The following sentences describe a market. Only the first and last sentences are in the correct spatial order. Rewrite the sentences as a paragraph that describes the market from side to side.

1. Our local farmers' market is a feast for the senses.

2. In the center of the market are baskets of plump strawberries.

3. To the left of the entrance are bins of red, ripe tomatoes.

4. Along the right side of the market are tables covered with gleaming jars of honey, jam, and pickles.

5. Next to the tomatoes are piles of crisp green lettuce, cucumbers, beans, and other delicious-looking vegetables.

6. By the strawberries are boxes of fat blueberries.

7. My mouth starts to water just thinking about it!

Activity B

Read the following details that describe Paul's physical appearance. Three of the details are irrelevant and should be left out. Put the other details in spatial order, starting with detail 1 and going from head to toe.

1. narrow head with messed-up brown curls
2. always sports the latest fashion in sneakers
3. greets everyone with a friendly grin
4. lives on Cornelia Street
5. usually wears a Phillies T-shirt
6. belongs to the chess club
7. always wears jeans
8. big brown eyes
9. small, freckled nose
10. likes playing the drums

Activity C

Use the details in Activity B to write a paragraph describing Paul. You may reword the details or combine more than one detail in a sentence to make your writing more interesting.

Activity D

Think of someone you know well. Write down a list of at least eight physical details you could use to describe that person. Check over your list. Are any of the details irrelevant? If any are, replace them with relevant ones.

Writer's Corner

Look at the list you wrote for Activity D. Number the details in the order you would use them in a description organized by spatial order. Then use the details to write a paragraph describing the person.

Chronological Order

Another way to describe something is by chronological, or time, order. Chronological order tells the order in which something happens from beginning to end. It is usually used to describe an event or a process. For example, if you wanted to describe carving a jack-o'-lantern, you might start with cutting out the lid and smelling the aroma of the pumpkin. Then you might describe the feel of the seeds as you scrape them out. Next you would describe designing and cutting out the face until the jack-o'-lantern is completed.

Activity E

Tell how you would organize a description of each of these topics. Would you use spatial order or chronological order?

1. decorating a birthday cake

2. a newborn kitten

3. your family's car

4. your winning home run

5. planting a garden

6. a local skate park

7. a fishing trip

8. a king salmon

9. a motorcycle

10. a motorcycle race

11. a slide down a toboggan run

12. your uncle

Activity F

Choose one of the topics in Activity E or think of a topic of your own. Write a list of five details that you would include in a description of that topic. Check to make sure that all your details are relevant. Then number the details in spatial or chronological order.

Activity G

The following sentences describe a trip to the beach. Only the first and last sentences are in the correct chronological order. Rewrite the sentences as a paragraph that describes what happened from beginning to end.

1. I came out of the dim woods into the bright sunshine.
2. My first step into the waves was a shock.
3. I sat down and put my shoes back on.
4. The first thing I noticed was the salty tang in the air.
5. I took off my shoes and started walking toward the water.
6. I jumped out and headed back toward the warmer sand.
7. I decided I might as well go home.
8. As I approached the water, I watched the waves roll in.
9. The water was as cold as ice.
10. There would be no more wading for me that day!

Activity H

Think of one of your favorite places. It might be a garden, a video arcade, or any other place you like. Decide whether you will use spatial order or chronological order to describe it. Then write a list of details about the place. Check to make sure that all the details are relevant. Last, number the details in the order you would use them in a description.

Our Wide Wide World

The Statue of Liberty, a gift to the United States from France, was designed by French sculptor Frederic Auguste Bartholdi. "Lady Liberty," which stands more than 2,000 feet high, is located on Liberty Island in New York Harbor, where she welcomes newcomers arriving by ship. She is holding a torch in her right hand and a tablet in her left with July 4, 1776, engraved on its cover.

Writer's Corner

Imagine you are walking through a park or down a familiar street. Write a paragraph to describe what you see, hear, taste, smell, and touch along the way. Write your description in chronological order.

Writing Skills

Graphic Organizers

A graphic organizer is a chart or diagram that a writer uses to map out ideas in a visual way.

Word Webs

A word web is a type of graphic organizer that can help you organize the details related to a chosen topic. It can also keep you from introducing irrelevant details.

Mary Jane is writing a description of her new kitten to send to her grandfather. She will use spatial order. She started by making a word web. First, she wrote the kitten's name and drew an oval around it. Around that oval she wrote the four parts of the kitten's body that she would describe and drew ovals around them. Last, she added details about the kitten's head, body, feet, and tail.

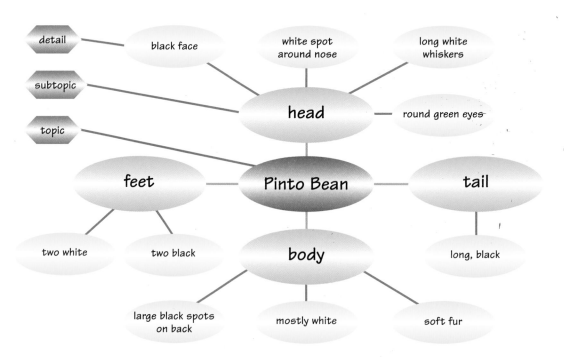

Activity A

Refer to the word web on page 130 and write a short description of the kitten's head, her body, her feet, and her tail.

Here is an example.
Pinto Bean has a black face with a white spot around her nose.

Activity B

Copy and add to this word web to describe Carrots the Clown. Use your imagination to fill in sensory details.

shoes — Carrots the Clown — hair

face — Carrots the Clown — costume

Activity C

Make word webs for three of the following topics.

A. your favorite childhood toy

B. an animal that lives in your part of the country

C. a storm you experienced

D. the front of your home

E. a warm spring day

F. a body of water you have visited

G. a costume you have worn

H. yourself

The Little Bighorn National Monument is near the Little Bighorn River in Montana. It stands in remembrance of the Battle of the Little Bighorn, sometimes called Custer's Last Stand. George Custer led the U.S. cavalry into battle against the Lakota Sioux and Cheyenne Indians that day. Under the leadership of Sitting Bull and Crazy Horse, a group of Native Americans had refused to accept life on an Indian reservation. The cavalry was sent to suppress their forces, but Custer's attack backfired, resulting in the death of more than 300 of his men.

Writer's Corner

Use one of the word webs you made for Activity C. Write a paragraph, using the ideas in your word web. Be sure to include sensory details in your description.

Venn Diagrams

Some descriptions compare and contrast two different topics. These descriptions tell how the two things are alike and how they are different. A Venn diagram is useful in organizing information for this kind of description.

Here are the steps for making a Venn diagram.

1. Draw two large overlapping circles.
2. Write the name of one of the two topics at the top of each circle.
3. Write "Both" in the section where the circles overlap.
4. Write things that are true of both topics in the section labeled "Both."
5. Write things that are true of only that topic under its name in the outer section of its circle.

Look at this Venn diagram that compares and contrasts frogs and toads. Can you think of a characteristic for the blank line? (Hint: To what class of animals do both belong?)

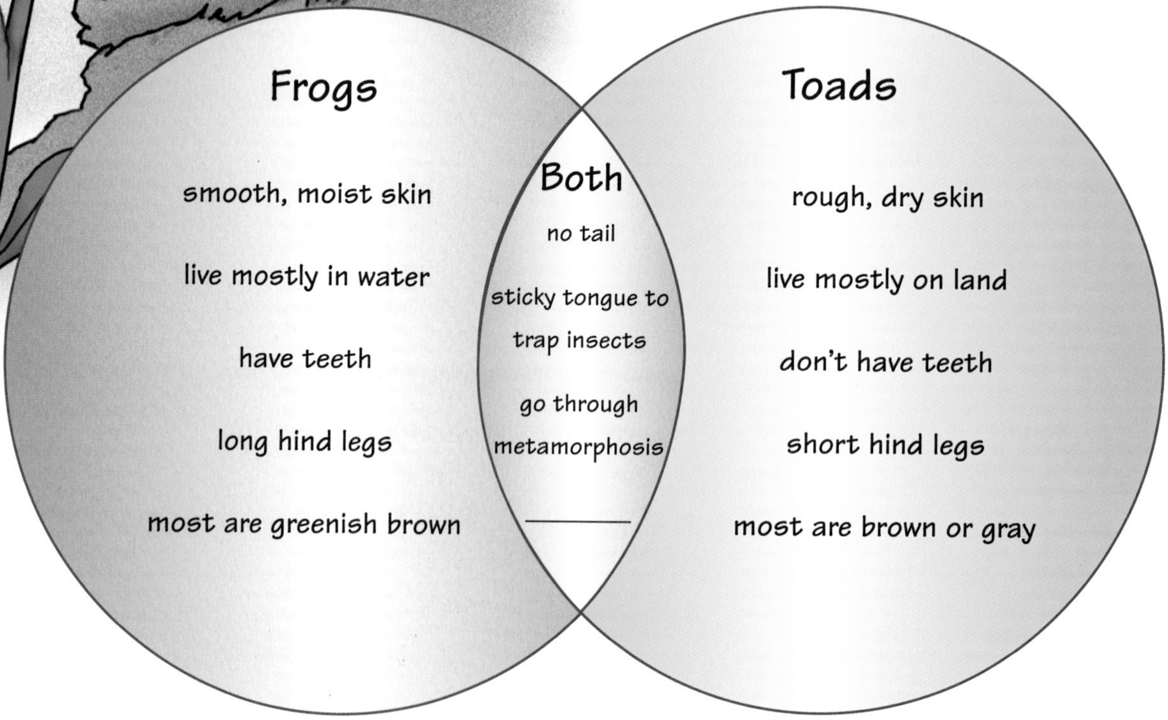

Frogs

smooth, moist skin

live mostly in water

have teeth

long hind legs

most are greenish brown

Both

no tail

sticky tongue to trap insects

go through metamorphosis

_____

Toads

rough, dry skin

live mostly on land

don't have teeth

short hind legs

most are brown or gray

Activity D

People often confuse alligators and crocodiles. Here are some details about these two animals. Put the facts into a Venn diagram. How would someone distinguish between these animals?

Crocodiles

reptile family

strong tail for swimming

long, pointed snout

two teeth show when mouth is closed

strong jaws to eat small animals

dark, scaly skin

Alligators

strong tail for swimming

no teeth visible with closed mouth

strong jaws to eat small animals

broad, rounded snout

reptile family

dark, scaly skin

Activity E

Read this paragraph that compares and contrasts two breeds of dogs. Then make a Venn diagram about the breeds.

At first glance, the 5-pound Chihuahua would seem to have nothing in common with the massive 200-pound St. Bernard. Less than a foot tall, the tiny Chihuahua is a snuggly dog who will curl up in your lap. Chihuahuas can live to be 20 years old. In contrast, the St. Bernard at almost 3 feet tall is not a cuddly lap dog. St. Bernards have a much shorter life span than Chihuahuas, usually around 10 years. Both breeds like lots of attention and are very loyal, affectionate pets. Both are good watchdogs. However, if you are thinking of buying one of these dogs, remember that a Chihuahua can get plenty of exercise running around in your kitchen. A St. Bernard needs a large yard in which to play.

Writer's Corner

Think of two animals that you could compare and contrast. The animals should be different from each other yet share some characteristics. Make a Venn diagram. Use an encyclopedia or the Internet to find facts. Then write a descriptive paragraph about the two animals.

Word Study

Suffixes

A suffix is a syllable or syllables added to the end of a base word to form a new word. Knowing the meanings of suffixes can help you increase your vocabulary.

Noun and Adjective Suffixes

Some suffixes change the part of speech of a word. The suffix *-er* *(-or)* can be added to verbs to make nouns. A *runner* is a person who runs. An *actor* is a person who acts. Other suffixes can change one noun into another. A *novelist* is a person who writes a novel.

Some suffixes change nouns to adjectives. Adding the suffix *-ful* to the noun *beauty* makes the adjective *beautiful.* Adding the suffix *-y* to the noun *star* makes the adjective *starry.*

Notice that sometimes there is a spelling change when you add a suffix to a base word. You may need to check a dictionary.

Adjective Suffixes

Suffix	Meaning	Example
-able	capable of being	climbable
-al	relating to	parental
-ful	full of	hopeful
-ic	like a, relating to	artistic
-ish	like a, resembling	childish
-y	full of	cloudy

Activity A

Tell the meaning and part of speech of each of these words containing a suffix. Use each word in a sentence.

1. teacher
2. sorrowful
3. chewable
4. inventor
5. colorful
6. personal
7. sunny
8. readable

Activity B

Copy the chart below and fill in the missing parts.

Base Word	Suffix	New Word	Meaning
1. snow	-y	_____	_____
2. _____	-ful	_____	full of tears
3. music	_____	musical	_____
4. baby	_____	babyish	_____
5. athlete	_____	athletic	_____

Activity C

Add an adjective suffix from the chart on page 134 to each base word below so that the new word correctly completes the sentence. Check a dictionary for spelling.

joy
move
fruit
fool
rhythm
ornament

1. The chorus sang a _____ song.
2. We discovered that the rock was not _____.
3. The _____ drink was sweet and delicious.
4. The _____ antics of the clown made me laugh.
5. The _____ sound of the train put me to sleep.
6. The path was lined with _____ bushes.

Writer's Corner

Brainstorm 10 words with the suffixes listed on page 134. Then write descriptive sentences. Use at least one of your words in each sentence.

Adverb and Verb Suffixes

Some suffixes are used to form adverbs and verbs. The suffixes *-ly* and *-ally* can be added to adjectives to form adverbs. *Sadly* means "in a sad way," and *terrifically* means "in a terrific way."

Some suffixes change adjectives to verbs. Adding the suffix *-ate* to the adjective *active* forms the verb *activate*. Adding the suffix *-fy* to the adjective *simple* forms the verb *simplify*.

Verb Suffixes

Suffix	Meaning	Example
-ate	make	activate
-en	become, make	deepen
-ize	cause to be	legalize
-fy	make	electrify

• Activity D •

Tell the meaning and part of speech of each of these words containing a suffix. Use each word in a sentence.

1. falsify   **3.** eagerly   **5.** blacken   **7.** magically

2. politely   **4.** popularize **6.** beautify   **8.** realize

• Activity E •

Add a suffix to each word to complete the sentence. Check a dictionary for spelling. Tell whether the new word is an adverb or a verb.

harmony   **1.** That barbershop quartet can _____ perfectly.

fierce   **2.** The wind howled _____ through the tunnel.

careful   **3.** I _____ aimed at the middle of the target.

active   **4.** The sun will _____ the solar panels.

nice   **5.** His poster was very _____ done.

sick   **6.** The smell of the fumes may _____ you.

simple   **7.** Please _____ the directions for the children.

rare   **8.** Peacocks are _____ seen in the United States.

Activity F

Read each pair of words and the sentences that follow. Complete each sentence with the correct word.

1. solidly, solidify

We set the fence post _____ into the concrete.

The concrete will _____ overnight.

2. shorten, shortly

Her new dress will be ready _____.

Her mother is going to _____ it.

3. apologize, apologetically

His father told him to _____.

He spoke _____.

4. clearly, clarify

Would you please _____ what you mean.

The teacher _____ explained the facts.

5. simplify, simply

I'd like to _____ this recipe.

It should be possible to make a cake more _____.

6. beautiful, beautify

Our garden looks _____ in the summer.

A few rosebushes would _____ it even more.

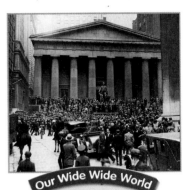

Our Wide Wide World

Federal Hall was located on Wall Street in New York City. It served as the first capital building of the United States but was demolished in the 19th century. Today the Federal Hall National Memorial is located in the building that replaced it, the U.S. Customs House. The first U.S. Congress met at Federal Hall. The building also hosted the inauguration of George Washington as the first president of the United States.

Writer's Corner

Reread some of the writing you have been working on recently. Find at least five words with suffixes. Look up each word in a dictionary to make sure you used and spelled it correctly. Rewrite your sentences if necessary. See if there are other places where you could use suffixes to make your writing clearer and more interesting.

Dictionary

Could you find a ptarmigan in your neighborhood? In what situations is it appropriate to use the word *aloha?* To what family of animals does a gibbon belong? A dictionary can give you the answers to these questions and many others.

A dictionary is a book of words that are listed in alphabetical order. When you look up a word, you find the spelling, pronunciation, part of speech, and definition of that word. The words that are defined in the dictionary are called entry words.

Alphabetizing

The entry words in a dictionary are arranged in alphabetical order. When words begin with the same letter, they are alphabetized by the second letter. For example, the word *pat* would come before *pot* because *a* comes before *o* in the alphabet. If words have the same first and second letters, they are alphabetized by the third letters, and so on. The word *pan* would come before *pat* because *n* comes before *t.*

Guide Words

At the top of each dictionary page, you will find two words. These are called guide words. The first guide word is the first entry word on the page. The second guide word is the last entry word on the page. Check the guide words to see whether the word you are looking for can be found on that page. For example, if you want to find the word *pelican,* first look for the guide words that begin with *p.* Then look at the second and third letters of the guide words. You might see the guide words *peg/pen.* Since *pel-* comes between *peg* and *pen,* you will know that you can find the word *pelican* on that page.

Activity A

Write each set of entry words in alphabetical order.

1.	2.	3.	4.
animated	dolphin	curious	soft
appealing	diver	cat	sandy
alien	delightful	cuddle	smooth
actual	deliberate	cute	seaside
anxious	direction	creep	seclude

Activity B

Look at each pair of guide words. Then look at the entry words that follow each pair. Write the word that does not come between those guide words.

1. web/week   weed, weep, wedding

2. about/absolute   absent, above, abound

3. dachshund/daisy   damage, dairy, dainty

4. sample/sandwich   sandal, sane, sand

5. magnify/maintain   magnet, mailbox, magpie

Activity C

Write three words that would be on a page with each pair of guide words below. You may use a dictionary for help.

1. contain/contest

2. lean/leavening

3. parody/participate

4. tinder/tire

5. neophyte/neuralgia

Writer's Corner

Use a dictionary to find where your first name would appear if it were an entry word. Write down the entry word just before and the entry word just after where your name would appear. Then write down the guide words for that page of your dictionary.

A Dictionary Entry

The parts of a dictionary entry give you important information about that word. The following example shows what is included in most dictionary entries.

<table>
<tr><td>

A B   C   D
cack•le (kak'əl) *v.* **1.** to make the shrill noise a hen makes after laying an egg **2.** to laugh or talk in a
E
shrill way *They cackled at the boy's silly behavior.*
n. **1.** the act or sound of cackling **2.** shrill laughter *The witch's cackle scared the villagers.* **3.** noisy chatter
The cackle from the cafeteria was deafening. -ling, -led
F

</td><td>

A. division into syllables
B. dictionary respelling for pronunciation
C. part of speech
D. definition
E. sample phrase or sentence
F. spelling of last syllable with endings added

</td></tr>
</table>

• Activity D •

Use the sample dictionary entry above to answer these questions.

1. What parts of speech are listed for *cackle*?

2. How many pronunciations are given for *cackle*?

3. How many meanings does *cackle* have as a noun?

4. How many meanings does *cackle* have as a verb?

• Activity E •

Use a dictionary to find out which of these things you would eat and which you would wear.

1. kohlrabi   **6.** fedora

2. amulet   **7.** papaw

3. oxford   **8.** puttee

4. flounder   **9.** tam

5. hominy   **10.** puree

Activity F

List how many different meanings and parts of speech your dictionary shows for each of these words. Then choose one of the words to use in three sentences, showing three different meanings of the word. Use the word as at least two different parts of speech.

1. strike
2. run
3. point
4. ring
5. nose
6. pop
7. mark
8. make
9. down
10. right

Activity G

Two of the words in each set rhyme. Look up the words in a dictionary and use the pronunciation key to find which one does not rhyme with the others.

1. chary	ferry	weary	6. grain	mien	dean
2. bier	ire	pyre	7. zeal	creel	cruel
3. pawl	haul	loll	8. panache	ache	hake
4. lurk	torque	dirk	9. quay	queue	lieu
5. urge	gorge	merge	10. league	fatigue	siege

Activity H

Choose five words that you found especially interesting in Activity G. Use each one in a sentence that shows what it means.

Writer's Corner

Look up the meanings of these words in a dictionary. Then use each word in a sentence that tells about something you did or something that happened to you recently.

lamentable	momentous	scrupulous
intriguing	vexatious	restorative

Speaking and Listening Skills

Oral Descriptions

Have you ever described a new shirt to a friend? Have you told your parents how your fifth-grade teacher looks and acts? If you did, you were giving an oral description. An oral description is a lot like a written description. You use vivid sensory details to paint a picture in your listeners' minds. You organize your description in a way that your listeners can follow.

The descriptions you tell to your friends and family are informal. At times you may need to give a more formal description. These are some things to keep in mind as you prepare an oral description

Audience

It is important to consider the audience as you plan your description. Choose a topic that your audience will find interesting. Plan your use of language. You will probably use different words if you are talking to five-year-olds than if you are talking to fifth graders.

Keep in mind how much your audience may already know about your topic. If you think they know very little about it, you will have to add some background information and use a lot of sensory details. If you think your audience may be completely unfamiliar with it, you may want to show a picture or diagram as a visual aid.

Sensory Details

To begin planning your oral description, visualize your topic. Jot down notes about how it appeals to each of the five senses: sight, hearing, taste, smell, and touch. You might make a five-senses chart or a word web to help you remember these details.

Look over your notes. Did you overuse words such as *nice, pretty, big,* or *good?* Use a thesaurus to find more exact, colorful language that will help your audience visualize your topic.

Organization

Think about the best way to organize your description. You don't want your audience to become confused because you jump around in your description. If you are describing a person, a place, or a thing, you may want to use spatial order. If you are describing a process or an event, chronological order may be better.

Whichever order you choose, lead your listeners logically from one detail to the next. Write your ideas on note cards and arrange the cards in your chosen order. Check to make sure all your details are relevant and help create a clear picture in your listeners' minds.

Activity A

Think of a special event you participated in recently. Perhaps it was a birthday party, a trip to the ballpark, or a family picnic. Make notes of everything you saw, heard, smelled, tasted, and touched. Decide what would be the best way to organize a description of the event and arrange your notes in that order. Check to see that your sensory details give an accurate picture of what you experienced.

Speaker's Corner

Work in small groups and share your notes about your special event. After each presentation, tell what you especially liked and offer suggestions about anything that might be rearranged or put into clearer sensory details. Make notes of your classmates' suggestions and keep them to use in planning an oral description to present for a larger audience.

Body Language and Voice

When you give an oral presentation, it is important to speak loud enough for everyone to hear and clearly enough for everyone to understand. Don't mumble. Don't use words such as *uh, um,* or *like.* Glance around at the audience so that each person feels like you are talking directly to him or her.

When you present an oral description, use your voice and body. Vary your tone to emphasize important parts of your description. Use body movements to show sensory details. You might use gestures to show size or movement. Let your enthusiasm for your topic be seen in your facial expressions.

Practice

Once you have your notes organized, you are ready to practice your presentation. First practice by yourself in front of a mirror. This way you can see and evaluate the expressions and body movements that you will use.

When you are ready, ask a friend or family member to listen to your presentation. Ask him or her to pay close attention to your delivery and your words. When you have finished, ask for suggestions for improving your presentation.

Listening Tips

When it is your turn to be a listener, it is important to be attentive. Keep these tips in mind when you listen to a description.

- Look at the speaker so he or she knows you are paying attention. Don't fidget or stare around the room.
- Listen for sensory details that will help you know how the topic looks, sounds, feels, tastes, and smells.
- Pay attention to the speaker's facial expressions and body language as well as his or her tone. This will help you visualize the topic.
- Do not interrupt the speaker.

When the speaker has finished, give him or her some feedback. Mention parts of the description that you especially liked. Ask questions about anything you didn't understand.

Activity B

Work with a partner. Take turns reading each sentence aloud. Vary your tone and expression. Use gestures to emphasize the meaning.

1. It smelled like a dirty, old tennis shoe.

2. The first bite was an explosion of delicious flavors.

3. The emerald green moss is as soft as a blanket.

4. The ferocious wind howled at the windowpanes.

5. His big brown eyes sparkle with mischief.

6. The fur on its back is rough and curly.

7. The fluffy clouds looked as tasty as cotton candy.

8. The sharp tang of the onions made my eyes water.

9. The bubbling stream splashed against the slippery rocks.

10. The soft wind in the pines creates a gentle, soothing sound.

Activity C

Choose an object in your classroom. Write five sentences to describe the object. Use as many sensory details as you can, but do not name the object in your sentences. Work with a partner. Take turns reading your sentences aloud one by one. Use your voice and gestures to help emphasize the meaning. Can your partner guess your object?

Speaker's Corner

Use your notes from the Speaker's Corner on page 143. Consider your classmates' suggestions for improvements. When you are ready, practice by yourself and then with a partner. Experiment with using your voice and gestures to help get your meaning across. Present your oral description to the class.

Descriptions

Prewriting and Drafting

Have you ever tried to explain what something is like to someone else? This is a description. Descriptions can be about anything. You can use sight, smell, taste, touch, and sound as tools to make your description come alive. The purpose of a description is to make the readers feel as if what is being described is right in front of them.

Prewriting

Noah is a fifth grader who was asked to help put together an exhibit for the Portland, Oregon, Cultural Center. The cultural center was making an exhibit about different festivals throughout the world from a student's point of view. Some students would write descriptions, and others would paint pictures or make other displays. Noah was asked to write a description. First he had to choose a topic and gather details about it.

Choosing a Topic

Noah thought about different festivals from around the world. He knew of many famous festivals, such as Chinese New Year. He decided to write a description about a less known festival, the International Bathtub Regatta. He also chose this topic because he had seen the race in person. He thought he would be able to write a strong description because he had seen it up close. Since the festival was a long event to describe, he decided to focus on three of the boats in the race.

Your Turn
Choose a topic that interests you. You might describe a place, a person, a thing, or an event. Make sure that it will be something you will enjoy writing about. Think about your audience when you choose your topic. Your audience will be your classmates. What do you think they would like to read about?

Making a Word Web

Now that Noah had a topic, he began gathering the details he would use to make his description strong and interesting. He started by visualizing the boats as he remembered them. He closed his eyes and thought about how the boats affected his five senses. He began making word webs. He made one word web for each of the three boats he wanted to describe. Noah jotted down notes about how the boats looked and sounded. He had trouble thinking of how to use touch, smell, and taste to describe the boats. He decided that he would use only the senses that would help him describe the boats. Here is one of his word webs.

Your Turn

Think about all of the details of your topic. Organize them in a word web. Try to think of ways of describing your topic by using all five of your senses. When you have finished, read over your word web. Add any more details that come to mind. Include only details that are relevant to the description of your topic.

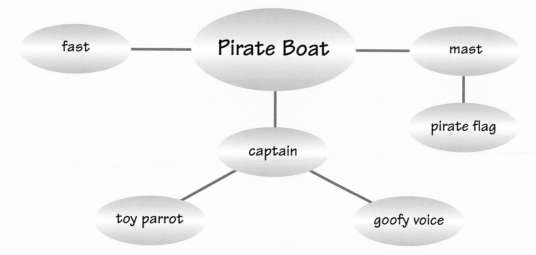

Drafting

Noah wrote his draft, using his word webs. He used sensory details because he wanted his readers to feel as if they were watching the boat race. He thought of his audience as he wrote. He wanted his description to be appropriate for the people visiting the cultural center.

The Tub Boat Races of Belgium

You would think not much would be happening on a hot August day in the small town of Dinant, Belgium. But once a year the town is crowded and noisy, and the Meuse river is filled with bathtubs. People from the town wait all year to try out their wacky bathtub boats in the race called the International Bathtub Regatta.

Last year, on the day of the race the narrow river was filled with homemade boats that had bathtubs as part of their hulls. All of the paddles from the bathtub boats splashing in the river sounded like giant fish jumping out of the water. The smell of the warm chocolate crepes from the outdoor cafés filled the air. The faster boat had a mast with a black pirate flag. The captain had a giant neon green toy parrot on his shoulder. He yelled out instructions in a goofy voice.

The slower boat was sinking into the water. The crew was dressed as cooks and paddled with oversized kitchen utensils. As their boat sank, the cooks threw their tall white chef's hats and giant wooden spoons and spatulas into the air. The crowd applauded and hooted, and it was as loud as a gym during a basketball game.

Another boat was built in the shape of a swan. Every few minutes a stream of water shot out of the swan's mouth. The crew of the swan boat aimed the water at the crowd. People in the crowd tried to get hit by the water so they could cool off their skin.

It's great. You've got to see it! With all the splashing water, cheering, and laughing, it sounds like a gigantic pool party. The bathtub inventions look like something out of another world. It is more of a party than a race. Sometimes in Belgium a bathtub is much more than just a bathtub.

Your Turn

Write a draft of your description, using the word web you made during prewriting. Remember to write a title and an introduction that names the topic of your description.

When you write the body, add as many relevant details as you can. End your description with a conclusion that brings all of your details together.

The audience you are writing for is your classmates. Make sure that the language and content of your description is understandable and appropriate for this audience.

Shaping Sensory Details

One way to make good sensory details for your description is to compare one thing to another. Instead of saying that the garbage falling out of the bag and tumbling down the stairs was loud, you might say that it was as loud as a tin can in a washing machine. This will show your audience a different way of thinking about what you are describing. Can you name some of the comparisons that use sensory details in Noah's draft?

Descriptions

Content Editing

Although Noah was happy with his draft, it could be made better through content editing. By content editing, Noah would check the structure of the description, its focus, and its tone.

Noah asked his friend Jude to content edit his description for him. Jude was familiar with the cultural center project because he was making a slide show for it about a festival he had been to in Brazil. Noah also asked Jude for help because he thought Jude might be able to catch mistakes that he hadn't noticed. This is the Content Editor's Checklist that Jude used.

Content Editor's Checklist

✓ Does the description stay focused on a topic?

✓ Are sensory details used so that readers can visualize what is being described?

✓ Does the introduction name the topic?

✓ Is the body well-ordered with logical connections?

✓ Does the conclusion summarize the description?

✓ Is the tone appropriate for the audience?

Jude read Noah's description. He saw that the introduction named the topic. Jude also liked how Noah tied his description together in the conclusion. He complimented Noah on the last line. Then Jude told Noah his ideas for making the description stronger.

- The sentence about the smell of the crepes doesn't fit the focus of the description.

- I think that you should add more details about the boats you're describing. It would make me feel more like I was there.

- You could order the body better. The description isn't in spatial or chronological order. Because of this, the description of the swan boat seems out of place.

Noah thanked Jude for his comments. He wasn't sure if he was going to use all of the ideas, but he was going to carefully consider each one. Noah then took time to content edit his own work, using the Content Editor's Checklist. He wanted to make sure that he could answer yes to each question.

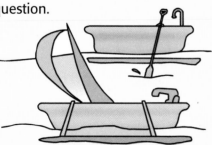

Your Turn

Exchange your description with a partner. Use the Content Editor's Checklist to check your partner's draft. Pay attention to one question at a time. Take notes on changes you would like to suggest to your partner about his or her description.

When you have finished, take turns talking about each other's drafts. Begin by telling your partner what you liked about his or her description. Write down your partner's ideas. If you have any questions about your own description, make sure you ask your content editor for help. Then use the Content Editor's Checklist to content edit your own description.

Chapter 4 Writer's Workshop

Descriptions

Revising

This is how Noah used ideas from content editing to revise his draft.

The Tub Boat Races of Belgium

You would think not much would be happening on a hot August day in the small town of Dinant, Belgium. But once a year the town is crowded and noisy, and the Meuse river is filled with bathtubs. People from the town wait all year to try out their wacky bathtub boats in the race called the International Bathtub Regatta.

Last year, on the day of the race the narrow river was filled with homemade boats that had bathtubs as part of their hulls. All of the paddles from the bathtub boats splashing in the river sounded like giant fish jumping out of the water. ~~The smell of the warm chocolate crepes from the outdoor cafés filled the air~~. The faster boat had a mast with a black pirate flag. The captain had a giant neon green toy
The people rowing the boat were dressed like pirates and all had eye patches.
parrot on his shoulder. He yelled out instructions in a goofy voice.

The slower boat was sinking into the water. The crew was dressed as cooks and paddled with oversized kitchen utensils. As their boat sank, the cooks threw their tall white chef's hats and giant wooden spoons and spatulas into the air. The crowd applauded and hooted, and it was as loud as a gym during a basketball game.

switch with next paragraph

Another boat was built in the shape of a swan , with the bathtub as the swan's belly . Every few minutes a stream of water shot out of the swan's mouth. The crew of the swan boat aimed the water at the crowd. The weather was so humid that the air felt like a wet sponge. People in the crowd tried to get hit by the water so they could cool off their skin.

The International Bathtub Regatta is a sight to see and to enjoy. It's great. You've got to see it! With all the splashing water, cheering, and laughing, it sounds like a gigantic pool party. The bathtub inventions look like something out of another world. It is more of a party than a race. Sometimes in Belgium a bathtub is much more than just a bathtub.

Here are changes Noah made to improve his description.

- Noah liked his sentence about the crepes. The sentence allowed him to include a sensory detail about a smell. However, he took it out because it had nothing to do with boats, the focus of his description.

- Noah agreed that he needed more details in his description. He added details about the pirate boat and the swan boat. He was pleased that he was able to add a detail involving the sense of touch.

- Noah chose to describe the boats in the order they passed him. He started with the fastest boat, then a second boat, and finally the slowest boat. He realized that his description would be in chronological order.

Noah also had an idea about something that Jude had not noticed. Noah didn't think that the tone at the start of the conclusion was appropriate for the cultural center audience. He wrote a new sentence to start his conclusion that made the tone seem more professional.

Your Turn
Revise your draft, using your ideas and those suggested by your content editor. Be sure to look over all of the possible changes before you make any of them.

Descriptions

Copyediting and Proofreading

Copyediting

Noah copyedited his description to make sure all of his sentences made sense and were the best that they could be. Noah used this checklist to help him with copyediting.

Copyeditor's Checklist

✓ Are all the sentences complete?

✓ Do the sentences follow each other in an order that makes sense?

✓ Are the sentences different lengths?

✓ Are exact words used?

Noah read his description one time for each of the questions in the checklist. He saw that all of his sentences were complete and in an order that made sense.

Noah thought that he could do a better job of using exact words to express exactly what he was describing. He knew that by using exact words, he would also improve the sensory details of his description. Noah made the *hot day* into a *sizzling hot day.* He also wanted to give the reader a better sense of the sound of paddles slapping the water. To make the sound seem louder, Noah said that the sound was more like a giant fish *leaping* in and out of the water. He thought that a leaping fish would make a bigger splash noise in his readers' imaginations.

Noah added the words *barked, sparkling,* and *sun-warmed.* Can you find the places where he might have decided to use these words to make his description stronger?

Your Turn

Copyedit your description. Use the Copyeditor's Checklist. Look for only one kind of mistake at a time. Make sure that you use exact words to make your description clear. What you are describing will be easier to see, hear, smell, taste, or feel if you use sensory details.

Proofreading

Noah thought that it was a good idea to have someone proofread his description. He had read his description many times, and he wanted someone who had not read it before to read it for mistakes that he might have missed. Noah asked his classmate Archer to proofread the description. Archer used this proofreader's checklist to help him.

Proofreader's Checklist

✓ Are the paragraphs indented?

✓ Are all the words spelled correctly?

✓ Are capitalization and punctuation correct?

✓ Is the grammar correct?

✓ Were any new mistakes added while editing?

Archer proofread Noah's description. He read for one type of mistake at a time. He found one capitalization mistake. The word *river* needed to be capitalized in one place. In the first paragraph, it is part of the proper noun Meuse River. This was the only place where it needed to be capitalized.

Archer also noticed two grammatical mistakes. In the second paragraph, the word *faster* should be *fastest.* Noah was describing more than two boats, so the *-est* suffix should be used. Noah found that he made the same mistake with a different word in another place in the description. Can you find it?

Your Turn

Read your description carefully, using the Proofreader's Checklist. Look for only one kind of mistake at a time.

When you have finished, ask a partner to proofread your description. Remind your partner to check for one kind of mistake at a time. Discuss any of your partner's changes that you do not agree with or understand.

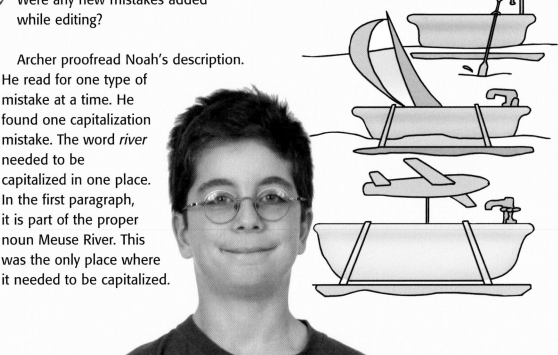

Descriptions

Publishing

Noah took his time making changes. He knew that it would be displayed in the cultural center, so he didn't want any mistakes in his published description. Here is Noah's final version.

The Tub Boat Races of Belgium
by Noah Friedlander

You would think not much would be happening on a sizzling hot August day in the small town of Dinant, Belgium. But once a year the town is crowded and noisy, and the Meuse River is filled with bathtubs. People from the town wait all year to try out their wacky bathtub boats in the race called the International Bathtub Regatta.

Last year, on the day of the race the narrow river was filled with homemade boats that had bathtubs as part of their hulls. All of the paddles from the bathtub boats splashing in the river sounded like giant fish leaping out of the water. The fastest boat had a mast with a black pirate flag. The people rowing the boat were dressed like pirates and all had eyepatches. The captain had a giant neon green toy parrot on his shoulder. He barked out instructions in a goofy voice.

Another boat was built in the shape of a swan, with the bathtub as the swan's belly. Every few minutes a sparkling stream of water shot out of the swan's mouth. The crew of the swan boat aimed the water at the crowd. The weather was so humid that the air felt like a wet sponge. People in the crowd tried to get hit by the water so they could cool off their sun-warmed skin.

The slowest boat was sinking into the water. The crew was dressed as cooks and paddled with oversized kitchen utensils. As their boat sank, the cooks threw their tall white chef's hats and giant wooden spoons and spatulas into the air. The crowd applauded and hooted, and it was as loud as a gym during a basketball game.

The International Bathtub Regatta is a sight to see and to enjoy. With all the splashing water, cheering, and laughing, it sounds like a gigantic pool party. The bathtub inventions look like something out of another world. It is more of a party than a race. Sometimes in Belgium a bathtub is much more than just a bathtub.

The Tub Boat Races of Belgium
by Noah Friedlander

You would think not much would be happening on a sizzling hot August day in the small town of Dinant, Belgium. But once a year the town is crowded and noisy, and the Meuse River is filled with bathtubs. People from the town wait all year to try out their wacky bathtub boats in the race called the International Bathtub Regatta.

Last year, on the day of the race the narrow river was filled with homemade boats that had bathtubs as part of their hulls. All of the paddles from the water. The boats splashing in the river sounded like giant fish leaping out of the water. The fastest boat had a mast with a black pirate flag. The people rowing the boat were dressed like pirates and all had eyepatches. The captain had a giant neon green toy parrot on his shoulder. He barked out instructions in a goofy voice.

Another boat was built in the shape of a swan, with the bathtub as the swan's belly. Every few minutes a sparkling stream of water shot out of the swan's mouth. The crew of the swan boat aimed the water at the crowd. The weather was so humid that the air felt like a wet sponge. People in the crowd tried to get hit by the water so they could cool off their sun-warmed skin.

The slowest boat was sinking into the water. The crew was dressed as cooks and paddled with oversized kitchen utensils. As their boat sank, the cooks threw their tall white chef's hats and giant wooden spoons and spatulas into the air. The crowd applauded and hooted, and it was as loud as a gym during a basketball game.

The International Bathtub Regatta is a sight to see and to enjoy. With all the splashing water, cheering, and laughing, it sounds like a gigantic pool party. The bathtub inventions look like something out of another world. It is more of a party than a race. Sometimes in Belgium a bathtub is much more than just a bathtub.

After Noah finished typing his work, he made a poster on which to mount his description. On his poster he put postcards from Dinant, photos of the bathtub boats, and a drawing of the cooks leaping from their sinking boat.

Your Turn
Make a final copy of your description. Add the changes from proofreading that you decided to use. Make sure that you don't add any new mistakes while making your final copy.

You might want to make a display to go along with your description. You can make a poster to show what you described. You might bring in an audio recording to let your classmates hear what you described. Be creative with your displays!

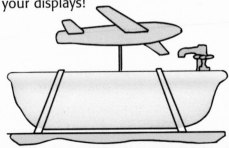

Our Wide Wide World

St. Paul is the state
capital of Minnesota.
The cities of St. Paul
and Minneapolis
are often referred to
as the "twin cities"
because the two
are located next to
one another on the
Mississippi River.
St. Paul got its start
as a focal point for
lumber and fur trading
because of its location
on the river. Father
Lucien Galtier, who
named the city in
1840, saved the young
town from the other
popular choice at the
time, Pigs Eye! Do
you know how your
hometown got
its name?

Book Reports

United Tates of America: A Novel With Scrapbook Art
by Paula Danziger
Reviewed by Mack47

United Tates of America, by Paula Danziger, is the story of Sarah Kate Tate, known to her friends as Skate Tate. Skate lives with her parents, her little sister, Emma, and her great uncle Mort (nicknamed GUM) in the small town of Chelsea, New Jersey. Comfortable with elementary school and the traditions of her family, she doesn't welcome the changes that begin on her first day at Biddle Middle.

Skate's cousin and best friend, Susie, quickly finds a new group of friends and has little time for Skate. The Happy Scrappys, Skate and Susie's scrapbooking club, continues to meet, but Skate senses that this group of close friends may be growing apart. Being chosen co-art director of the school paper with good-looking Garth Garrison helps Skate realize that new things can be good things.

GUM, one of Skate's favorite people in the whole world, encourages her artistic streak as he shares his travel adventures. GUM teaches Skate lessons about life. He gives her confidence to face tragedy and to deal with it in a way that would make him proud.

This book helps middle school readers realize that their mixed feelings about growing up are natural. GUM wanted Skate to know how to deal with whatever happens, even if it's not always fun, and then to move on in life.

I enjoyed this story about growing up. I identified with Skate and her feelings, and I laughed at Ms. Danzigers puns. For example, the D.D.T., the Donald Duck Trio—Huey, Duey, and Louie—enjoy quacking until the teacher says there'll be no more "fowl behavior."

I also liked the actual scrapbook pages at the end of the book. They made the Tate family and Skate's friends come alive for me. The pictures of the family trip to Plymouth, Massachusetts, for example, are arranged and annotated in a way that connects the trip to the Tate family. This alone makes the trip far livelier than most sleep-inducing vacation slide shows.

Page 1 of 1

What Makes a Good Book Report?

Writing a book report gives you the opportunity to tell others about a book you have read. In a book report, you give information about a book through description, explanation, and example. Then you give your personal opinion about the book, stating the reasons why you feel as you do about it.

Keep these things in mind when writing a book report.

Characters and Setting

An effective book report describes the important characters in a book and the setting of the story. Characters are the people, animals, or other beings in stories. The setting is where and when the story takes place.

How much your book report describes the characters and the setting will depend on how important each is to the story. For example, the book *United Tates of America* takes place in today's New Jersey. The setting is not unusual, so the writer of the book report on page 159 doesn't describe the setting in much detail.

Some settings are very important to a book and can play a larger role than the characters. In Jonathan Swift's *Gulliver's Travels,* the reader learns very little about Gulliver himself. But the reader learns a great deal about the strange lands he visits, such as Lilliput and Brobdingnag.

Plot Summary

Plot is what happens in the book, the major events. Much of a book report summarizes the plot of a book. A plot summary might start by describing the characters' situation at the beginning of the story. The summary might also tell what happens next, but it should never tell how the story ends.

Plot summaries tell only the important parts of the plot. Just like unnecessary details in other kinds of writing, if some parts of the story do not seem to be related to the main characters, leave them out.

• Activity A •

Read the following plot summaries of the book *A Week in the Woods* by Andrew Clements. Tell which one would be better in a book report and why.

A. At first Mark remains aloof from others. Why should he take the trouble to make friends when he'll be going to an expensive boarding school next year? Mr. Maxwell thinks Mark is a know-it-all and seems to be punishing him for it. The approach of the fifth-grade environmental camping trip makes Mark realize how he's been acting. He changes his ways and makes new friends. But unexpected events follow when Mark gets caught with a knife. What will this do to the relationship between Mark and Mr. Maxwell? Read this book to find out.

B. Mark doesn't try to make friends at first because he'll be going to a boarding school next year. Mr. Maxwell doesn't give Mark a chance. When Mark realizes he's been acting stuck-up, he changes and makes friends. The fifth-grade camping trip begins well. But when Mark is discovered with his friend Jason's knife and takes the blame when it's found, things take a turn for the worse. Leaving the car instead of waiting for Mr. Maxwell to drive him home, Mark starts on a dangerous adventure. Mr. Maxwell follows and gets hurt. Mark rescues him, and Mr. Maxwell apologizes for the way he treated Mark. They return to the camp as friends.

Writer's Corner

Write a plot summary of a book you like. Save your summary.

Our Wide Wide World

Montgomery is the state capital of Alabama. Montgomery has been the site of many major civil rights accomplishments including the Montgomery Bus Boycott of 1955. A courageous black woman named Rosa Parks refused to give up her seat on a bus and was arrested. In protest, supporters across the city refused to ride the bus. The boycott continued for 381 days, when the U.S. Supreme Court ruled that the segregation of bus service was illegal.

Theme

The theme is the idea that sums up the whole book. The theme might be the importance of friendship or the challenges of being in middle school. In a book report, you might state the theme as a life lesson that applies to everyone. The theme is part of the body of your book report.

Personal Opinion

In the conclusion, give your personal opinion of the book. Tell whether or not you liked the book and why. Be specific. Use examples from the book that led you to your opinion. Tell whether you recommend the book to others.

• Activity B •

Tell which of these examples might be a good statement of the theme of *A Week in the Woods*.

A. A boy and his teacher make up and realize they can be friends.

B. Mr. Maxwell was a knowledgeable and experienced science teacher.

C. Most people when given a chance will do the right thing and shouldn't be prejudged.

D. Mark felt that he was different but not better than the kids at Hardy Elementary School.

• Activity C •

These four paragraphs are from a book report about *Frindle* by Andrew Clements. Match the paragraphs with the following parts of a book report.

A. personal opinion; B. plot summary;
C. title, author, characters and setting; D. theme

1. *Frindle* by Andrew Clements is a clever story about a very clever boy named Nick Allen. Nick lives with his parents in a small New Hampshire town and is known for turning classrooms upside down. Will fifth grade be different with Mrs. Granger, a language arts teacher who doesn't let anybody get away with anything?

2. Trying one of his tricks to distract the teacher at the end of class so she won't assign homework, Nick innocently asks where words come from. Mrs. Granger's answer inspires Nick to invent a new word. He calls a pen a *frindle*, and soon everyone in the school, the town, and beyond does the same. Mrs. Granger is up to Nick's challenge. The local paper hears about it, and it becomes important news. A local businessman becomes involved. Where will it end? Nick found out, but not until ten years later.

3. This book helps readers understand the true nature of words, especially that they are important and are needed by everyone. The dictionary endures, as do words, and it changes and grows through the years and never goes out of date.

4. I thought this was a very good book. It was really neat that a fifth grader could make up a word that became known all over the world. Nick, an ordinary kid, became wealthy because of his creativity and persistence. All kids could relate to Mrs. Granger and her x-ray vision. It was ordinary, yet extraordinary! I loved the illustrations in this book. Often books do not have many pictures, but these pencil sketches emphasized the book's humor.

Writer's Corner

Look at the plot summary that you wrote for the Writer's Corner on page 161. Think about the theme of the book. Write an explanation of the theme of the book.

Writing a Book Report

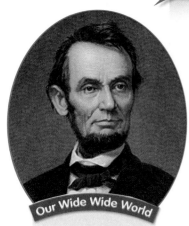

Springfield is the state capital of Illinois. It was made the capital in 1837, and the first state legislature met here in 1839. Springfield is probably best known as the home of U.S. President Abraham Lincoln, who freed the slaves. The Springfield Race Riots of 1908 led to the beginnings of the NAACP (National Association for the Advancement of Colored People), an influential civil rights organization.

Once you have identified all of the information that will go into a book report, the next step is to write the information in a way that makes a reader interested in the book.

Purpose

Effective book reports show a clear understanding of their purpose. When you write a book report, think about what you want the reader to know about the book. Think of how you can best organize and present your information to make it interesting and memorable.

Introduction

Book reports begin by telling what the title of the book is and the name of the author. The introduction of a book report tells who the main characters are and where the story takes place. It also gives an idea of what the book is about.

Body

The body of a book report gives more details about the plot and the theme of the book. The body of a book report tells what happens in the book, but it doesn't give away the ending. If you tell the ending, why would your audience want to read the book?

Conclusion

The conclusion of a book report tells the reader your opinion of the book. The conclusion should also give reasons and examples for your opinion.

Activity A

Tell what important information is missing in this introduction of a book report for the novel *Skylark*.

Readers who met the characters in *Sarah, Plain and Tall* will be excited to find out in this next book if they lived happily ever after. This story tells what happens when drought forces the family to leave their prairie home in the West and travel east to Maine.

Activity B

Read the following conclusions from book reports on *United Tates of America*. Decide which conclusion supports the writer's opinions with strong reasons and examples.

1. I liked this book a lot. It's about kids our age and some of the struggles that they go through when they start middle school. The characters, especially Skate and GUM, seemed like real people. The scrapbook at the end made the story seem even more real.

2. I really didn't like this book. But then again, I don't like many books. This one just seemed boring. I also didn't like the characters or the plot.

3. My opinion of this book is very favorable. It's a definite must-read! The characters were good and so was the story. The author's use of humor added a lot. You should put it on your list of books to read.

Writer's Corner

Choose one book from the library that you have read. Write an introduction for a book report. Save your introduction to use later.

Planning a Book Report

Before writing a book report, a writer should write down all of the important information to include. The book report should name the title and the author, and include the main events of the book in chronological order. The book report should also include the theme of the book and your opinion of the book based on examples from the plot.

A book report should include the features listed below.

Features of a Book Report

Title
Underline the title if you write it or use italics if you work on a computer.

Author
Copy the author's name exactly as it appears on the cover.

Setting
Describe the setting in as much detail as you need. If the setting is important to understand the story, describe it in as much detail as you can.

Characters
Name the main characters in the book and tell a little bit about them.

Plot Summary
The plot summary describes the main events in chronological order without giving away the ending.

Theme
The theme is the general idea or "life lesson" of the book.

Personal Opinion
Include your personal opinion, giving reasons and using examples from the book.

• Activity C •

Review the book report on page 159 and answer the following questions.

1. What information is included in the first paragraph of the book report?

2. What information is included in the second and third paragraphs of the report?

3. What was the theme of *United Tates of America?*

4. What was the writer's personal opinion about this story? What were some of the things the writer especially liked?

5. Have you read this book? If so, do you agree with the writer's opinion? Why or why not? If you haven't read this book, do you think you would like to read it? Why or why not?

• Activity D •

Find in the library three or four fiction books that you have not read. Write down the titles and authors. For each book write a sentence that tells why you might want to read the book. For example, you might say that you have read other books by the same author or that something on the cover caught your attention.

Writer's Corner

Read a book report or book review in a magazine or on the Internet. Answer the following questions. Use complete sentences.

1. **Who are the main characters?**
2. **What is the setting of the book?**
3. **What main events are included in the plot summary?**
4. **What is the theme of the book?**
5. **What is the writer's opinion of the book?**

Revising Sentences

Our Wide Wide World

Honolulu is the state capital of Hawaii. *Honolulu* means "sheltered bay" or "place of shelter" in the Hawaiian language. Honolulu is known as a popular tourist destination but also for the attack on Pearl Harbor. On December 7, 1941, Japanese planes bombed Pearl Harbor, a U.S. naval base located west of Honolulu. It was this attack that forced the United States to become involved in World War II.

Rambling Sentences

Sentences that have too many words or too many ideas are called rambling sentences. Rambling sentences can be difficult to read and make readers lose interest. Some rambling sentences are just a string of short sentences linked together by words such as *and*, *but*, or *or*.

Effective writers use a variety of sentence lengths. Doing this keeps the reader interested. Read these two examples. Notice how they are alike and how they are different. Which example is easier to read?

A. On Saturday my family took a trip to Independence Mall, and we saw the Liberty Bell and Constitution Hall, and then we watched a film on Benjamin Franklin at the end of the day.

B. On Saturday my family took a trip to Independence Mall. There we saw the Liberty Bell and Constitution Hall. At the end of the day, we watched a film on Benjamin Franklin.

Both examples include a description of a trip to Independence Mall. Example B, however, breaks the same information into three sentences that are easier to read. When you use shorter sentences, the reader has a chance to take in each idea.

If you are using several conjunctions in one sentence, you may be writing a rambling sentence. Try beginning a new sentence each time that a conjunction appears.

Another way to find a rambling sentence is to look for sentences with many ideas. When you revise these sentences, try to write a new sentence for each idea.

Activity A

Revise the following rambling sentences by breaking them up into shorter sentences. Add words such as *and* or *then* where needed.

1. Our science class had a video camera to use for a week, and we made a tape showing chicks hatching, and we showed our tape to the first graders.

2. The boots in the store are on sale, and my mother is going to buy them for me, or if she doesn't I will buy them myself.

3. Japan is a group of islands in the sea off the continent of Asia, and its land area is less than that of California, and it gets much of its food from other countries.

4. Doing chores at home is one common job for young people, and mowing lawns is another, but some young people have unusual jobs such as acting as clowns at children's parties.

5. My cousin's favorite activity is canoeing, and every summer he goes on canoe trips, and he has traveled thousands of miles by canoe.

Activity B

The following paragraph is one long, rambling sentence. Break it up into shorter sentences.

I love Karen Cushman's books, and *Rodzina* is no exception, and this historical fiction story is about the orphan trains that carried children to the West to be adopted and work as farm laborers, and Rodzina herself tells the story, but the way she tells it made me feel like I was living it with her, and now I can appreciate that time in our history.

Writer's Corner

Use your imagination and write a long sentence with several conjunctions. Then exchange your sentence with a partner and break up the sentence you receive into several shorter sentences. Compare the finished sentences with the original sentence.

Run-on Sentences

A run-on sentence is two or more sentences put together without correct punctuation. Run-on sentences confuse readers. One way to fix a run-on sentence is by adding correct punctuation to make two or more sentences. Read the run-on sentence and the revision below.

A. We went to the arboretum to see many varieties of trees most interesting to me were the gingko trees.

B. We went to the arboretum to see many varieties of trees. Most interesting to me were the gingko trees.

In example A the run-on sentence had no punctuation between the two ideas. In example B a period after *trees* makes the second idea into a separate sentence.

Read the next pair of examples. The first example is a run-on sentence that has the wrong punctuation mark, a comma, after the first idea. In the revised sentence, the comma is replaced by a period.

A. The study of plants is called botany, there are at least 300,000 different kinds of plants in the world.

B. The study of plants is called botany. There are at least 300,000 different kinds of plants in the world.

Another way to fix a run-on sentence is to add a conjunction and turn it into a compound sentence. A comma should be added before the conjunction. Be sure that the ideas in the run-on sentence fit together before you revise the sentence with a conjunction. Here is a run-on sentence that was revised, using a conjunction.

A. We didn't want to go home it was getting late.

B. We didn't want to go home, but it was getting late.

Activity C

Correct the following run-on sentences by separating them into more than one sentence.

1. Joan and I like to show each other our artwork sometimes we go to the art museum together Joan likes the paintings while I prefer the sculptures.

2. In the 1700s a Frenchman built a three-foot high robot, the robot could write and when it wrote, its eyes would follow the pen, it would even dot its *i*'s.

3. Uncle Owen gave me a large package for my birthday I shook it before I opened it in the package I found a new football.

Activity D

Correct the following run-on sentences by separating them into more than one sentence or by adding a conjunction and the correct punctuation.

1. We planted beans in our garden, we had no idea how quickly they would grow.

2. In August we take a family vacation this year we will visit the Grand Canyon.

3. My little brother can be very helpful around the house sometimes he hides to avoid housework.

4. Our public library always sponsors Battle of the Books, I hope I can qualify for this year's battle.

5. I heard my mom and dad whispering about puppies I hope they're thinking of getting one for our family.

6. For my report I have to use encyclopedias, I'll have to go to the library after school.

Writer's Corner

Look at your work from a previous Writer's Corner in this chapter. Check your work for rambling or run-on sentences. Revise any rambling or run-on sentences that you find.

Word Study

Prefixes

A prefix is a syllable, or syllables, added to the beginning of a base word that changes the meaning of the word. Knowing what prefixes mean can help you figure out the meaning of new words as you read.

The prefixes *dis-*, *un-*, *im-*, and *in-* have similar meanings. These prefixes mean "not." Notice how these prefixes change the meanings of these base words.

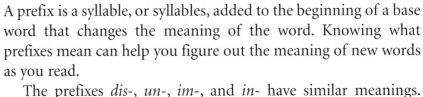

dis- + honest = dishonest   im- + perfect = imperfect

un- + even = uneven   in- + correct = incorrect

Although these prefixes have similar meanings, each prefix fits only with certain words. If you are unsure which prefix to add to a base word, you can check a dictionary.

Here are some other common prefixes and their meanings.

Prefix	Meaning	Example
mis-	badly, wrongly	misunderstand
re-	again	rejoin
pre-	before	predawn

If you know that the prefix *pre-* means "before," it will help you remember that a prefix is added before the base word.

Activity A

Complete these sentences by adding words that use a prefix that means "not." Use the words in italics as the base words.

1. If you are not *satisfied* with the ending of a story, you are _____.

2. If you think the smell of dirty socks is not *pleasant*, you think it is _____.

3. If you do not *continue* your subscription to a soccer magazine, you _____ it.

4. Bats are not *active* during the day; they are _____.

5. If sunny days are not *frequent*, they are _____.

6. If he is not *loyal* to his team, he is _____.

Activity B

Use the chart of prefixes on page 172 to tell what these words mean. Use a dictionary to check your answers.

1. mislead

2. reabsorb

3. misread

4. reuse

5. recharge

6. precut

7. misbehave

8. prepay

Writer's Corner

Pick one prefix from this lesson. Then brainstorm a list of as many words as you can that begin with that prefix. Write five sentences. Use one or more words from your list in each sentence.

Number and Amount Prefixes

Many prefixes have meanings that tell a number or an amount. For example, the word *bicycle* has a prefix. Can you see it? What do think the prefix means?

Here is a list of prefixes that tell a number or an amount.

Prefix	Meaning	Example
uni-	one	unicycle
mono-	one	monorail
bi-	two	biweekly
tri-	three	triangle
quad-	four	quadrangle
cent-	hundred	centimeter
mega-	million	megaton
poly-	many	polygon
multi-	many	multicolored

• Activity C •

Use the prefix chart above to answer these questions.

1. How many *centiliters* are in one liter?

2. How many events does a *biathlete* compete in?

3. How many watts are in a *megawatt*?

4. How many things can a *multitalented* dinosaur do?

5. How many colors are on a *tricolor* flag?

6. Who speaks more languages—someone who is *monolingual* or someone who is *multilingual*?

Activity D

Read the following sentences and find the words that use prefixes from the list on page 174. Define the words. Use a dictionary if you need help.

1. The speaker talked in a monotone voice.

2. The filmmaker was a multimillionaire.

3. The mayor holds town meetings triweekly.

4. Some scientists believe the first life on earth was unicellular.

5. Democrats and Republicans formed a bipartisan committee.

Activity E

Copy the chart below and fill in the missing parts.

Prefix	Base Word	New Word	Meaning
1. _____	step	misstep	_____
2. dis-	_____	_____	not organized
3. in-	_____	incomplete	_____
4. im-	pure	_____	_____
5. multi-	stage	_____	many stages
6. uni-	_____	unicycle	_____
7. bi-	_____	_____	twice weekly

Writer's Corner

Imagine that you are writing a letter to your favorite author. Write some questions and comments you might include in your letter. Use words with prefixes from this lesson.

Study Skills

Fact and Opinion

Both facts and opinions are used in book reports. A fact is a statement that can be proved true. You can use the library or the Internet to find out if the fact is true. Here is an example of a fact.

> Franklin D. Roosevelt was the 32nd president of the United States.

An opinion states a person's judgments or beliefs about a subject. Opinions cannot be proved true or untrue because they reflect a person's feelings. Here is an example of an opinion.

> Franklin D. Roosevelt was the best president since Thomas Jefferson.

A person might believe that this statement is true, but it cannot be proved true or untrue.

When writers give their opinion, they try to support their opinion with facts. For example, a writer trying to support the opinion above might list good things that President Roosevelt did for the United States.

The introduction and body of a book report may contain many facts, such as what the characters do or where they live. Most statements in the conclusion of a book report are opinions. By using facts from the book, a writer can persuade the reader to agree with his or her opinion.

Activity A •

Identify the statements below as fact or opinion. Explain your answers.

1. **a.** Dinosaurs became extinct about 65 million years ago.

   b. Dinosaurs would be more fun to ride than elephants.

2. **a.** The Vikings built a colony on Greenland.

   b. The Vikings were the toughest people in Europe.

3. **a.** The Irish Sea has the biggest waves you'll ever see.

   b. The Irish Sea separates Ireland from Great Britain.

4. **a.** The four-string banjo is easier to play than the guitar.

   b. An open-back banjo doesn't have a resonator.

Activity B •

Read these facts and opinions. Tell whether the fact supports the opinion. Explain your answers.

1. Opinion: "A Haunted Attic" is a scary story.
   Fact: The main character hears a howling noise in the attic at night.

2. Opinion: No one can write like C. S. Lewis.
   Fact: He wrote *The Lion, the Witch and the Wardrobe*.

3. Opinion: Science fiction stories can help you see things that are wrong with the present.
   Fact: H. G. Wells wrote a book about a Martian invasion called *War of the Worlds*.

4. Opinion: Isaac Asimov was a fast writer.
   Fact: He wrote or edited over 500 books.

Writer's Corner

Write one positive opinion about your school. Then research and write one fact that supports your opinion.

Opinion Words

Knowing opinion words can help you decide if what you are reading is fact or opinion. Opinion words signal that the writer is telling his or her opinion on a subject. Here are some common opinion words you might find.

believe	good	bad
think	favorite	horrible
should	ugly	beautiful
feel	best	worst

Activity C

Pick the words in these opinions that signal that they are opinions. Explain your answers.

1. I believe that this is the best football team our school has ever had.

2. I feel that the new school logo is awful.

3. Mysteries are my favorite kind of fiction.

4. That is the most beautiful roller coaster I've ever seen.

5. Bowling is the best sport for building your strength.

6. Ours is the mightiest wrestling team in Texas.

Activity D

Tell whether each statement is a fact or an opinion. Explain your answers.

1. Baseball is the most elegant American sport.

2. Baseball players use a bat to hit the ball.

3. The pitcher stands on a mound to throw pitches.

4. All boys should play baseball.

5. Baseball games have nine innings, unless the score is tied.

6. Hot dogs are the best baseball food.

7. A home run is always the most exciting part of a game.

Activity E

Read each of these opinions. Tell whether the supporting statement is a fact or an opinion.

1. Opinion: *The Lord of the Rings* trilogy is too long.
   Support: Each book is hundreds of pages.

2. Opinion: *Bud, Not Buddy* is a funny book.
   Support: Bugs is the funniest character.

3. Opinion: I think biographies are more exciting than fiction.
   Support: A biography is the story of a person's life.

4. Opinion: Huck Finn has exciting adventures.
   Support: In one part of the book, he rides down the Mississippi River on a raft.

5. Opinion: King Arthur's story is inspiring and sometimes sad.
   Support: One of the best parts is when he pulls the sword from the stone.

Our Wide Wide World

Salt Lake City is the state capital of Utah. The city takes its name from nearby Great Salt Lake. The city was founded in 1847 when Brigham Young led members of the Church of Jesus Christ of Latter-day Saints (Mormons) to the West to find a location where they could practice their religion openly.

Activity F

Choose two of the following items. Use opinion words to write a few sentences about each.

A. year-round school

B. curfews

C. skateboarding

D. horseback riding

E. dress codes

F. exercise

G. watching television

Writer's Corner

Think of a book you have recently read. Write two opinions you have about the book. Then support your opinions by writing a fact for each opinion.

Oral Book Reports

Think of your favorite book. What did you do when you finished it? Did you tell your friends about it? Did you tell them that they just had to read it? An oral book report is a chance to share with an audience a book that you enjoyed.

Audience

Keep in mind the audience you will be speaking to. Will it be an audience of friends or younger children? When you choose a book to talk about for an oral book report, try to pick one that fits your audience.

You can give an oral book report about a book you liked or a book you disliked. To keep your audience interested, choose a book that you have strong feelings about.

Organization

Start by telling the title and author of your book. Then describe the setting of the book and some of the main characters. You might also say why you think the book is worth reading. That can grab the audience's attention.

Next tell about a few things that happen in the book without giving away the ending. Use characters' names and details to keep the audience interested.

End by telling the audience your opinion of the book. Be sure to include examples from the book to support your opinion.

Delivery

You can do some things in an oral book report that you cannot do in a written one. Here are a few ideas.

- Use your voice. You can interest your audience in your book by speaking in a lively way. You can also emphasize your opinions by using your voice and gestures in the conclusion. Show how you feel about the book through the way you talk about it.

- Use visual aids. Show your audience what the cover of the book looks like. You might show illustrations of characters, pictures of the setting, or photos of the author.

- Read part of the book aloud. Try to find a paragraph or scene that you think is especially good. The audience might like to hear what the author's writing sounds like. Be sure that you keep your reading short. The audience wants to hear what you have to say.

Activity A

Make a list of books you have read. Try to think of more than one kind of book. Discuss your list with a partner. Talk about which books might be most interesting for an audience of your classmates. Then choose a book for an oral book report.

Activity B

Think about the book you chose in Activity A. Plan a book report by listing all of the important information you should include. Use the chart on page 166. Then think about a passage from the book you could read aloud. Also think of a visual aid to include in your report.

Speaker's Corner

Look at the personal opinion that you listed in Activity B. Write down reasons and examples that support it. Share with a partner your reasons and examples.

Prepare

After you choose a book, prepare your oral book report. Write the information you need for the introduction on one or two note cards. You might want to include a few comments you have about the book that you think might grab the attention of the audience.

Write on note cards the major events that happen in the book. Use words to remind you of what you want to say. Describe the important parts, but don't give away the ending.

Write a few note cards for the conclusion. Include examples that support your opinion. Don't write down everything you are going to say. The audience wants to hear you talk, not read from your note cards.

Practice

Practice giving your oral book report, using your note cards. If you have trouble remembering something, you may want to add new note cards. Practice in front of a mirror. As you practice, try using your note cards less and less. If you plan to use a visual aid, such as the book or a picture, practice using your visual aid.

When you are ready, practice with a friend or family member. Here are some questions you might want to ask your listener.

- Am I speaking clearly and loudly enough?

- Can you see my visual aid?

- Did I tell about the plot and characters clearly?

- Do I speak with enough or too much enthusiasm?

- Do I give examples to support my opinions?

Listening Tips

Listen carefully to your classmates' book reports. You might discover a book you would like to read. Here are some tips for being a good listener.

- Pay attention to the speaker. Try to picture the characters and setting that the speaker describes.

- Don't interrupt. If you have questions about something, write them down. You might be able to ask questions at the end of the book report.

- As you listen, think about whether the book sounds like something you might like to read.

- Listen to the speaker's opinions. If you have read the book, think about whether you agree with the speaker. Do the examples that the speaker gives support his or her opinions?

• Activity C •

Copy this chart to help you organize your ideas. Fill out the Introduction and Body columns with the information you need for those parts of your book report. For the Conclusion column, you can use the reasons and examples you wrote for the Speaker's Corner on page 181. After you organize your ideas in the chart, use the chart to make note cards for an oral book report.

Introduction	Body	Conclusion

Speaker's Corner

Practice giving your oral book report with a partner. When you have finished, ask your partner the questions on page 182. Then let your partner practice his or her book report.

Book Reports

Prewriting and Drafting

Have you ever read about a book that sounded so good that you couldn't wait to read it? Have you ever read about a book that sounded awful? You might have been reading a book report. Book reports tell others about a book and what the writer thought about it.

Prewriting

Holden's fifth-grade class was making a class magazine. Holden was going to write a book report about a book that kids his age might like to read. His book report would be printed in the magazine for the whole school to read.

Before Holden wrote his book report, he knew he would have to do prewriting. He would choose a book, free write details about the book, and organize his ideas.

Choosing a Book

Holden made a list of some books that he enjoyed. He asked other kids in his class what they liked and added those books to his list. He included a short summary of each book so that he wouldn't mix them up. Look at his list.

> _The Witch of Blackbird Pond_ by Elizabeth Speares. Set in the colony of Connecticut in the late 1600s.
>
> _The Lion, the Witch, and the Wardrobe_ by C.S. Lewis. Four kids travel to a magic land.
>
> _Bud, Not Buddy_ by Christopher Paul Curtis. An orphan looks for his father during the Great Depression.
>
> _From the Mixed-up Files of Mrs. Basil E. Frankweiler_ by E.L. Konisburg. A sister and brother run away from home and live in a museum.

He had already read _The Lion, the Witch, and the Wardrobe_. He chose _Bud, Not Buddy_ because he had never read the book and didn't know much about the Great Depression.

Your Turn

Make a list of books and write a sentence or two about each one. Now read your list. Is there a book you want others to know about? Is there a book that might teach you about an unfamiliar time or place? Consider these questions and choose your book.

Free Writing

Holden checked out *Bud, Not Buddy* from the library and read it. He knew he was going to write about it, so he wrote notes about the book as he read. He jotted down important things that happened in the story. He wrote his ideas about the theme. He also wrote notes about the things that he liked. Here are Holden's free-writing notes about the first part of the book.

> Bud was 6 when his mom died. He didn't know who his dad was.
>
> Story starts when Bud is 10. He lives in an orphanage in Flint, Michigan.
>
> Bud's special suitcase—blanket, flyers of a jazz musician (Bud's dad?), stones with dates on them from mom, mom's picture
>
> Bud's Rules and Things for Having a Funner Life—FUNNY!
>
> awful foster home—Bud runs away
>
> Before she dies, Bud's mom tells him no matter how bad things get, when one door closes, another one opens. (theme?)

Your Turn

Read your book and make free-writing notes about it. If you have already read the book, skim through it to help remember the important things that happen. Write down a lot of details. Don't forget to write some things that you liked.

Organizing Ideas

Holden had a lot of notes about his book. Here are some of his notes.

> Title
> Bud, Not Buddy
>
> Author
> Christopher Paul Curtis
>
> Setting
> Flint and Grand Rapids, Michigan; Great Depression during 1930s; On the road
>
> Plot Summary
> Characters: Bud, Herman E. Calloway, Lefty Lewis, Miss Thomas, the Amoses
>
> Bud the orphan runs away from the foster home. He travels from Flint to Grand Rapids looking for his dad. Along the way he meets a lot of people who are poor because of the Depression. He meets some band members who help him find Herman E. Calloway.
>
> Theme
> When one door closes, another one opens.
>
> Personal Opinion
> I liked Bud's story because I could share his happiness and sadness.

Your Turn

Organize your notes the way Holden did. Describe the events of the plot in chronological order. Remember that you can add more details as you write your draft.

Drafting

After taking detailed notes and organizing them, Holden was ready to start writing. He wanted to give people enough information to make them want to read the book, but not so much that he told the whole story. Holden looked over his notes and wrote his first draft, adding information and details as he went along.

My Review of <u>Bud, Not Buddy</u>

by Holden Barrow

<u>Bud, Not Buddy</u> is the name of the book and the name of the book's main character, Bud. The story is set during the 1930s. As 10-year-old Bud travels, he makes friends like Lefty Lewis, Miss Thomas, and gruff Herman E. Calloway.

Bud's mother died when he was six and ever since, he's been shuffled from the orphanage to foster homes. He takes off from an abusive foster home to find his father. The family Bud stays with locks him in a shed after he gets into a fight with their son. Bud spends a scary night thinking that vampire bats are going to bite him. Bud thinks his father is jazz musican Herman E. Calloway. He travels alone from Flint to Grand rapids in search of Mr. Calloway. He uses flyers of Mr. Calloway left by his mother as clues. Along the way, Bud meets people whose lives have been changed by the Great Deppresion. He has many adventures that are funny and sad at the same time.

His courage leads him to the truth what he learns about his mom, himself, and the love of family may surprise you as much as it did Bud!

I liked this book a lot. I liked the character of Bud and his suitcase of memories, which was so special to him? I also liked Bud's Rules and Things for Having a Funner Life because it was hilarious. His mom's picture, the flyers about Herman E. Calloway, and his precious rocks are all things that help him remember his family. I also think that the author did a great job of having Bud tell the story. I felt like I was sharing Bud's happiness and sadness.

If you like stories about brave kids and like stories set in different times in American history, I'm sure you'll like Bud's journey too.

Your Turn

Use your organized free-writing notes to write a draft of your book report. Be sure to include important information such as characters, setting, plot, and personal opinion. Tell the main events of the story in chronological order, but don't give away too much.

Words with Feeling

Make the characters or events come alive for your readers. Choose words that show how you feel. Holden wrote about Bud's *precious rocks*. He refers to Bud's foster home as *abusive*.

Using exact words will help your audience feel what you felt when you read the book. A thesaurus can help you find the exact words that you need.

Book Reports

Content Editing

Holden had worked hard on his book report. He was happy with his first draft. But he knew that it could be made better by content editing. A content editor could check his ideas for logic, order, and clarity. A content editor could also tell him if he gave away too much information or if he needed to add more details.

Holden asked his cousin Daisy to content edit his draft. Daisy was the editor of her high school newspaper, and she often wrote reviews of movies, plays, and music. Daisy used this Content Editor's Checklist to check Holden's draft.

Content Editor's Checklist

✓ Does the book report have a clear purpose?

✓ Does the introduction tell the title and author of the book?

✓ Does the introduction tell the main characters and the setting, and hint at why the book is worth reading?

✓ Does the body give details about the plot in logical order?

✓ Does the body give enough information about the plot without giving away too much?

✓ Does the body state the theme of the book?

✓ Does the conclusion give the writer's opinion?

Daisy read Holden's book report carefully. Then she used the Content Editor's checklist to content edit the draft. Daisy checked for one question at a time and made notes and suggestions about what she read. Then she and Holden talked about the draft.

Daisy first told Holden about the things she liked. She liked how Holden wrote the conclusion with so much feeling. It was clear that Holden liked the book. Daisy also liked that the purpose of the book report was clear and that the body told the plot in logical order. Here are Daisy's other comments.

- You say what the book's title is, but you don't say who wrote it. People who read your book report might use the author's name to find the book.

- You did a great job of naming the characters in the introduction. But can you say more about the setting? You say when the book takes place, but not where.

- I think you should take out the part about Bud getting locked in the shed and being afraid of the vampire bats. It's interesting, but people might rather read about it in the book.

- I like what you say about Bud in the third paragraph. But is there a theme in the book that applies to everyone?

Holden thanked Daisy for her help. He thought that Daisy had made some really good suggestions. Holden was glad that he had asked his cousin to content edit the book report.

Your Turn

Read the draft of your book report. Then read it again, using the Content Editor's Checklist. Have you included the introduction, body, and conclusion? Try to put yourself in the place of your readers. Do you think that readers will trust your opinion about whether to read the book after reading your book report?

Ask a classmate to be your content editor. There may be a classmate who likes the same books as you do. You might content edit each other's work.

Content edit your partner's draft. Then meet with your content editor and discuss his or her suggestions. Think carefully about what your content editor says. Remember that your content editor may see things in a way that you cannot. But keep in mind that you will make the final decision about what you will change.

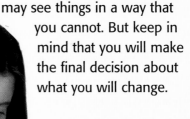

Book Reports

Revising

Look at how Holden used Daisy's suggestions and his own ideas to revise his draft.

Great, Not Good

~~My Review of Bud, Not Buddy~~

by Holden Barrow

by Christopher Paul Curtis. It is also

<u>Bud, Not Buddy</u> is ~~the name of the book and~~ the name of the book's main

in Flint and Grand rapids, Michigan

character, Bud. The story is set during the 1930s. As 10-year-old Bud travels,

he makes friends like Lefty Lewis, Miss Thomas, and gruff Herman E. Calloway.

Bud's mother died when he was six and ever since, he's been shuffled from

the orphanage to foster homes. He takes off from an abusive foster home to

find his father. ~~The family Bud stays with locks him in a shed after he gets into~~

~~a fight with their son. Bud spends a scary night thinking that vampire bats are~~

mysterious

~~going to bite him.~~ Bud thinks his father is jazz musican Herman E. Calloway. He

travels alone from Flint to Grand rapids in search of Mr. Calloway. He uses

flyers of Mr. Calloway left by his mother as clues. Along the way, Bud meets

people whose lives have been changed by the Great Deppresion. He has

many adventures that are funny and sad at the same time.

Before Bud's mom died, she told him that when one door closes, another opens. Everyone should remember

that. Bud

His courage leads him to the truth what he learns about his mom, himself,

did, and

and the love of family may surprise you as much as it did Bud!

I liked this book a lot. I liked the character of Bud and his suitcase of

memories, which was so special to him? I also liked Bud's Rules and Things for

Having a Funner Life because it was hilarious. His mom's picture, the flyers about Herman E. Calloway, and his precious rocks are all things that help him remember his family. I also think that the author did a great job of having Bud tell the story. I felt like I was sharing Bud's happiness and sadness.

   If you like stories about brave kids and like stories set in different times in American history, I'm sure you'll like Bud's journey too.

Holden used proofreading marks to mark changes in his draft. Look at how he revised his book report.

- Holden added the author's name. An introduction should always include the author's name.

- He added the names of the cities in which most of the story takes place. He thought that they were important to the setting.

- Holden took out the part about Bud getting locked in the shed. He agreed with Daisy that it was too much information.

- Holden thought that Daisy was right about the theme. Holden reread his notes about the theme and found an idea that might apply to every reader.

Holden changed the title. He thought that the new title was more interesting because it told how he felt about the book. His new title was also similar to the title of the book.

Holden also added the word *mysterious* to his description of Herman E. Calloway. He thought that *mysterious* described Mr. Calloway perfectly.

Your Turn
Use your ideas and the ideas from your content editor to revise your book report. When you have finished, go over the Content Editor's Checklist again. Can you answer yes to each question?

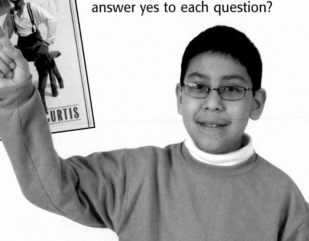

Copyediting and Proofreading

Copyediting

Holden knew that Daisy's suggestions and his own changes had made his book report better. He thought that now the plot summary gave just enough information to get people interested in the book. But he knew that there were additional changes to be made. He wanted to make sure that all his sentences were correct and that his word choices were exact. He used this Copyeditor's Checklist to copyedit his book report.

Copyeditor's Checklist

✓ Are there any run-on or rambling sentences?

✓ Are there any sentences that should be combined?

✓ Is each sentence grammatically correct?

✓ Are words with prefixes used correctly?

✓ Do all the words mean what I think they mean?

Holden carefully checked for one checklist question at a time. He paid special attention to word meaning.

Holden found a rambling sentence in the second paragraph of his draft. He decided to make it into two sentences. Look at how Holden revised the rambling sentence.

Old Sentence: Bud's mother died when he was six and ever since, he's been shuffled from the orphanage to foster homes.

Revision: Bud's mother died when he was six. Ever since, he's been shuffled from the orphanage to foster homes.

Holden also spotted a run-on sentence in his draft. Can you find it? How would you revise the sentence?

Holden did not like the word *sadness* at the end of the fourth paragraph. Bud had a lot of things happen to him, but he hadn't been sad about them. He checked a thesaurus and found the word *disappointments*. It was the exact word he needed.

After making his copyediting changes, Holden used the Copyeditor's Checklist again to check his changes.

Your Turn

Look over your revised draft. Use the Copyeditor's Checklist to copyedit your book report. Make sure that every sentence is clear, logical, and correct.

After making your changes, check your draft again. Pay special attention to the revisions you made.

Proofreading

Holden knew that he should proofread his draft before writing his final copy. Daisy had told Holden that proofreading was very important. A proofreader would check for spelling, capitalization, and punctuation mistakes in the draft.

Daisy's friend Jay was the proofreader for his high school newspaper. He offered to proofread Holden's book report. He used this Proofreader's Checklist.

Proofreader's Checklist

✓ Are the paragraphs indented?

✓ Are all the words spelled correctly?

✓ Are capitalization and punctuation correct?

✓ Is the grammar correct?

✓ Were any new mistakes added while editing?

Jay found two misspelled words in the draft. In the second paragraph, Holden misspelled *musician*. Can you find the other misspelled word?

Jay noticed one mistake in capitalization and one in punctuation. He thought that *Grand rapids* should be *Grand Rapids*. He checked a Michigan state map to be sure and saw that he was correct. Can you find the mistake in punctuation?

Holden thanked Jay for his help. He was so excited to have had high-school newspaper editors edit his book report!

After making sure that he made all of the changes, Holden proofread his draft again. He wanted to make sure that he had not made any new mistakes.

Your Turn

Read your book report carefully, using the Proofreader's Checklist. Check to make sure that your paragraphs are indented and that your words are correct. Check for misspelled words and correct grammar, capitalization, and punctuation. Finally make sure that you did not make any new mistakes while revising.

After you have proofread your draft, trade book reports with a partner. Go through your partner's report carefully, using the Proofreader's Checklist. Remember to keep a dictionary nearby.

Publishing

Holden carefully typed the draft on his computer. Then he printed it out and checked it one last time, using the Proofreader's Checklist. Here is the copy of Holden's book report that was published in his class magazine.

Great, Not Good

by Holden Barrow

Bud, Not Buddy is by Christopher Paul Curtis. It is also the name of the book's main character. The story is set in Flint and Grand Rapids, Michigan, during the 1930s. As 10-year-old Bud travels, he makes friends like Lefty Lewis, Miss Thomas, and gruff Herman E. Calloway.

Bud's mother died when he was six. Ever since, he's been shuffled from the orphanage to foster homes. He takes off from an abusive foster home to find his father. Bud thinks his father is mysterious jazz musician Herman E. Calloway. He travels alone from Flint to Grand Rapids in search of Mr. Calloway. He uses flyers of Mr. Calloway left by his mother as clues. Along the way, Bud meets people whose lives have been changed by the Great Depression. He has many adventures that are funny and sad at the same time.

Before Bud's mom died, she told him that when one door closes, another one opens. Everyone should remember that. Bud did, and his courage leads him to the truth. What he learns about his mom, himself, and the love of family may surprise you as much as it did Bud!

I liked this book a lot. I liked the character of Bud and his suitcase of memories, which was so special to him. I also liked Bud's Rules and Things for Having a Funner Life because it was hilarious. His mom's picture, the flyers about Herman E. Calloway, and his precious rocks are all things that help him remember his family. I also think that the author did a great job of having Bud tell the story. I felt like I was sharing Bud's happiness and disappointments.

If you like stories about brave kids and like stories set in different times in American history, I'm sure you'll like Bud's journey too.

Your Turn

Look over your book report one last time before you publish it. If you typed your book report, use your computer's spell checker. Print out your final copy and check it one last time, using the Proofreader's Checklist.

Book reports are fun to share. They give you a chance to share your opinion with others. They are also a good way for you to learn about books you have not read. One way that you can publish is by sharing your book report with your classmates. You might inspire someone else to read the book!

Another way that you might publish your book report is to find an Internet site on which to post it. Ask your teacher or librarian to help you find one. When you have found one, read over the guidelines that are posted to make sure that your book review fits the site.

If you publish your book report online, don't use your full name. You might choose a screen name instead. Or you can just use your first name. Remember to follow the rules for Internet safety whenever you publish your work online.

CHAPTER 6

The Mississippi River, when combined with the Missouri River, is part of the largest river system in North America. On its own the Mississippi River is the second longest river in the United States. The Mississippi River was important to America's development. It was used heavily to transport goods and passengers during the 19th century. What bodies of water are located near where you live?

Creative Writing

Paul Bunyan

Long ago when our country was young, the biggest baby on record was born. His name was Paul Bunyan, and he was so big that it took a whole herd of cows to fill up his bottle. By the time he was a year old, his clothes were so large that he had to use wagon wheels for buttons.

At that time settlers on the frontier needed lumber to build houses, stores, barns, and churches. Most loggers were big and strong. Paul grew up to be the biggest, strongest, toughest logger in the country. His voice was so loud that the other loggers had to wear earmuffs all year long. Whenever he sneezed, the roof blew off his cabin. Paul could chop down six acres of trees with one mighty swing of his giant steel ax.

During the winter of the Blue Snow, Paul found a baby ox lying in a drift and carried it home to his logging camp. When the ox thawed out, his color stayed as blue as the snow. Paul named the ox Babe. Babe grew fast and soon measured more than 42 ax handles between the eyes. The tips of his horns were so far apart that it took a bird a whole day to fly from one to the other. Paul soon learned that Babe was not only big, but that he was also very, very strong. Babe could haul logs as fast as Paul could chop them.

Babe helped Paul in other ways too. Once Paul hooked him up to the end of a crooked road through the logging camp, and Babe pulled all the kinks out of it. In fact, when all the curves were pulled straight, there were 10 miles of road left over. Paul rolled it up and gave it to a nearby town to use as Main Street.

Creative Writing

What Makes a Good Tall Tale?

Tall tales were the movies, TV, and video games of America in the 1800s. Pioneers of the time traveled to the West across territory in which everything seemed huge and dangerous—dark forests, vast prairies, tall mountains, arid deserts, and ferocious animals. Everything seemed bigger than life, so their stories were about people who were bigger than life.

Some of their stories were based on real people such as Johnny Appleseed and Davy Crockett. Others were about made-up characters like Paul Bunyan and Pecos Bill. The one thing the stories had in common was that everything was exaggerated.

Larger-than-Life Hero

The hero of a tall tale always has a specific job, such as cowboy, logger, railroad worker, or steelworker. He or she is always the biggest, bravest, strongest, fastest worker of them all, able to do things that no ordinary human could do. Tall tales often start by telling amazing things about the hero's childhood.

Problems, Solutions, Explanations

The hero of a tall tale often has a problem that he or she solves in an exaggerated and humorous way. For example, Sourdough Sam, Paul Bunyan's camp cook, had to make a lot of pancakes to feed all the loggers. Sam solved the problem by making a big griddle. It was so big that it had to be greased by skaters wearing slabs of bacon strapped to their feet.

Often a tall tale will explain how some familiar thing began. It is said that Babe the Blue Ox was so big and heavy that his footprints created Minnesota's 10,000 lakes.

Everyday Language

Tall tales are told using everyday language about ordinary things. Tall tales use exaggeration to create surprising and amusing pictures in the reader's mind.

Characters in tall tales speak in the everyday language of the people of their time and place. They use slang, contractions, and the vocabulary that a logger, a cowboy, or a railroad worker would use.

• Activity A •

Answer the following questions about the tall tale on page 197.

1. What was Paul Bunyan's job?

2. What problem did Paul have, and how did he and Babe solve it?

3. What are some exaggerated details about Paul's size?

4. What are some exaggerated details about Babe's size?

5. What ordinary things does the author mention to make exaggerated points about Paul and Babe?

Writer's Corner

Reread the model on page 197. Think about what else Paul might have eaten or worn. Write a few sentences giving exaggerated details about Paul's food and clothing.

At 2,565 miles in length, the Missouri River is the longest river in the United States. It joins the Mississippi River near St. Louis, Missouri. Together the two rivers make up the fourth-longest river system in the world. The Missouri River played an important role in the westward expansion of the United States. It was used to transport goods and passengers. It was also used by early explorers, most notably Lewis and Clark.

Activity B

Read the following adventure of tall-tale hero Pecos Bill. Then answer the questions.

When Pecos Bill was just a baby, his family headed west all the way into Texas with a caravan of covered wagons. Baby Bill was so big that he wrestled grizzly bears for fun. One day, unnoticed by his parents, he fell out of the wagon and into a river.

Bill was rescued by coyotes and raised as part of their family. His happy days as a teenager coyote were interrupted when a cowboy came riding through and spotted him. "Howdy, pardner, who are you?" asked the cowboy. After about a week of trying, the cowboy convinced Bill that he was a human and not a coyote. "Wanna head for the nearest ranch? Just follow me, fella," offered the cowboy.

Before leaving, Bill tamed himself a mountain lion. He rode his lion instead of a horse. On the way, he encountered a huge rattlesnake and a pack of vicious Gila monsters that a normal person would have tried to avoid. Not Bill. He grabbed the snake and whipped it around, beating the poison out of it. He made a rope out of the flattened snake and used it to lasso the Gila monsters. When he got to the ranch, Bill said, "How da ya like my herd, fellas?" Then he showed the ranch hands how to rope cattle with his rattlesnake lasso!

1. What are some amazing stories about Pecos Bill's childhood?

2. What is another example of exaggeration in the story?

3. What problem did Pecos Bill solve in an unusual way?

4. What unusual item did Pecos Bill invent?

5. How would you describe the way the characters speak in the story? Read the characters' exact words the way the characters might have said them.

Activity C

Tell why each sentence is from a tall tale.

1. John Henry drove spikes into railway ties faster than a steam engine could.

2. Pecos Bill rode a tornado and carved out the Grand Canyon.

3. Davy Crockett killed a bear when he was just three years old.

4. Three hours after Paul was born, he weighed 80 pounds, and his family had to use a lumber wagon as a baby carriage.

5. Annie Christmas was almost 10 feet tall.

6. Slue-foot Sue rode up on the Rio Grande on a catfish as big as a whale.

7. "By golly, I'm gonna tame that river or die trying!" said Paul.

Activity D

Tell whether each of the following sentences describes a larger-than-life hero.

1. The baby fussed and cried all night.

2. The boy studied six hours for his final exams.

3. The girl whooped so loud that the moon started to spin.

4. The bricklayer worked so fast that he could build a whole town in an hour.

5. The children skied to school after the big blizzard.

6. The woman was so hungry that she ate three cheese sandwiches.

Writer's Corner

Choose one of the sentences in Activity D that does not describe a larger-than-life hero. Rewrite it, using exaggeration to make it fit in a tall tale.

Writing a Tall Tale

The people who told tall tales in the 1800s told stories about the things they knew best. Loggers told stories about Paul Bunyan. Railroad workers told stories about John Henry. Cowboys told stories about Pecos Bill. The storytellers took things that happened in their own lives and exaggerated them to make them funny and entertaining. If there was a lot of snow, they said that the snow was so deep that loggers had to dig down to find the trees. If it was hot, they said it was so hot that the corn popped right on the stalks in the fields. The bigger the exaggeration, the more amusing the story would be.

Tall-tale writers of today write about things they know. You might write about the world's best soccer player or the world's fastest skater. Someone who likes to travel might write about the world's greatest explorer.

Creating a Character

The first step in writing a tall tale is choosing the hero. The hero should have a job that the writer is familiar with. Then the writer needs to decide what things can be exaggerated about that hero to make the hero larger than life. A baseball player must be able to throw, hit, and run. A baseball player who is the hero of a tall tale should be able to throw harder, hit farther, and run faster than any other baseball player. This baseball player might be able to run fast enough to catch the ball that he or she hit!

Activity A

Complete each of the following sentences to exaggerate something about the hero of a tall tale.

Example: The boy was so tall that _____.

The boy was so tall that he could wash the windows of a skyscraper without a ladder.

1. The wrestler was so strong that _____.
2. The teacher had such good vision that _____.
3. The bike rider pedaled so fast that _____.
4. The week-old baby was so big that _____.
5. The baker could make cakes so good that _____.
6. The musician could hear so well that _____.
7. The figure skater jumped so high that _____.

Activity B

Think of a special quality that each of these people might have. Then write a sentence that makes the person larger than life.

Example: fifth grader

The fifth grader was so smart that she could finish a whole math chapter in less than a minute.

1. football player
2. news reporter
3. zoo keeper
4. deep-sea fisher
5. in-line skater
6. taxi driver

Our Wide Wide World

The Gulf of Mexico is a body of water that extends from the Florida Keys to the eastern shore of the Yucatán Peninsula in Mexico. The Gulf of Mexico may appear to be part of the Atlantic Ocean, but it is actually a semi-enclosed sea. The Gulf had a major economic impact on the history of the United States because it allowed the country to import and export goods easily via the Mississippi River.

Writer's Corner

Imagine that you are the hero of a tall tale. Write a list of exaggerated things that you could do.

Creating Problems and Solutions

The problem that the hero faces in a tall tale should be an exaggeration of something that could happen in real life. In real life it would get cold in the winter at the logging camps. One story of Paul Bunyan says it got so cold that when he spoke, his words froze in mid-air. Paul's companions had to thaw the words out over the fire to find out what he had said.

Solutions also involve exaggeration and humor. Once Paul's foreman sent the wrong logs all the way down the Mississippi River from Minnesota to New Orleans. Paul had Babe the Blue Ox take a huge gulp from the river to reverse its course and bring the logs back to the camp.

As the writer of a modern tall tale, you should do as the storytellers of old and let your imagination run wild. Think of a problem your hero might have and then exaggerate it. Does he meet up with a strange dog? Then it should be the biggest, meanest dog in town. Is she caught in the rain? Then it should be the worst storm of the century.

The solution to the problem should also be exaggerated. Perhaps the hero tricks the dog by throwing a stick so far that the dog chases it all the way to South America. Perhaps the hero stays dry by running in a path so crooked that the raindrops don't touch her.

Remember that in a tall tale, everything is superlative. It's the hottest, coldest, wettest, driest, tallest, shortest, biggest, loudest, strongest, worst, or best.

Vocabulary

When you are writing a tall tale, use vocabulary that your hero would use. If you are writing about a baseball player, use words like *sinker* and *grounder*. If you are writing about a skateboarder, use words like *halfpipe* and *freestyle*. This will give a sense of reality and make the exaggerations even funnier.

Activity C

Match each problem with a possible solution from the list.

1. The logging-camp table was two miles long.

2. A drought has dried up the prairie.

3. Lucy the Purple Cow was happy only when the grass was green.

4. A wagonload of rice and vegetables fell into a lake.

5. Johnny Inkslinger was running out of ink.

a. Paul gave her green-tinted glasses to wear in the wintertime.

b. Pecos Bill lassoed a thundercloud and squeezed it until it rained.

c. Boys on bicycles rode down the middle to deliver the salt and pepper.

d. He saved five barrels by not dotting his *i*'s or crossing his *t*'s.

e. The cook built bonfires on the shore and boiled the lake to make soup.

Activity D

Write a humorous or an exaggerated explanation to answer each of these questions.

1. Why is the sky blue?

2. Why can't dogs talk?

3. What caused the Rocky Mountains?

4. Why does it get cold in the winter?

5. Why does the moon glow?

Writer's Corner

Write down a problem that the hero of a tall tale would need to solve. Trade papers with a partner. Write a solution to your partner's problem. Use exaggeration to make your problem and solution as humorous as possible.

Figurative Language

Good writers try to create vivid pictures in their readers' minds. One way to do this is to use sensory language—words and ideas that appeal to sight, hearing, taste, touch, and smell. Another way is to use figurative language—language that compares one thing to another in a new and revealing way. Here are some types of figurative language.

Exaggeration

Exaggeration is used to make a dramatic or humorous point by describing something in impossible terms. Real loggers did chop down trees, but no real logger could chop down six acres of trees with one swing of an ax. The teller of the tall tale used exaggeration to show that Paul Bunyan was larger than life.

Many exaggerations use expressions such as *it was so hot that*, *he was so tall that*, or *she was so strong that*. Exaggerations often contain superlatives such as *coldest*, *deepest*, *fastest*, *loudest*, and *biggest*.

Simile

A simile describes one thing by telling how it is like something else. A simile uses the word *like* or *as*. In the examples below, Annie Christmas's height is compared to a paddle wheel, and her voice is compared to thunder. These details help create a vivid picture of Annie.

> Annie Christmas was *as* tall *as* a paddle wheel
>
> Her voice was *like* a roll of thunder.

Some similes have been so overused that they have become clichés. *As quiet as a mouse* and *as old as dirt* are clichés. Good writers try to think of a fresh comparison that will give readers a new idea of the thing they are describing.

Our Wide Wide World

The Great Lakes are located on or near the northeastern border of the United States. They are five fresh-water lakes— Lake Huron, Lake Ontario, Lake Michigan, Lake Erie, and Lake Superior. The lakes are not interconnected, but a series of man-made canals allows ships to travel the lakes during the warmer months.

Activity A

Complete each of the following similes. Be creative.
Try not to use clichés.

1. Danny is shy. His voice is as quiet as _____.

2. Molly is nervous. Her mouth feels as dry as _____.

3. Jacob took swimming lessons. Now he swims like _____.

4. Cara was very happy. She was smiling like _____.

5. Ryan is a fast runner. He's as fast as _____.

6. José makes a lot of noise. He's as loud as _____.

Activity B

Work with a partner to write a simile to describe each of these people. You may use exaggeration to make your similes humorous.

1. someone who is strong

2. someone who dances well

3. someone who is tall

4. someone who is friendly

5. someone who plays guitar well

6. someone who reads quickly

Writer's Corner

Choose a pet or an animal in the zoo. Write sentences to describe something about it, such as its eyes, ears, tail, or paws. Include exaggeration and similes.
Example: **The monkey's tail was as long as a jump rope.**

Metaphor

A metaphor is a way of comparing two things without using *like* or *as*. A simile states that one thing is like another thing. A metaphor states that one thing is another thing.

> The preschool classroom is a beehive of activity.
>
> The stream is a green snake slithering through the woods.
>
> The jets are enormous silver birds against the blue sky.

These sentences say that the classroom is a beehive, the stream is a snake, and the jets are birds. Using metaphors can make writing interesting and colorful by creating a vivid picture in readers' minds.

Activity C

Tell whether the comparison in each of these sentences is a simile or a metaphor. Tell how you know.

1. The inside of the car was a blast furnace.
2. The water lilies covered the pond like a heavy blanket.
3. The sunset is a fire in the evening sky.
4. When Kelly dances she's as graceful as a swan.
5. John rushed through the door like a tornado.
6. The track team members are racehorses approaching the finish line.
7. The woods were a cool umbrella on a hot, sunny day.

Activity D

Explain each of these metaphors by telling what two things are being compared and how they are alike.

1. His laughter is sunshine on a gloomy day.
2. My room was a refrigerator when I got home.
3. The snow was a white blanket on the lawn.
4. Her hat was a garden of wildflowers.
5. The party was a three-ring circus.

• Activity E •

Match the metaphor parts in Column A with those in Column B to make complete sentences.

Column A	Column B
1. The aroma of breakfast cooking	**a.** was a volcano about to erupt.
2. The child's messy room	**b.** were the warning flags for the storm.
3. The astronomy book	**c.** is the captain of our learning ship.
4. The tall hedge	**d.** is my personal alarm clock.
5. The black clouds	**e.** was the guardian of the garden.
6. Our teacher	**f.** is his window on the world.
7. The bubbling coffeepot	**g.** was her private spaceship.
8. His new computer	**h.** is a wastebasket with windows.

• Activity F •

Write a sentence using a simile or a metaphor to describe each of these things.

1. rush hour in a big city

2. a mountain road

3. a sleeping baby

4. an old car

5. a worn-out baseball glove

6. a playful kitten

7. a new skateboard

Writer's Corner

Think of a person you admire. It can be a person you know or a character you have read about in a book. Write a description of the person, using similes and metaphors. You may use exaggeration to make your description humorous or dramatic.

Word Study

Homophones

Homophones are words that sound alike but have different spellings and meanings. There are many homophones in the English language. They can sometimes be confusing for writers. Here are two sentences with pairs of homophones. What is the meaning of each word in italics?

> I saw the cat *peek* around the corner to watch the birds on the *peak* of the roof.

> Don't lose your bus *fare* or you'll have to walk home from the *fair*.

Peek and *peak* are homophones, and so are *fare* and *fair*. Because homophones have different meanings, make sure to use the correct one when you write. Check a dictionary if you are unsure of the spelling.

Activity A

Choose the correct homophone for each of these definitions. Then use the word you did not choose in a sentence. Use a dictionary if necessary.

1. a material used in making paper (would, wood)

2. a survey of people's opinions on an issue (poll, pole)

3. a time of calm and quiet (piece, peace)

4. a place to dock a boat (pier, peer)

5. the head of a school (principle, principal)

6. a word used in asking a question (witch, which)

7. a street or highway (road, rode)

8. a period of seven days (week, weak)

Activity B

Complete each sentence with the correct homophone.
Use each word only once.

paws, pause	wood, would	ate, eight
break, brake	moose, mousse	scent, sent

1. The bear held the food in its huge _____ while
   it _____ its dinner.

2. Speeding downhill, I was afraid that the _____
   on my bike _____ not work.

3. Did you see the _____ at the zoo?

4. Paul Bunyan helped the pioneers get _____ to
   build their towns and villages.

5. The fragrant _____ of the roses made me _____
   for a few moments to smell them.

6. I was afraid the window would _____ if I tried to
   force it to open.

7. My uncle _____ me _____ comic books for my
   birthday.

8. Carmen loves chocolate _____.

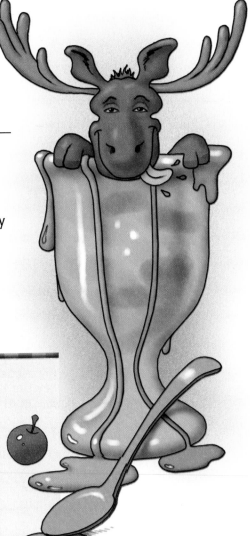

Writer's Corner

**Work with a partner to write a homophone for
each of these words. Then try to use each pair of
homophones in one sentence. Be creative and write
some fun sentences. Use a dictionary if necessary.**

made	seller	urn	prints
hare	hour	allowed	doe

The following homophones are often confusing for writers. Do you use these words correctly when you write?

Homophone	Meaning or Use	Example
your	possessive adjective	Your drawing is beautiful.
you're	contraction for *you are*	You're very kind.
there	adverb that tells *where*	I put it there.
their	possessive adjective	Their books are lost.
they're	contraction for *they are*	They're late.
to	preposition meaning "toward"	Let's go to the store.
too	adverb meaning "also" or "overly"	It's too bright!
two	adjective meaning "one more than one"	I have two cats.

Did you notice that sometimes three words are homophones? Some other examples are *so*, *sew*, and *sow* and *rein*, *rain*, and *reign*. You have to be especially careful when you use one of these words.

Activity C •

Rewrite these sentences. Choose the correct homophone from the chart to fill in each blank.

1. If you're not _____ tired, we can go _____ the drive-in for an ice-cream cone after dinner.

2. _____ parents asked the girls to be home early, but _____ walking home now in the dark.

3. _____ going to brush _____ teeth before bed, aren't you?

4. Put these _____ books on the shelf _____.

Activity D

Tell which of the three homophones belongs in each blank. Use a dictionary if necessary.

1. When the —————— started, Katy held tight to the horse's ————————. (rein, reign, rain)

2. The —————— was resting under the branches of the straggly ————————. (yew, you, ewe)

3. Put your —————— into the water and row fast, ———————— we won't have a chance to win the race. (or, ore, oar)

4. On the high ———————— the pirates were about to ———————— the unsuspecting ship. (sees, seas, seize)

5. My jacket is ———————— torn that my aunt will have to ———————— it. (so, sow, sew)

Activity E

Rewrite these sentences to make sense by finding and correcting the incorrect homophones. Check a dictionary if necessary. Each sentence has more than one incorrect homophone.

1. She was so vein that she looked at herself in the mirror for ours.

2. He cent an e-mail to his friend, who replied write away.

3. My sister has a knew diamond engagement wring.

4. We're going too take a sightseeing crews on Lake Michigan.

5. The Straight of Gibralter connects the Mediterranean See and the Atlantic Ocean.

Writer's Corner

Write five sentences with incorrect homophones like those in Activity E. Trade papers with a partner and correct each other's sentences.

Nonsense Verse

Nonsense verse is poetry that is completely silly. It describes things that are so strange that they could never happen in the real world. Writers of nonsense verse dream up weird creatures and unbelievable situations. Poets use rhyme, choose funny-sounding words, and even make words up. The purpose for writing nonsense verse is to have fun and make readers laugh.

Poet Jack Prelutsky likes to have this kind of fun with words. Here are two examples of his nonsense verse.

A Foolish Cow
A foolish cow, declining greens,
ate jumping and vanilla beans.
Now she quivers, now she quakes,
now she gives vanilla shakes.

The Otter and the Ocelot
The otter and the ocelot,
as fortunate as they could be,
now sail the seas upon their yacht—
they won the OCELOTTERY.

What silly, impossible thing happens in each poem? What picture of the cow do the words *quivers* and *quakes* help form in your imagination? What words did the poet use to make up *ocelottery*? Which words in each poem rhyme?

Activity A

Which of these characters do you think might appear in a nonsense verse? Tell why you think so.

1. a cow that jumps over the moon

2. a girl and boy who fall down a hill

3. a flying groundhog

4. a rooster that lives in a barn

5. an ostrich ballerina

Activity B

The characters from tall tales can be good subjects for nonsense verse. Copy these couplets and fill in the blanks with rhyming words.

1. Paul Bunyan sneezed a mighty sneeze

   And felled an acre full of _____.

2. Sourdough Sam cooked eggs and ham

   And served them up with toast and _____.

3. Pecos Bill gave the snake a terrible shake

   And said, "A fine lasso you'll _____."

4. Sue rode a fish as big as a whale.

   It had flashing eyes and a lashing _____.

Writer's Corner

Choose an idea from Activity A or one of your own to use in a rhyming nonsense couplet. You might try making up an animal name combination.

Examples: The ostrich spins with style and grace,
But sometimes she falls on her face.

When the alligatortoise comes over to play,
Will the eerie elephantom scare him away?

Rhyme Scheme

Rhyme is one of the features that make nonsense verses fun to read. There are many ways to make a rhyming verse. Look back at Jack Prelutsky's poems on page 214. The first one is written in rhyming couplets. Each pair of lines rhymes. In the second poem, every other line rhymes. These are examples of rhyme schemes. A poet usually uses the same rhyme scheme throughout a poem.

Meter

In a word with more than one syllable, one syllable is always stressed. It is pronounced more loudly than the other syllables. When you speak, you also stress, or emphasize, different words within a sentence. In a poem these stressed words and syllables fall in a regular pattern. This pattern is called meter.

Read the poem and notice how the syllables are marked. The checks are above the stressed syllables. Each line has four stressed syllables. There is one unstressed syllable between each pair of stressed syllables.

> ᵕ ✓ ᵕ ✓ ᵕ ✓ ᵕ ✓
> A foolish cow, declining greens,
>
> ᵕ ✓ ᵕ ✓ ᵕ ✓ ᵕ ✓
> ate jumping and vanilla beans.
>
> ✓ ᵕ ✓ ᵕ ✓ ᵕ ✓
> Now she quivers, now she quakes,
>
> ✓ ᵕ ✓ ᵕ ✓ ᵕ ✓
> now she gives vanilla shakes.

A poem can have a different number of stressed syllables in each line and a different number of unstressed syllables between the stressed ones. The beginning of this nursery rhyme has just two stressed syllables in each line and two unstressed syllables between the stressed ones.

> ✓ ᵕ ᵕ ✓ ᵕ
> Little Jack Horner
>
> ✓ ᵕ ᵕ ✓ ᵕ
> Sat in a corner

Activity C

Read each line of poetry. Tell how many stressed syllables it has.

1. The owl and the pussycat went to sea

2. Simple Simon met a pieman

3. Peter Piper picked a peck of pickled peppers

4. Betty Botter bought some butter

5. Whether the weather be fine

Activity D

This is the beginning of a nonsense verse by Laura Richards. Copy it on a sheet of paper. Circle the pairs of rhyming words. Mark the stressed and unstressed syllables. Then underline the made-up words.

Peter Piper pick'd a Peck of Pickled Peppers:
Did Peter Piper pick a Peck of Pickled Peppers?
If Peter Piper pick'd a peck of Pickled Peppers,
Where's the Peck of Pickled Peppers Peter Piper pick'd?

Eletelephony

Once there was an elephant,

Who tried to use the telephant—

No! No! I mean an elephone

Who tried to use the telephone—

(Dear me! I am not certain quite

That even now I've got it right.)

Writer's Corner

Write a nonsense verse that is at least four lines long. You can use your couplet from the Writer's Corner on page 215 or think of a new idea. Choose a rhyme scheme and use it throughout your poem. Try to keep the same number of stressed syllables in each line.

Storytellers' Contests

Imagine a group of loggers or cowboys sitting around a campfire in the 1800s. There is no radio or TV, so they are telling stories to one another. Each one tries to get the biggest laugh by making his story funnier and more exaggerated than anyone else's. These stories might even have become part of the tall tales about Paul Bunyan and Pecos Bill.

The same kind of thing happens today when storytellers enter storytelling festivals or liars' contests. The point of these contests is to win the prize by telling the funniest, most outrageous story of all the contestants.

The stories told in these festivals and contests have many of the same features as tall tales.

- There may be a main character who is larger than life.
- There is often a problem that needs to be solved or something that needs to be explained.
- The solution or explanation might involve things that cannot happen in the real world.
- Exaggerations, similes, and metaphors are used to make the story funny.

Audience

A storyteller needs to think about the ages and interests of the audience. Young children may not understand similes and metaphors that older students would. People in the country might find different things funny than people in the city. Adults might not get the exaggeration in a story about playing video games. You will be telling a story to your classmates. Keep their interests—and senses of humor—in mind.

Body Language and Voice

Storytellers in festivals and contests generally do not use props. They use their voices and body language to win over the audience and to make people laugh.

When you tell your story, speak loudly enough so everyone can hear you. If your story includes dialog, try to change your voice for each character. Use your voice to make your exaggerations more effective. Emphasize actions by using appropriate body language. For example, use your arms to show size and movement. Smile to let everyone know that you are enjoying the humor in your story.

• Activity A •

Take turns reading aloud these selections from tall tales. Read the dialog the way you think the character might have said it. Discuss the differences in the way your classmates perform.

1. John Henry was anxious to prove that he could beat the steam drill that threatened his job. Determined, he insisted, "A man ain't nothing but a man. I'm gonna do my best and beat that machine."

2. Johnny Appleseed carried his apple seeds all across the country. When settlers tried to pay him for the seeds, he'd say, "No, no, I don't want any money. Just take and plant the seeds. Sow them and wait for the harvest."

3. Stormalong was 20 feet tall before he was 12. That year he strolled down to the wharf and said to a boat captain, "There's nothing I can't do; I want to hire on to your boat. I'm a fighter and a worker. I'll make you proud."

Speaker's Corner

Your class is going to have a storytellers' contest. The topic is "why I can't turn in my homework today," and the story cannot be longer than two minutes. Start writing down ideas. Make them as wild and as imaginative as possible. Remember that this story is not supposed to be true. It's supposed to make people laugh.

New York City may sit directly on the Atlantic Ocean, but is was the Hudson River that allowed the surrounding areas to develop while New York City was still a young metropolis. In 1825, the Erie Canal was built, connecting the Hudson River to Lake Erie, and in turn, the Great Lakes to the Atlantic Ocean. The canal's opening caused a major population increase in western New York as well as a drop in transportation costs to the West by as much as 90 percent.

Prepare Your Story

Telling a funny story requires careful preparation. Look over your ideas from the Speaker's Corner on page 219. Choose the one that you can expand with the most exaggerated details. Maybe a spaceship full of pirates landed in your backyard, and the pirates stole your homework paper to draw a treasure map. Think of the wildest ideas you can of how the pirates looked, what they wore, and how they talked.

Make notes or a graphic organizer to help you come up with details. Write down any similes and metaphors that will help you describe these foul fiends. Use the wildest exaggerations you can to make your story funny. Remember that in a story like this, anything is possible.

Practice

Before you present a funny story to an audience, practice telling it several times in front of a mirror. Experiment with different voices, facial expressions, and body language to see which ones best convey the meaning. Choose words and expressions that seem the funniest when you say them aloud.

When you are satisfied with your presentation, ask a friend or family member to be your audience. Tell your story, paying attention to the parts that make your listener laugh. Check that there are no "dead spots" where your listener does not seem at all amused. Ask your listener to give you suggestions for making your storytelling even better.

Listening Tips

Just as practice makes you a better speaker, practice can make you a better listener. Here are some things that you will want to keep in mind when you are listening to a storyteller.

- Keep your eyes on the speaker so he or she will know you are listening.
- Pay attention to the speaker's tone of voice and body language so you do not miss any clues about what happens in the story.
- Listen carefully for figurative language and use it to create pictures in your imagination.
- Show that you are enjoying the story and its humor. Laugh!

• Activity B •

Complete the story you began in the Speaker's Corner on page 219. Write details on note cards that you can refer to as you talk. Jot down exaggerations, similes, and metaphors that you want to use. Experiment with different ways to use your voice and body to make your story as funny as you can.

• Activity C •

Practice telling your story to a classmate. Use the practice tips from page 220. Have your listener time you to make sure your story is not longer than two minutes. Ask your listener to give you ideas for which parts of your story work and which do not. Ask the person to identify any details that he or she did not understand or did not find funny. You may want to change those details before presenting your story.

Speaker's Corner

Take turns with your classmates in telling your stories. As each person finishes, you might jot down a few notes about his or her story so that you can remember who gave what explanation for the missing homework. When everyone has finished, talk about your favorite parts of each other's stories.

Chapter 6 Writer's Workshop

Tall Tales

Prewriting and Drafting

Tall tales are fun to read and to write. Now it is time to use what you have read about in this chapter to write your own tall tale.

Prewriting

Imogen's family was having a party to celebrate her grandfather's birthday. At the party each family member was going to perform something special. Imogen's grandfather loved tall tales, so she decided to write a tall tale and read it aloud at the party.

Imogen began by choosing a hero and a setting, free writing her ideas, and then organizing her ideas.

Choosing a Hero and a Setting

Imogen liked tall tales about super-strong heroes of the frontier. But she thought that a modern hero might be fun too. She made a list of some ideas for both.

- a cowgirl who can run faster than any person or animal
- a boy who has a computer for a brain
- a very tall boy who can jump over mountains

Imogen's grandfather was the tallest person Imogen knew. So she decided to write about a tall boy. She even decided to name the character Jack, after her grandfather.

Imogen's family lived near Sequoia National Park in California. Imogen once went on a hike there with her grandfather. She thought it might be fun to set her tall tale in a familiar place.

Imogen thought that Jack could be a park ranger. She imagined many ways that a very tall boy could be helpful as a park ranger.

Your Turn

Choose your hero and setting. If you are having trouble, answer the following questions.

- Is my hero a boy or a girl?
- What is my hero's special ability?
- Is my hero's special ability better suited to the city or to a rural setting?
- What job does my hero have? How does my hero's special ability help him or her do that job?

Pick the hero that interests you the most. Which one makes you think of a lot of ideas for your tall tale?

Free Writing

Imogen thought about her hike at Sequoia National Park. A ranger had told them about a huge snowstorm a few years earlier. Imogen thought that a snowstorm might create a good problem for Jack to solve.

Imogen started writing notes about Jack's childhood, his abilities, a problem, and how Jack solves the problem. Here is a part of Imogen's notes.

- *Jack Johnson, a big, bouncy baby, is born in a town right by the park.*
- *huge snowstorm hits and buries the whole town in snow*
- *Jack is the only one who can get anywhere because he can do stuff that real people can't do.*
- *went up to the clouds and made snowballs out of them*
- *found out that the clouds tasted like ice cream*
- *He became a park ranger.*

Your Turn

Free write your ideas about your tall tale. If you have chosen a character and setting that are based on real life, write down what you know about the person or place.

Free write your ideas about what made your hero's childhood unusual. Include details about your hero's abilities and job. Think about the problem he or she will face and how that problem will be solved.

Organizing Ideas

Imogen had to organize her notes before she started to write. Here is the plan that Imogen made.

Setting: Sequoia National Park

Hero: Jack Johnson

Jack's Life: born in town near park, popular athelete, becomes a park ranger

Problem: snowstorm that traps the townspeople in their houses

Solution: Jack gets rid of clouds by making them into scoops of ice cream. He invites the town to celebrate with him by eating snow-cloud ice cream.

Your Turn

Use your free-writing notes to organize your tall tale. Look at Imogen's plan if you need help. Organize your notes by naming your setting, hero, hero's life, problem, and solution.

Drafting

Imogen was ready to begin writing her tall tale. She used her plan and her free-writing notes to begin her draft. As she wrote, she realized that she would have to exaggerate the details of her tale more to fit the style of a tall tale. She also added some dialog so that readers could get an idea of Jack's personality. Here is Imogen's first draft.

Jumping Jack Johnson

Jack Johnson was born in a town just outside of Sequoia National Park in central California. He was a happy baby who just wasn't still in his crib for a moment. He was a bouncing ball that never stopped. By the time Jack was in his teens, his legs were as long as stilts and he spent his high school years as captain of the basketball team, high-jumping champion, and the county's undefeated pole-vaulter. He was very popular. He was never alone at the lunch table. Everyone new him as Jumping Jack.

When he applied to become a park ranger at Sequoia National Park, he was immediately accepted. "In a single jump, I'll reach people who are lost," said Jack. "I can care for the trees and the animals. My gifts can help everyone." By the time Jumping Jack was 20, he could jump higher than a sequoia tree, higher than a skyscraper, even higher than a bird could fly. The townspeople would whisper "That young Jack must have springs in his feet." But Jack was more than his jumps. He also had the nicest personality of anyone in town.

Nature didn't wait long to put Jumping Jack to the test. On a cold day in January, a sudden snowstorm blue up. Snow fell for three days straight. When the snow finally stopped, all that could be seen were the tips of chimeneys peaking out of the snow. The thick snow clouds would not let a ray of sunshine through. The townspeople were buried in a sea of white.

Only Jumping Jack had no problems getting to work. Jack waited for several hours for the head ranger, but he never came. No one came. It was then that Jack realized the townspeople couldn't leave their homes. So Jack went back to the town to come to their rescue. He jumped as straight and as high as he could. Then he grabbed a corner of one of the snow clouds. He formed a small snowball. He did this again and again. When he got hungery, he took a bite from one of these snowballs. "Yummy! Ice cream," he said in surprise. Soon he had turned the snow clouds into thousands of scoops of ice cream.

Jack came back down. The sun was shining. The snow melted in minutes. The townspeople flooded out of their houses, cheering. "celebrate with me!" invited Jack. "Let's all share this delicious solushun to our problem." That night everyone had ice cream for dessert.

Your Turn

Use your plan and free-writing notes to write your first draft. Remember to describe your hero's childhood. Include details about your hero's special ability. Make the problem or the solution exaggerated and funny. Tell the events in time order. Double-space your draft so that you will have room to make changes later.

Say Something!

Just as in other kinds of stories, dialog can be important in a tall tale. When characters speak, they often reveal something about their feelings, personalities, or thoughts. Dialog can help to make your tall tale more interesting.

When you write dialog for your characters, remember to use words that are appropriate to the time in which they live. Put each character's exact words within quotation marks.

Chapter 6 Editor's Workshop

Tall Tales

Content Editing

Imogen liked what she had written so far. She was sure that her grandfather would enjoy the fact that the main character of the tall tale was named after him. But Imogen knew that the tall tale could be made better by content editing. She used the following checklist to content edit her draft.

Content Editor's Checklist

✓ Does the story revolve around a larger-than-life hero?

✓ Is there an interesting setting?

✓ Are the events told in time order?

✓ Are the hero, main events, and details described in an exaggerated way?

✓ Are all of the details necessary?

✓ Are similes and metaphors used in the descriptions?

✓ Is the tale told in everyday language?

✓ Does the hero solve the problem in a funny way?

When Imogen was finished, she asked her friend Viola to content edit her draft. Viola was in a book club at school. The club talked often about what was good and bad about stories. Imogen knew that Viola would be able to give her helpful feedback. Viola would check to make sure that the ideas were clear. She could also suggest things that Imogen might delete or ways in which Imogen might improve her tall tale.

Viola read Imogen's tall tale once to get an idea of the story. She laughed out loud when she got to the part about the ice cream. Then Viola read the draft a few more times, checking for each item on the checklist. She

wrote some notes and suggestions to talk with Imogen about later. When Viola was finished, she and Imogen looked at the draft together.

Viola liked Imogen's idea. She thought that it was a funny tall tale. She thought that Imogen had made Jack very likable. Viola also thought that the draft had a nice conversational tone. Here are some of Viola's suggestions.

- I like the way you describe Jack. But can you add any more details that describe him as a baby?

- Can you give more description of the town? At first I pictured a big city.

- The second paragraph is kind of confusing. Does Jack become a ranger before he is 20 or after?

- The part about Jack being popular at school seems unnecessary.

- I like the metaphor he was a bouncing ball. You might add a simile in the second paragraph when you describe Jack's jumps. Maybe graceful as a swan.

- I really like the way that you exaggerated the details. But can you add more? I think they would make your tall tale even funnier.

Imogen thought that Viola had some good ideas. She really liked Viola's suggestion about the simile. Imogen always had trouble thinking of similes. She went right to work making her changes.

Your Turn

Read your tall tale again. Do the characters come alive? Did you include enough dialog? Use the Content Editor's Checklist to remind you of things to look for as you content edit your draft. Remember to read for one item on the checklist at a time.

Work with a partner to content edit each other's drafts. Take notes as you content edit. Be positive in your comments.

Meet with your partner and discuss each other's suggestions. Remember to compliment your partner on the things you liked in his or her draft. Listen carefully to the suggestions that your partner has. Consider his or her suggestions, but remember that the final decisions are yours.

Tall Tales

Revising

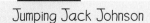

This is Imogen's revised draft.

Jumping Jack Johnson

sleepy, little
Jack Johnson was born in a town just outside of Sequoia National Park in

central California. He was a happy baby who just wasn't still in his crib for a

He jiggled and wiggled and giggled.
moment. He was a bouncing ball that never stopped. By the time Jack was in

his teens, his legs were as long as stilts and he spent his high school years

as captain of the basketball team, high-jumping champion, and the county's

undefeated pole-vaulter. ~~He was very popular. He was never alone at the~~

~~lunch table.~~ Everyone new him as Jumping Jack.

> When he applied to become a park ranger at Sequoia National Park, he
> was immediately accepted. "In a single jump, I'll reach people who are lost,"
> said Jack. "I can care for the trees and the animals. My gifts can help
> everyone." By the time Jumping Jack was 20, he could jump higher than a

sequoia tree, higher than a skyscraper, even higher than a bird could fly.

When Jack jumped, he was as graceful as a swan.
The townspeople would whisper "That young Jack must have springs in his

feet." But Jack was more than his jumps. He also had the nicest personality

of anyone in town.

Nature didn't wait long to put Jumping Jack to the test. On a cold day in

as thick as cotton
January, a sudden snowstorm blue up. Snow fell for three days straight.

When the snow finally stopped, all that could be seen were the tips of

chimeneys peaking out of the snow. The thick snow clouds would not let a

ray of sunshine through. The townspeople were buried in a sea of white.

He just jumped through the mountain of snow that covered his house and landed in the park eight miles away.

Only Jumping Jack had no problems getting to work. ∧ Jack waited for several hours for the head ranger, but he never came. No one came. It was then that Jack realized the townspeople couldn't leave their homes. So Jack ~~went~~ jumped back to the town to come to their rescue. He jumped as straight and as high as he could. Then he grabbed a corner of one of the snow clouds. He formed a small snowball. He did this again and again. When he got hungery, he took a bite from one of these snowballs. "Yummy! Ice cream," he said in surprise. Soon he had turned the snow clouds into thousands of scoops of ice cream.

Jack came back down. The sun was shining. The snow melted in minutes. The townspeople flooded out of their houses, cheering. "celebrate with me!" invited Jack. "Let's all share this delicious solushun to our problem." That night everyone had ice cream for dessert.

Here are the changes Imogen made.

- Imogen added the words *jiggled*, *wiggled*, and *giggled* to describe Jack as a baby. She also added the words *sleepy* and *little* to describe the town.

- Imogen saw that the order in the second paragraph was confusing. She moved four sentences to the end of the paragraph.

- She agreed that the part about Jack being popular in school was unnecessary.

As Imogen was revising, Viola suggested another simile. Do you see it? Imogen added another exaggerated detail and changed the word *went* to *jumped* in the fourth paragraph. She thought that both changes made her tall tale funnier.

Your Turn

Use your own ideas and suggestions from your content editor to improve your tall tale. When you have finished, go over the Content Editor's Checklist again. Can you answer yes to each question?

Tall Tales

Copyediting and Proofreading

Copyediting

Imogen was glad that Viola had content edited her draft. But she knew that her tall tale would be even better after she copyedited it. She wanted to make sure that the sentences in her draft were correct and that the words she used were exact. Imogen used this Copyeditor's Checklist.

Copyeditor's Checklist

✓ Has the writing been checked for rambling or run-on sentences?

✓ Are short, choppy sentences combined?

✓ Is there a variety in sentence length?

✓ Do all the words, especially those that are homophones, mean what I think they mean?

Imogen found a run-on sentence in the first paragraph. Look at how she revised it.

Revision:

By the time Jack was in his teens, his legs were as long as stilts. He spent his high school years as captain of the basketball team, high-jumping champion, and the county's undefeated pole-vaulter.

In the fourth paragraph, Imogen combined *Then he grabbed a corner of one of the snow clouds* and *He formed a small snowball* into one sentence. Do you see another place where Imogen might combine sentences?

Imogen found three homophone mistakes. In the first paragraph, she wrote *new* when she meant to write *knew*. In the third paragraph, she wrote that the chimneys were *peaking out* instead of *peeking out*. Can you find the other homophone mistake?

Your Turn

Use the Copyeditor's Checklist to copyedit your draft. Remember to look for one kind of mistake at a time. Reading aloud your draft might help you hear rambling and run-on sentences. It also might help you hear places where sentences might be combined. Pay special attention to your word choice. Don't forget to check that homophones are spelled correctly.

Proofreading

Because Imogen would be reading her tall tale aloud, she did not want to get tripped up at the party over misspelled words or incorrect grammar. A proofreader would check for misspelled words and mistakes in capitalization, grammar, and punctuation.

Imogen's brother Edmund was in seventh grade. He was really good at language arts and agreed to proofread Imogen's draft. Edmund used this checklist.

Proofreader's Checklist

✓ Are the paragraphs indented?

✓ Are all the words spelled correctly?

✓ Are capitalization and punctuation correct?

✓ Is the grammar correct?

✓ Were any new mistakes added while editing?

Edmund found three misspelled words. In the third paragraph, he changed *chimeneys* to *chimneys*. He also changed *hungery* to *hungry*. What was the third misspelled word that Edmund found?

He also spotted a capitalization mistake in the fifth paragraph. Do you see Imogen's mistake?

Your Turn

Read your tall tale carefully, using the Proofreader's Checklist. Look for only one kind of mistake at a time. Each time you read you have another chance to find mistakes that you missed. Pay special attention to the dialog in your tall tale. Make sure that spoken parts follow the rules for the capitalization and punctuation of dialog.

When you have finished proofreading your draft, trade drafts with a partner. Go through each other's drafts carefully. Be sure to have a dictionary nearby.

Chapter 6 · Writer's Workshop

Tall Tales

Publishing

Imogen read her draft with the revisions one last time to make sure that she had included all of her corrections. Then she was ready to write the final copy. She used a computer to type her tall tale.

Jumping Jack Johnson

Jack Johnson was born in a sleepy little town just outside of Sequoia National Park in central California. He was a happy baby who just wasn't still in his crib for a moment. He jiggled and wiggled and giggled. He was a bouncing ball that never stopped. By the time Jack was in his teens, his legs were as long as stilts. He spent his high school years as captain of the basketball team,

high-jumping champion, and the county's undefeated pole-vaulter. Everyone knew him as Jumping Jack.

By the time Jumping Jack was 20, he could jump higher than a sequoia tree, higher than a skyscraper, even higher than a bird could fly. When Jack jumped, he was as graceful as a swan. The townspeople would whisper "That young Jack must have springs in his feet." But Jack was more than his jumps. He also had the nicest personality of anyone in town. When he applied to become a park ranger at Sequoia National Park, he was immediately accepted. "In a single jump, I'll reach people who are lost," said Jack. "I can care for the trees and the animals. My gifts can help everyone."

Nature didn't wait long to put Jumping Jack to the test. One cold day in January, a sudden snowstorm blew up. Snow as thick as cotton fell for three days straight. When the snow finally stopped, all that could be seen were the tips of chimneys peeking out of the snow. The thick snow clouds would not let a ray of sunshine through. The townspeople were buried in a sea of white.

Only Jumping Jack had no problems getting to work. He just jumped through the mountain of snow that covered his house and landed in the park eight miles away. Jack waited for several hours for the head ranger, but he never came. No one came. It was then that Jack realized the townspeople couldn't leave their homes. So Jack jumped back to the town to come to their rescue. He jumped as straight and as high as he could. Then he grabbed a corner of one of the snow clouds and formed a small snowball. He did this again and again. When he got hungry, he took a bite from one of these snowballs. "Yummy! Ice cream," he said in surprise. Soon he had turned the snow clouds into thousands of scoops of ice cream.

When he came back down, the sun was shining. The snow melted in minutes. The townspeople flooded out of their houses, cheering. "Celebrate with me!" invited Jack. "Let's all share this delicious solution to our problem." That night everyone had ice cream for dessert.

Imogen drew a picture of Jack. Her mom took the completed tale and picture and had them bound between two covers. After Imogen read her tall tale at the party, she was going to give the tale to her grandfather as a gift.

Your Turn

Before you write or print your final copy, read your tall tale one more time. If you type your tall tale, use your computer's spell checker. Then write or print your final copy. You might make a drawing of your hero to include with your tale, just like Imogen did.

Decide as a class how you will publish your tall tales. One way is to share your tall tales orally. A few students each day might read aloud their tall tales until they have all been shared.

You might also share your tall tales with other classes, especially classes of younger kids. The tall tales could be read to a whole class, or each person could read to one or two younger kids.

The first 10 amendments to the U.S. Constitution are called The Bill of Rights. These amendments outline and guarantee the rights of citizens under the federal government. The Bill of Rights was controversial at first. Some people worried that the rights covered would be the only rights citizens would ever have. But supporters argued that it was the job of the courts to interpret them as needed. Do you agree that it was important to guarantee citizens' rights? Why or why not?

Persuasive Writing

HILLSDALE HERALD

Founded 1882
Premier Publications, Inc.

Monday, April 18, 20–

Page 8   Section 1

Put That Helmet On!

It's that time of year again. Spring is in the air, and bicycles are on the highways and byways. One thing that we aren't seeing enough of, however, is the vision of brightly colored helmets on the heads of bikers. Our city should pass a helmet law for bike riders, both young and old alike.

Sadly, when it comes to wearing a helmet while biking, the statistics speak for themselves. According to the Bicycle Helmet Safety Institute in Arlington, Virginia, more than 800 lives per year are lost as a result of bike accidents in the United States. Almost all of them involve collisions with cars. About three-fourths of them involve head injuries. Hundreds of thousands of bicyclists with injuries visit emergency rooms each year. More than half of these are children and young teens.

A Mayo Clinic report to CNN confirms the Institute's findings and agrees that wearing a helmet can prevent head injury and death. The National Highway Traffic Safety Administration and the American Automobile Association both stress the importance of bike helmets.

The cost of a helmet is a small price to pay for the safety it can provide. Safety-approved helmets for children can be purchased for about $30.

There are no federal laws regulating bicycle helmets, but 20 states and more than 100 communities nationwide have helmet laws. Increasing numbers of states and localities are enacting laws covering bikes. Only 17 states have no state or local laws concerning helmets. While most of the current laws apply only to younger riders, police and public safety officers tell parents to set a good example for their children by wearing helmets themselves.

In our opinion, adults must take a stand on this issue. The statistics are clear, authoritative voices agree, and the price is right. Let's use our heads and join the states and cities that can say "It's the law."

What Makes Good Persuasive Writing?

Persuasive writing tries to make readers agree with a position on a topic. Stating a position is easy, but persuading others to agree with you often requires presenting reasons that are supported by evidence. You can find examples of persuasive writing almost anywhere, such as advertisements, letters to the editor, newspaper editorials, and political speeches.

Position

Before drafting a persuasive article, a writer must choose a topic that has two sides, which are sometimes called opposing views. Then the writer chooses one side, or viewpoint, taking a clear position on the topic. The position appears in the introduction of the article and should tell exactly where the writer stands on the topic. The position is summarized again in the conclusion.

Introduction

The introduction to a persuasive article is where you state your position on a topic. The introduction is also a place to grab the reader's attention and to explain your purpose for writing.

Body

The body of your persuasive article is where you will convince your audience. This is where you present your reasons and evidence in detail. Each reason often has its own paragraph with statistics, facts, or examples that support it.

You can also use the body of your persuasive article to rebut arguments against your position. State the opposing arguments, then show why they are weak or unimportant.

Activity A

Persuasive writing starts with a topic that has two sides. Choose three questions below and write one reason for each side.

Example: Should school lunchrooms have vending machines that sell cold drinks and snacks?
Yes These foods and drinks taste good.
No Most of these kinds of foods and drinks are not nutritious snacks.

A. Should our school have a "no homework on weekends" policy?

B. Should dog owners be made to keep their dogs on leashes?

C. Should students be able to use the school library after school or on Saturday?

D. Should all schools have swimming pools?

E. Should students be able to play radios on the school bus?

F. Should students get a longer summer break?

G. Should students be fined if they litter?

H. Should parents pay their kids for doing chores?

I. Should kids be allowed to skip one test per school year?

Activity B

Brainstorm four topics that might be good topics for a persuasive article. Be sure that there are two sides to each topic.

Writer's Corner

Choose a topic from Activity B that you feel strongly about. Write an attention-grabbing position that might be found in the introduction to a persuasive article. Share your position with the class.

Conclusion

The conclusion to a persuasive article briefly summarizes the strongest reasons for your position. Avoid adding new reasons in the conclusion. Restate your position in a positive, convincing way. A persuasive conclusion should leave readers thinking about the topic. A well-written persuasive article might even cause a reader to take action in support of the writer's position.

• Activity C •

Read the following pairs of introductions to persuasive articles. Tell which is the better introduction. Explain your answers.

1. **A.** The beauty of our national parks is unequaled in any other country. If we want that beauty to last, we must limit automobile traffic in the parks.
   B. There is a need for limiting automobile traffic in our national parks. I will present several good reasons for you to think about.

2. **A.** Even if you like to choose the outfits you wear to school each day, you ought to support the vote for uniforms in our school.
   B. Students in crisp shirts and blouses and coordinated slacks and skirts could soon describe a typical classroom in our school. Best of all, no more worrying about what to wear! Uniforms will take care of that decision.

3. **A.** If the new after-school program passes, you can visit with your friends after school. You might even work on projects together.
   B. Students should have an opportunity to stay in their own school after the day is over. This is only fair.

• Activity D •

Write a position for each of these topics for a persuasive article.

1. the installation of traffic signals at a busy corner near school

2. a special area for skateboarding in a new park

3. a proposal to extend the school day by a half hour

Activity E

Rewrite each position to reflect your own feeling on the issue. Then write a reason for supporting it.

1. I believe we (should/should not) have tests in two subjects on the same day.

2. We (should/should not) be expected to clean our lunch tables before going outside.

3. I believe our city (must/must not) enact a bicycle licensing law.

4. I believe the gym (should/should not) be open for all students after school.

Activity F

Read this paragraph from a newspaper about the need for a community library. Write another paragraph that features a different reason for the library. Use your imagination and include explanations or evidence to support your reason.

One reason that our community must build a library is so our children and adults will have a resource for knowledge and pleasure. Statistics show that teenagers are more likely to excel in school if there is a library within three miles of their home. Besides books and magazines, public libraries offer computers with Internet access.

Activity G

Choose a position that you wrote in Activity D. Then think of one reason for your position on the issue. Write a paragraph giving supporting evidence for that reason.

Writer's Corner

Use the paragraph you wrote for Activity G and write a conclusion for a persuasive article. Remember to briefly summarize the reason and restate the position in a positive way.

Writing a Persuasive Article

Deciding what your topic is and your position on it are the first decisions you make when writing a persuasive article. Once you decide what your position is, the next step is to craft the evidence you gather into a clear and convincing article.

The prospect of a permanent base on the moon is exciting. We could use the forces of the universe for an easier and cheaper mission to Mars. Just think of it! A spacecraft flying to Mars from the moon would need only one-sixth the amount of thrust to lift off from the surface of the moon compared with lifting off from Earth. Why is this? Because the moon's gravity is only one-sixth that of Earth's. The craft could be much lighter. It would not need to be aerodynamically built, because there is no atmosphere on the moon to cause drag on the spacecraft.

Persuasive Voice

A writer's voice, or tone, is one of the best tools to use in a persuasive article. The way you state your opinion and reasons affects the way your readers receive your message.

Here are some of the tones that writers use in persuasive writing.

uplifting	confident	enthusiastic
hopeful	concerned	warning

Effective persuasive writing shows readers that you care about your position on a topic. Your choice of words shows that you are confident and that your position and evidence are reasonable.

The writer of this paragraph about a possible permanent base on the moon used an enthusiastic tone to encourage readers to support the position.

Activity A

Tell which sentence in each pair is written in a more confident voice. Explain your answers.

1. **A.** A new Olympic-sized pool will meet the needs of our town on those hot summer days when we all want to relax in the sun and not be crowded.
   B. Our town could really use a second public pool.

2. **A.** If the curfew is passed, we can expect teens to be home earlier and to be less likely to get into trouble.
   B. Teens will be teens, but passing the new curfew might help families in our community.

3. **A.** The school district needs your vote next week to provide money for after-school activities.
   B. Computer experts, photography buffs, and avid book reviewers are just a few examples of what our children can become if we give them the opportunity for after-school activities. That is why we should pass next week's referendum.

4. **A.** Perhaps the county needs another fire station to keep up with growth in the population.
   B. Population growth in this county requires us to add a new fire station.

5. **A.** The city's water supply is in danger of drying up if we don't think about how to cut back on the amount we use.
   B. I think the city's water supply might dry up sometime, so maybe we should not use so much.

6. **A.** Undersea research seems like a good idea to me.
   B. Undersea research will have benefits for all forms of life.

Writer's Corner

Think about writing an article on a position you wrote for the Writer's Corner on page 237. Talk with a partner about what tone is best for your topic. What are some ways you could revise your paragraph to make your tone stronger and clearer?

Audience

Writers often write differently for different audiences. When you write a persuasive article, think about whom you are trying to convince. Think of reasons that appeal to that audience. For example, a person who is trying to persuade Congress to provide money for a new highway knows that politicians are concerned about the people they represent. The presenter might discuss how the highway would provide jobs for the representative's district.

Opinions

In Chapter 5 you discussed the difference between facts and opinions. When you write a persuasive article, your opinions should be supported by practical, logical ideas and facts. Opinion words are useful tools for expressing your position. Use words such as *should, ought, must,* and *best* to express your opinion.

• Activity B •

Identify the words or phrases that make each sentence below an opinion. Then use your imagination to write one reason that supports each opinion.

1. The most amusing animal is the penguin.

2. Shel Silverstein is one of the funniest poets for kids.

3. Going to the beach is the best way to cool off on a hot day.

4. The trees in our neighborhood must be preserved.

5. I believe yellow, red, and blue are the prettiest colors.

6. Babe Ruth ought to be considered the best baseball player ever.

• Activity C •

Think of an issue that is related to your school, community, or state. Write a position on the issue and identify who would be the best audience for it.

Activity D

Rewrite the following paragraph, changing the voice from uplifting to warning. Use your imagination.

An after-school reading program is needed. It would bring the students closer together and give us a sense of community. Together we can work for a common cause to improve students' reading ability. At the same time, we can greatly improve overall test scores. An after-school reading program is the perfect way to enrich the learning environment, both in and out of school.

Activity E

Read the following sentences. The first sentence in each pair is an opinion. Tell whether the second sentence is a convincing reason. Explain your answers.

1. *Number the Stars* by Lois Lowry should be on our historical fiction book list.
   It won the Newbery Award and the Rebecca Caudill Award and is set in World War II.

2. *Wayside School Is Falling Down* by Louis Sachar should be on our list of humorous books.
   The paperback costs only $5.99.

3. Cantigny Park would be a good place for an educational end-of-year picnic.
   The First Division Museum there has historical information from World War I to the present.

4. The Museum of Science and Industry is a great place for an educational field trip.
   There are a really great gift shop and restaurant.

Our Wide Wide World

The Second Amendment guarantees the right to keep and bear arms and the right to form a militia. When the Constitution was being drafted, some Americans were afraid that the government might abuse its military power. Many people wanted to be able defend themselves in the form of a militia—an army of ordinary citizens, not professional soldiers—that could act in an emergency.

Writer's Corner

Choose a tone for the position you wrote in Activity C. Then write an introduction for a persuasive article on that position.

Expanding Sentences

Our Wide Wide World

The Third Amendment guarantees that the government won't "quarter," or house, troops in private citizens' homes during times of peace. Before the American Revolution, Britain often forced citizens to house British troops, especially when those troops were located in foreign lands. The Constitution does allow quartering troops during times of war but only in accordance with law.

Good writers vary the lengths of their sentences. You can make sentences longer by expanding them, using adjectives, adverbs, and prepositional phrases. Expanding sentences makes your sentences clearer and more interesting. Here are some ways to expand your sentences.

Expanding Sentences with Adjectives

You can write sentences that are colorful and interesting by adding adjectives before nouns. Colorful adjectives will expand sentences and help paint a mental picture for the reader. Look at the two sentences below.

> Brian discovered a trunk in the corner of the attic.

> Brian discovered a *dusty metal* trunk in a *gloomy* corner of the attic.

The writer expanded the sentence by adding the adjectives *dusty* and *metal* before the noun *trunk*. The writer also added the adjective *gloomy* before the noun *corner*.

Expanding Sentences with Adverbs

Adverbs also help to expand sentences. Adverbs can tell *how, when,* or *where.* Adverbs usually come at the beginning of a sentence or after a verb. Look at the two sentences below.

> The rain began to fall.

> *Suddenly* the rain began to fall *furiously.*

The writer improved the sentence by adding the adverb *suddenly,* which tells *when* the rain fell, and the adverb *furiously,* which tells *how* it fell. Both words expand the sentence and help readers better understand when and how the rain fell.

Activity A

Write two adjectives that could describe each noun in different ways.

ocean	car	picture	man	road

Activity B

Expand these sentences by using colorful adjectives.

1. A _____ kite soared in the _____ sky.

2. The _____ snow cone was a treat on a _____ day.

3. We spotted a _____ whale not far from our _____ boat.

4. A _____ tourist wandered through the _____ streets.

5. The _____ tick of the clock echoed throughout the _____ house.

6. Chris bought a _____ pen at the _____ store.

Activity C

Expand these sentences by using adverbs.

1. The roller coaster sped _____ down the tracks.

2. Two astronauts floated _____ in space.

3. A cheetah walked _____ toward its prey.

4. _____ I picked up the crystal vase.

5. The ballerina danced _____ before the audience.

Writer's Corner

Write a descriptive paragraph about a house. Trade paragraphs with a partner. Rewrite each other's paragraphs, adding adjectives and adverbs to make the paragraph more interesting.

Expanding Sentences with Prepositional Phrases

Prepositional phrases can also help to expand sentences. A prepositional phrase is a group of words that begins with a preposition and ends with a noun or pronoun. *In the morning, behind the door,* and *over the moon* are prepositional phrases. Prepositional phrases can be used as adjectives or adverbs. They can begin a sentence or follow a noun or verb. Look at the two sentences below.

> The boat floated slowly.

> The boat *with the broken mast* floated slowly *down the river.*

The prepositional phrase *with the broken mast* describes the boat. *Down the river* tells where it floated. The prepositional phrases add descriptive details that give a clearer picture to the reader.

Activity D

Expand these sentences with prepositional phrases.

1. Jon and Jan looked at the constellations _____.

2. I heard a loud noise _____.

3. Miguel carried his backpack _____.

4. _____ fell a shower of confetti.

5. The penguin waddled _____.

6. _____ the campers swam _____.

7. Stan cannot play baseball _____.

8. Put the cake _____.

9. _____ is where you'll find the treasure chest.

10. The band played "The Star-Spangled Banner" _____.

11. _____ is where you will see the spotted owls.

12. _____ the submarine lurked.

13. Theo played the movie _____.

Activity E

Expand these sentences with adjectives, adverbs, or prepositional phrases.

1. I heard the _____ stairs creaking _____.

2. The _____ bear walked toward me _____.

3. The _____ cat crept _____.

4. _____ icicles hung _____.

5. A _____ spider skittered _____.

Activity F

Rewrite the following paragraph, expanding the sentences by adding adjectives, adverbs, and prepositional phrases. You may change or add other words to make the paragraph more interesting.

Jennifer was reading. She heard a noise. She got up from her chair. She crept up the stairs to the bedroom. She pushed open the door. The noise was louder. She realized it was a tree branch scraping the window.

Activity G

Write sentences using the following adjectives, adverbs, and prepositional phrases.

1. delicious
2. terrific
3. tremendously
4. on time
5. thoughtfully

6. down the stairs
7. miniature
8. gratefully
9. over the road
10. useful

Writer's Corner

Write four persuasive sentences to convince people to buy a product. Use adjectives, adverbs, and prepositional phrases to make your statements more convincing. Think of TV commercials or magazine ads for ideas.

Word Study

Antonyms

Antonyms are words that have opposite meanings. Here are a few antonym pairs.

familiar	unknown
simple	elaborate
calm	frantic
permanent	temporary

Many words have more than one antonym. How many words can you think of that are opposite of *small?*

Words that have more than one meaning might have antonyms for each different meaning. The words *dark* and *heavy* are both antonyms of the word *light.* Can you explain why?

• Activity A •

The chart below shows one antonym each for four words. Copy the chart and add more antonyms to each column.

little	special	rude	happy
huge	common	pleasant	sad

Activity B

Match each word in Column A with its antonym in Column B.

Column A	Column B
1. vain	a. firm
2. soothing	b. rare
3. bored	c. modest
4. end	d. refuse
5. agree	e. stressful
6. unsteady	f. whisper
7. yell	g. beginning
8. believe	h. decrease
9. abundant	i. excited
10. increase	j. doubt

Activity C

Rewrite each sentence by replacing the word in italics with an antonym of that word.

1. A *harsh* wind blew across Crocodile Lake.

2. Do you think Raoul is *foolish* to play pinball on crutches?

3. Sammy *remembered* that he left his friend Jake on the porch.

4. Does that superhero *shrink* or does he fly?

5. Your invention is so *simple.*

6. Just as we arrived on the scene, the monster in the lake *disappeared.*

Writer's Corner

Read a short persuasive article, such as a letter to the editor of a newspaper. List five words from the article that have antonyms. Then list antonyms for the five words.

Activity D

Each word in italics is followed by three words. Tell which of the three words is not an antonym of the word in italics.

1. *alert*   sleepy, observant, inattentive
2. *sour*   tart, sugary, sweet
3. *sick*   healthy, hardy, ailing
4. *violent*   fierce, peaceful, calm
5. *funny*   serious, sad, amusing
6. *empty*   full, vacant, occupied
7. *amazing*   boring, dull, thrilling
8. *cooperate*   refuse, agree, resist

Activity E

The word pairs in parentheses are antonyms. Choose the word that makes sense in each sentence.

1. Because of his (indifferent inquisitive) nature, Giles just had to know what was in the shed behind the old house next door.

2. His shaking hands showed how (apprehensive fearless) he felt.

3. His (graceful clumsy) brother Xander started to follow, until he tripped on a garden hose in the grass.

4. The dark, (serene agitated) clouds rumbled with thunder overhead.

5. It felt good to be (idle active) outside after a long day reading at the library.

6. As he approached the shed, he realized there was a (strange normal) glow inside.

7. The (menacing harmless) light made him think twice about his exploration.

8. "Hey, Giles!" his brother (wailed whispered) from the back porch of the house. "Time for dinner!"

9. As he ran home, Giles felt (genuine fake) relief that it was time to eat.

Activity F •

Tell which pairs of words are synonyms and which are antonyms.

1. bashful, timid
2. powerful, weak
3. mistaken, accurate
4. parched, drenched
5. flawless, perfect
6. appreciative, ungrateful
7. magnificent, splendid
8. cautious, careless

Activity G •

Read the following descriptive paragraph. Then rewrite the paragraph to give an opposite description by replacing the words in italics with their antonyms.

It was a scene to *remember.* The lake was *peaceful* and *quiet.* A *smooth* beach led to a single *lovely* cottage. *Healthy* bushes surrounded the *clean* cottage. *Bright* curtains decorated the *spotless* windows. The whole family filled the *enormous* rooms with *laughter* and *cheerful* voices. What a *wonderful* place to be!

Writer's Corner

Write a comparison of something you like to do at home with something you do not like to do at home. Use at least three pairs of antonyms in your comparisons.

Study Skills

Library

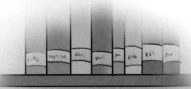

Libraries have a lot of books and research materials. Some libraries are several stories tall and packed with information. No matter what their size, all libraries use specials systems to organize their resources and to make information easy to find. Here are a few tips for finding books in a library.

Fiction

Fiction books usually have a section of their own. Books in the fiction section are arranged alphabetically by the author's last name. If several authors have the same last name, the books are usually further alphabetized by the authors' first names. If an author has written more than one book, the books will be alphabetized again by title. Some libraries label the spine of a fiction book with the letter *F* and the first three letters of the author's last name.

Nonfiction

Nonfiction books are grouped by subject. If you look for a book about whales, the books around it will also be about whales and other marine life. Because nonfiction books are grouped by subject, they are arranged using call numbers. Books with a call number of 505 are next to the books with a call number of 506. Each nonfiction book is assigned a call number according to the subject of the book.

   A book's call number appears on the spine of the book. Just below the call number, you will find the first three letters of the author's last name. Use the card catalog or computer catalog in your library to find the call number of a book.

Reference Books

Some nonfiction books are put in a separate section called the reference section. Reference books include dictionaries, encyclopedias, almanacs, and atlases. Reference books cannot be checked out because people use them often and because they are very expensive. Books in the reference section are also arranged numerically by call number.

Other Materials

Many libraries offer videos, music, new and old issues of magazines, and computer software. Individual libraries organize these materials differently. Ask a librarian for help finding these materials.

• Activity A •

Tell in which section of the library—fiction, nonfiction, or reference—you would find these books.

1. *Huckleberry Finn* by Mark Twain
2. *The American Heritage Dictionary of the English Language*
3. *A History of American Whaling* by Fred Darling
4. *Bud, Not Buddy* by Christopher Paul Curtis
5. *Archery for Amateurs* by Neil Gaby
6. *The Planets of Our Solar System* by Denise O'Malley
7. *An Atlas of Europe*

Writer's Corner

List the titles of three books that you know are in each of the three main sections of the library. Remember, the three main sections are fiction, nonfiction, and reference.

Card Catalogs

To find the call number of a book you are searching for, you will need to use a library's catalog. Some libraries organize this information in a card catalog. A card catalog is a cabinet with drawers of cards. The cards have the information you need to find a book. There are three kinds of cards in a card catalog. Each kind allows you to search for books in different ways. All of the cards are combined in alphabetical order.

Author Cards

Author cards are arranged by the authors' last names. These cards can be helpful if you are looking for an author, but you do not know the titles of the author's books.

Title Cards

Title cards are arranged by title. The words *A, An,* or *The* at the beginning of a title are ignored. For example, the card for *The Grape Escape* would be in the G section. These cards are helpful if you know the title of a book, but can't remember the author's name.

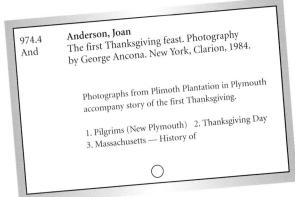

Subject Cards

Subject cards have subjects at the top. These cards provide titles and authors of books about that subject.

Look at these cards from card catalogs. Under what letter of the alphabet would you find each card?

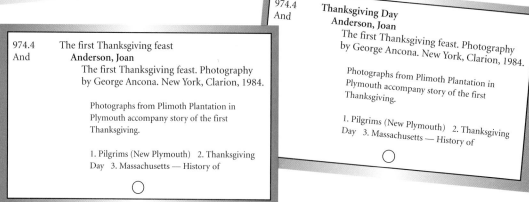

Computer Catalogs

Today many libraries use computer catalogs. A computer catalog provides the same information as a card catalog. You can usually search by title, author, or subject. Computer catalogs can be different from library to library. Ask a librarian if you need help.

Activity B

Imagine you are looking for a book in the library. You have only the information below. Tell whether you would use the title, author, or subject to find the book you need.

1. pets
2. *The Rose Parade*
3. *Lava in Hawaii*
4. Beverly Cleary
5. James Howe
6. earthquakes

Activity C

Visit your school library and use the card catalog or computer catalog to find the following information.

1. Titles of books by
   a. Jerry Spinelli
   b. Karen Hesse
   c. Phyllis Reynolds Naylor

2. The author of the book
   a. *Catherine, Called Birdy*
   b. *What Would Joey Do?*
   c. *Bridge to Terabithia*

3. Books on the subject of
   a. automobiles
   b. Russian history
   c. Henry James

4. The titles and call numbers for books by
   a. Jack Prelutsky
   b. Jim Arnosky
   c. Seymour Simon

Writer's Corner

Suppose you are doing research on each of these topics. For each topic write a list of subjects you could search under in the card catalog or computer catalog.

monkeys   lava   jet airplanes

Speaking and Listening Skills

Persuasive Speaking

Have you ever seen the president, a mayor, or a governor give a speech? Most political speeches are a form of persuasive speaking. You use persuasive speaking too. You are using persuasive speaking when you try to convince your parents to let you stay up later. Any time you try to convince someone to agree with you, you are using persuasive speaking. Here are a few things to think about when preparing a persuasive speech.

Audience and Position

Think about what your audience already knows about your topic. If they already agree with you, you might be able to make them agree more strongly and take action. If they disagree, you might be able to change their minds. Be sure to pick a topic and position that you care strongly about.

Knowing your audience can help you prepare the reasons and evidence you will use in your speech. What kinds of reasons and evidence will show your audience that your position affects their lives?

Introduction

State your position early in your speech. Try to grab the audience's attention. A personal story or an example that illustrates how your position affects people can often get an audience interested.

Body

Present your reasons and evidence in the body of your speech. Be sure to give your reasons clearly and in logical order. Speak slowly and clearly to emphasize your points. Your audience cannot go back and reread your reasons if something is not clear.

Conclusion

Use your conclusion to summarize your position and briefly restate the reasons you used in the body. Be sure to speak calmly and confidently in your conclusion. It is often a good idea to tell your audience in the conclusion what action they can take if they agree with you.

Body Language and Voice

Your voice and your body language are important in persuasive speaking. Stand straight as you speak. It will help you breathe and will show that you are confident. Use gestures to emphasize important points. With your voice and your body language, you can make your persuasive speech even more persuasive.

• Activity A •

Brainstorm a list of after-school activities or student clubs you would like to have in your school. Think about hobbies, sports, and interests you have and could share with others. Then meet with a partner to talk about the activities on your list. Choose an activity from your list that you feel strongly about and that would be interesting to an audience of your classmates.

• Activity B •

List a few reasons you might use in a persuasive speech about activities or clubs you would like your school to start. Think about evidence you might use to support your reasons.

Speaker's Corner

Write an introduction for a persuasive speech on the topic you chose for Activity A. If you chose a hobby or an activity you already enjoy, you might tell a story about it. Then practice your introduction with a partner.

The Eighth
Amendment protects
against excessive
bail or fines and
from cruel or
unusual punishment
at sentencing.
This means that
if a charge is
serious, then the
punishment, whether
it be jail time or
a fine, may be
significant. If a
charge is less
serious, then the
punishment should
reflect that.

Organize

Organize your persuasive speech in the same way you might organize a persuasive article. Once you decide on an introduction, write a few notes on a note card to remind you what your position is and how you plan to grab your audience's attention.

For the body of your speech, write each reason on the top of a separate note card. Write your evidence underneath each reason. You might number your reasons if you want to present them in a particular order.

Write on a note card a few ideas for your conclusion. You might include notes about what the audience can do if they agree with you.

Practice

Practicing is a chance to get comfortable with your speech. Being comfortable with your speech will allow you to be confident as you talk. It helps you become familiar with using note cards to deliver your speech. Practicing is also a chance for you to experiment with different gestures and tones of voice. Practice in front of a mirror and try emphasizing your points in different ways. If you find a gesture or tone of voice that you think is effective, write a reminder on one of your note cards.

When you think you are ready, practice with a friend or family member. Here are some questions you might ask your listener.

- Was my position clear?
- Were my reasons in a clear, logical order?
- Do my reasons support my topic?
- Did I support my reasons with strong evidence?
- Did I appear confident as I spoke?
- Did I use gestures and tone of voice to emphasize my points?
- Did I convince you to agree with me?

Listening Tips

When you listen to a persuasive speech, be a critical listener. Listen to the speaker's reasons and think about whether they make sense. Listen to the evidence and decide if it is convincing. Here are a few more tips for listening to a persuasive speech.

- Listen to find out the speaker's position.
- Write down or try to remember each of the speaker's reasons.
- Think about whether the evidence presented supports those reasons.
- You might disagree with the speaker. If so, still listen to the speaker and respect his or her position. Think about how you might argue your own side.
- Wait until the end of the speech to ask questions. Then ask your questions politely.

Activity C

Organize your notes from Activity B on page 257. Write ideas for kinds of evidence you could use to support your reasons. Then gather evidence that supports your reasons. Write your reasons and evidence on note cards.

Activity D

Write a conclusion that summarizes your position and your reasons. If you can, tell your audience what action they could take if they agree with you. Use what you write to make a note card for your conclusion. Then write notes on a note card for the introduction you wrote for the Speaker's Corner on page 257.

Speaker's Corner

Practice your persuasive speech with a partner. When you have finished, ask your partner the questions on page 258. Then let your partner practice his or her persuasive speech. Remember the listening tips above as you listen to your partner's speech.

Persuasive Writing
Prewriting and Drafting

Persuading other people to agree with you is not always easy. But if you choose a topic that you care about, state your position clearly, give reasons to support it, and back up your reasons with evidence, you have a better chance of persuading others.

Prewriting

Greta's dad told her about "The Best Town in Michigan" contest. Kids from all over the state would send articles to the *Lansing Gazette,* trying to persuade others that theirs was the best town. Greta thought her town was the best town in the world. So she decided to enter the contest.

Greta began by prewriting. She needed to think of a strong sentence stating her position. She also had to think of reasons to support her position, back up her reasons with evidence, and organize her ideas.

Position and Reasons

Greta's position was easy. She thought that River City was the best town in Michigan. Now she needed to think of reasons to support her position.

Greta listed her position and reasons on a sheet of paper. Here is Greta's list.

> Position:
>   River City is the best town in Michigan!
> Reasons:
> * It is beautiful.
> * It is a fun place to live.
> * There are lots of cool things to do.
> * Everyone loves it here.

Your Turn

Choose a topic that you care about. Think about your audience. Think of reasons that support your position. Then write a sentence that states your position. List reasons why people should agree with you. The more reasons you have to support your position, the better chance you have of convincing your audience to agree with you.

Evidence

In order to persuade the judges of the contest, Greta would need evidence that backed up her reasons. She made a list of her own ideas that backed up her reasons. Then she went online and found some more evidence.

Your Turn

Now it's time to back up your reasons with evidence. Remember that opinions without support are not likely to persuade your audience. Make some notes about why you think each reason is a good one. Then use the library or the Internet to find more evidence.

Organizing Ideas

Greta saw that some of her evidence was not effective. She organized her notes, including evidence for each reason. She took out information that she didn't need. Here are her notes.

Introduction:
- *River City is the best town in Michigan. (position)*

Body:

Reason One: It is beautiful.
- *parks built on the waterfront*
- *historic buildings from 1800s*
- *mansions on Center Ave. built by lumber barons*

Reason Two: It has a lot of festivals.
- *Independence Day Fireworks Festival: three days long, fireworks each night, music groups, food*
- *River Roar: boat race down Saginaw River, music, food*

Reason Three: There are things for families to do.
- *Deer Run: pet and feed deer, amusement park, restaurant*
- *Sunshine Stables: trail rides, hay rides, horse shows*

Conclusion:
- *River City is an interesting and beautiful town. (restate position)*

Your Turn

Look at your notes. Organize them with an introduction, a separate section for each reason, and a conclusion. Include your evidence for each reason. Organize your notes in a way that makes sense to you. If necessary, do additional research to strengthen your reasons.

Drafting

Greta used her organized notes as a guide to write her article. She made sure to include opinion words to make her writing sound confident. Here is Greta's first draft.

Why River City Is Michigan's Best Town

River City is the best town in Michigan! Other towns aren't as good as we are. Every year it gets better and better. I think that River City can win the <u>Lansing Gazette</u>'s contest for "Michigan's Best Town."

River City is one of the most beautiful towns in Michigan. River City, which is split in half by the Saginaw river, now has beautiful parks. The buildings along the river can be traced back to the earliest settlements. People can also travel down Center Avenue, which is only a short walk from the river, to see mansons and churches.

Now that people are starting to notice the beauty of River City, it has fun and interesting festivals. The most well known is the Independence Day Fireworks Festival. This festival lasts for three days. Besides the fireworks show each night, there are also music and comedy acts, rides, food, and arts and crafts shows in Waterfront Park. There is also the River Roar, an exciting boat race down the Saginaw river. The River Roar also has a lot of fun entertainment, like magicans, music, and food! There are also lots of fun things for families to do all year. One place to go is Deer Run.

Deer Run has an amusement park. There is a restaurant that has good food like hot dogs and candy apples. Or families can go to Sunshine Stables. They have guided trail rides through River City State Park. They also have hay rides in the fall and sliegh rides in the winter.

We should win the <u>Lansing</u> <u>Gazette</u>'s contest for "Michigan's Best Town." With our beautiful rivers and parks, old buildings, and fantastic festivals, how could anyone disagree?

Your Turn

Use your notes to write your first draft. Remember to double-space your lines so that you will have room to make changes later. Keep in mind that you will probably revise your draft several times.

Establishing Tone

It is important to establish a tone that will make your readers like what you are saying. The more positive your tone is, the more effective your writing will be. You don't want your audience to think that your persuasive article has reasons based on anger or bias. Greta made a negative comment in the first paragraph that she might want to delete. Her article is more persuasive if she says positive things about River City that she can prove, rather than saying negative things that are her personal opinion.

Persuasive Writing

Content Editing

Greta had worked hard on her persuasive article. But she knew her article could be stronger. She asked her best friend, Zosia, to content edit her draft. A content editor could check to make sure her reasons were logical and well supported. Zosia used this checklist to content edit Greta's draft.

Content Editor's Checklist

✓ Does the introduction state the position clearly?

✓ Does the body have logical reasons that support the position?

✓ Is each reason written in a separate paragraph, and are the reasons well supported?

✓ Are all of the details necessary and important to the position?

✓ Does the conclusion restate the position and give readers an action to take?

✓ Are opinion words used to express the position?

Zosia read Greta's draft several times. She made notes about what she liked and listed her suggestions. Then Greta and Zosia met to talk about the draft.

Zosia told Greta that she had written good reasons to support her position. She also thought that Greta had stated her position well. Here are Zosia's suggestions for improvement.

- In the second paragraph, you say that River City has beautiful parks. Do you mean the parks on the river or the state park? The state park isn't on the river.

- The second reason is kind of confusing. It seems like you're saying we've had festivals only since people started noticing River City.

- Maybe you should mention that the Fireworks Festival is one of the largest in the Midwest.

- You should mention the Munger Potato Fest. It's a lot of fun too.

- The third paragraph has two reasons. I think that you should make the sentence "There are also lots of fun things for families to do all year" the beginning of a new paragraph.

- You talk about the amusement park and the restaurant at Deer Run, but you don't mention the deer! People might wonder why it's called Deer Run.

- I don't see an action readers can take.

Greta appreciated Zosia's suggestions. She hadn't realized that she forgot to mention the deer at Deer Run. Greta thought that it was the best part about the place.

Greta looked over Zosia's suggestions carefully. Then she checked the draft herself, using the Content Editor's Checklist. She found two things that Zosia forgot to check for. Do you see what Zosia forgot?

Your Turn

Work with a partner and content edit each other's persuasive articles. Make notes as Zosia did, using the Content Editor's Checklist to content edit your partner's draft. See if you are convinced by your partner's persuasive article.

When you have both finished, meet with your partner and discuss your suggestions. Remember to begin by telling your partner what was strong about his or her draft. Point out anything you really liked. Then tell your suggestions in a positive and helpful way.

It is also a good idea to use the Content Editor's Checklist to content edit your draft yourself. You might find, as Greta did, that your content editor missed something. Take some time to make sure that you can answer yes to every question on the checklist.

Chapter 7 Writer's Workshop

Persuasive Writing

Revising

This is Greta's revised persuasive article.

River City Is the Place to Be!

~~Why River City Is Michigan's Best Town~~

River City is the best town in Michigan! ~~Other towns aren't as good as we are!~~ Every year it gets better and better. I ~~think~~ believe that River City ~~can~~ should win the Lansing Gazette's contest for "Michigan's Best Town."

River City is one of the most beautiful towns in Michigan. River City, which is split in half by the Saginaw river, now has beautiful waterfront parks. The buildings along the river can be traced back to the earliest settlements. People can also travel down Center Avenue, which is only a short walk from the river, to see mansons and churches.

Now that people are starting to notice the beauty of River City, it has started hosting some of the most fun and interesting festivals in the state. The most well known is the Independence Day Fireworks Festival which is one of the largest in the Midwest. This festival lasts for three days. Besides the fireworks show each night, there are also music and comedy acts, rides, food, and arts and crafts shows in Waterfront Park. There is also the River Roar, an exciting boat race down the Saginaw river. The River Roar also has a lot of fun entertainment, like magicans, music, and food! There are also lots of fun things for families to do all year. One place to go is Deer Run.

You can actually feed and pet baby deer there!
∧Deer Run has an amusement park. There is a restaurant that has good food like hot dogs and candy apples. Or families can go to Sunshine Stables. They have guided trail rides through River City State Park. They also have hay rides in the fall and sliegh rides in the winter.

River City is the most interesting and beautiful town in Michigan.
∧ We should win the Lansing Gazette's contest for "Michigan's Best Town." With our beautiful rivers and parks, old buildings, and fantastic festivals, how could anyone disagree? Vote for River City!
∧

Look at how Greta improved her persuasive article.

- She added the word *waterfront* in the second paragraph. She didn't want people to think she was talking about the state park.

- Greta revised the second reason to mean that more new festivals were being held in River City.

- Greta thought that saying the Fireworks Festival was one of the largest in the Midwest was a good idea.

- She disagreed with Zosia about the Munger Potato Fest. The Potato Fest was held in Munger, so it wasn't good evidence for why River City had fun things to do.

- Greta followed Zosia's suggestion to divide the third paragraph into two paragraphs.

- She added a sentence to help explain the name of Deer Run.

- Greta revised her conclusion to include an action. She also added a sentence to make the restatement of her position stronger.

Greta revised her title and added some more opinion words in her introduction. She also deleted the sentence about other towns. It was an unsupported opinion that did not strengthen her position.

Your Turn
Use your content editor's suggestions and your own ideas to revise your draft. Make any other changes that you notice as you go along. Then use the Content Editor's Checklist again to make sure you can answer yes to all the questions.

Chapter 7 Editor's Workshop

Persuasive Writing

Copyediting and Proofreading

Copyediting

Now that the reasons and evidence in her article were solid, Greta wanted to copyedit it. She knew that she would have a better chance of persuading her audience if they weren't distracted by confusing sentences or by unclear word choices. Greta used this checklist to copyedit her draft.

Copyeditor's Checklist

✓ Are there any sentences that could be expanded with adjectives, adverbs, or prepositional phrases?

✓ Are there any rambling or run-on sentences?

✓ Are there sentences that could be combined?

✓ Is there a variety of word choice?

✓ Are exact words used?

Greta used adjectives to expand a sentence in the third paragraph. Look at how she revised it.

Revision: This colorful and exciting festival lasts for three days.

She combined two sentences in her new fourth paragraph. Do you see where Greta might combine sentences?

Greta noticed that she used the word *also* a lot in her draft. She decided to take out *also* in some places.

Greta didn't like the word *old* in the last paragraph. She decided to replace it with the word *historic,* which meant "being important to history." Greta thought that *historic* described the buildings much better.

Your Turn

Use the Copyeditor's Checklist to copyedit your draft. Look for ways to make your sentences more persuasive. Try expanding sentences to make your draft come alive for your audience. Be sure that your feelings are clearly conveyed through your word choice. If your readers don't think that you feel strongly about your position, they won't be persuaded to agree with you!

Remember to check for one item on the checklist at a time. You might miss mistakes if you check for too many things at once. When you have finished, check your draft again, using the Content Editor's Checklist to make sure that your sentence changes did not change any of your content ideas.

Proofreading

Before she sent her article to the *Lansing Gazette,* Greta wanted to make sure someone proofread it. She knew that a proofreader would check for errors in spelling, capitalization, punctuation, and grammar. A checklist like this can help when proofreading.

Proofreader's Checklist

✓ Are the paragraphs indented?

✓ Are all the words spelled correctly?

✓ Are capitalization and punctuation correct?

✓ Is the grammar correct?

✓ Were any new mistakes added while editing?

Greta had read her persuasive article so many times that she knew she was seeing what she wanted to see. So she asked her dad to proofread her draft.

In the fourth paragraph, Greta's dad, Mr. Ingram, saw two words that should have been one compound word. Do you see the words he found?

Mr. Ingram found three misspelled words. In the second paragraph, Greta misspelled *mansions.* She had written *mansons.* In the third paragraph, she had left out the second *i* in *magicians.* Do you see the other misspelled word in Greta's draft?

Mr. Ingram also found a capitalization mistake that appeared twice in Greta's revised draft. *Saginaw river* should be *Saginaw River,* because it is a proper noun.

Your Turn

Read your draft carefully, using the Proofreader's Checklist. Check for one item at a time. This is a good way to spot mistakes and to make last-minute changes to improve your draft.

When you have finished, trade drafts with a partner. Use the Proofreader's Checklist to proofread your partner's draft. Remember to use a dictionary to check the spelling of words that you aren't sure of. Then meet with your partner to discuss any mistakes that you each found.

Persuasive Writing

Publishing

Greta was confident that she had written a very persuasive article. She typed her article carefully on her dad's computer. Then she checked her typed copy one last time, using the Proofreader's Checklist. She didn't find any more mistakes, so she knew her article was ready. Greta knew that just having people at the *Lansing Gazette* read her work was a form of publishing. Even if she didn't win the contest, Greta was glad that she had worked so hard.

River City Is the Place to Be!
by Greta Ingram

River City is the best town in Michigan! Every year it gets better and better. I believe that River City should win the <u>Lansing Gazette</u>'s contest for "Michigan's Best Town."

River City is one of the most beautiful towns in Michigan. River City, which is split in half by the Saginaw River, now has beautiful waterfront parks. The buildings along the river can be traced back to the earliest settlements. People can also travel down Center Avenue, which is only a short walk from the river, to see mansions and churches.

Now that people are starting to notice the beauty of River City, it has started hosting some of the most fun and interesting festivals in the state. The most well known is the Independence Day Fireworks Festival, which is one of the largest in the Midwest. This colorful and exciting festival lasts for three days. Besides the fireworks show each night, there are music and comedy acts, rides, food, and arts and crafts shows in Waterfront Park. There is also the River Roar, an exciting boat race down the Saginaw River. The River Roar has a lot of fun entertainment, like magicians, music, and food!

There are lots of fun things for families to do all year. One place to go is Deer Run. You can actually feed and pet baby deer there! Deer Run has an amusement park and a restaurant that has good food like hot dogs and candy apples. Or families can go to Sunshine Stables. They have guided trail rides through River City State Park. They also have hayrides in the fall and sleigh rides in the winter.

River City is the most interesting and beautiful town in Michigan. We should win the Lansing Gazette's contest for "Michigan's Best Town." With our beautiful rivers and parks, historic buildings, and fantastic festivals, how could anyone disagree? Vote for River City as Michigan's Best Town!

Your Turn

The moment that you share your work with your audience is the moment that you publish. Follow these steps to prepare your persuasive article for publishing.

- Read your article one more time to make sure that you haven't left out any facts or evidence. Remember to content edit, copyedit, and proofread any additional changes that you make.

- Use your neatest handwriting or a computer to produce the final copy of your draft.

- Proofread your final copy one more time to make sure that there are no misspelled words or mistakes in capitalization, punctuation, or grammar.

Decide with your classmates and teacher how you will publish your work. One good way is to post your persuasive article on a school bulletin board. You might convince students and teachers from all over the school to agree with you.

If your persuasive article is about an issue or a change in your school or community, talk with your teacher and parents about how you might share your viewpoint with a wider audience. For example, you might send your article to the local newspaper or post it on a community Internet site.

Our Wide Wide World

A mayor is usually the elected executive of a town or city. There are no universal responsibilities of a mayor, as they vary from place to place. Most mayors, however, work with a legislative body, such as a city council, to decide municipal policy. Do you know if your town has a mayor? Do you know who it is?

Research Reports

Why All the Hoopla?

As a new basketball season gets under way, millions of Americans will be engaged in this popular sport. Did you know that the first basketball was a soccer ball and the first hoop a wooden peach basket? Some things about the game have evolved—equipment, rules, leagues—but basketball is considered the invention of one man. Unlike most sports, which evolved from sports in other countries, basketball is truly an American game.

Basketball's inventor, Dr. James Naismith, was born in Ontario, Canada, in 1861. Later he moved to the United States to study and then teach at the YMCA Training School in Springfield, Massachusetts. In 1891, while teaching physical education, Naismith created an indoor team game that students could enjoy during the winter months. The game of basketball was born.

At first Naismith considered playing outdoor games indoors but thought the play would be too rough. He also recognized that all team games used some kind of ball, and he liked the idea of using a soccer-like ball because it would be easy to handle.

For baskets, he used two wooden peach baskets, which he attached to the railings at either end of the gym balcony. Naismith greeted his physical education class of 18 students with his 13 rules of basketball, a soccer ball, and the peach baskets. Soon the entire school and their families and friends were playing.

The game quickly caught on in YMCAs all over the country. As teams began to play outside of the Y, professional basketball began. The first professional league, the National Basketball League, was formed in 1898. Other leagues were founded and eventually merged to become the National Basketball Association (NBA), which we have today.

The impact of basketball on American athletics has been great. For the father of basketball, the fun of playing the game was more important than the competition and the score. Maybe this is the reason for all the hoopla!

Fall Issue 209

What Makes a Good Research Report?

A research report is a kind of writing that tells readers factual information about a topic in an organized way. A research report shares ideas that a writer has read and collected from a variety of sources.

Writers of research reports first gather information about a topic, then organize the information, and finally write the report. A research report might be about almost any topic—a person, a place, or an event. It could be about T. S. Eliot, Yellowstone Park, or the Fourth of July.

Choose a Topic

Choose a topic that interests you. Your interest and enthusiasm for the topic will show through in your report. Sometimes your choice of a topic will be up to you. Other times your teacher might give you guidelines. Then you can brainstorm and choose an aspect of the topic that you want to write about.

Narrow the Topic

Once you have chosen your topic, you need to make sure it is narrow enough for an effective research report. Be specific about what you want to know. The history of England might be too broad a topic. The War of the Roses would be a more narrow topic, because it could be more easily covered in a research report.

Asking questions about your topic gives you a chance to focus your thoughts about it. Questions can guide your research and let you decide what information is important to your report and what isn't.

Research

Research reports require research. That means you will need to spend some time gathering information from sources. The information for your report can come from a wide variety of sources, such as books, encyclopedias, or Web sites.

It's difficult to remember everything you read, so you will want to take good, organized notes as you research. Write down everything that is relevant to your topic. Your notes will help you organize an effective research report.

Activity A

Read these pairs of topics. Tell which topic in each pair is the narrower topic for a research report.

1. **a.** birds of North America

   b. the bald eagle

2. **a.** Colonial Williamsburg

   b. Colonial America

3. **a.** exploring outer space

   b. expeditions to Mars

4. **a.** Casimir Pulaski

   b. Revolutionary War heroes

Activity B

The following topics are too broad for a research report. Narrow each of them until it is a suitable topic for a research report.

1. insects

2. dinosaurs

3. endangered animals

4. geology

Writer's Corner

Write three questions you have about a narrow topic you identified in Activity B. Save your work.

Topic Sentence

As you do your research, you will probably find more information than you can use. To guide your research, develop a topic sentence. The topic sentence is a sentence that briefly describes or explains the topic of your research report. Read this example.

Broad topic: sports

Narrow topic: football

Topic sentence: Football is a popular sport.

By narrowing the topic to a topic sentence, this writer has a focus for the rest of the report. With a topic sentence, the writer can use the body of the report for the reasons why football is a popular sport.

Introduction

Like other kinds of writing, an effective introduction catches the reader's attention. In a research report, a catchy introduction might start with an interesting fact about your topic. The introduction should also include the topic sentence of the report.

Body

The body of a research report is the place to present what you have discovered. As in other types of writing, the body is the longest part of a research report. It can be one page or many pages long. Usually each paragraph of the body covers one main idea that supports your topic sentence. Imagine you are writing a research report about why football is a popular sport. One paragraph might be about the increased television ratings for football. Another paragraph might be about the rise in stadium attendance. A third paragraph might be about the growing popularity of the Super Bowl.

Conclusion

A good conclusion briefly summarizes the topic sentence of the research report. It also leaves the reader with a sense that the topic was covered well and nothing important was left out.

• Activity C •

Tell which idea in each group does not go with the topic sentence.

1. *topic sentence:* Stars are more than just lights in the sky.

   a. what stars are made of

   b. how "The Star-Spangled Banner" was written

   c. solar radiation

   d. types of stars

2. *topic sentence:* Hurricanes are a powerful force of nature that affects millions of people every year.

   a. effects of hurricanes

   b. how earthquakes occur

   c. causes of hurricanes

   d. where hurricanes occur

3. *topic sentence*: Ferdinand Magellan lived a fascinating and accomplished life.

   a. when and where Magellan lived

   b. the kinds of expeditions Magellan made

   c. what Balboa found

   d. Magellan's discoveries

4. *topic sentence:* One of history's greatest puzzles is whether King Arthur was real or fictional.

   a. how swords are made

   b. factual accounts of King Arthur

   c. theories of who King Arthur really was

   d. fictional stories of King Arthur

Use your work from the previous Writer's Corner on page 275 to write an introduction for a research report. Include your topic sentence in your introduction.

Gathering and Organizing Information

You will do a lot of reading as you gather information. If you have narrowed your subject and found good sources, you will be able to include many details in your report. Here are some things to keep in mind as you take notes and organize your information.

Taking Notes

When you find a source that you want to use in your report, you should read only the information that deals with your topic. If you are looking for information about your topic in a book, read the contents in the front of the book or the index in the back of the book. Find and read the pages that relate to your topic.

To take notes on a source, read a paragraph and write down in your own words what the source is saying. Write important words and phrases that will help you recall the ideas in your source. Writing in your own words helps you understand and remember what you have read.

Using Note Cards

Using note cards is a handy way to take notes. Note cards are small enough to organize easily, yet large enough for writing down important information. One way to keep your notes in order is to write each note on a separate card. Once you have finished your note cards, put cards with information about the same thing into piles. Make separate piles for each idea that you researched.

To help you remember where each piece of information came from, write the name of the source, the author, and the page number at the bottom of the card.

These two note cards were written by a student writing a research report on humpback whales.

The scientific name for humpback whales
is _Megaptera novaeanglia._

"Humpback Whales,"
Animal Encyclopedia, p. 284.

Humpback whales eat almost 1½ tons of
small fish per day.
What Whales Eat, by Colleen Richardson
p. 77.

• Activity A •

**Here are some ideas you might want to cover if
you were doing a research report about fireflies.**

1. why and how fireflies light up

2. the life of a firefly

**These are notes from note cards for ideas 1 and 2. Which
notes would go in a pile for idea 1 and which would go
in a pile for idea 2?**

timing of flashes controlled by nerves
average life span = 5 to 30 days
lay eggs in moist places
chemical reaction causes light to flash
to attract mates or prey
larvae eat snails, worms, and insects

Writer's Corner

**Find two sources of information, such as an encyclopedia
and a nonfiction book, about planets in the solar system.
Make two note cards like the cards above. Write the
sources of the information on the note cards. Save your
work.**

Works Cited Page

An important part of a research report is the Works Cited page. The Works Cited page is found at the end of the report. It lists all the sources you used in your report in alphabetical order, according to the author's last name.

Each entry of a Works Cited page is a source that you used in your report. It does not include sources that you read but did not use. Start each entry with the author's name, last name first. If you cannot find an author listed, use the title of the source in place of the name. The titles of books are underlined, and the titles of articles are put between quotation marks.

You will probably take notes from many different kinds of sources. As you take notes, record on separate note cards the information about each source that you will need for your Works Cited page. Here is the information you will need for different kinds of sources.

Book

For most books, you will need the name of the author, the title of the book, the publisher, the location of the publisher, and the year the book was published. You can usually find this information on the title page or the copyright page. The entry on the Works Cited page for a book would look like the one below.

> Swinburne, Stephen R. The Woods Scientist. Boston: Houghton Mifflin, 2002.

Encyclopedia

Most encyclopedias do not list the names of the people who wrote each article. For these encyclopedias, you will need only the name of the article, the title of the encyclopedia, and the edition or year of the encyclopedia.

> "Tigers." World Book Encyclopedia. 2003 ed.

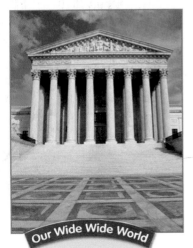

Our Wide Wide World

The U.S. Supreme Court is the judicial branch of the federal government. Supreme Court justices are appointed by the U.S. president and approved by the U.S. Senate. In all, there are nine Supreme Court justices, including the Chief Justice, who hear every case accepted by the Court.

Web Site

If a Web site gives the author's name, be sure to include it along with the name of the article, the date that you looked at the Web site, and the Web site address. Put the Web site address between angle brackets (< >).

> Brody, Valerie. "Common Dolphin." 20 Nov 2004
> <www.acsonline.org/factpack/common.htm>.

Many Web sites do not tell who wrote them. If a Web site does not give the author's name, begin the entry with the name of the article.

• Activity B •

Here are some sources for the firefly research report. Use this information to write a Works Cited page. Alphabetize the entries.

1. An article titled "A Beacon in the Night" by Lana Unger, looked up on November 20, 2004, Web site address: www.uky.edu/Agriculture/Entomology.

2. An article titled "Firefly" by James E. Lloyd, in *World Book Encyclopedia*, 2003 edition.

3. A book titled *Fireflies* by Sally M. Walker, published by Lerner Publications in Minneapolis in 2001.

• Activity C •

Look for three sources of information about an animal or insect. For example, you might use an encyclopedia, a nonfiction book, and a Web site. Write a Works Cited page for the three sources. Remember to put the entries in alphabetical order.

Writer's Corner

Use your notes from the previous Writer's Corner on page 279. Write a Works Cited page for your two sources. Use the correct form for each entry.

Outlines

Our Wide Wide World

The vice president is the second in command in the executive branch of the U.S. federal government. The vice president's primary responsibility is to fill the role of president when the president is unable to fulfill his duties. The vice president is also the president of the U.S. Senate, where he can cast a tiebreaking vote if need be.

After you have finished doing research and writing note cards, the next step in writing a research report is to organize your information. An effective way to organize information is to write an outline. An outline is like the skeleton of a research report. It helps you decide which information you want to use and how to present that information in an order your readers can follow.

An outline can let you know if you have more information than you need. It can also let you know if you need to look for additional information.

Parts of an Outline

An outline lays out ideas as they will appear in a research report. Main ideas are labeled with Roman numerals (I, II, III, IV, and so on). Each main idea will be explained in a paragraph in your report.

Details support the main ideas in research reports. They are listed below the main ideas and are labeled with capital letters (A, B, C, D, and so on). If a main idea has details, there should always be two or more details.

Outline Structure

Outlines should be written neatly so that they are easy to follow. For example, the periods for the Roman numerals should line up with one another. The detail letters should line up too. Use a ruler to line up your main ideas and details if you need help keeping them straight.

Outlines list all ideas in complete sentences, in phrases, or in single words. Sentences, phrases, and words should not be mixed in an outline.

Here is an outline of a research report about the life of turtles.

I. where turtles live
   A. deserts
   B. rivers and ponds
   C. seas
II. what turtles eat
   A. plants
   B. small animals
III. turtle life span
   A. longer than people
   B. can live 100 years
IV. turtle growth
   A. small one, 3 inches
   B. long one, 8 feet
   C. most in-between

• Activity A •

Use the following word web to create an outline. Use the above outline as a guide.

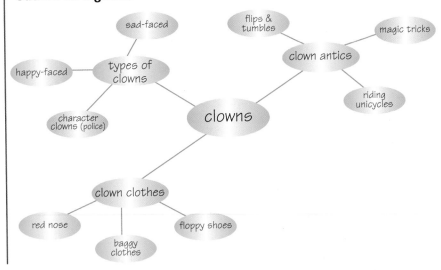

Writer's Corner

Add another main idea to the outline about clowns.
Under the main idea, write at least two details.

Activity B

Below are parts of two outlines. Identify the detail in each outline that doesn't support the main idea.

Outline 1

    I. Olympic Games
       A. discus throw
       B. javelin throw
       C. business sponsors
       D. 100-m dash

Outline 2

    I. wonders of the ancient world
       A. Great Pyramid of Egypt
       B. Grand Canyon
       C. Hanging Gardens of Babylon
       D. Colossus of Rhodes

Activity C

Below is a list that contains two main ideas and their details. They are part of an outline for a research report about polar bears. The ideas are out of order. Write them in outline form by finding the two main ideas and putting the appropriate details under each main idea. Use Roman numerals for the main ideas and capital letters for the details.

what a polar bear looks like

body with thick white fur

five claws on each foot

northern coasts of Canada, Russia, and Greenland

islands in the Arctic Ocean

where polar bears live

long body and neck

northern coast of Alaska

Activity D

These are the details for a main idea of a research report about clouds. Write a main idea for the details. Then write this part of the outline in outline form.

stratus clouds like blankets or sheets of fog

cumulus clouds like puffy white masses

cirrus clouds curly or wispy ice-crystal forms

Activity E

Read the notes that follow the main ideas below and choose which is the best main idea to describe all of the notes. Then write an outline of the main idea and the four details from the notes.

Main Ideas

what a gemstone is

the value of gemstones

making imitation gemstones

Gemstones are treasured by many people. The value of these treasures is determined by many factors.

The brilliance and color of a stone determines its worth.

The hardness of the gem is important because the harder the gem, the longer it will last.

The way a stone is cut and polished affects its value. The rarest gemstones are the most valuable.

Writer's Corner

Choose a story or book that you like. Make an outline that summarizes the plot of the story. Choose at least three major events as main ideas. Remember to include at least two details for each main idea.

Compound Words

Compound words are two words joined together to form one word. In the research article on page 273, the sportswriter wrote about the sport of basketball. *Basketball* is a compound word. So is the word *sportswriter*. What other compound words are used in games?

What two words make up each of these compound words?

airport	sunflower	snowflake
farmyard	carefree	daydream
raincoat	hairbrush	lighthouse

The compound word *snowflake* is made up of *snow* and *flake*. Recognizing the two words that make up a compound word can help you figure out its meaning. A snowflake is a flake of snow.

Some compound words are written as two words. The words *firehouse* and *firefighter* are written as one word. But *fire station* and *fire engine* are not. Here are some other examples.

One Word	Two Words
airmail	air bag
waterbed	water bug

Compound words may also be hyphenated. For example, *half-dollar, great-grandson,* and *forget-me-not* are hyphenated compound words. Be sure to check a dictionary if you are not sure whether to write a compound word as one word, as two words, or as a hyphenated word.

• Activity A •

Tell the two words that make up each of these compound words. Then think of one or more compound words using the first part of each of these compound words.

newsstand   all-around

eyesight   everyone

hairbrush   sunlight

raincoat   seacoast

full-length   fingernail

• Activity B •

Make compound words by matching each word in Column A with an appropriate word in Column B.

Column A	Column B
1. head	a. mate
2. gold	b. strip
3. fire	c. bolt
4. class	d. phone
5. life	e. fish
6. thunder	f. guest
7. water	g. book
8. house	h. melon
9. air	i. cracker
10. match	j. saver

Writer's Corner

Write three sentences using as many compound words as you can. Be sure to write sentences that make sense. When you have finished, use a dictionary to check your compound words.

• Activity C •

Complete the sentences below by filling in the blanks to complete each compound word.

1. I think the baseball game will be rained out. I see thunder_____.

2. The first time Jake rode in a bumpy two-seat plane, he became air_____.

3. Our grandfathers were class_____ 60 years ago.

4. The life_____ wore sunblock to protect her from the sun.

5. Tim's mother bakes gooey home_____ cookies every Sunday.

6. My goggles are always full of water. They're not water_____.

7. My uncle loves the ocean so much that he's living in a house_____ in the San Diego harbor.

8. It's not cold at all, but my dad is still starting a fire in the fire_____.

• Activity D •

Form compound words by answering the questions below. The first part of the compound word is provided.

1. I am at the end of a fishing line. What am I? fish_____

2. I am a mark you leave on wet sand. What am I? foot_____

3. I will protect your horse's hoof. What am I? horse_____

4. I am a helper who cares for a baby. Who am I? baby_____

5. I am a container for a plant. What am I? flower_____

6. I am the residence for your pet dog. What am I? dog_____

7. I am the part of your home in which you sleep at night. What am I? bed_____

8. I am a delicious food made by cooking and crushing apples. What am I? apple_____

Activity E

Many compound words have a different meaning from that of the two words being combined. The pictures below represent two words that make up a compound word. Identify the two words that each picture represents. Then guess the compound word and look for its meaning in a dictionary.

1. _____

2. _____

3. _____

4. _____

5. _____

Writer's Corner

Write a sentence for each of the compound words in Activity E. Be sure your sentences show the actual meaning of the compound word.

Study Skills

Library Reference Materials

Reference books give information and facts about a wide variety of topics. They are kept in the reference section of the library. Reference books cannot be checked out, so they will always be available for you. Each reference book has a special purpose. Here are some common reference materials.

Encyclopedia

An encyclopedia is usually a set of books that contains articles about people, places, things, and events. The articles are often illustrated with pictures, diagrams, and maps.

Topics in encyclopedias are organized alphabetically. Each book, or volume, of an encyclopedia has a letter or letters on the spine that show the first letter of the topics in that book. Guide words can also help you find your topic.

You might need to look for keywords for your topic, just as you do when you search for information on the Internet. If you were researching cameras, you would probably look in the *C* volume. But if you wanted to find out how film is developed, you might need to brainstorm keywords such as *film* and *darkroom* to find the articles containing that information. Some encyclopedias have an index in the last volume. You might look up your keywords there to find which articles have information about your topic.

Atlas

An atlas is a book of maps. There are many kinds of maps. Some are like maps you've probably seen before that include roads, cities, and state and country borders. There are also maps that show climate, elevation, and geographical features. Some maps show information about where people live in an area and what goods are produced there. Some maps show the mountains and trenches under the ocean. And some maps show the average income of people who live in certain areas of a city.

Historical atlases can show you all the above information as it was in the past. For example, if you looked at a historical atlas of the United States, you could see how the borders have changed over the centuries.

Activity A

Read the questions below. Write the keyword or words under which you might look in an encyclopedia to find the answer to each question.

1. Who were the first people to settle in California?

2. How are clouds formed?

3. What were some of Julius Caesar's major accomplishments?

4. In what ways can solar energy be used?

5. What are the parts of the brain?

6. What are some of the important monuments in Greece?

7. What is the life cycle of a dragonfly?

8. How was the first computer invented?

Writer's Corner

Choose one of the questions from Activity A. Use an encyclopedia to find the answer to the question. Write a brief report to share your findings.

Almanac

An almanac is a reference book that is published every year. Much of the information in an almanac is facts and statistics that change often. In the most recent almanac, you can find up-to-date information about countries, governments, sports teams, and many other subjects. You can find out who won the last World Series and who the current ruler of Estonia is—or even if it's still called Estonia.

Specialized almanacs publish up-to-date information in a specific area. For example, a sports almanac lists historical and recent sports statistics.

Periodicals

Magazines are called periodicals because they are published periodically, such as once a month. Periodicals provide up-to-date information. Most libraries have recent issues of periodicals for you to browse. Older issues of periodicals are sometimes bound together as a large book. Another way of collecting older issues of periodicals is to put them on microfilm or microfiche. A librarian can show you how to use these materials. Sometimes an old periodical article can be useful to show you how people felt about a historical event at the time it happened.

Information in older issues of periodicals can be found by using an index or the *Readers' Guide to Periodical Literature*. A librarian can help you use these guides to find the articles you need.

Activity B

Tell whether you would use an encyclopedia, atlas, or almanac to find the following information. You might use more than one reference book for each topic.

1. the names of three different types of dinosaurs

2. how coal is formed

3. how many people live in China

4. the city where the tallest building in the United States is located

5. the name of a river that runs through Pennsylvania

Activity C

Tell which of these children's magazines, or periodicals, would most likely have information about the following topics.

Odyssey   *Cobblestone*
Ranger Rick   *Time for Kids*
Sports Illustrated for Kids

1. current political election results
2. life in colonial America
3. viewing the constellations
4. squirrels, raccoons, and other neighborhood animals
5. biographies of rookie baseball players

Activity D

Use a current almanac to answer these questions.

1. What is the population of New Zealand?
2. Who won last year's Nobel Peace Prize?
3. Who was Major League Baseball's Rookie of the Year last year?
4. Who is the current Prime Minister of Great Britain?
5. Who is the current governor of Texas?
6. What is the current population of Alaska?
7. What is the average age of people living in Iceland?
8. What won the National Book Award for fiction last year?

Writer's Corner

Choose a state in the United States that you would like to know more about. Use an encyclopedia, almanac, and atlas to find interesting facts about that state. Record two or more facts from each kind of reference book. Write a brief report that summarizes what you found.

Speaking and Listening Skills

Oral Research Reports

You will probably need to research things throughout your life for school, for work, and for your own information. You might research the history of a Caribbean island you plan to visit. You might research the diet of an iguana you want to buy as a pet. You might one day report groundbreaking research in front of a group of listeners. Here are some ideas for how to prepare and present an oral research report.

Purpose and Audience

Think about why you are sharing your information. The purpose of your talk can help you think about how you want to present your information. Are you trying to get others interested in something that interests you? Are you giving others information that will help them later?

Think about your audience. Keep in mind that your listeners have not done as much research as you have. Be sure to explain technical terms that they may not know.

Organization

Organize your oral research report the way you would organize a written research report. Making notes and an outline can help you organize the information you researched. Speak slowly and let your audience know how the parts of your research report are connected. Remember that a confused listener cannot go back and reread something the way that a reader can.

Visual Aids

Research reports have a lot of information. Listeners have to try hard to understand how all of that information is connected. One way you can help listeners is by providing one or more visual aids.

Visual aids can include pictures, maps, models, diagrams, posters, or drawings. Be sure that your visual aid will help readers understand, rather than get distracted from, the information. If your research report is about the Brazos River in Texas, listeners might find it helpful to see a map of where the Brazos River flows. It probably wouldn't be helpful if you showed them a glass of water from the river.

Make sure that everyone can see your visual aid. You might use a slide projector, make a poster, or have enough copies for all of your listeners.

Our Wide Wide World

A sheriff is usually the elected chief police officer of a county. A sheriff's responsibilities include overseeing jails, supervising deputy sheriffs, summoning individuals to court, and all-purpose police work.

• Activity A •

Reread the brief report that you wrote for the Writer's Corner on page 293. Then take turns sharing facts from your report with a group of your classmates. See whether they can guess which state you wrote about from the facts you present orally.

Speaker's Corner

Work with a partner to browse encyclopedias or Web sites to find an exotic location. It can be in the United States or in a different country. Decide with your partner which topic you would like to talk about in an oral research report. Work with your partner to check other reference books and Web sites. Collect information on your location and write on note cards the notes from your research.

Introduction and Conclusion

As in other kinds of writing and speaking, you will need an introduction and a conclusion. Begin with an introduction that grabs the audience's attention. You might start with an interesting question that you will answer in your report or an interesting fact that you discovered. In your conclusion, briefly restate your topic sentence. Emphasize what you want the audience to remember about your topic.

Prepare

If you have taken good notes and written an outline for your research report, much of your work is already done. Your outline can help you make note cards for your speech.

Write one or two note cards for your introduction. Be sure to include your topic sentence so that your audience knows what you will be talking about.

Use your outline to make note cards for the body of your report. Write the main ideas for the body at the top of several note cards. Then write supporting information for each main idea.

Write note cards for your conclusion. Think of a brief way to restate your topic sentence. Make a note card with a statement you want your audience to remember.

Practice

As with other kinds of speaking, it is important to practice. Be sure to speak clearly and slowly. Speak loudly enough for everyone to hear. If you plan to use a visual aid, practice using it. Be sure that everyone will be able to see it.

After you have practiced your oral research report a few times, you might want to practice with a friend or family member. Be sure to get feedback from your listener. See if you can make your oral research report clearer. Ask if your delivery was loud enough and slow enough for your listener to follow the information that you presented.

Listening Tips

Listening to a research report is a chance to learn something new. Here are some tips for listening to an oral research report.

- Make notes of what the speaker's topic sentence is and what each of the main ideas are. Think about whether the details support the main ideas.

- Pay attention to the speaker's visual aids. They may help you understand more about what the speaker is saying.

- If you are confused or if you want to know more, you may be able to ask questions after the speaker has finished.

Activity B ●

Use the notes you made for the Speaker's Corner on page 295 to write a topic sentence and an outline for a research report.

Activity C ●

Write an introduction and a conclusion for a research report on the exotic location you have been researching. Try to grab the reader's attention with an interesting question or fact.

Activity D ●

Use your outline and the introduction and conclusion you wrote to make note cards for an oral research report. Be sure you do not write your entire report on your note cards. Practice speaking your report, using your note cards.

Speaker's Corner

Practice your oral research report with the same partner who helped you research your topic. Talk with your partner about how your oral research reports are different, even though you started with the same information. Discuss why you organized your notes the way you did.

Research Reports

Prewriting and Drafting

In this chapter you have practiced the skills you need to write a research report. Now is the time to apply these skills to write your draft.

Prewriting

The sixth graders at Max's school go on an overnight field trip every year. The place the sixth graders visit is chosen from the suggestions made by students when they are in fifth grade.

Max decided to submit a research report for a place to visit next year. He knew that he would have to write a report that was neither too broad nor too narrow, that included many details, and that would be well researched.

Choosing a Topic

Max had always wanted to visit Mesa Verde National Park. Max decided to write his report about the park.

Because there was so much to write about, Max's father suggested that he narrow his topic. Since he was suggesting the park for a school trip, Max thought that a research report about the history of the park and some educational activities for students would be a good topic.

Your Turn

A research report is a chance for you to learn more about something that you are interested in. It can be related to anything you might want to know more about.

Choose a topic that is not too broad. Think about specific people, places, or events. Then decide what you want to know about your topic.

Researching

Max had two questions that he wanted his report to answer: "What is the history of Mesa Verde National Park?" and "What activities are there for kids to do?"

Keeping his questions in mind, Max went to the library and found some good sources. Then he did some research online. As he researched, he started thinking of other questions. He wrote a note card for each source with the information he would need for a Works Cited page.

Your Turn

What questions do you want your report to answer? Look for information to answer these questions. As you research, you might think of more specific questions. Write these questions at the tops of note cards and write the answers to the questions below. Write the source, author, and page number at the bottom of each note card.

Organizing Information

Max had gathered a lot of note cards with researched facts. He organized his cards into two piles. One pile was information about the history of the park. The other pile was about things to do at the park. He used the note cards to write an outline for his report. This is a part of Max's outline.

Max included on his outline a section each for his introduction, body paragraphs, and conclusion. He wrote a Roman numeral before each main idea. Then he listed details under each main idea and lettered them.

Your Turn

Organize your note cards in a way that makes sense to you. Sort your notes so that cards with related ideas are together.

Use your organized note cards to write an outline. Include sections on your outline for each part of your draft.

III. original inhabitants

    A. Anasazi, or ancient pueblos

    B. from AD 550 to about 1300

    C. reasons for disappearance

IV. Anasazi homes

    A. underground "pithouses"

    B. above-ground adobe villages

    C. cliff houses

Drafting

Max typed his first draft on a computer. The following paragraphs are from the introduction, the body, and the conclusion of Max's draft.

A Gift from the Past

At the southwestern tip of Colorado is a place known as the Four Corners. It is also where you can find Mesa Verde National Park. There are a lot of unusual trees there. Mesa Verde National Park has a rich and interesting history.

The Anasazi, or the ancient pueblos, were the first people to make their home in this area. They arrived in AD 550 and stayed for about 700 years. The Anasazi spread thrughout the South west and then in about 1300, all of the people disappeared and no one is sure what happened. They may have moved south along the Rio Grande and Colorado Rivers. Some people believe that droughts and dry land forced them to move on. Other people believe that the tribes had gotten too big and had used up all of the area's natural resources.

The next big discovery at Mesa Verde was made by Richard Wetherill and Charles Mason. Because of their discovery, they decided to explore some more. Richard Wetherill and his brothers went back many times between 1889 and 1892. Over that time they gathered eight different collections of Anasazi artfacts. They were out searching for lost cattle when they saw the Cliff Palace dwelling. Over the next two days, they found two more dwellings. Many explorers went to Mesa Verde to collect artifacts, which they would later sell. Finally, in 1906, Mesa Verde was made a national park. After that explorers could not collect and sell artifacts or destroy any part of the park.

Visiting Mesa Verde National Park is like taking a really awesome trip through time. Seeing the history of the park, and knowing just a little bit about the people who lived there, shows how even 1000 years ago people were different from us but like us at the same time.

Your Turn

Use your prewriting notes to write your first draft. Keep in mind the questions that you asked about your topic.

As you write your draft, you may find that some of your research does not fit in your report. You may find that you have to do additional research to support the direction your draft is taking. Make sure you give yourself enough time to make these changes as you work on your draft.

Research Reports

Content Editing

Max had found a lot of interesting information about Mesa Verde National Park. He was happy that he was able to use so many facts in his draft. But Max had read so much about the park that he wasn't sure if what he wrote in his draft made sense.

Max's next-door neighbor, Becky, was in his class at school. Becky was also writing a research report about a place for the sixth-grade class to visit. Max and Becky decided to content edit each other's reports. Here is the checklist they used.

Content Editor's Checklist

✓ Does the introduction include a topic sentence?

✓ Does each main idea support the topic sentence?

✓ Is each main idea supported with researched details?

✓ Does the conclusion summarize the topic sentence? Does it leave the readers with a sense that the topic was covered well?

✓ Does the report use formal language and a confident tone?

Becky read Max's draft. She told Max that Mesa Verde sounded like more fun than the place she had written about!

Becky then read the draft a few more times, using the Content Editor's Checklist. As she worked, she made notes about what she wanted to tell Max when they met to discuss their reports.

First Becky told Max that she hoped the principal chose Max's suggestion. She thought the park sounded like a lot of fun. She also told Max that she liked how his topic sentence was clearly stated in the introduction and how the main ideas of each paragraph supported the topic sentence. Then Becky gave Max her suggestions for improvements.

- You talk about the Four Corners in your introduction. Where is that?

- I don't think that the sentence about the trees in the introduction is necessary. You don't ever talk about them again in your report.

- The paragraph about Wetherill and Mason is confusing.

- In the very last paragraph, the words *really awesome* stick out. I don't think they are very formal.

Max was glad that Becky had content edited his draft. She had found a lot of things that he had missed.

Max used the Content Editor's Checklist to content edit the draft himself. He found a few more things that he wanted to change and one thing on the checklist that Becky had missed. Do you see what Becky forgot to check?

Your Turn

Work with a partner to content edit each other's work. Read the draft once to get an idea of what the report is about. Then read it again, using the Content Editor's Checklist. Take notes about your suggestions.

Meet with your partner to discuss your drafts. Don't forget to tell your partner what you liked about the report. Remember to give your suggestions in a constructive and positive way. Listen to your partner's suggestions with an open mind, but use only the suggestions that you think will improve your report.

Remember that it is also a good idea to content edit your own work. You might find something that your content editor missed. You might see places that need further revision.

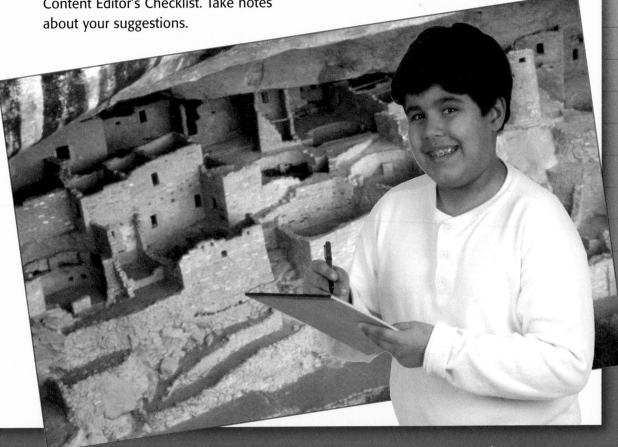

Revising

Here are the changes that Max made to his draft.

A Gift from the Past

At the southwestern tip of Colorado is a place known as the Four

It is the only place in America where four states touch. Utah, Colorado, Arizona, and

Corners. It is also where you can find Mesa Verde National Park. New Mexico meet there.

~~There are a lot of unusual trees there.~~ Mesa Verde National Park has

a rich and interesting history.

The Anasazi, or the ancient pueblos, were the first people to make their home in this area. They arrived in AD 550 and stayed for about 700 years. The Anasazi spread thrughout the South west and then in about 1300, all of the people disappeared and no one is sure what happened. They may have moved south along the Rio Grande and Colorado Rivers. Some people believe that droughts and dry land forced them to move on. Other people believe that the tribes had gotten too big and had used up all of the area's natural resources.

The next big discovery at Mesa Verde was made by Richard Wetherill and Charles Mason. Because of their discovery, they decided to explore some more. Richard Wetherill and his brothers went back many times between 1889 and 1892. Over that time they gathered eight different collections of Anasazi artfacts. They were out searching for lost cattle when they saw the Cliff Palace dwelling. Over the next two days, they found two more dwellings. Many explorers went to Mesa Verde to collect artifacts, which they would later sell. Finally, in 1906, Mesa Verde was made a national park. After that explorers could not collect and sell artifacts or destroy any part of the park.

You can Visiting Mesa Verde National Park is like taking a ~~really awesome~~ trip imagine yourself there weaving baskets, making pots or climbing a ladder to your room. through time. Seeing the history of the park, and knowing just a little bit about the people who lived there, shows how even 1000 years ago people were different from us but like us at the same time.

Look at the changes Max made.

- Max added a couple of sentences that explained the location of the Four Corners.

- He took out the unnecessary sentence mentioning trees.

- He took out the words *really awesome.* He agreed that the language wasn't very formal.

- Max agreed that the paragraph about Wetherill and Mason needed to be reordered.

Max added a sentence that summarized how the park is educational to make his conclusion stronger.

Your Turn
Use your partner's suggestions and your own ideas to revise your draft. When you have finished, use the Content Editor's Checklist again to check your draft.

Chapter 8 Editor's Workshop

Research Reports

Copyediting and Proofreading

Copyediting

Now that the ideas of his draft were strong, Max took some time to copyedit. He used this checklist to copyedit his draft.

Copyeditor's Checklist

✓ Has the writing been checked for rambling and run-on sentences?

✓ Are compound words used correctly?

✓ Is there variety in sentence length?

✓ Are exact words used to give the writing a confident tone?

✓ Do all the words mean what I think they mean?

Max found one place where he had written two separate words that should be one compound word. He changed *South west* to *Southwest* in the first paragraph of the part about the Anasazi.

Max found a place in the paragraph about Wetherill and Mason where he could combine sentences. Look at his revision below.

Revision: Because of their discovery, Richard Wetherill and his brothers came back many times between 1889 and 1892.

Max added the word *severe* to describe *droughts*. He thought that adding this descriptive word made his writing sound more confident.

Max found a run-on sentence in the first paragraph of the part about the Anasazi. He revised the sentence that begins *The Anasazi spread throughout . . .* into three separate sentences.

Your Turn

Read aloud your draft to hear how the language and tone sound. Then use the Copyeditor's Checklist to copyedit your draft.

It is always a good idea to have someone else check your work. Ask someone at home to use the Copyeditor's Checklist to copyedit your work.

Proofreading

Max wanted to have someone proofread his draft to make sure that there were no errors in spelling, punctuation, capitalization, or grammar.

Max's neighbor across the street, Professor Danvers, taught at the state university. Max asked her to proofread his research report. Professor Danvers used this checklist to proofread Max's draft.

Proofreader's Checklist

✓ Are the paragraphs indented?

✓ Have all the words been checked for spelling?

✓ Is the grammar correct?

✓ Are the sentences and proper nouns capitalized correctly?

✓ Has the writing been checked to make sure no new mistakes have been added?

Professor Danvers found only two misspelled words. One was in the part about the Anasazi. She changed *thrughout* to *throughout.* The other misspelled word was in the part about Wetherill. What word did Max misspell?

Professor Danvers noticed *pueblos* in the first sentence of the part about the Anasazi. She marked the change to *Pueblos*, because she knew that it was a proper noun.

She found one punctuation mistake. In the conclusion, Max had forgotten to put a comma between *pots* and *or* in the second sentence.

Your Turn

Read your draft again. Use the Proofreader's Checklist to check for misspelled words and mistakes in grammar, punctuation, and capitalization.

Trade drafts with a partner. Use the Proofreader's Checklist to proofread your partner's draft. Be sure to double-check whether the misspelled words you mark are really incorrect. Then return each other's papers and discuss the mistakes that you found.

Research Reports

Publishing

After a lot of work and several revisions, Max felt that his research report was ready to hand in to the principal. He made sure to include a Works Cited page so that the principal would know where he got all of his information. Now that he had learned so much about the park, he really hoped that his class would be going there next year!

A Gift from the Past

At the southwestern tip of Colorado is a place known as the Four Corners. It is the only place in America where four states touch. Utah, Colorado, Arizona, and New Mexico meet there. It is also where you can find Mesa Verde National Park. Mesa Verde National Park has a rich and interesting history.

The Anasazi, or the ancient Pueblos, were the first people to make their home in this area. They arrived in AD 550 and stayed for about 700 years. The Anasazi spread throughout the Southwest. Then, in about 1300, all of the people disappeared. No one is sure what happened. They may have moved south along the Rio Grande and Colorado Rivers. Some people believe that severe droughts and dry land forced them to move on. Other people believe that the tribes had gotten too big and had used up all of the area's natural resources.

The next big discovery at Mesa Verde was made by Richard Wetherill and Charles Mason. They were out searching for lost cattle when they saw the Cliff Palace dwelling. Over the next two days, they found two more dwellings. Because of their discovery, Richard Wetherill and his brothers went back many times between 1889 and 1892. Over that time they gathered eight different collections of Anasazi artifacts. Many explorers went to Mesa Verde to collect artifacts, which they would later sell. Finally, in 1906, Mesa Verde was made a national park. After that explorers could not collect and sell artifacts or destroy any part of the park.

Visiting Mesa Verde National Park is like taking a trip through time. You can imagine yourself there weaving baskets, making pots, or climbing a ladder to your room. Seeing the history of the park, and knowing just a little bit about the people who lived there, shows how even 1000 years ago people were different from us but like us at the same time.

Works Cited

Arnold, Caroline. *The Ancient Cliff Dwellers of Mesa Verde.* New York: Clarion Books, 1992.
Fisher, Leonard Everett. *Anasazi.* New York: Atheneum Books for Young Readers, 1997.
Hester, Thomas R. "Anasazi." *World Book Encyclopedia.* 2004 ed.
"Mesa Verde National Park." 16 Nov 2004 <www.mesa.verde.national-park.com>
Petersen, David. *Mesa Verde National Park.* Chicago: Children's Press, 1992.

Your Turn

Carefully copy your report in your neatest handwriting or type it on a computer. Don't forget to include a Works Cited page. Remember to proofread your Works Cited page to make sure that you have used the correct punctuation for each entry.

Decide as a class the best way to publish your reports. You might make a mini-encyclopedia by combining everyone's research reports within a single cover. Arrange the reports in alphabetical order and create a contents page. You might ask the librarian if it can be included with the library's reference materials.

PART
2

Grammar

Nouns

1.1   **Common Nouns and Proper Nouns**

1.2   **Singular Nouns and Plural Nouns**

1.3   **More Singular Nouns and Plural Nouns**

1.4   **Possessive Nouns**

1.5   **Collective Nouns, Count and Noncount Nouns**

1.6   **Nouns as Subjects and Subject Complements**

1.7   **Nouns as Objects**

1.8   **Nouns as Indirect Objects**

1.9   **Nouns in Direct Address**

1.10   **Words Used as Nouns or as Verbs**

1.11   **Words Used as Nouns or as Adjectives**

Noun Challenge

1.1 Common Nouns and Proper Nouns

A **noun** is a word that names a person, a place, or a thing.

A **common noun** names any one of a class of persons, places, or things.

Person	Place	Thing
skater	rink	ice skates
citizen	country	flag
writer	library	book
president	park	award

A **proper noun** names a particular person, place, or thing. Proper nouns begin with capital letters.

Person	Place	Thing
Michelle Kwan	California	Olympics
Nelson Mandela	South Africa	Nobel Peace Prize
Columbus	Spain	*Santa Maria*
Jimmy Carter	Disneyland	Bill of Rights

Exercise 1

Tell whether each of these nouns names a person, a place, or a thing. Tell whether each is a common noun or a proper noun.

1. James Naismith
2. Massachusetts
3. inventor
4. Central Park
5. artist
6. gym
7. soccer
8. Canada
9. United Nations
10. governor
11. teacher
12. scoreboard
13. Indiana Pacers
14. Pablo Picasso
15. surfboard

Exercise 2

Identify the nouns in each sentence. Tell whether each names a person, a place, or a thing. Tell whether each is a common noun or a proper noun. The number of nouns in each sentence is shown in parentheses.

1. Michael Jordan was born in New York. (2)
2. When Michael was a baby, his family moved to North Carolina. (4)
3. Jordan played basketball in high school. (3)
4. The teen was cut from the team. (2)
5. His determination and his practice got the young man back on the team. (4)
6. The young athlete later led the University of North Carolina to a national championship. (3)
7. Jordan helped the United States win a gold medal at the Olympics. (4)
8. The now-respected player joined the Bulls, the professional team in Chicago. (4)

Exercise 3

Complete each sentence with nouns.

1. I like to play _____ and _____.
2. My favorite athletes are _____ and _____.
3. Sports I like to watch are _____ and _____.
4. The _____ and the _____ are places where I play sports.

Practice Power

Write as many nouns as you can think of related to an athlete or a sport that interests you. Identify each as a common or a proper noun.

1.2 *Singular Nouns and Plural Nouns*

A **singular noun** tells about one person, place, or thing. A **plural noun** tells about more than one.

> Sally Ride was an *astronaut.* (singular)
> Sally Ride and Kathryn Sullivan were *astronauts.* (plural)

The plural of most nouns is formed by adding *-s* to the singular form.

Singular	Plural	Singular	Plural
ship	ships	airport	airports

Add *-es* to form the plural of nouns ending in *s, x, z, ch,* and *sh.*

Singular	Plural	Singular	Plural
box	boxes	watch	watches
gas	gases	dish	dishes

For nouns ending in *y* after a consonant, change the *y* to *i* and add *-es.*

Singular	Plural	Singular	Plural
baby	babies	cherry	cherries

For nouns ending in *y* after a vowel, simply add *-s.*

Singular	Plural	Singular	Plural
day	days	valley	valleys

For most nouns ending in *f* or *fe*, add *-s.*

Singular	Plural	Singular	Plural
roof	roofs	safe	safes

For some nouns ending in *f* or *fe,* form the plural by changing the *f* or *fe* to *v* and adding *-es.*

Singular	Plural	Singular	Plural
leaf	leaves	shelf	shelves

Exercise 1
Write the plural of each noun.

1. journey
2. airplane
3. lunch
4. ray
5. machine
6. loss
7. penny
8. thief
9. bus

Exercise 2
Find the nouns in each sentence. The number of nouns is shown in parentheses. Tell whether each noun is singular or plural.

1. Sally Ride first wanted to be a tennis player but later studied science. (3)
2. Ride heard that NASA was looking for astronauts. (3)
3. Her studies included jumps with parachutes. (3)
4. Ride was the first U.S. woman to orbit Earth. (3)

Exercise 3
Complete each sentence with the plural of the nouns in parentheses.

1. Sally Ride went on two space _____ (flight), spending a total of 14 _____ (day) in space.
2. Her _____ (duty) included helping during _____ (launch) and conducting _____ (experiment).
3. On one mission the _____ (astronaut) took peanut butter, _____ (loaf) of bread, and _____ (candy).
4. Sally is one of the _____ (advocate) of science education.

Practice Power

Choose one paragraph from a newspaper article. List each noun. Write *S* if the noun is singular and *P* if it is plural.

1.3 *More Singular Nouns and Plural Nouns*

For a noun ending in *o* after a vowel, form the plural by adding *-s* to the singular.

Singular	Plural	Singular	Plural
radio	radios	rodeo	rodeos

For a noun ending in *o* after a consonant, form the plural by adding *-es* to the singular.

Singular	Plural	Singular	Plural
potato	potatoes	hero	heroes

For some nouns ending in *o* after a consonant, however, the plural is formed by simply adding *-s*.

Singular	Plural	Singular	Plural
piano	pianos	solo	solos

Some singular nouns use a different word to show the plural.

Singular	Plural	Singular	Plural
goose	geese	man	men
woman	women	ox	oxen
child	children	mouse	mice
tooth	teeth	person	people

Some nouns use the same word for both singular and plural.

Singular	Plural	Singular	Plural
deer	deer	fish	fish
sheep	sheep	series	series
Iroquois	Iroquois	species	species

Use a dictionary to check plural forms.

Exercise 1
Write the plural of each noun.

1. tomato
2. studio
3. shrimp
4. silo
5. foot
6. moose
7. echo
8. trio
9. alto
10. mosquito
11. salmon
12. corps

Exercise 2
Complete each sentence with the plural of the noun or nouns in parentheses.

1. In colonial days _____ (person) did different tasks.
2. The _____ (woman) often gathered to make quilts.
3. The _____ (man) worked together to build houses.
4. The _____ (child) did work in the home.
5. The girls would cook the meals and do the _____ (dish).
6. The boys would feed the farm _____ (animal): _____ (turkey), _____ (chicken), _____ (goose), and _____ (calf).
7. Instead of horses, farmers sometimes used _____ (ox).
8. The _____ (sheep) provided wool to make clothing.
9. Warm _____ (scarf) and _____ (shawl) were made from this animal fiber.
10. Crops grown in the _____ (colony) included _____ (tomato), _____ (bean), and _____ (pumpkin).

Practice Power

Write the plural form of these nouns. Use each in a sentence of your own.

1. **hero**
2. **photo**
3. **statue**
4. **fish**
5. **chimpanzee**
6. **country**

1.4 *Possessive Nouns*

The **possessive form** of a noun expresses possession, or ownership. The apostrophe (') is the sign of a possessive noun.

> *Kevin's* tuba is in its case.

The tuba belongs to Kevin. The word *Kevin's* is a possessive noun.

To form the singular possessive, add an apostrophe and *s* to the singular form of the noun.

> The *singer's* voice was powerful.

To form the possessive of plural nouns ending in -*s*, add an apostrophe only.

> The *singers'* voices were loud.

To form the possessive of plural nouns that do not end in -*s*, add -*'s*.

> The *women's* voices were beautiful.

The possessive of a singular proper noun ending in *s* is formed by adding -*'s*. The plural possessive of a proper noun is formed just as the plural possessive of a common noun is formed.

> *James's* song in the recital was in Spanish.
> The *Phillipses'* home was the site of many concerts.

Exercise 1

Write the singular possessive and the plural possessive form of each noun.

Example: baby   baby's   babies'

1. sister
2. child
3. puppy
4. goose
5. teacher
6. player
7. bear
8. dinosaur
9. athlete

Exercise 2

Identify the possessive noun in each sentence. Tell whether it is singular or plural in form.

1. Andres Segovia's work elevated the place of the guitar in classical music.

2. Before Segovia many people's view was that the guitar was neither a serious nor an important instrument.

3. Composers' works for orchestras did not include guitar.

4. Segovia played classical musicians' works on his guitar.

Exercise 3

Rewrite the following phrases, using singular possessive nouns.

Example: the performance of the guitarist
     the guitarist's performance

1. the guitar of the musician
2. the efforts of this man
3. the music of Bach
4. the lessons of the teacher
5. the applause of the audience
6. the sound of the orchestra

Exercise 4

Rewrite the following phrases, using plural possessive nouns.

Example: the performances of the guitarists
     the guitarists' performances

1. the legacy of the musicians
2. the voices of the sopranos
3. the cases of the violinists
4. the lessons of my teachers
5. the sound of the drums
6. the works of classical composers

Practice Power

Write about a famous musician or singer. Include at least three possessive nouns in your writing.

1.5 *Collective Nouns, Count and Noncount Nouns*

A **collective noun** names a group of persons, animals, places, or things that are considered a unit. A collective noun usually acts as a singular noun.

The *public* likes stories of impossible victories.

Here is a list of some common collective nouns.

army	couple	herd
audience	crowd	jury
bunch	faculty	orchestra
cast	family	staff
class	flock	swarm
club	government	team
committee	group	troop

Count nouns name items that can be counted separately. These nouns have singular and plural forms: *one player, two players.*

Noncount nouns name items that cannot be counted separately. These nouns usually do not have plural forms. Noncount nouns generally take singular verbs.

Lasting *fame* was gained by the 1980 U.S. hockey team.

Here is a list of some common noncount nouns:

butter	flour	nature
clothing	hair	salt
cotton	homework	sugar
dirt	luggage	traffic

Many noncount nouns name ideas:

advice	faith	independence
childhood	freedom	liberty
courage	happiness	loyalty
education	hope	sportsmanship

Exercise 1
Write a collective noun for each word. Use it in a sentence.

Example: players   team   I am on the soccer team.

1. students
2. grapes
3. sheep

4. soldiers
5. teachers
6. spectators

7. relatives
8. actors
9. musicians

Exercise 2
Identify the collective noun in each sentence.

1. The 1980 U.S. Olympic hockey team won a gold medal.
2. This bunch of players obviously was skilled.
3. The audience filled the arena at Lake Placid, New York, for the final game against the Soviet Union.
4. The home crowd was excited and boisterous.
5. A committee voted them into the Hockey Hall of Fame.

Exercise 3
Tell whether each noun in italics is a count noun or a noncount noun.

1. The coach, Herb Brooks, and his *assistants* studied the other teams closely and came up with game plans.
2. The coach's *leadership* was important.
3. He emphasized speed and *discipline.*
4. The U.S. team scored four *goals* against the Russians.
5. *People* around the world heard the news of their victory.

Practice Power

Choose three collective nouns and three noncount nouns that relate to things in your life. Use them in sentences about yourself.

1.6 *Nouns as Subjects and Subject Complements*

A noun can be the **subject** of a verb. The subject tells what a sentence is about.

> *Martin Luther King, Jr.,* was born on January 15, 1929.

The subject of this sentence is *Martin Luther King, Jr.* To find the subject, ask *who* or *what* before the verb. Who was born? The answer is *Martin Luther King, Jr.*

A noun can be a **subject complement.** A subject complement follows a linking verb, such as *am, is, are, was,* or *were.* It renames the subject.

> Martin Luther King was a *minister.*
> (Martin Luther King = minister)

The subject complement in this sentence is *minister.*

Exercise 1

Complete each sentence with a subject noun. Use each of these nouns only once.

hometown	marches	King	country	people

1. King's childhood _____ was Atlanta, Georgia.

2. His _____ helped Americans understand the existence of inequality in the country.

3. _____ used words to win fights, not violence.

4. _____ crowded his church for his powerful sermons.

5. The _____ changed because of his work.

Exercise 2
Identify the subject in each sentence.

1. Martin Luther King, Jr., skipped ninth and twelfth grades.

2. Morehouse College admitted him at the age of fifteen.

3. His ordination as a minister occurred in 1948.

4. A church in Montgomery, Alabama, offered him the position of pastor.

5. The young minister became an important figure in the civil rights movement, a crusade for equal rights for blacks.

6. A national holiday in January marks his birthday.

7. People admire King for his courage.

Exercise 3
Identify the subject in each sentence. Then identify the subject complement.

1. Gandhi was an inspiration to Martin Luther King, Jr.

2. Gandhi was a supporter of nonviolent protest in India.

3. King was a determined leader.

4. King was a powerful speaker.

5. His speech was an invitation to action.

6. King was the youngest winner of the Nobel Peace Prize.

7. King was the victim of an assassination in 1968.

8. King's widow is Coretta Scott King.

Practice Power

Write six sentences about Martin Luther King, Jr. Use encyclopedias, books, or the Internet for information. Use at least two nouns as subject complements. Underline the subjects and the noun subject complements in your sentences.

1.7 Nouns as Objects

A noun can be used as a **direct object** of a verb. The direct object answers the question *whom* or *what* after an action verb.

In this sentence the direct object is *cartoons*. It answers the question *What did Charles Schultz draw?*

Charles Schultz drew *cartoons*.

In this sentence the direct object is *Charles Schultz*. It answers the question *Whom did the readers of Peanuts appreciate?*

Readers of the *Peanuts* comic strip appreciated *Charles Schultz*.

A noun can be the **object of a preposition.** Prepositions show place, time, direction, and relationship. Some prepositions are *at, by, for, from, in, into, of, on, to, with,* and *without.* A prepositional phrase consists of a preposition and a noun or a pronoun, which is the object of the preposition. In the first sentence, *of* is the preposition and *children* is the object of the preposition. In the second sentence, *in* is the preposition and *newspapers* is the object of the preposition.

The *Peanuts* comic strip featured a group <u>of</u> <u>children.</u>
The strip appeared <u>in</u> many <u>newspapers</u>.

Exercise 1
Complete each sentence with a direct object.

1. I really enjoy _____.
2. I read _____.
3. I watch _____.
4. I play _____.
5. I study _____.
6. I am learning _____.
7. I might get _____.
8. I often eat _____.

Exercise 2
Identify the direct object in each sentence.

1. Charles Schultz created famous characters.
2. Schultz created Charlie Brown.

3. Readers loved the ordinary boy.

4. Charlie had problems.

5. For example, he didn't often win his baseball games.

6. Schultz had a smart dog with the name of Spike.

7. Spike inspired the creation of the dog Snoopy.

8. We read Snoopy's thoughts in cartoon bubbles.

9. One character, Linus, always carries a blanket.

10. The character Lucy has superior knowledge about everything.

Exercise 3
Identify the preposition or prepositions in each sentence. Then identify the object of each.

1. Charles Schultz wrote about everyday problems.

2. Newspapers throughout the world published his comics.

3. *Peanuts* reached millions of readers in 75 countries.

4. Fans of the cartoonist read his comic strips eagerly.

5. People identified with Schultz's characters.

6. Experiences with failure are part of everyone's life.

7. Schultz worked primarily in his studio in California.

8. He wrote and drew *Peanuts* for 50 years.

9. Charles Schulz left his imprint on people's lives.

10. The work of Schultz still makes us think—and smile.

Practice Power

Write six sentences about a character from a cartoon or a fiction book. Underline each direct object and each object of a preposition. You might start this way:

I like [name of the character]. I like ____ about ____.
I first read ____ in ____.

1.8 Nouns as Indirect Objects

A noun can be the indirect object of a verb. The **indirect object** tells *to whom, to what, for whom,* or *for what* the action was done. In this sentence the direct object is *compassion.* The indirect object is *people.* It answers the question *to whom* after the verb: *To whom did Mother Teresa show compassion?*

	Verb	Indirect Object	Direct Object
Mother Teresa	showed	*people*	*compassion.*

Here is a list of verbs that can take indirect objects.

assign	get	owe	send
bring	give	pay	show
buy	hand	promise	teach
deny	lend	read	tell
forgive	offer	sell	write

A sentence can have an indirect object only if it has a direct object. The indirect object always comes after the verb and before the direct object. Can you find the verb, the direct object, and the indirect object in this sentence?

Mother Teresa offered poor people help.

You're correct if you said the verb is *offered.* What did Mother Teresa offer? The answer is *help,* the direct object. To whom did she offer help? The answer is *people,* the indirect object.

Exercise 1
Identify the indirect object in each sentence. The direct object is italicized.

1. The young Agnes Gonxha Bojahiu offered God her *life.*

2. At first, as a nun in India, she taught young girls *religion.*

3. In 1948 the Church granted Sister Teresa *permission* for a different kind of work.

4. She offered the very poorest people *service.*

Exercise 2

Identify the direct object and indirect object in each sentence.

1. Many women gave Mother Teresa their help.

2. Mother Teresa and her nuns gave the hungry food.

3. They offered homeless people shelter.

4. Her work gained the dedicated nun international attention.

5. People gave her causes both money and help.

6. According to Mother Teresa, she owed God all her success in the service of others.

7. The Nobel Committee awarded the nun its peace prize in 1979 for her service to others.

8. In 2003 Pope John Paul II gave Mother Teresa the title of *Blessed*, a step toward sainthood.

Exercise 3

Rewrite the sentences, adding indirect objects. Use the nouns in parentheses.

1. The schoolwide committee told its plans for the fundraising project—a secondhand-item sale. (classes)

2. Many students promised their help. (the committee)

3. People gave old clothes and other items. (the students)

4. The students sold these items at low prices. (customers)

5. The students gave the money to help the poor in India. (a charity)

Practice Power

Choose five verbs from the list of verbs that can take indirect objects. Use the verbs in sentences with indirect objects.

1.9 *Nouns in Direct Address*

A noun in **direct address** names the person spoken to. A noun used in direct address is set off from the rest of the sentence by a comma or commas.

> *Class,* here are the scripts for our play on the American Revolution.
> Do you know your lines, *Alicia?*
> Be sure, *Ryan,* that you bring your costume.

In the first sentence *class* names a group of people being spoken to and is, therefore, a noun used in direct address. *Alicia* and *Ryan* name individuals being spoken to and so are nouns in direct address. Because *Ryan* appears in the middle of the sentence, it is set off by two commas, one before and one after the noun.

Exercise 1
Identify the noun in direct address in each sentence.

1. Do you want to help make the costumes, Louise?

2. Doug, are you making the scenery?

3. Lee, help me make signs for the colonists to carry.

4. Mei Ling, do you have the No Taxation Without Representation sign?

5. What's your role in the play, Jason?

6. Here is your Betsy Ross costume, Amanda.

7. I lost my tricorn, Ms. Bryne.

8. Go to your place, Jack, with the rest of those in the Boston Tea Party.

9. Please hand me my wig, Rosalie.

10. Ben is sick today, so, Kevin, you'll play John Adams.

Exercise 2

Rewrite the sentences. Use commas to set off the nouns of direct address in these sentences.

1. Say your lines louder Elaine.

2. Michael where is the script for the narrator?

3. Lilian put your hat on straight.

4. Students it's time for the play to start.

5. Congratulations fifth graders on a great job.

Exercise 3

Tell how the italicized nouns are used in the sentences. Tell whether each is a subject, a subject complement, a direct object, an indirect object, or a noun in direct address.

1. The 13 colonies wanted *independence* from Britain.

2. The colonies paid *England* taxes.

3. The *colonies* had no voice in the decisions of the British government.

4. At the Boston Tea Party, colonists threw tea into the *harbor* as a protest against unfair taxes.

5. Paul Revere was a *leader* of the protest.

6. John Adams was a lawyer from *Massachusetts.*

7. He supported *independence* for the colonies.

8. According to tradition, Betsy Ross sewed the first American flag, with 13 *stars* in a circle.

9. Who was the first signer of the declaration, *Mr. Daniels*?

Practice Power

Pretend you are cleaning out the garage or attic with your family. Write a script about things you find and give directions about what to do with the items.

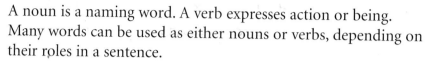

1.10 *Words Used as Nouns or as Verbs*

A noun is a naming word. A verb expresses action or being. Many words can be used as either nouns or verbs, depending on their roles in a sentence.

In this sentence *practice* is a noun because it names a thing.

> Our *practice* lasted for about an hour.

In this sentence *practice* is a verb because it tells about an action.

> We *practice* soccer every day.

Tell whether each word in italics is a noun or a verb.

> **A.** Leg *stretches* are really important.
> **B.** Each team member *stretches* before practice.

You're correct if you said *stretches* is a noun in the first sentence. It is the subject of the verb *are*. In the second sentence *stretches* is a verb. It describes an action performed by the subject.

Exercise 1

Tell whether each italicized word is a noun or a verb.

1. If I stretch before a game, I usually *play* better.
2. The coach always goes over each *play* before a game.
3. In practice we always work on our *passes.*
4. Our coach always *passes* the ball to each player.
5. Last night I missed my first *pass.*
6. This was really a *surprise* to me!
7. It *surprised* the coach too.
8. The next thing we worked on was *kicks.*
9. My first *kick* missed the goal.
10. I didn't *kick* the ball hard enough.

Exercise 2

Tell whether each italicized word is a noun or a verb. If the word in italics is a verb, write a new sentence using it as a noun. If the word in italics is a noun, write a new sentence using it as a verb.

1. During each soccer *practice* our coach instructs us on technique.

2. These drills greatly *help* our playing skills.

3. We worked on push *passes* last night.

4. According to our coach, we will *try* this movement several times each day.

5. The coach said a player should *approach* the ball with his or her foot aligned with the ball.

6. My first *attempt* was not very successful.

7. I didn't *address* the ball at an angle.

8. We will *study* passes again during our next session.

Exercise 3

Write sentences, using each word as a noun and as a verb. Tell how you use each.

1. dance
2. photograph
3. pilot
4. camp
5. work
6. dream
7. stay
8. plant
9. shop
10. blossom
11. copy
12. drop

Practice Power

Write a short paragraph about an experience you had while trying to learn something new. Include some of these words. Then tell whether they serve as nouns or verbs: *study, try, experiment, surprise, play, step, cause, start, result, hope, end, plan.*

1.11 Words Used as Nouns or as Adjectives

A noun names a person, place, or thing. An adjective describes a noun. Many words can be used as either nouns or adjectives.

In this sentence the word *baseball* is a noun because it names a thing. It acts as the direct object of the verb *enjoy*.

We really enjoy *baseball.*

In this sentence the word *baseball* is an adjective because it describes the noun *team*.

I play on the *baseball* team at school.

Tell whether each italicized word is a noun or an adjective.

A. It is important to be a *team* player.
B. Our *team* got ready for the game by stretching.

You are correct if you said that the word *team* is an adjective in sentence A. It describes the noun *player*. The word *team* is a noun in sentence B. It is the subject of the sentence.

Exercise 1
Tell whether each italicized word is a noun or an adjective.

1. Do you know any *woman* who played professional baseball?

2. *Women* players helped keep baseball alive during World War II.

3. Philip K. Wrigley was the owner of the Wrigley Company and of a baseball *team* called the Chicago Cubs.

4. A league of women's *teams,* called the All American Girls Softball League, was organized in 1943 with his support.

5. The teams played *professional* baseball and had more than a million fans.

6. Each woman player earned a good salary and was pleased to be a *professional.*

Exercise 2

Complete each sentence with one of the following words. Tell whether it is used as a noun or an adjective.

women	baseball	public	spring	league

1. Baseball played by _____ players was somewhat different.

2. During the early years of the league, the _____ used a large ball and pitched it underhand.

3. Later the _____ was smaller and they threw overhand.

4. The women included some outstanding _____ players.

5. _____ interest in the league was high.

6. The _____ loved going to see these professional players.

7. In the _____ the women would train.

8. _____ training began in May.

9. The _____ championship was decided by play-off games.

Exercise 3

Write two sentences with each word, using it once as a noun and once as an adjective. Tell how you use the word in each sentence.

1. ocean
2. newspaper
3. school
4. kitchen
5. rain
6. street
7. forest
8. farm
9. computer
10. sale
11. apple
12. holiday

Practice Power

Use your imagination. Write a story that uses as many of the words below as you can. Tell whether you use the words as nouns or adjectives.

prize   garden   family   city   newspaper   house

school   television   zoo   surprise   silver

Noun Challenge

Read the selection and answer the questions.

1. Did you know, class, that some plants live on insects? 2. For instance, the butterwort plant catches its prey on its sticky leaves. 3. The plant's leaf rolls up on the trapped insect. 4. Juices from the leaf dissolve the insect's body. 5. Like the leaves of a butterwort, the sticky leaves of a sundew plant are a trap for a careless intruder. 6. Another plant, the Venus's flytrap, captures its dinner in its "fingers." 7. Slowly, the liquid from the leaf digests the victim. 8. Nature's insect-eating plants have given writers ideas for many horror books and movies!

1. In sentence 1 name a noun in direct address.

2. In sentence 2 how would you write the singular form for the word *leaves*?

3. In sentence 3 name the subject of the sentence.

4. In sentence 4 name the direct object of the verb *dissolve.*

5. In sentence 5 name a subject complement.

6. In sentence 6 name a prepositional phrase. What is the object of the preposition?

7. In sentence 6 is the noun *plant* count or noncount?

8. In sentence 7 name the direct object.

9. In sentence 7 is the noun *liquid* count or noncount?

10. In sentence 8 name the possessive noun.

11. In sentence 8 what is the indirect object?

12. List at least four singular nouns and four plural nouns from this paragraph.

13. In sentence 2 is the word *prey* a noun or a verb?

14. In sentence 8 is the word *horror* a noun or an adjective?

Pronouns

2.1   Singular Pronouns and Plural Pronouns

2.2   Personal Pronouns

2.3   Subject Pronouns

2.4   Object Pronouns

2.5   Indirect Objects

2.6   Uses of Pronouns

2.7   Possessives

2.8   Intensive Pronouns, Reflexive Pronouns

2.9   Antecedents

2.10   Pronouns and Contractions

2.11   Demonstrative Pronouns, Interrogative Pronouns

Pronoun Challenge

2.1 *Singular Pronouns and Plural Pronouns*

A **pronoun** takes the place of a noun. A **personal pronoun** changes form depending on who or what is referred to and on the role it plays in a sentence.

> Homer was a famous Greek writer. *Homer* lived many hundreds of years ago.
>
> Homer was a famous Greek writer. *He* lived many hundreds of years ago.

Pronouns help avoid repetition of the same word. In the second set of sentences above, the pronoun *he* is used instead of the noun *Homer*. In this way *Homer* does not need to be repeated.

A personal pronoun is **singular** when it refers to one person, place, or thing. The pronoun *he* is singular.

> *He* is famous for writing poems of adventure.

A personal pronoun is **plural** when it refers to more than one person, place, or thing. The pronoun *we* is plural.

> *We* are going to read about the adventures of Odysseus.

Here is a list of the personal pronouns.

Singular	Plural
I, me, mine	we, us, ours
you, yours	you, yours
he, him, his	they, them, theirs
she, her, hers	
it, its	

Exercise 1
Identify the personal pronoun in each sentence.

1. We still read stories from ancient Greece.

2. They frequently tell about gods and goddesses.

3. Some, however, tell us about the deeds of human heroes.

4. Do you know much about Mount Olympus?

5. It was the home of the gods.

6. Aphrodite was a Greek goddess, and she was beautiful.

7. Have you heard of Odysseus?

8. His was an epic tale that included many adventures.

9. They were written about in two long poems by Homer.

10. One of them is called *The Odyssey.*

Exercise 2

Identify the personal pronoun in each sentence. Tell whether it is singular or plural.

1. We read about the Trojan War.

2. It was won by the crafty Greeks.

3. Tricks are often used in wartime, and theirs helped to conquer the Trojans.

4. The Greeks fooled them with a wooden horse filled with soldiers.

5. Odysseus was clever, and he thought of the trick.

6. Homer gave us the story of the war in *The Iliad.*

7. He tells the story of Odysseus's long journey home to his wife, Penelope, in *The Odyssey.*

8. She waited for Odysseus's return for many years.

Practice Power

Paint a picture of someone with words. Choose one person—a friend, a family member, or a neighbor. Tell about things you and this person do together. Write five sentences. Use the personal pronouns you studied in this lesson.

2.2 *Personal Pronouns*

A personal pronoun names the speaker; the person spoken to; or the person, place, or thing spoken about.

The personal pronouns that name the speaker are *I, me, mine, we, us,* and *ours.* These are **first person** pronouns.

> *I* read the stories from *The Odyssey* in class last year.
> The teacher told *us* about Homer.

The personal pronouns that name the person spoken to are *you* and *yours.* These are **second person** pronouns. *You* and *yours* can be singular or plural.

> What do *you* know about Odysseus?

The personal pronouns that name the person, place, or thing that is spoken about are *he, him, his, she, her, hers, it, its, they, them,* and *theirs.* These are **third person** pronouns.

> *She* offered to lend me a copy of *The Odyssey.*
> *They* wanted to read more myths.
> I lent my copy of the book to *him.*

Exercise 1
Identify the personal pronoun that names the speaker in each sentence.

1. We studied ancient Greece.

2. Our teacher assigned us a project.

3. She said that ours could be on mythology.

4. I chose the adventures of Odysseus as my topic.

Exercise 2
Identify the personal pronoun that names the person spoken to in each sentence.

1. Have you ever read *The Odyssey*?

2. I told you about this wonderful story, didn't I?

3. When can you help me with this project on *The Odyssey*?

4. Is this project yours?

Exercise 3

Identify the personal pronoun or pronouns that name the person or thing spoken about in each sentence.

1. Odysseus wanted to go home after the Trojan War, but he and the crew encountered many problems along the way.

2. At one point, they arrived at the island of Lotus Eaters.

3. The people there gave them a magical flower to eat.

4. It made the crew forget about their homes and wives.

5. Odysseus had to force the crew to return to the ships, and thus he saved them from the flower's spell.

Exercise 4

Complete each sentence with a personal pronoun. Use the directions in parentheses.

1. _____ read about the Lotus Eaters. (speaker, plural)

2. Do _____ know the story? (person spoken to)

3. The flower filled the men's minds with music, and _____ didn't want to leave. (person spoken about, plural)

4. Odysseus's wife was waiting for him; _____ was named Penelope. (person spoken about, singular)

Practice Power

Write an e-mail with at least four sentences to a friend. Tell the friend about a book you have read. Explain why it would be enjoyable to read. Use personal pronouns in your sentences.

2.3 *Subject Pronouns*

A personal pronoun may be used as the subject of a sentence. Here is a list of the **subject pronouns.**

Singular	Plural
I	we
you	you
he, she, it	they

A subject pronoun tells who or what the sentence is about. To find the subject of a sentence, ask *who* or *what* before the predicate.

> *They* came upon an island.

Who came upon an island? The answer is *they.* The pronoun *they* is the subject of the sentence.

A subject pronoun can also take the place of a noun used as a subject complement. A subject complement follows a linking verb and refers to the same person, place, or thing as the subject of the sentence.

> The captain of the ship was *he.*

The pronoun *he* is a subject complement in this sentence. *He* renames the subject, *captain.*

Exercise 1
Identify the pronoun used as a subject in each sentence.

1. He landed on Circe's island with his crew.

2. It was a beautiful island.

3. She was a bewitching enchantress.

4. They became friends.

5. I wondered about the dangers ahead on the trip.

6. Do you know the story of any of these dangers?

Exercise 2
Replace the italicized noun or phrase in each sentence with the correct pronoun.

1. *Circe* warned Odysseus to beware of the singing Sirens.
2. *Their music* was both sweet and bewitching.
3. *Ships* tried to draw near the music but hit sharp rocks.
4. *Odysseus* didn't put wax in his ears as his men did.
5. *The song* enticed him to join the Sirens.
6. *Ropes,* however, held him tightly to the mast.

Exercise 3
Identify the pronoun used as a subject complement in each sentence.

1. The person who faced many dangers was he.
2. The creatures who enticed Odysseus were they.
3. The sailors who bound Odysseus to the mast were they.
4. The person Odysseus wanted to see again was she.

Exercise 4
Replace the italicized noun or phrase in each sentence with the correct pronoun.

1. The woman who warned Odysseus was *Circe.*
2. The person tied to the mast was *Odysseus.*
3. The voyagers from Ithaca were *Odysseus and his crew.*
4. The creatures whose songs were deadly were the *Sirens.*

Practice Power

Imagine you are introducing your family to the class. Use personal pronouns as subjects and subject complements to describe hobbies and activities that you all enjoy.

2.4 *Object Pronouns*

A personal pronoun may be used as the direct object of a verb. Here is a list of the **object pronouns.**

Singular	Plural
me	us
you	you
him, her, it	them

Use object pronouns for direct objects. A **direct object** names the receiver of the action of the verb. To find a direct object, ask *whom* or *what* after the predicate.

> Odysseus heard *them.*

Odysseus heard what? The answer is *them,* the direct object.

An object pronoun may be used as the object of a preposition. A preposition shows a relationship between two words in a sentence. An **object of a preposition** follows a preposition, such as *about, at, between, by, for, from, in, into, of, on, to, under, next to, under,* and *with.*

> The crew sailed *with him.*

In this sentence the preposition is *with.* The object of the preposition is *him.*

Exercise 1

Identify the pronoun used as a direct object in each sentence.

1. Odysseus's friend Circe told him about the dangers of Scylla and Charybdis.

2. He thanked her for the warnings.

3. Odysseus and his men saw them in the distance.

4. The swirling waters of the whirlpool Charybdis, on the left, identified it.

5. Scylla's cave, on the right, hid her.

Exercise 2

Replace the italicized noun or phrase in each sentence with the correct pronoun.

1. The whirlpool Charybdis might pull *the ship* down.

2. The six-headed monster Scylla ate *sailors*.

3. How could the ship pass *Scylla and Charybdis* safely?

4. The problem intrigued *my friend and me*.

Exercise 3

Identify the pronoun used as an object of a preposition in each sentence.

1. Circe gave warnings, and Odysseus listened to her.

2. Odysseus saw two cliffs and had to sail between them.

3. On the left was Charybdis, and the ship could easily be swallowed by it.

4. On the right Scylla's arms and heads were a danger to him.

Exercise 4

Replace the italicized noun or phrase in each sentence with the correct pronoun.

1. Odysseus and his crew were frightened by *the dangers*.

2. Scylla was hidden in *her cave.*

3. She sprang out and grabbed six men in *her powerful jaws.*

4. The ship passed, however, without any more danger from *Scylla.*

Practice Power

You and a friend have been chosen to take a magic-carpet ride to an exotic place. You see unusual things and meet many interesting people. Write a paragraph about your trip. Use as many object pronouns as you can.

2.5 *Indirect Objects*

Some sentences contain two objects: a direct object and an indirect object. The direct object is the receiver of the action. The **indirect object** tells *to whom, for whom, to what,* or *for what* the action is done.

> Circe gave *him* advice.

The direct object answers *whom* or *what* after the verb. *Circe gave what?* The answer is *advice,* the direct object. *To whom did Circe give advice?* The answer is *him. Him* is the indirect object. *Him* tells *to whom* the advice was given.

A noun used as an indirect object can be replaced by an object pronoun.

> Odysseus gave *the sailors* their orders.
> Odysseus gave *them* their orders.

Object pronouns are used as indirect objects: *me, us, you, him, her, it,* and *them.*

Here are some verbs that may take indirect objects: *assign, bring, buy, deny, do, forbid, give, grant, hand, lend, offer, pay, promise, read, refuse, sell, send, show, sing, teach, tell, wish,* and *write.*

Can you identify the indirect object in this sentence? What pronoun can replace the indirect object?

> Odysseus told Circe his story.

The indirect object is *Circe.* The pronoun *her* can replace *Circe.*

> Odysseus told *her* his story.

Exercise 1

Identify the personal pronoun used as an indirect object in each sentence. The direct object is italicized.

1. Prometheus stole fire from Olympus for humans and gave them this *gift.*

2. Zeus had denied them *fire.*

3. Zeus sent him a cruel *punishment.*

4. Calling an eagle, he assigned it a *task:* to gnaw at Prometheus's body every day.

5. To punish humans, Zeus sent them the first *woman.*

6. He gave her a *box.*

7. He told her the *dangers* of opening the box.

8. Pandora's opening of the box brought them many *evils,* such as greed and envy.

Exercise 2

Replace the italicized noun or phrase in each sentence with the correct pronoun.

1. Eos, the goddess of dawn, offered *a handsome king* eternal love.

2. The gods granted *Eos* a request.

3. They gave *her husband* eternal life but not youth.

4. Her husband grew old and shriveled, and she made *the now-old man* a home in a tiny box.

5. Athena, the goddess of wisdom, taught *pupils* crafts.

6. One of her pupils, Arachne, showed *people* her work.

7. People told *the goddess* stories of Arachne's skills as a weaver.

8. Eventually her mocking of the gods cost *Arachne* her human life, and she was turned into a spider by Athena.

Practice Power

Write several sentences about gifts that you have given friends and family members for Christmas or birthdays. Explain who each person is. Use personal pronouns.

Example: Sarah is my best friend. I gave her a CD of a favorite singer.

2.6 Uses of Pronouns

Pronouns are used in different ways in sentences. The **subject pronouns** are *I, you, he, she, it, we,* and *they.* Each can be used as the subject of a sentence or as a subject complement.

> *I* would like to read the adventures of Odysseus. (subject)
> The owner of the book is *she.* (subject complement)

The **object pronouns** are *me, you, him, her, it, us,* and *them.* Each can be used as the direct object or the indirect object of a sentence, or as the object of a preposition.

> I told *them* about Odysseus's adventures. (direct object)
> I loaned *her* my copy of *The Odyssey.* (indirect object)
> The stories about *him* are fascinating. (object of a preposition)

Can you choose the correct pronoun to complete the sentence?

> My friend and (I me) are doing a report on *The Iliad.*

You are correct if you said *I.* It is part of the compound subject of the sentence. Don't be confused if a pronoun is part of a compound. Look for how the pronoun acts in the sentence.

Exercise 1
Complete each sentence with the pronoun *I* or *me*.

1. Will you lend ____ your copy of Homer's *Iliad?*

2. ____ need to go to the library for a copy.

3. My friend and ____ enjoyed the story of the Sirens.

4. Tell ____ the story of the Sirens.

5. That copy of *The Odyssey* belongs to ____.

Exercise 2
Complete each sentence with the pronoun *he* or *him*.

1. ____ arrived back in his country after 20 years.

2. A goddess warned ＿＿ of dangers.

3. ＿＿ and his son plotted to destroy his wife's suitors.

4. The beggar in Penelope's home was ＿＿.

5. No one recognized ＿＿.

Exercise 3
Complete each sentence with the pronoun *she* or *her*.

1. Odysseus's wife was Penelope; he had left ＿＿ many years before to fight in the Trojan War.

2. ＿＿ and her son did not know whether Odysseus was alive.

3. Many suitors wanted to marry ＿＿.

4. ＿＿ began to weave a tapestry.

5. ＿＿ promised to marry when it was finished.

Exercise 4
Complete each sentence with the pronoun *they* or *them*.

1. ＿＿ believed Penelope's promise to ＿＿.

2. Penelope didn't tell ＿＿ her secret.

3. She would weave the threads during the day and then rip ＿＿ out each evening.

4. She was waiting for her husband's return and wasn't interested in ＿＿.

5. ＿＿ fled or were killed by Odysseus and his son.

Practice Power

Write a paragraph about an activity that you have participated in, such as baking cookies or going to a ball game. Use personal pronouns in your paragraph. When you are finished, circle each pronoun and note whether it is a subject pronoun or an object pronoun.

2.7 Possessives

A **possessive pronoun** shows possession, or ownership. A possessive pronoun takes the place of a possessive noun.

> This report on the Sirens is *Sarah's.* (possessive noun)
> This report on the Sirens is *hers.* (possessive pronoun)

Here is a chart of the possessive pronouns.

	Singular	Plural
First person	mine	ours
Second person	yours	yours
Third person	his, hers, its	theirs

Note the spelling of the forms. Unlike possessive nouns, possessive pronouns do not contain apostrophes. A possessive pronoun stands alone and is not followed by a noun.

A **possessive adjective** also shows possession. A possessive adjective is always used with a noun. Remember that a possessive pronoun stands alone and a possessive adjective always precedes a noun.

> The book is *mine.* (possessive pronoun)
> This is *my* book. (possessive adjective)

Here is a chart of the possessive adjectives.

	Singular	Plural
First person	my	our
Second person	your	your
Third person	his, hers, its	their

Exercise 1

Identify the possessive pronoun in each item.

1. Helen was a beautiful woman. According to tradition, the fault for the Trojan War was hers.

2. Hercules was superhuman. An extraordinary strength was his.

3. The gods ruled from Mount Olympus. Theirs were special golden thrones on the mountain.

4. The Muses were each associated with one of the arts, and theirs was the gift to make magnificent music together.

5. Atlas was a powerful creature finally defeated by Zeus; his was the job of holding up the world.

Exercise 2
Identify the possessive adjective in each item.

1. Bellerophon was a hero in Greek mythology. The ability to tame horses was one of his special gifts.

2. Pegasus was a winged flying horse. Its job was to carry Zeus's thunderbolts.

3. Bellerophon and Pegasus acted as a team in facing their very difficult task of defeating the Chimera.

4. The Chimera was a hideous monster. Her body had parts of a lion, a goat, and a snake.

5. Many men had tried to slay the Chimera, but all their attempts were unsuccessful.

Exercise 3
Tell whether the possessives in the following sentences are adjectives or pronouns.

1. The students displayed their projects on ancient Greece.

2. His was made of balsa and tissue paper.

3. Ours was devoted to Pegasus, the winged horse.

4. Your model of Mount Olympus was the best!

5. Medusa's head with its many serpents was spectacular.

Practice Power

Imagine that you went to a science fair or an art show at school. Tell about the projects you saw. Use possessive pronouns and possessive adjectives in your writing.

2.8 *Intensive Pronouns, Reflexive Pronouns*

Intensive and reflexive pronouns end in *-self* or *-selves*.

	Singular	Plural
First person	myself	ourselves
Second person	yourself	yourselves
Third person	himself, herself, itself	themselves

An **intensive pronoun** is used to emphasize a noun that comes before it. In this sentence *himself* emphasizes *Odysseus,* the noun that comes before it.

Odysseus *himself* devised a plan to win the Trojan War.

A **reflexive pronoun** is used as the direct or indirect object of a verb or the object of a preposition. It generally refers to the subject of the sentence. In this sentence *himself* is an indirect object. It refers to the subject of the sentence, *Odysseus.*

Odysseus earned *himself* a reputation as a smart leader.

Can you find the reflexive pronoun in the following sentence? What role does it play in the sentence? What word does it refer to?

Some Greeks hid themselves inside a large horse to get within the gates of Troy.

You are correct if you said that the reflexive pronoun is *themselves.* It is the direct object of the verb *hid,* and it refers to the third person plural noun *Greeks.* The words *hisself* and *theirselves* are not acceptable terms and should never be used in speaking or writing.

Exercise 1
Identify the intensive or reflexive pronoun or pronouns in each sentence. Tell what word each refers to.

1. Zeus himself, the chief god, was the father of Hephaestus.

2. Hera herself, the chief goddess, was his mother.

3. The gods often bickered among themselves.

4. Once Hephaestus tried to break up a quarrel between his parents and was thrown to earth by the angry Zeus himself.

5. Hephaestus injured himself badly when he fell.

6. A sea goddess found him and nursed him herself.

7. From then on, Hephaestus couldn't walk by himself.

8. He built himself two special robots of gold and silver who were able to think for themselves.

9. They themselves were large enough to help the husky Hephaestus move himself around.

10. The powerful Hephaestus himself was actually most famous as the blacksmith for the gods.

Exercise 2

Complete the sentences with intensive or reflexive pronouns. Each should refer to the italicized word in the sentence.

1. *We* decided on our project for the unit among _____.

2. *I* made a chart of the gods by _____.

3. *Amy* _____ could name 20 gods and goddesses.

4. *Mr. Peterson* _____ praised our work.

5. Dave, *you* can see our project _____ in the library.

6. The *projects* _____ show a lot of hard work.

7. The model *robot* can move by _____.

8. The *students* are very proud of _____.

Practice Power

Imagine that you are giving a surprise party for your parents. What do you need to do by yourself? What do your brother and sister need to do by themselves? Write a detailed account of the planning procedure. Use intensive and reflexive pronouns in your writing.

2.9 *Antecedents*

The word to which a pronoun refers is its **antecedent.** The antecedent is the word that the pronoun replaces.

> Did *Odysseus* return home? Yes, *he* did, but only after many difficulties.

The pronoun *he* refers to the noun *Odysseus* in the question. *Odysseus* is the antecedent of *he*.

> *The Iliad* is an epic poem. *It* was written by Homer.

The pronoun *it* refers to *The Iliad* in the previous sentence. The antecedent of *it* is *The Iliad*.

The pronoun must agree with its antecedent in person and number and in whether it refers to a male, a female, or a thing. In the first example *he* is the third person singular male to agree with *Odysseus*. In the second example *it* agrees with a third person singular thing, *The Iliad*.

What is the antecedent of the italicized pronoun in this set?

> Sarah worked on a project on Odysseus. *She* looked for information about him on the Internet.

You are correct if you said the antecedent is the noun *Sarah*. *She* is third person singular female; it agrees with *Sarah*.

Exercise 1
Identify the pronoun for the italicized antecedent.

1. *Orpheus* was a figure in Greek myth, and he had an interesting story.

2. Orpheus had a special *ability.* It was to make beautiful music.

3. His mother was one of the *Muses.* They were patron goddesses of such arts as painting, dance, and music.

4. When *Orpheus* was grown, he brought music to the earth.

5. He fell in love with a *woman,* and she loved him in return.

6. *Orpheus and Eurydice* married, and they were happy.

Exercise 2
Identify the antecedent for the italicized pronoun.

1. One day a snake bit Eurydice; *it* had a deadly poison.

2. Eurydice fell to the ground, where *she* died.

3. Hermes, the messenger god, came for Eurydice, and *he* gently carried her to the underworld.

4. Orpheus was sad, and *he* lost all joy in life.

5. He searched for the underworld's entrance and found *it.*

6. As *he* walked, Orpheus played sad music.

7. He wanted to meet Hades and ask *him* to free Eurydice.

8. Hades and his queen were crying; the music moved *them.*

9. The queen was sad, and *she* begged for Eurydice's release.

10. Hades consented, but *he* set a condition.

Exercise 3
Complete each sentence with a pronoun. The antecedent for the pronoun is italicized.

1. Orpheus agreed to the *condition*; _____ was to not look at Eurydice until they were outside of the underworld.

2. If Orpheus looked at his *wife* on the way, _____ would have to return to the underworld forever.

3. *Orpheus* started out eagerly, but then _____ began to doubt.

4. He heard *footsteps* behind him, but were _____ Eurydice's?

5. Orpheus turned and got just a brief glimpse of *Eurydice* before _____ was banished to the underworld forever.

Practice Power

Write about a Greek myth. Use the library or the Internet for information. Use personal pronouns. Remember to match pronouns with antecedents.

2.10 Pronouns and Contractions

Personal pronouns can be joined with some verbs to form contractions. An apostrophe (') replaces the missing letter or letters in contractions.

Here is a list of common **contractions** that contain pronouns:

I'm = I am	I've = I have
you're = you are	you've = you have
he's = he is *or* he has	she's = she is *or* she has
it's = it is *or* it has	
we're = we are	we've = we have
they're = they are	they've = they have

Will can also be joined with pronouns to form contractions: *I'll, you'll, we'll, she'll, he'll,* and *they'll.*

I've read about Gaia. = *I have* read about Gaia.
She's been called Mother Earth. = *She has* been called Mother Earth.

Possessive adjectives are often confused with contractions. Possessive adjectives express possession but do not contain apostrophes.

Pronoun + Verb	Possessive Adjective
You're (= You are) late.	Your report is late.
It's (= It is) long.	Its title is "Greek Gods."
They're (= They are) old.	Their story is long.

Exercise 1
Identify the contraction in each sentence. Write the words that make up the contraction.

1. I've read an interesting Greek myth.

2. It's about two strong brothers, Otus and Ephiatles.

3. "I'm worried about Otus and Ephiatles," said Zeus.

4. "They're more than 60 feet tall and still growing."

Exercise 2
Write the contractions for the italicized words.

1. Mother Earth, an enemy of Zeus, said, "*You are* strong."
2. "*You will* be able to overthrow Zeus."
3. The brothers said, "*She has* given us good advice."
4. They said, "*We are* going to build a mountain."
5. "*It is* going to be as big as Mount Olympus."
6. From its top, they called, "Zeus, *you have* ruled too long."
7. Otus said, "I love Artemis, and *I will* marry her."
8. Zeus said, "*I am* sending thunderbolts against you."
9. Ephiatles shouted, "*They are* not strong enough to hurt us."
10. Apollo said to Zeus, "*I have* got a plan."
11. Apollo shouted, "Artemis said *she is* willing to marry you."
12. "*She will* meet you on the island of Naxos."

Exercise 3
Choose the correct word or words to complete each item.

1. Apollo told Artemis, "Go to Naxos. There (your you're) going to change yourself into a deer."
2. "(You're Your) going to dart between the brothers."
3. "Instead of shooting the deer, (their they're) going to shoot each other, and the victory will ours."
4. (It's Its) exactly what happened.

Practice Power

Write clues to the identification of a character from Greek mythology or from a subject you're studying in class. Use contractions with pronouns in them. Exchange your clues with classmates. How many characters can you name?

2.11 *Demonstrative Pronouns, Interrogative Pronouns*

Demonstrative pronouns are used to point out people, places, and things.

Singular	Plural
this	these
that	those

Use *this* and *these* to point out things that are near.

> **These** are books of myths.

Use *that* and *those* to point out things that are farther away.

> **That** was my favorite book.

Because *this* and *that* are pronouns, they stand alone.

An **interrogative pronoun** is used to ask a question. The interrogative pronouns are *who, whom, what,* and *whose.*

> **What** happened after Pandora opened the box?

The interrogative pronoun *who* is used when the person is the subject of a sentence.

> **Who** opened the box that released evils into the world?

Who is the subject of *opened.*

The interrogative pronoun *whom* is used when the person is the object of a verb or a preposition.

> **Whom** did Prometheus help?

Whom is the direct object of the verb *help.*

The interrogative pronoun *whose* is used to ask about ownership.

> **Whose** was the punishment that resulted in being gnawed by an eagle?

Exercise 1

Identify the demonstrative pronoun in each sentence. Tell whether it is singular or plural.

1. Those are nonfiction books.
2. This is the section with fiction books.
3. These are all books of myths.
4. Is that a good book to read?

Exercise 2

Complete each sentence with a demonstrative pronoun. Follow the directions in parentheses.

1. I found _____ in the library. (singular, far)
2. _____ are all books from the library. (plural, near)
3. _____ are all myths. (plural, far)
4. Have you read _____? (singular, near)

Exercise 3

Complete each sentence with the correct interrogative pronoun.

1. (Who Whom) was Zeus?
2. To (whom who) did Prometheus give fire?
3. (What Whose) was Prometheus's punishment?
4. (Whose Whom) was the job of bringing life to earth?
5. (Whose Who) was the box that released evils into the world?
6. (Who Whom) gave Pandora the box?
7. (Who Whom) did Zeus send to the world with a box?

Practice Power

Write five questions about Greek myths. Use interrogative pronouns. Ask about characters and things that you want to know more about.

Pronoun Challenge

Read the paragraph and answer the questions.

1. In 1804 Meriwether Lewis and William Clark set out on their famous expedition. 2. They wanted to explore the western United States and find a water route connecting the Mississippi River and the Pacific Ocean. 3. At this time only Native Americans lived there. 4. One Soshoni woman, Sacagawea, guided them on their journey. 5. In addition, she obtained food and ponies for them by trading with the Native American peoples. 6. Without her help, the trip could not have continued. 7. In their diaries Lewis and Clark praised her. 8. What would they have done without her help? 9. This is a question historians often ask. 10. She herself is one of the reasons for their success. 11. We Americans should thank her because a good deal of the credit for the success of the expedition is hers.

1. Name the personal pronoun in sentence 2.
2. Tell whether the pronoun in sentence 2 is singular or plural.
3. In sentence 3 substitute a personal pronoun for *Native Americans.*
4. In sentence 4 is the personal pronoun a subject or an object pronoun?
5. Name the pronoun used as the subject of the sentence in sentence 5.
6. In sentence 5 the pronoun *she* takes the place of what noun?
7. Name a pronoun used as an object in sentence 7.
8. Name the interrogative pronoun in sentence 8.
9. Name the demonstrative pronoun in sentence 9. Is it singular or plural?
10. Find the intensive pronoun in sentence 10.
11. Name a possessive pronoun in sentence 11.
12. In sentence 11 find a pronoun naming the speaker.

Adjectives

3.1   Descriptive Adjectives

3.2   Proper Adjectives

3.3   Articles

3.4   Repetition of Articles

3.5   Demonstrative Adjectives

3.6   Adjectives That Tell How Many

3.7   Subject Complements

3.8   Adjectives That Compare

3.9   *More, Most* and *Less, Least*

3.10 *Fewer, Fewest* and *Less, Least*

3.11 Interrogative Adjectives

Adjective Challenge

3.1 Descriptive Adjectives

An **adjective** describes a noun. Adjectives that tell about the size, shape, color, or weight of the things they describe are called **descriptive adjectives.** They can tell how something looks, tastes, smells, or feels.

> Mark made a model of a dinosaur with claws.
> Mark made a model of a *gigantic brown* dinosaur with *long, sharp* claws.

The words *gigantic, brown, long,* and *sharp* were added to the second sentence. These words are adjectives. *Gigantic* and *brown* tell about the noun *dinosaur. Long* and *sharp* tell about the noun *claws.*

A descriptive adjective generally comes before a noun. Can you find the descriptive adjectives in these sentences? Which noun does each describe?

> Dinosaurs are large animals.
> Dinosaurs could be fierce hunters.

In the first sentence the adjective *large* describes the noun *animals.* In the second sentence the adjective *fierce* describes the noun *hunters.*

Exercise 1

Find the descriptive adjectives in these sentences. The number of adjectives in each is in parentheses.

1. *Dinosaur* means "terrible lizard." (1)

2. Dinosaurs were the dominant species on earth for millions of years. (1)

3. Like modern reptiles, dinosaurs probably had green or brown skin. (3)

4. Small dinosaurs that ate meat were usually speedy animals so that they could escape large predators. (3)

5. Dinosaurs that ate plants were often huge animals. (1)

6. Tracks show that big dinosaurs walked in long, easy steps. (3)

Exercise 2
Find the descriptive adjectives in these sentences. Tell which noun each describes.

1. Paleontologists have difficult jobs.

2. They spend long hours looking for fossils of dinosaurs.

3. They do slow, painstaking work.

4. New dinosaurs are always being discovered.

5. Fossils form as the hard, bony parts of an animal turn to stone.

6. The soft parts just dissolve and disappear.

7. Brittle fossils can easily break up as they are being removed, and so they need to be handled with special care.

8. Fossils are generally found in dry, rocky areas.

Exercise 3
Add a descriptive adjective before each noun.

1. _____ dinosaurs

2. _____ snakes

3. _____ skyscraper

4. _____ artist

5. _____ sandwich

6. _____ movie

7. _____ jacket

8. _____ story

Exercise 4
Add a noun after each descriptive adjective.

1. loud _____

2. delicious _____

3. muddy _____

4. smooth _____

5. polite _____

6. swift _____

7. green _____

8. funny _____

Practice Power

Choose three objects or people. Use three descriptive adjectives to describe each.

3.2 *Proper Adjectives*

A proper noun names a particular person, place, or thing. Some descriptive adjectives come from proper nouns and are called **proper adjectives.** Like proper nouns, proper adjectives begin with capital letters.

Proper Noun	Proper Adjective
Africa	African
America	American
Arab	Arabic, Arabian
Celt	Celtic
France	French
Freud	Freudian
Greece	Greek
Hungary	Hungarian
Japan	Japanese
Jefferson	Jeffersonian
Mexico	Mexican
Moses	Mosaic
Poland	Polish
Rome	Roman
Shakespeare	Shakespearean
Sweden	Swedish
Victoria	Victorian

Exercise 1

Write a proper adjective for each proper noun. Use a dictionary to check your spelling.

1. Russia _____
2. George _____
3. Spain _____
4. Carolina _____
5. Bible _____
6. Cuba _____
7. Edward _____
8. Ireland _____
9. Amazon _____
10. Egypt _____
11. Elizabeth _____
12. Vietnam _____

Exercise 2

Choose five proper adjectives that you wrote in Exercise 1. Write five sentences, each using one of the proper adjectives.

Exercise 3

Complete each sentence with a proper adjective formed from the proper noun in parentheses.

1. Fossils of one of the largest plant-eating dinosaurs, *Argentinosaurus,* are found only on the _____ continent. (South America)

2. A complete skeleton of *Tyrannosaurus rex* is in a _____ museum. (Midwest)

3. Mary Anning, a _____ fossil hunter of the nineteenth century, found many important fossils. (Britain)

4. _____ scientists began discovering and studying other fossils at about the same time. (Europe)

5. A large armored dinosaur, *Minmi,* was named after an _____ town. (Australia)

6. *Huayangosaurus* is named after a _____ province. (China)

7. *Edmontonia,* a spiked dinosaur, is named after a _____ city. (Canada)

8. *Triceratops* was as big as a present-day _____ elephant. (Africa)

9. The *Leaellynasaura* lived in the cold climate of the _____ Circle. (Antarctica)

10. One amazing fossil, now in an _____ museum, shows a *Velociraptor* attacking another dinosaur. (Asia)

Practice Power

Imagine you have just returned from a trip around the world. Use proper adjectives in sentences that tell about five things you brought back with you as souvenirs.

3.3 *Articles*

A, an, and *the* are **articles.**

A and *an* are **indefinite articles.** An indefinite article refers to any one of a class of things.

> *A* fossilized cockroach that lived in North America many years ago was discovered by geologists.
> *An* estimate of its age is 300 million years.

A is used before words beginning with a consonant sound. *An* is used before words beginning with a vowel sound.

Vowel Sounds	Consonant Sounds
an iceberg	a stone
an egg	a nest
an hour	a unit

If the article precedes a descriptive adjective, the article agrees with the vowel sound of the adjective: a *large* microscope, an *old* microscope.

The is the **definite article.** It refers to one or more specific persons, places, or things.

> *The* fossil of this cockroach was discovered by geologists from Ohio State University.
> *The* roach lived 55 million years before *the* dinosaurs!
> *The* scientist told us that crocodiles, crabs, and some roaches lived at *the* same time as *the* early dinosaurs.

Exercise 1
Write the correct indefinite article, *a* or *an*, before each item.

1. _____ ocean
2. _____ pebble
3. _____ archaeologist
4. _____ bug
5. _____ web

6. _____ insect
7. _____ eagle
8. _____ geologist
9. _____ fossil
10. _____ ancient fossil

Exercise 2

Identify the articles in each sentence. Tell whether each is a definite article or an indefinite article.

1. A fossil of a cockroach was found by geologists, and the ancient insect was about three-and-a-half inches long.
2. The insect was twice as large as the typical modern roach.
3. It was discovered in a coal mine in Ohio.
4. The color pattern of the ancient cockroach was still visible.
5. The well-preserved cockroach was a welcome find, but a live roach generally remains an unwelcome guest in most places!
6. Geologists discovered a fossil of another insect.
7. The prehistoric creature was five feet long and one foot wide!

Exercise 3

Complete the sentences by adding an indefinite article (*a* or *an*) or the definite article (*the*) in each blank. More than one choice may be correct for some blanks.

1. What is _____ palmetto bug?
2. Believe it or not, _____ insect is really _____ kind of roach!
3. It is _____ largest cockroach in North America and is most common in _____ Deep South.
4. _____ person might find _____ insects under _____ sink or in _____ closet.
5. _____ discovery of palmetto bugs is usually _____ surprise—and _____ unpleasant one at that!
6. I saw _____ palmetto bug when I was in Florida.
7. It was _____ strange sight!

Practice Power

Write about any strange animal that you know about. Underline each article you use in your sentences.

3.4 *Repetition of Articles*

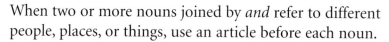

When two or more nouns joined by *and* refer to different people, places, or things, use an article before each noun.

> *The* paleontologist and *the* geologist worked together to find the fossils.

In the above example two different people are mentioned. The repetition of the article before the two nouns shows this.

When two or more nouns joined by *and* refer to the same person, place, or thing, use an article before the first noun only.

> *The* paleontologist and professor organized a dig.

In the above example one person is mentioned. The article *the* is used only before the first noun.

Which of the following refers to more than one person?

A. a student and aspiring paleontologist
B. the photographer and the biochemist
C. the professor and leader of the dig crew

The correct answer is B because the photographer and the biochemist are two different people.

Exercise 1

Tell whether each italicized phrase refers to one person, place, or thing or to more than one. Check for repetition of the article.

1. *A writer and an illustrator* worked together on the book about dinosaurs that I used for my report.

2. *A writer and editor* has written an interesting book about dinosaurs.

3. *A young rancher and rodeo cowboy* discovered a dinosaur skeleton in 1998.

4. *The museum guide and volunteer* gave us a lecture about dinosaurs.

5. *Scientist and professor* Paul Sereno has made some amazing discoveries of early dinosaurs in Argentina.

Exercise 2

Add an article where an article is needed. Put an X if none is needed. Look at the description of the number of people.

1. *There was one judge*: _____ science teacher and _____ fair director picked the best project.

2. *There were two presenters*: _____ principal and _____ district superintendent presented the prize.

3. *One student did the project*: _____ writer and _____ illustrator of the project on dinosaurs was a fifth grader.

4. *Two students worked on the project together, doing different tasks*: _____ writer and _____ illustrator of the winning project on dinosaurs were fifth-grade students.

Exercise 3

Complete the paragraph with articles. Put an X if no article is needed. More than one article may be correct in some cases.

My class and I went to visit (1) _____ museum with many exhibits on dinosaurs. There was even (2) _____ dig site where visitors to (3) _____ museum could actually look for fossils. I used (4) _____ chisel and (5) _____ brush to uncover my fossil! In another area I touched (6) _____ tooth from (7) _____ *T. rex* and (8) _____ horn from (9) _____ *Triceratops.* Bold visitors put their hands between (10) _____ sharp teeth of a dinosaur skull. (11) _____ museum also featured (12) _____ skeleton of (13) _____ *Gigantosaurus.* Some say that it was (14) _____ largest meat eater ever to walk the earth! (15) _____ volunteer guide and (16) _____ former teacher was working preparing fossils in a lab. We were able to see her work and ask her questions.

Practice Power

Have you ever seen a dinosaur exhibit in a museum? Have you ever watched a film about dinosaurs? Write a letter to a friend about what you saw. Underline the articles in your sentences.

3.5 Demonstrative Adjectives

A **demonstrative adjective** points out a specific person, place, or thing and is more specific than an *a, an,* or *the.* The demonstrative adjectives are *this, that, these,* and *those.* They come before nouns and point out *which one* or *which ones.*

This and *that* point out one person, place, or thing. *These* and *those* point out more than one person, place, or thing.

This and *these* point out items that are near. *That* and *those* point out items that are farther away.

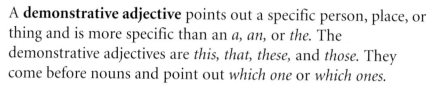

> *This* fossil belonged to a raptor. (singular, near)
> *That* tool is used by paleontologists. (singular, far)

> *These* teeth are from a *T. rex.* (plural, near)
> *Those* horns are from a *Triceratops.* (plural, far)

Which nouns do the demonstrative adjectives point out?

> I think these skeletons are amazing.
> That dinosaur is a *Velociraptor.*

In the first sentence *these* points out the plural noun *skeletons.* In the second sentence *that* goes with the singular *dinosaur.*

Exercise 1
Put the correct demonstrative adjective before each noun to name an object or objects near at hand.

1. _____ skeleton
2. _____ guide
3. _____ eggs

4. _____ pictures
5. _____ fossils
6. _____ tool

Exercise 2
Put the correct demonstrative adjective before each noun to name an object or objects far away.

1. _____ plants
2. _____ skull
3. _____ trees

4. _____ nest
5. _____ behavior
6. _____ exhibit

Exercise 3

Identify the demonstrative adjective in each sentence. Tell whether it is singular or plural and tell the noun it goes with.

1. This skull is from a *Herrerasaurus,* an early dinosaur from the Triassic period.

2. That period is often called "the age of reptiles."

3. These drawings show the plants that grew during the Jurassic period.

4. During this period dinosaurs were dominant.

5. Look at those two huge skeletons of *Tyrannosaurus rex.*

6. They're attacking that *Triceratops.*

7. Those animals lived during the Cretaceous period.

8. At the end of that period, dinosaurs became extinct.

Exercise 4

Write the correct word to complete each sentence. Follow the directions in parentheses.

1. _____ exhibit at the museum is amazing. (near)

2. _____ workers are actually preparing and cleaning fossils. (far)

3. _____ brushes are used to remove dirt from fossils. (near)

4. _____ tool looks like a dentist's drill; it removes extraneous material from fossils. (far)

5. Let's ask _____ woman about her work. (far)

6. _____ are real dinosaur eggs—or at least fossils. (near)

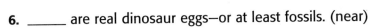

Practice Power

Write a paragraph that details a tour of a place you find interesting—any place, such as the school cafeteria, a museum, or even a room in your home. Use demonstrative adjectives as you point out objects. Underline those adjectives in your writing.

3.6 *Adjectives That Tell How Many*

Some descriptive adjectives tell *how many* or *about how many*. Each of these adjectives comes before a count noun.

A number can be used as an adjective that tells how many.

   one photograph   *fifty* bones   *20* tour guides

A word that tells number order can be an adjective that tells how many.

   the *first* visit   the *10th* trip   the *hundredth* visitor

The following words can be used as adjectives that tell about how many.

all	each	few	much	some
any	either	many	neither	
both	every	most	several	

All dinosaurs died out millions of years ago.
Every student in my class is interested in dinosaurs.

What is the adjective that tells how many in the sentence?

   The huge *Brachiosaurus* ate many plants in order to survive.

You're correct if you said *many*. It tells about the noun *plants*.

Exercise 1
Add an adjective that tells how many or about how many. The adjective should go with the noun.

1. _____ horns

2. _____ bones

3. _____ feet

4. _____ miles per hour

5. _____ teeth

6. _____ years

7. _____ scientists

8. _____ fossil

Exercise 2
Use the phrases you wrote in Exercise 1 in sentences of your own.

Exercise 3

Identify the adjective that tells how many or about how many in each sentence. There may be more than one adjective in a sentence.

1. The *Brachiosaurus* weighed about 80 tons!

2. It had two front legs that were longer than its back legs.

3. It was a plant-eating dinosaur that walked on four legs.

4. A few scientists believe that it never stopped growing.

5. This could be the reason that a *Brachiosaurus* could reach up to 50 feet when it stretched its long neck!

6. Every *Brachiosaurus* had two nostrils on top of its head.

7. Many paleontologists believe that this permitted the *Brachiosaurus* to eat constantly.

8. Two almost-complete *Brachiosaurus* skeletons have been discovered.

9. One skeleton is in Germany, and the second fossil is in Chicago.

10. Some *Tyrannosaurus rex* grew to be 40 feet tall.

11. After many years of evolution, they became the perfect killing machine.

12. Each *T. rex* had two large feet and two short arms.

13. One *T. rex* tooth that was found was 14 inches long.

14. Many scientists believe that the *T. rex* could run as fast as 35 miles per hour.

15. Some scientists, however, think that it was slow moving and would wait hidden in foliage to attack its prey.

Practice Power

Describe an animal that interests you. Give facts about it, using adjectives that tell how many or about how many in your paragraph. Underline the adjectives you use.

3.7 Subject Complements

An adjective that follows a linking verb and completes the sentence is called a **subject complement.** The subject complement describes the subject of the sentence.

> The *T. rex* was *powerful.*

The adjective *powerful* is a subject complement. It follows the linking verb *was* and it describes the subject *T. rex.* Common linking verbs are forms of the verb *be* and words such as *become, feel, grow, look, remain, seem, smell, sound,* and *taste.*

Can you identify the adjective subject complements in these sentences?

> **A.** The *T. rex's* teeth were sharp with cutting edges.
> **B.** *T. rex* was not necessarily green, as some myths claim.

You're right if you said that in sentence A *sharp* describes *teeth,* and in sentence B *green* describes *T. rex.*

An adjective usually comes before a noun. A subject complement, however, follows a linking verb and comes after the noun it describes.

> The *fierce T. rex* preyed on animals. (before a noun)
> The animal was *frightening.* (subject complement)

Exercise 1
Identify the subject complement in each sentence. Then identify the noun it describes.

1. The *Triceratops* was huge.

2. Its three horns were gigantic.

3. The horn on its nose was smallest.

4. The creature's body seems bulky.

5. The dinosaur looks clumsy to me.

Exercise 2
Identify the position of each italicized adjective. Tell whether it appears before a noun or as a subject complement.

1. The *Triceratops* is *famous* for its horns.
2. *Triceratops* traveled in *large* groups.
3. This *massive* dinosaur was a herd animal.
4. *Triceratops* usually ate *low* plants.
5. Each one ate an *enormous* amount of food.
6. Their skulls were *remarkable* for their size and strength.
7. A *Triceratops* was fairly *tall*—the height of a basketball hoop.
8. Its head was *long*—about the length of a human adult.
9. The animals engaged in *fierce* fights among themselves.
10. A *Triceratops* probably charged its enemies, and its horns were an *effective* defense.

Exercise 3
Add adjectives to complete the sentences. Tell whether the adjective comes before the noun or whether it is a subject complement.

1. The work of a paleontologist seems _____ to me.
2. To me, dinosaurs are _____.
3. Dinosaurs were _____ animals.
4. I saw _____ skeletons at a museum.
5. The _____ *T. rex* fascinates many people.

Practice Power

Write two sentences for each of the following adjectives. Use the adjective before a noun in one sentence and as a subject complement in the other.

1. unusual	3. adventurous	5. hot
2. colorful	4. green	6. beautiful

3.8 Adjectives That Compare

Most adjectives have three degrees of comparison: positive, comparative, and superlative. The **positive** degree of an adjective shows a quality of a noun. The **comparative** degree is used to compare two items or two sets of items. It is often used with *than*. The **superlative** degree is used to compare three or more items.

> The *T. rex* was a *large* predatory dinosaur. (positive)
> The *Carcharodonotosaurus* may have been *larger* than the *T. rex*. (comparative)
> The *Giganotosaurus* may have been *largest* of all predatory dinosaurs. (superlative)

For adjectives of one syllable and some adjectives of two syllables (generally those ending in *y*), the comparative is formed by adding *-er* to the positive. The superlative is formed by adding *-est* to the positive.

Positive	Comparative	Superlative
smart	smarter	smartest
narrow	narrower	narrowest

To form the comparative and superlative degrees, follow these rules.

- If an adjective ends in *e*, just add *-r* or *-st*.
  tame   tamer   tamest

- If an adjective ends in *y* preceded by a consonant, change the *y* to *i* before adding *-er* or *-est*.
  clumsy   clumsier   clumsiest

- If a single-syllable adjective ends in a consonant preceded by a vowel, double the consonant before adding *-er* or *-est*.
  hot   hotter   hottest

Some adjectives have irregular forms of comparison.

Positive	Comparative	Superlative
good	better	best
well	better	best
bad	worse	worst

Exercise 1

Write the comparative and the superlative forms of these adjectives.

1. tiny
2. sad
3. brave
4. pretty
5. good
6. thin
7. light
8. happy

Exercise 2

Identify the adjective in the comparative or the superlative degree in each sentence. Tell the degree of each adjective.

1. The earliest dinosaurs lived during the Triassic period.
2. The Jurassic period was later than the Triassic.
3. During the Jurassic period, the climate was wetter and warmer than before, and dinosaurs flourished.
4. The longest dinosaur was probably *Seismosaurus,* a sauropod that was 120 to 150 feet long.

Exercise 3

Choose the correct form to complete each sentence.

1. The (bigger biggest) dinosaurs of all were the long-necked plant eaters called sauropods.
2. Meat-eating dinosaurs had (stronger strongest) legs and jaws than plant-eating dinosaurs had.
3. Plant-eating dinosaurs had (larger largest) stomachs than meat eaters because plants are (harder hardest) to digest.
4. The (smaller smallest) dinosaur was probably *Compsognathus,* a three-foot-long, meat-eating dinosaur.

Practice Power

Use each of these adjectives in a sentence.

1. scarier
2. hardest
3. softest
4. smarter
5. crunchier
6. longest

3.9 More, Most *and* Less, Least

Most adjectives of three or more syllables and some adjectives of two syllables do not add -*er* or -*est* to form the comparative and superlative degrees.

Instead, the comparative is formed by adding *more* or *less* before the positive form of the adjective. Form the superlative by adding *most* or *least* before the positive form of the adjective.

Positive	Comparative	Superlative
mysterious	more mysterious less mysterious	most mysterious least mysterious
famous	more famous less famous	most famous least famous

Dinosaurs can be *more mysterious* than suspense novels.
   (comparative)
I think the really huge dinosaurs are *most mysterious* of all.
   (superlative)
Insects are *less interesting* than *T. rex.* (comparative)
What is the *least interesting* dinosaur? (superlative)

You can check a dictionary for the proper forms of adjectives. It is incorrect to use *more* or *less* and -*er* together, or *most* or *least* and -*est* together. Do not say "the more smarter dinosaur" or "the most smartest dinosaur."

Exercise 1
Write the comparative and superlative degrees for each positive degree adjective. Use *more* or *less* and *most* or *least*.

1. powerful
2. difficult
3. generous
4. important
5. intelligent
6. courteous
7. frightful
8. fortunate
9. courageous

Exercise 2

Choose the correct adjective to complete each sentence.

1. Many people think that dinosaurs were the (more fascinating most fascinating) animals that ever lived.

2. Blue whales are actually (more massive most massive) than any of the dinosaurs were.

3. (More intelligent Most intelligent) of all the dinosaurs was *Troodon,* a small meat-eater.

4. It had to make rapid decisions as it pursued its prey, so it needed a (more efficient most efficient) brain.

5. The large, plant-eating sauropods were probably (less intelligent least intelligent) of all the dinosaurs.

6. *T. rex* was (more successful most successful) than other hunters because of its size and its sharp teeth and claws.

7. (More enormous Most enormous) of all dinosaur eggs was one about the size of a soccer ball.

8. The (more widespread most widespread) dinosaur was probably *Iguanodon.*

9. Were horns (more effective most effective) weapons for dinosaurs than clubs at the end of tails?

10. I think that paleontologists need to be (more patient most patient) than people in most other jobs.

11. Dinosaurs may have been (more agile less agile) than early researchers thought.

12. The earth's climate was (more moderate most moderate) during the age of the reptiles than it is today.

Practice Power

Write your opinion about two or more movies, TV shows, foods, or another general topic. Use these adjectives in the comparative or superlative form: *interesting, boring, delicious, humorous, difficult.*

3.10 Fewer, Fewest *and* Less, Least

Less, least, fewer, and *fewest* are used in comparing things. Use *less* and *least* with noncount nouns. Use *fewer* and *fewest* with count nouns.

Count nouns name things that can be counted: *birds, trees, children.* They have plural forms. **Noncount nouns** name things that cannot be counted: *water, food, patience.* They do not have plural forms.

Less and *fewer* are comparative forms and are used to compare two things or two sets of things.

Least and *fewest* are superlative forms and are used to compare more than two things.

Comparative

There were *fewer* types of plants during the Jurassic period
    than during the Cretaceous. (with a count noun)
There was *less* rain during the Triassic period. (with a noncount
    noun)

Superlative

The *fewest* plants existed during the Triassic period. (with a
    count noun)
The *least* moisture was present during the Triassic period. (with
    a noncount noun)

Tell whether *less* or *fewer* should be used with each of these nouns.

    A. dinosaurs   **B.** food   **C.** footprints

You are correct if you said the following:

    A. fewer dinosaurs   **B.** less food   **C.** fewer footprints

Tell whether *least* or *fewest* should be used with these nouns.

    A. forests   **B.** rain   **C.** sunlight

You are correct if you said the following:

    A. fewest forests   **B.** least rain   **C.** least sunlight

Exercise 1

Write phrases with each noun and *less* or *fewer.* Tell if each noun is a count or a noncount noun.

Example: creatures   fewer creatures, count

1. mammals
2. water
3. interest
4. information
5. time
6. teeth

Exercise 2

Write phrases with each noun and *least* or *fewest.* Tell if each noun is a count or a noncount noun.

1. land
2. eggs
3. evidence
4. bones
5. intelligence
6. babies

Exercise 3

Choose the correct word to complete each sentence.

1. The (fewest fewer) animals are at the top of a food chain.

2. (Less Fewer) food for animals at the bottom of the food chain can mean starvation for animals at the top.

3. (Fewer Less) grass for animals at the bottom of the food chain can affect the entire chain.

4. (Fewer Less) trees can also have a negative effect.

5. There were (fewer less) carnivores than herbivores because the carnivores were at the top of the food chain.

6. There are (fewer less) fossils of dinosaurs than most people think.

7. Scientists have (fewer less) evidence about individual dinosaurs than a person might expect.

Practice Power

Write sentences using five phrases from those you wrote for Exercises 1 and 2.

3.11 *Interrogative Adjectives*

An **interrogative adjective** is used in asking a question. The interrogative adjectives are *what, which,* and *whose.* An interrogative adjective comes before a noun.

> *What* prey did *T. rex* eat?
> *Which* dinosaurs had spoon-shaped teeth?
> *Whose* dinosaur sketches are on the table?

What is used for asking about people or things.

> *What* animals should we have in our classroom?

Which is usually used to ask about one of two or more people or things.

> *Which* dinosaur was bigger—*Argentinosaurus* or *Seismosaurus?*

Whose asks about possession.

> *Whose* model of a *T. rex* is this?

Can you identify the interrogative adjective in this question and the noun it goes with?

> What plants did *Brachiosaurus* eat?

You are correct if you said that *what* is the interrogative adjective and that *plants* is the noun it goes with.

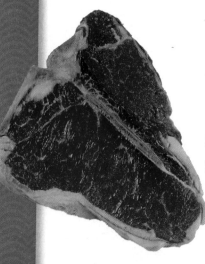

Exercise 1
Identify the interrogative adjective in each sentence. Then identify the noun it goes with.

1. Which dinosaur had long, sharp, curved claws?

2. What discoveries did Paul Sereno make?

3. Which dinosaur was a meat eater—*Brachiosaurus* or *Gigantosaurus?*

4. Whose presentation on the *Allosaurus* was best?

5. What question would you like to ask about *T. rex?*

6. Which carnivore was the largest member of the *Allosaurid* family?

7. Which dinosaur ate fish primarily—*Baryonyx* or *Velociraptor?*

8. Whose favorite dinosaur is the *Spinosaurus?*

Exercise 2

Complete each sentence with the correct interrogative adjective. More than one choice may be correct.

1. _____ large group of animals did dinosaurs belong to?

2. _____ group of dinosaurs had clubs on their tails— *Ankylosaurs* or *Ceratopsians?*

3. _____ event might have ended the era of the dinosaurs?

4. _____ theory is it that a meteorite caused the extinction of the dinosaurs?

5. _____ tools do paleontologists use?

6. _____ turn is it to make the next presentation on dinosaurs?

7. _____ interesting fact did you learn about dinosaurs?

8. _____ presentation was most interesting?

Practice Power

Work with a partner to choose a topic you are studying in class. Write 10 questions with interrogative adjectives to ask about the topic. Use encyclopedias, library books, and the Internet to help find the answers. How many answers did you find?

Adjective Challenge

Read the paragraph and answer the questions.

1. Which state is the youngest state in the United States?
2. Hawaii became a state in 1959, and it consists entirely of islands. 3. Hawaii is beautiful at any time of year. 4. On the islands you are surrounded by sparkling blue seas, clear waterfalls, beautiful palms, and colorful flowers. 5. Polynesian wanderers first settled Hawaii, and most Hawaiians of today are descended from them. 6. These settlers also started many of Hawaii's most delightful customs. 7. The first and last word the visitor to Hawaii hears is *aloha*. 8. *Aloha* means "love" and is used for both *hello* and *goodbye*. 9. According to Hawaiians, however, this word has a deeper meaning than hello or goodbye.

1. In sentence 1 is the adjective *youngest* in the positive, comparative, or superlative degree?

2. In sentence 1 what kind of adjective is *which*?

3. What is the article in sentence 2? Is it definite or indefinite?

4. In sentence 3 find an adjective used as a subject complement.

5. In sentence 4 find at least three descriptive adjectives.

6. In sentence 5 what kind of adjective is *Polynesian*?

7. In sentence 5 what kind of adjective is *most*?

8. In sentence 6 find the demonstrative adjective. Is it singular or plural?

9. In sentence 6 find a descriptive adjective. What degree is it in?

10. In sentence 9 is the article definite or indefinite?

11. In sentence 9 find all the adjectives and tell what kind they are.

Verbs

4.1   Action Verbs and Being Verbs

4.2   Verb Phrases

4.3   Principal Parts of Verbs

4.4   Irregular Verbs

4.5   More Irregular Verbs

4.6   Simple Tenses

4.7   Progressive Tenses

4.8   Present Perfect Tense

4.9   Past Perfect Tense

4.10   Future Perfect Tense

4.11   Linking Verbs

Verb Challenge

4.1 Action Verbs and Being Verbs

A **verb** is a word used to express action or being.

> The ice cream *melts* in the sun. (action verb)
> The ice cream *is* delicious. (being verb)

In each sentence the subject is *ice cream*. In the first sentence *melts* expresses action. In the second sentence *is* expresses being. Both words are verbs.

An **action verb** expresses action. Here are a few action verbs: *dance, run, dream, write, sing, study, ring, chime, clang, toll,* and *jingle*.

A **being verb** expresses a state of being. The verb *be* and its various forms are the most common being verbs: *is, are, was, were, am, be, been,* and *being*.

Can you find the verb in each of these sentences? Is it an action verb or a being verb?

> There are many fascinating stories about ice cream.
> Marco Polo possibly tasted ice cream in Asia in about 1254.

You are correct if you said *are* is the verb in the first sentence. It expresses being. You are correct if you said *tasted* is the verb in the second sentence. It expresses action—the act of tasting.

Exercise 1
Identify the action verb or verbs in each sentence.

1. Americans eat a lot of ice cream.

2. I read a fascinating article about the history of ice cream.

3. The Chinese discovered an ice-preservation method—the use of ice houses.

4. They used this technique three thousand years ago.

5. Over time, people added syrups and flavorings to the ice.

6. At first chefs kept the addition of cream to the ice a secret.

7. Only royalty served ice cream at meals in the 1600s.

8. By the 1700s, however, many people made and sold ice cream.

Exercise 2
Identify the being verb in each sentence.

1. Crushed ice with syrup or fruit was probably the original iced dessert.

2. The Emperor Nero's favorite dessert was snow mixed with honey and fresh fruit.

3. Fruit, ice, and milk are the typical ingredients for sherbet.

4. The major ingredient of ice cream is cream.

5. Various sweet syrups are still popular additions to ice cream.

Exercise 3
Add a verb to each sentence. Tell whether each is an action verb or a being verb.

1. The most popular ice cream flavor _____ vanilla.

2. Many people also _____ chocolate.

3. Many people _____ sprinkles on their ice cream.

4. Fruit _____ a healthful addition to many snacks.

5. People _____ ice cream in cones.

Practice Power

Supply at least two action verbs for each of the following nouns. Write two sentences with each noun as a subject.

| chefs | volcanoes | acrobats |
| musicians | boats | horses |

4.2 *Verb Phrases*

A **verb phrase** is a group of words that does the work of a single verb. A verb phrase contains a main verb and one or more **helping verbs** such as *is, are, has, have, can,* and *do.*

One-Word Verb	Verb Phrase
Manufacturers *use* cacao beans for chocolate.	Manufacturers *have used* cacao beans for chocolate for hundreds of years.
Rain forests in the Americas *have* cacao trees.	The cacao tree *can be found* in the rain forests of the Americas.

In each sentence in the left column, the verb is only one word. In the right column the verbs are verb phrases of two or more words. Groups of words such as *have used* and *can be found* are verb phrases. Each phrase does the work of a single verb.

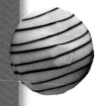

In questions and some statements the parts of the verb phrase may be separated.

> *Did* chocolate *originate* in the Americas?
> Chocolate bars *were* not *invented* until 1876.

Here are some common helping verbs.
> *am, is, are, was, were, be, being, been*
> *has, have, had*
> *do, does, did*
> *may, can, might, could, must, should, would, will*

Can you identify the verb phrase in each sentence?

> Cacao beans were used as money by early Americans.
> You can see cacao trees at most botanical gardens.

You are correct if you said *were used* is the verb phrase in the first sentence and *can see* is the verb phrase in the second sentence.

Exercise 1
Identify the verb phrase in each sentence.

1. The seeds from a cacao tree are processed for chocolate.
2. The ancestors of people in Mexico and Central America have been credited with the discovery of chocolate.
3. The Maya and the Aztec peoples did process chocolate centuries ago.
4. Did they mix the ground seeds with spices and water?
5. Such a mixture could have been the first chocolate drink.
6. By the 1600s hot chocolate had become popular in Europe.
7. Its taste and texture have changed over the years.
8. Its many varieties are enjoyed by people the world over.

Exercise 2
Identify the main verb and the helping verb in each sentence.

1. Have you ever read anything about the cacao tree?
2. It can grow only in tropical climates.
3. Cacao trees are usually planted in shady areas.
4. After a few years they are transplanted to sunny areas.
5. A full-grown cacao tree can be 25 feet tall.
6. Some trees, though, have grown to 60 feet or more.
7. Twenty to fifty cacao beans can be found in a pod.
8. The cacao beans are dried for the production of chocolate.
9. How many beans does it take for a pound of chocolate?
10. It may take about 400 beans!

Practice Power

Write sentences using these verb phrases: can eat, will finish, have been, have seen, had traveled, might try.

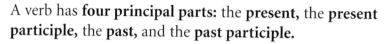

4.3 *Principal Parts of Verbs*

A verb has **four principal parts:** the **present,** the **present participle,** the **past,** and the **past participle.**

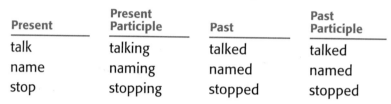

Present	Present Participle	Past	Past Participle
talk	talking	talked	talked
name	naming	named	named
stop	stopping	stopped	stopped

- The present participle is formed by adding *-ing* to the present. The present participle is often used with a form of the helping verb *be* (*am, is, are, was, were,* and *been*).

  My friend *prepares* delicious salads. (present)
  He *is preparing* a chicken salad for lunch. (present participle)

- The past and the past participle of regular verbs are formed by adding *-d* or *-ed* to the present. The past participle is often used with the helping verb *has, have,* or *had.*

  My friend *prepared* a shrimp salad yesterday. (past)
  He *has prepared* a different salad each day. (past participle)

- To form the present participle of verbs ending in *e,* drop the final *e* and add *-ing: prepare + ing = preparing.*

- To form the present participle of a verb ending in a consonant following a vowel, double the consonant before adding *-ing: wrap + ing = wrapping.* Likewise, to form the past participle, double the consonant before adding *-ed: wrap + ed = wrapped.*

- When the subject is a singular noun or *he, she,* or *it,* add *-s* to the present part of the verb: My friend *prepares* delicious salads. He often *serves* his salads to friends.

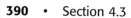

Exercise 1

Write the present participle, the past, and the past participle of each verb.

1. call
2. skate
3. visit
4. serve
5. explore
6. skip
7. look
8. carry

Exercise 2

Tell whether the verb in italics is present, present participle, past, or past participle. For verbs ending -ed, look for a helping verb to see if the form is a past participle.

1. People are *consuming* more and more yogurt nowadays.
2. People *obtain* it in small cartons in supermarkets.
3. Yogurt has *existed* for thousands of years.
4. Yogurt is *produced* by special bacteria in milk.
5. The Bulgar people are *credited* with the discovery of yogurt.
6. Yogurt *remained* a European food until the early 1900s.

Exercise 3

Complete each sentence with the form of the verb in parentheses.

1. Fruit is often _____ to yogurt. (add—past participle)
2. People _____ its flavor in the yogurt. (like—present)
3. I'm _____ berries into mine. (stir—present participle)
4. Have you ever _____ strawberry yogurt? (taste—past participle)
5. I _____ yogurt at home for a project. (prepare—past)

Practice Power

Write a sentence using each verb in the principal part noted in parentheses.

1. describe (present)
2. try (past participle)
3. study (present participle)
4. provide (past)

4.4 *Irregular Verbs*

The simple past and the past participle of irregular verbs do not end in *-ed*. These parts of irregular verbs take a variety of forms.

Present	Past	Past Participle
bring	brought	brought
come	came	come
have	had	had
know	knew	known
teach	taught	taught

I sometimes *buy* lunch in the cafeteria. (present)
I *bought* lunch there yesterday. (past)
I have *bought* macaroni and cheese for lunch on occasion.
    (past participle)

Which word correctly completes the sentences?

    We (knowed knew) what was for lunch.

You're correct if you said *knew*. The simple past part of *know* is *knew*.

Exercise 1

Write the present, the past, and the past participle of each verb. Check a dictionary if you need help.

1. give
2. leave
3. fall
4. do

5. stand
6. swim
7. write
8. sink

9. grow
10. make
11. hurt
12. see

Exercise 2

Complete each sentence with the past or the past participle of the irregular verb in parentheses. Remember to use the past participle if the sentence has a helping verb.

1. The Spanish explorers _____ (find) many foods new to Europe in South America.

2. Potatoes were _____ (grow) in the Andes.

3. Fried potatoes _____ (become) popular in the 1800s.

4. Joseph Malines, a British restaurant owner, _____ (put) a dish of fried fish and fried potatoes on his menu.

5. This _____ (become) Britain's national dish, under the name of "fish and chips."

6. The French also _____ (make) fried potatoes.

7. In World War I, American soldiers _____ (eat) them there.

8. These soldiers _____ (give) the fried potato a new name.

9. They _____ (say) it should be called the "French fry."

10. Billions of French fries are _____ (eat) each year!

Exercise 3

Complete the paragraph by using either the past or the past participle of the word in parentheses. Some verbs are regular.

People all over the world have _____ (1. put) ketchup on their French fries for years. Did you know that people _____ (2. have) ketchup in the 1600s? It _____ (3. begin) in China as a fish sauce and was _____ (4. call) kechiap. Travelers _____ (5. bring) it to the United States, but they _____ (6. use) somewhat different ingredients in their ketchup. I have _____ (7. hear) that some ketchup originally _____ (8. have) nuts in it! Enjoying ketchup (without the nuts!) on fries has _____ (9. become) an American tradition!

Practice Power

Write a paragraph about the origin of something that interests you—a food, a sport, a type of clothing. Underline the irregular verbs and tell whether each is simple past or past participle.

4.5 *More Irregular Verbs*

Here are the principal parts of some other irregular verbs.

Present	Present Participle	Past	Past Participle
break	breaking	broke	broken
choose	choosing	chose	chosen
go	going	went	gone
see	seeing	saw	seen
take	taking	took	taken

Which verb form completes the sentence correctly?

Have you (went gone) to the new pizzeria already?

You are correct if you chose *gone.* The helping verb *have* precedes it, so the past participle is correct.

Exercise 1
Complete each sentence with the correct part of *break.*

1. We _____ the bread and dipped it into the olive oil.

2. I almost _____ the glass when I reached for the salt.

3. I seldom _____ things by being careless.

4. After I had _____ the fortune cookie, I read the fortune.

Today is your lucky day

Exercise 2
Complete each sentence with the correct form of *see.*

1. I _____ Hilda at the pizzeria last night.

2. We _____ the chef making pizza.

3. Earlier Hilda had _____ the pizza with no cheese.

4. We usually _____ kids from school at the pizzeria.

Exercise 3
Complete each sentence with the correct form of *go.*

1. Our family always _____ to Pizzeria Luigi's on Friday.

2. We _____ there two weeks ago.

3. Friends and I had _____ to Pizzeria Luigi's before bowling on my last birthday.

4. My mom and I are _____ there right now.

Exercise 4
Complete each sentence with the correct form of *choose*.

1. Bob _____ mushrooms as a topping for his pizza today.

2. He always _____ mushrooms.

3. Greg and I are _____ our toppings now.

4. I have _____ onions and blue cheese before.

5. What toppings have you _____ for your pizza?

Exercise 5
Complete each sentence with the correct form of *take*.

1. We are _____ our leftover pizza home.

2. We have _____ the leftover pizza out of the refrigerator and put it into the microwave.

3. Sandie had _____ her pizza home before we arrived.

4. She _____ it to school for lunch.

Practice Power

Imagine that you and a friend spent the summer working on a special tree house. Use the irregular verbs on page 394 and at least four other irregular verbs to write a paragraph about what happened as you worked on the tree house. Answer these questions in the paragraph.

1. How did you get ready to build?

2. Did you have any problems during construction?

3. What did you choose to include in the tree house?

4.6 Simple Tenses

The **tense** of a verb shows the time of its action. There are three simple tenses: the present, the past, and the future.

The **simple present tense** tells about something that is always true or about an action that happens again and again. Use the present part of the verb to form the present tense. If the subject is a third person singular noun or *he, she,* or *it,* add *-s* to the end of the verb.

The **simple past tense** tells about an action that happened in the past. Use the past part of the verb to express the past tense. The past tense of regular verbs ends in *-ed.*

The **future tense** tells about an action that will happen in the future. Use *will* or a form of *be* with *going to* and the present part of the verb to express future tense.

Simple present:	We eat Greek salad for lunch every Tuesday.
	She eats shrimp salad every Friday.
Simple past:	We ate tossed salad last night.
Future:	We will eat Caesar salad tomorrow.
	We are going to have fruit salad for dessert.

What is the verb in each sentence? What is its tense?

   A. We always make our dinner salad in a wooden bowl.
   B. Last night we put tomatoes and olives on our salad.
   C. I will order a taco salad for lunch tomorrow.

You are correct if you said the following:

A. The verb is *make*; the tense is simple present.
B. The verb is *put*; the tense is simple past.
C. The verb phrase is *will order*; the tense is future.

Exercise 1
Find the verb or verb phrase in each sentence. Tell whether the tense of each is simple present, simple past, or future.

1. Many cultures make a food similar to pizza.

2. The ancient Greeks baked a similar flat, round bread.

3. Tomatoes possess a fairly recent history in Europe.

4. Explorers took tomatoes to Europe from the Americas in the 1500s.

5. When will the tomatoes and the bread finally come together as pizza?

6. According to tradition, the combination of the two into pizza occurred in Naples in the 1800s.

7. Raffaele Esposito created a special pizza for Queen Margherita of Italy in 1899.

8. People still eat a "margherita" pizza today.

9. You are going to taste it also.

Exercise 2
Complete each sentence with the verb and tense in parentheses.

1. The Italians _____ pizza to the United States in the late 1800s. (introduce–simple past)

2. During the late 1950s a company _____ the frozen pizza. (develop–simple past)

3. I often _____ frozen pizza in the microwave oven after school. (cook–simple present)

4. I usually _____ pizza with mushrooms. (eat–simple present)

5. I _____ a different pizza tomorrow. (try–future)

Practice Power

Write six sentences about things you do every day. Change the time and tense, but keep the same verb for all. Go back a hundred years. Then go forward a hundred years.

Example: I watch television every day.
I watched the first airplane flight by Orville Wright.
I will watch people ride bicycles that can fly.

4.7 *Progressive Tenses*

The **progressive tenses** consist of a form of the verb *be* (*is, am, are, was, were*) and the present participle.

The **present progressive tense** tells what is happening now. It is used for ongoing actions. The present progressive tense uses a present form of the verb *be* (*am, is, are*) and the present participle.

> My mother *is cooking* a pot roast for dinner.

The **past progressive tense** tells what was happening in the past. The past progressive tense uses a past form of the verb *be* (*was, were*) and the present participle.

> We *were eating* our roast when the doorbell rang.

The **future progressive tense** tells about something that will be happening in the future. The future progressive uses *will, is going to,* or *are going to* with *be* and the present participle.

> Mom *will be serving* leftover pot roast tomorrow.
> She *is going to be preparing* several vegetables also.

What is the verb phrase in each sentence? What is its tense?

    A. I was looking for new pot-roast recipes.
    B. I am making a spicy side dish tonight.
    C. My sister will be reading the recipe as I mix the ingredients.

You are correct if you said the following:

A. The verb phrase is *was looking*; it is past progressive. It has *was,* a past form of the verb *be,* and the present participle.

B. The verb phrase is *am making*; it is present progressive. It has *am,* a present form of the verb *be,* and the present participle.

C. The verb phrase is *will be reading*; it is future progressive. It has *will* with *be* and the present participle.

Exercise 1

Identify the verb phrases in the progressive tenses in the sentences. Tell whether each is in the present progressive, the past progressive, or the future progressive tense.

1. We were planning our meals for the week yesterday.

2. We are going to be making pasta primavera for dinner.

3. I am cutting the onions now.

4. My eyes are tearing a little.

5. Ron is cutting the zucchini and the carrots.

6. Harry is putting garlic and oil in the pan.

7. My sister will be helping us if she gets home in time.

8. We were measuring the olive oil when the phone rang.

9. The pasta was boiling while we were cleaning up.

Exercise 2

Complete each sentence with the verb and the tense given.

1. We _____ dad cook last night. (help—past progressive)

2. I _____ the flour in a bowl when the phone rang. (put—past progressive)

3. The bowl slipped from my hands and broke as I _____ for the phone. (reach—past progressive)

4. We _____ curry for dinner. (have—future progressive)

5. The telephone _____ now. (ring—present progressive)

6. I _____ the sauce, and I don't plan to answer the telephone! (stir—present progressive)

Practice Power

Write a letter to someone you haven't talked to in more than a year. Make comparisons between then and now. Use present progressive and past progressive tenses.

4.8 *Present Perfect Tense*

The **present perfect tense** uses the past participle and a form of *have* (*have* or *has*).

The present perfect tense tells about an action that happened at some indefinite time or an action that started in the past and continues into the present time.

The students *have learned* about ethnic foods.
He *has helped* in the kitchen since he was seven.

What are the verb phrases in the present perfect tense in these sentences?

I have chosen some recipes from that cookbook.
Louis has never tasted squid.

You are correct if you said that in the first sentence *have chosen* is in the present prefect, and in the second sentence *has tasted* is in the present perfect.

Exercise 1
Identify the present perfect tense verb phrase in each sentence.

1. Our class has organized an international food day.

2. The students have decided to bring dishes characteristic of various countries.

3. Some students have already chosen what dishes to bring.

4. We have decorated the cafeteria for the event.

5. Sergio has come with an Italian dish with eggplant.

6. His grandmother has used the recipe for many years.

7. Nguyen has brought the ingredients for Vietnamese spring rolls with rice paper and mint.

8. I have used my mother's instructions to make a German potato salad.

Exercise 2

Identify the verb phrases in the present perfect tense in these sentences. Not all sentences are in the present perfect tense.

1. Richard has a recipe for peanut butter soup from Ghana.

2. He has put peanut butter, yams, and chicken into the soup.

3. I have not tasted it yet, but I love peanut butter, so I think I'll like it.

4. Pedro's dad has prepared his specialty, a paella.

5. The Spanish dish contains rice, tomatoes, and shellfish.

6. Bina has prepared a chicken curry from India.

7. Around it she has placed small dishes of condiments.

8. Elaine and I have placed some coconut and raisins on top of our curry.

Exercise 3

Complete each sentence with the verb in parentheses in the present perfect tense.

1. Arun _____ (mix) watermelon, ice, and honey for a Thai dessert.

2. We _____ (put) it into the refrigerator to stay cool.

3. Marta _____ (bring) some tortillas.

4. She _____ (get) some cheese, lettuce, and beans as filling to make tacos.

5. Jane's parents _____ (make) their own scones from scratch.

6. We _____ (spread) a special cream on ours.

Practice Power

Write four sentences about interesting foods that you have tried and four sentences about foods that you haven't tried but would like to try sometime. Use present perfect tense in your sentences.

4.9 *Past Perfect Tense*

The **past perfect tense** tells about a past action that was completed before another past action started.

The past perfect tense is formed by using *had* and the past participle of the verb.

> After Italians *had introduced* pizza to the United States, it became a popular food here.
> Before I tasted pizza with pineapple topping, I *had* not *thought* of it as an appealing ingredient.
> By the 1950s the Chicago deep-dish pizza *had become* popular.

In the first sentence the action of the verb phrase in the past perfect (*had introduced*) occurred before the action of the other verb (*became*). In the second sentence the action of the verb phrase in the past perfect (*had thought*) occurred before the action of the verb *tasted*. In the third sentence the action of the verb in the past perfect (*had become*) occurred before the time given (*the 1950s*).

Can you identify the verb in the past perfect in this sentence? Can you tell what action it preceded?

> I had cooked supper before mom arrived home.

You are correct if you said the verb *had cooked* is in the past perfect. Its action occurred before the action of the verb *arrived*.

Exercise 1
Identify the verb phrases in the past perfect tense in these sentences.

1. I wrote my report on food history after I had gathered a lot of information from books and Web sites.

2. Before 10,000 BC people had developed bread making.

3. By 2400 BC people in China had discovered the pleasures of tea.

4. According to legend, after a Chinese emperor had ordered the boiling of water for health reasons, some tea leaves fell into the hot water by accident and he enjoyed the flavor.

5. By 100 AD the Chinese had formed rice and wheat into long noodles for ease in eating.

6. Before the Spanish came to the Americas, people in Europe had not known about tomatoes, potatoes, squash, or corn.

7. Before 1870 bananas had been rare in the United States; now they are America's most popular fruit.

8. Peanut butter had not joined jelly in sandwiches until the 1900s.

Exercise 2

Complete each sentence with the verb in parentheses in the past perfect.

1. I decided to try a simple recipe for frozen yogurt treats after I _____ (find) it while doing research on my food project.

2. After I _____ (got) a cup of yogurt, a cup of fruit juice, and a teaspoon of vanilla, I mixed them together.

3. After I _____ (pour) the mixture into paper cups, I put a stick into each one and put the cups into the freezer.

4. Before I ate one of the frozen treats, I _____ (run) hot water over the cup and _____ (remove) the treat.

5. After we _____ (eat) all the treats, we decided to make another batch.

Practice Power

Write a paragraph about the steps required in making one of your favorite foods. Use the past perfect tense in your writing. When you are finished, circle each verb phrase in the past perfect tense.

4.10 *Future Perfect Tense*

The **future perfect tense** is used to talk about a future event that will be started and completed before another future event begins. It is formed by using *will have* and the past participle.

> Jan and Ben *will have made* supper by the time you arrive home.

The verb in the future perfect tense is *will have made.* It indicates something that will start in the future but that will be finished before the action described by the other verb, *arrive,* begins.

> We *will have eaten* supper by 7 o'clock tonight, and then I'll watch the game on TV.

The verb in the future perfect tense is *will have eaten.* It tells about an action that will begin in the future but will be completed before the time mentioned, 7 o'clock.

Can you identify the verb in the future perfect in this sentence? Can you tell the action it will precede?

> Our group will have decided on the topic for our project by next Monday, after which we will assign roles.

You are correct if you said that the verb in the future perfect is *will have decided.* It describes an action that will start and end before next Monday, the time given. It will also be completed before the group assigns roles.

Exercise 1
Identify the verb phrases in the future perfect tense in these sentences.

1. By Friday night we will have finished the preparations for the big family picnic on Saturday.

2. By then Uncle Joe will have raised the tent in our yard.

3. Aunt Sally will have made eight apple pies.

4. Dad will have bought lots of juice and soda.

5. Mom will have phoned everyone to confirm arrivals.

Exercise 2
Complete each sentence with the verb in parentheses in the future perfect tense.

1. By Saturday morning I _____ all the platters. (wash)

2. Susan _____ the decorations on the table. (place)

3. Uncle Peter _____ lots of tomatoes and carrots from his garden for the salads. (pick)

4. Our cousins from out of town _____. (arrive)

5. We _____ chairs from our neighbors. (borrow)

Exercise 3
Complete each sentence with the verb *attend* in the tense indicated. All are perfect tenses.

1. Susan _____ many family reunions. (present perfect)

2. In fact, she _____ one before she was one year old—her parents took her as a baby. (past perfect)

3. She _____ every reunion for the last 10 years. (present perfect)

4. By next month she _____ 12 reunions in all. (future perfect)

Practice Power

You or your family are planning a party. Write sentences about what you will do in the meantime to prepare for it. Use the future perfect tense.

Example: By two weeks before the party, we will have sent invitations.

A **linking verb** links, or joins, a subject with a subject complement that identifies or describes the subject. The subject complement may be a noun, a pronoun, or an adjective.

The verb *be* and its various forms are the most common linking verbs: *am, is, are, was, were, have been, has been, had been,* and *will be.* Some other common linking verbs are *become, feel, grow, look, remain, seem, smell, sound,* and *taste.*

Broccoli *is* an extremely healthful vegetable.

In this sentence the linking verb is *is.* The subject complement is the noun *vegetable*; it renames the subject *broccoli.*

These bananas seem ripe.

In this sentence the linking verb is *seem.* The subject complement is the adjective *ripe*; it describes the subject *bananas.*

The health teacher *will be* she.

In the sentence the linking verb is *will be.* The subject complement is the pronoun *she.* It renames the subject *teacher.*

Can you find the linking verb in the following sentence? Can you name both the subject complement and its part of speech?

These peaches look rotten with their darkened skin.

The linking verb is *look.* The subject complement is *rotten,* which is an adjective.

Exercise 1
Identify the linking verb in each sentence. Tell whether the italicized subject complement is a noun, a pronoun, or an adjective.

1. A food pyramid is a *picture* of a recommended diet.

2. The designer of the American food pyramid is a *department* of the U.S. government.

3. The foods at the bottom are most *essential.*

4. Fruits and vegetables are important *foods* in the pyramid.

5. Bread, pasta, and grain are *rich* in carbohydrates.

6. Carbohydrates are important *nutrients* for the body.

7. Some foods are *high* in calories.

8. Such foods, however, may be *low* in nutritional value.

9. Sweets, for example, taste *good.*

10. Sweets, however, are not very healthful *foods.*

11. Daily exercise remains a necessary *component* of a person's health.

12. The nutritionist who explained the pyramid was *he.*

Exercise 2
Identify the linking verb and the subject complement in each sentence.

1. Diets in different places have become quite different.

2. In the Asian diet rice is the basic grain.

3. Tea is a common beverage.

4. Olive oil is essential in the Mediterranean diet.

5. Italy, Spain, Greece, and Tunisia are several Mediterranean countries.

6. Pasta is basic in that diet.

7. Bread and couscous are other grain products in that diet.

8. In several diets fresh fruit remains the typical dessert.

Practice Power

Write a paragraph about your favorite foods—for example, foods that you prefer for breakfast, lunch, dinner, and snacks. Explain why you like them. Include linking verbs. When you have finished, circle the linking verbs and underline the subject complements.

Verb Challenge

Read the selection and answer the questions.

1. We are studying about Egypt and the Nile River in school. 2. I had known that Egypt is in Africa. 3. I didn't know, however, that the Nile River passed through Egypt. 4. It is the longest river in the world. 5. It flows northward, providing water to more than one million square miles of African land.

6. Every year the Nile overflows its banks, leaving behind rich, fertile soil. 7. Because of this, the river has supported farming along its banks for thousands of years. 8. The Nile had flooded its banks annually since 5,000 BC—until the building of the Aswan Dam.

9. The Nile River makes it possible for Egypt to be one of the major producers of cotton in the world. 10. Egypt is a fascinating country. 11. We will have learned many interesting facts about Egypt and the Nile by the end of the semester.

1. Name the verb phrase in sentence 1. Is it present progressive or past progressive?

2. Name the verb phrase in sentence 2. What is its tense?

3. What is the helping verb in sentence 2?

4. Name the verb in sentence 4. Does it express action or being?

5. Name the subject complement in sentence 4. Is it a noun, a pronoun, or an adjective?

6. Name the verb phrase in sentence 7. What is its tense?

7. Name the verb in sentence 8. Is it regular or irregular?

8. Name the verb in sentence 9. Name its principal parts.

9. Find a sentence with a verb that is in the future perfect tense.

10. Find any regular verb in this paragraph. Name the principal parts of the regular verb you chose.

Adverbs

5.1   Adverbs of Time, Place, and Manner

5.2   Adverbs That Compare

5.3   Troublesome Words, Negative Words

5.4   *There Is* and *There Are*

5.5   Adverb Clauses

Adverb Challenge

5.1 *Adverbs of Time, Place, and Manner*

An **adverb** describes a verb. Adverbs tell *when, how often, where,* or *how* an action happens.

> John Chapman worked *tirelessly* on his special mission.

The word *tirelessly* tells *how.* It is an adverb that describes the action of the verb *worked.*

An **adverb of time** answers the question *when* or *how often.*

> John Chapman *always* carried a bag of apple seeds.

Here is a list of common adverbs of time.

again	early	immediately	often	then
already	finally	late	once	today
always	frequently	now	seldom	usually

An **adverb of place** answers the question *where.*

> Johnny Appleseed walked *far* each day.

Here is a list of common adverbs of place.

above	back	everywhere	here	out	up
ahead	below	far	in	there	within

An **adverb of manner** answers the question *how.*

> He *carefully* planted each apple seed.

Here is a list of some common adverbs of manner.

carefully	fast	kindly	swiftly
correctly	gracefully	quickly	truthfully
courageously	hard	smoothly	well

Exercise 1
Tell whether the adverb in italics indicates time, place, or manner.

1. Americans *sometimes* told stories about Johnny Appleseed.

2. *Usually* the stories were made up or exaggerated.

3. John Chapman grew up in Massachusetts in the 1700s, but he didn't stay *there.*

4. He walked *far* on foot, through the country to the western frontier.

5. He started a farm and worked *hard.*

6. *Carefully* he tended his apple orchard.

7. *Soon* he realized that his mission was to encourage planting trees throughout the country.

8. *Generously* he gave seeds and seedlings to all settlers.

9. He had few possessions himself, and *often* he had no shoes and wore a soup pot on his head for a hat.

10. The legends of Johnny Appleseed continue to delight people *today.*

Exercise 2

Find the adverb in each sentence. Tell whether it is an adverb of time, place, or manner.

1. Johnny Appleseed treated people and animals kindly.

2. Once he was walking on a cold, snowy winter evening.

3. Then he saw a hollow log.

4. He quickly crawled into it.

5. A family of bears was sleeping there!

6. Slowly he backed out of the log.

7. He refused to chase the bears away.

8. He himself slept outside in the cold!

Practice Power

Write eight sentences, using one of the verbs and one of the adverbs below in each.

Verbs		Adverbs		
finish	sing	quickly	often	completely
dance	shop	happily	well	cheerfully

5.2 Adverbs That Compare

Like adjectives, some adverbs can be compared. These adverbs have three degrees of comparison: positive, comparative, and superlative.

The **positive degree** of an adverb is the base form. It describes one action. The **comparative degree** is used to compare two actions. It is often used with *than*. The **superlative degree** is used to compare three or more actions.

My father reads the newspaper *quickly.* (positive)
My brother reads *more quickly* than I do. (comparative)
My sister reads *most quickly* of anyone in my family.
    (superlative)

The comparative degree of most adverbs that end in *-ly* is formed by adding *more* or *less* before the positive form. The superlative degree is formed by adding *most* or *least* before the positive.

Positive	Comparative	Superlative
quickly	more (less) quickly	most (least) quickly
carefully	more (less) carefully	most (least) carefully
politely	more (less) politely	most (least) politely

My sister goes to the library *more frequently* than I do.
My sister listened to the storyteller *least attentively* of all.

The comparative of many adverbs that do not end in *-ly* is formed by adding *-er.* The superlative is formed by adding *-est.*

Positive	Comparative	Superlative
fast	faster	fastest
near	nearer	nearest
late	later	latest

We got to the library *sooner* than our friends.
Jackson arrived *latest* and missed the start of the presentation.

Exercise 1
Write the comparative and superlative degrees of the adverbs.

1. swiftly
2. carefully
3. hard
4. brilliantly
5. smoothly
6. long
7. noisily
8. diligently
9. faithfully

Exercise 2
Identify the adverb in the comparative or the superlative degree in each sentence. Tell the degree of each.

1. Of all folk heroes those in American tall tales seem to act most amazingly.
2. Figures such as Paul Bunyan worked more powerfully than any real human could.
3. Characters like Pecos Bill act more daringly than most folk heroes—even riding a tornado.
4. John Henry acted most nobly of all the folk heroes.

Exercise 3
Choose the correct form to complete each sentence.

1. John Henry could drive steel (fastest faster) of all the workers cutting tunnels for the railroads.
2. He worked (harder hardest) than any ordinary human.
3. In a contest he drove steel (more rapidly most rapidly) than a machine, but he died as a result of the effort.
4. He showed (more impressively most impressively) of all the folk heroes the power of the human spirit.

Practice Power

Choose four of the comparative and superlative adverbs listed in Exercise 1 and use them in sentences.

5.3 Troublesome Words, Negative Words

Good and Well

Good is an adjective that answers the question *what kind* about a noun. *Well* is generally an adverb that answers the question *how* about a verb. Be careful not to use *good* when the adverb *well* is needed.

> Pecos Bill was a good cowboy. (*What kind of cowboy? A good* cowboy. *Good* tells what kind about the noun *cowboy.*)
> He could twirl a lasso well. (*How could he twirl a lasso?* He could twirl it *well. Well* tells how about the verb *twirl.*)

Well can be used as an adjective but only in reference to a person's health.

> I'll bet Pecos Bill felt *well* every day—never sick for a minute.

Real and Very

Real is an adjective that means "genuine" or "true." *Very* is an adverb that describes an adjective or another adverb. It means "extremely" or "to a high degree." Be careful not to use *real* when the adverb *very* is needed.

> Pecos Bill was not a real person. (*What kind of person? Real* tells about the noun *person.*)
> Pecos Bill was *very* clever. (*How clever was he? Very* clever. *Very* tells more about the adjective *clever.*)

No, Not, and Never

A negative idea is expressed by using one negative word. This negative word may be *no, not, none, never,* or *nothing.* If a sentence already has a negative adverb, avoid using another negative word. Use a word like *any* or *ever* instead.

> There is no cowboy more famous than Pecos Bill. (one negative word, *no*)
> There isn't any cowboy more famous than Pecos Bill. (one negative word, *n't [not],* used with *any*)

Exercise 1
Complete each sentence with *good* or *well*.

1. Swamp Angel did _____ deeds for the people of Tennessee.
2. The settlers spoke _____ of her.
3. She was _____ at such pioneer skills as building cabins.
4. She could rope _____ too—once even roping a tornado.
5. There are several _____ stories about Swamp Angel.

Exercise 2
Complete each sentence with *real* or *very*.

1. Swamp Angel's _____ name was Angelica Longrider.
2. Actually Swamp Angel is not a _____ character from the past.
3. According to her creator, Swamp Angel grew _____ big and tall.
4. She was _____ strong—once lifting a wagon train out of a bog.
5. I think the stories about her are _____ entertaining.

Exercise 3
Choose the correct word to complete each sentence.

1. I haven't read (any no) stories more enjoyable than tall tales.
2. There wasn't (any no) person in Tennessee more appreciated than Swamp Angel.
3. (Any No) creature did more harm than the hungry bear.
4. There wasn't (anyone no one) who could defeat it.
5. There was (no any) battle more fierce than the one between that bear and Swamp Angel.

Practice Power

Write one sentence for each of these words: *good, well, real, very, no, not, never.*

5.4 There Is *and* There Are

When a sentence begins with *there* followed by a form of the verb *be*, the subject of the sentence comes after the verb.

There <u>is</u> a famous *spider* in many folk tales.
There <u>are</u>, in fact, many *stories* about the trickster spider.

In the sentences above, the subjects are in italics and the verbs are underlined. The subject follows the verb in each sentence.

There is or *there was* is used with a singular subject. *There are* or *there were* is used with a plural subject.

	Verb		Singular Subject	
There	*is*	a	*tale*	about Anansi in this book.

	Verb		Plural Subject	
There	*are*	several animal	*characters*	in this tale.

What verb correctly completes the sentence?

There (is are) tales from Africa and from the Caribbean.

You are correct if you chose *are*. This verb form goes with the plural subject *tales*.

Exercise 1

Identify the subject in each sentence. Tell whether it is singular or plural.

1. There is one major contribution of spiders.

2. There are fewer harmful insects because of them.

3. There are some poisonous spiders.

4. So there is a good reason to avoid some spiders.

5. There is a major difference between a spider and an insect.

6. There are eight legs on a spider's body—not six.

7. There is oil on the tips of spiders' legs—so the spiders won't get caught in their own webs.

8. There is no fiber in nature stronger than spider's silk.

Exercise 2
Choose the correct form to complete each item.

(**1.** There is There are) a well-known story about Anansi, the trickster spider. (**2.** There is There are) two other characters in the tale—Firefly and Tiger.

Anansi said to Firefly, "Let's go egg hunting tonight." (**3.** There was There were) fields nearby, and the pair started to look for eggs in them. (**4.** "There is "There are) no light," said Anansi. "Firefly, please light your light." Every time Firefly did this Anansi picked up any eggs that could be seen. Soon (**5.** there was there were) many eggs in Anansi's basket, but (**6.** there wasn't there weren't) even one egg in Firefly's basket. Firefly, seeing that it was being tricked, flew away. Now (**7.** there was there were) a big problem for Anansi—he couldn't see in the dark.

He heard a noise. Suddenly (**8.** there was there were) a big tiger in front of him. Tiger said, (**9.** "There is "There are) many eggs in your basket. Let's go to my home and eat them." Anansi was too afraid to say no. At Tiger's house (**10.** there was there were) a big pot. Soon Tiger was hungrily eating all the eggs. (**11.** There was There were) nothing left for Anansi! After Tiger went to bed, Anansi looked into the pot. (**12.** There was There were) some eggshells on the bottom. Anansi put his arm into the pot to get a shell, but (**13.** there was there were) also a live crab in the pot, and it bit him! Tiger had put the crab there to scare Anansi away. So (**14.** there was there were) no dinner for Anansi that night. And worse, (**15.** there was there were) no way for Anansi to find the field with the eggs. It was Firefly's secret.

Practice Power

Write four clues about a well-known book or story you read. Use *There is* and *There are* in the clues. Trade your clues with a partner to have him or her guess the title of the book or story.

Example: There is a magic cupboard.
There are several children.

5.5 Adverb Clauses

A **clause** is a group of words with a subject and a predicate. A **dependent clause** does not express a complete thought. In a sentence it is used together with an **independent clause,** which does express a complete thought.

An **adverb clause** is a dependent clause that is used as an adverb. An adverb clause often answers the question *when.*

> My mother often read me fables *when I was little.*

In this sentence *My mother often read me fables* is the independent clause. *When I was little* is a dependent clause. It has a subject and a verb, but it cannot stand alone as a sentence. The dependent clause is an adverb clause because it begins with the conjunction *when* and answers the question *When did mother read me fables? When I was little.*

Common conjunctions used to introduce adverb clauses include *after, as, as soon as, before, once, since, until, when, whenever,* and *while.*

Can you find the adverb clause in this sentence?

> After the hungry billy goat had searched for food all day, it found a patch of chili peppers.

You are correct if you said *after the hungry billy goat had searched for food all day.* It is introduced by *after* and tells when.

An adverb clause generally comes at the beginning or at the end of a sentence.

> The hungry billy goat found a patch of chili peppers after it had searched for food all day.

Exercise 1
Identify the adverb clause in each sentence. Look for the conjunctions for help.

1. The farmer yelled when the hungry billy goat started eating peppers in her field.

2. After it heard the farmer's cries, a dog came to help her.

3. The farmer was talking to the dog while the goat kept crunching the peppers.

4. When the dog barked loudly and asked the goat to leave the pepper patch, the goat simply said, "No!"

5. Other animals offered their help too once they became aware of the problem.

6. Whenever an animal talked to the goat, it just laughed and ate more peppers.

7. When an ant offered to help, the farmer almost refused the small and powerless creature.

8. The ant crept up silently until it reached the goat.

9. Once it climbed up to the goat's ear, the ant took a big bite out of the ear!

10. The goat ran out of the pepper field as soon as he felt the ant's bite!

Exercise 2

Complete each sentence with an adverb clause.

1. I read books _____.

2. I saw many interesting books _____.

3. I usually go to the library _____.

4. I haven't been to the bookstore _____.

5. I will read that book _____.

Practice Power

Write the plot of a story that you remember. Use adverb clauses and underline them in your retelling of the story.

Adverb Challenge

Read the paragraph and answer the questions.

1. "Swish, step, crack." 2. You might not immediately recognize these noises as the sounds of a dance. 3. The sounds are part of doing the *tinikling*, a traditional dance of the Philippines. 4. The dance gets its name from the long-legged tinikling birds. 5. These birds hop swiftly between tall reeds and the branches that hang overhead. 6. Dancers imitate the bird's hop as they jump gracefully up and down between two sticks. 7. Two other people hold the sticks and move them rhythmically to the music. 8. As the dance continues, the sticks begin to move back and forth more rapidly. 9. People dancing the tinikling wear loose, bright clothes. 10. They usually dance barefoot. 11. They themselves look a little like the birds.

1. In sentence 2 is the adverb *immediately* an adverb of time, place, or manner?

2. In sentence 5 find an adverb of manner. In what degree is the adverb?

3. In sentence 5 find an adverb of place.

4. In sentence 6 find the adverbs of place.

5. In sentence 7 find the adverb. What kind of adverb is it?

6. In sentence 8 find an adverb in the comparative degree. What are its positive and superlative degrees?

7. What is the adverb clause in sentence 8?

8. What is the adverb of time in sentence 10?

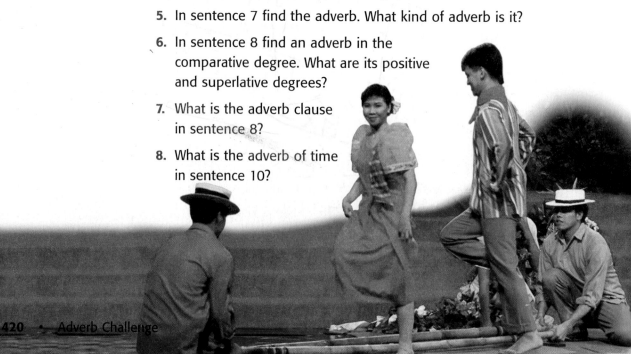

Prepositions, Conjunctions, and Interjections

6.1   Prepositions and Their Objects

6.2   Prepositional Phrases as Adjectives

6.3   Prepositional Phrases as Adverbs

6.4   Coordinating Conjunctions

6.5   Subordinate Conjunctions

6.6   Interjections

Section 6 Challenge

6.1 *Prepositions and Their Objects*

A **preposition** is a word that shows the relationship between a noun or a pronoun and another word in the sentence. The noun or pronoun that follows the preposition is called the **object of the preposition.**

	Preposition	Object
My mother read me a story	*by*	Aesop.

	Preposition		Object
Aesop lived	*in*	ancient	times.

In the first sentence the preposition is *by.* The object of the preposition is the noun *Aesop.* In the second sentence the preposition is *in.* The object of the preposition is *times.*

Common prepositions include the following.

about	around	by	near	through
above	at	down	like	to
across	before	during	of	toward
after	behind	for	off	under
against	beside	from	on	up

What are the prepositions and objects in these sentences?

Aesop's fables become famous during his lifetime.
Some fables are retellings of older stories.

In the first sentence *during* is the preposition and *lifetime* is the object. In the second sentence *of* is the preposition and *stories* is the object.

Exercise 1
Identify the preposition in each sentence.

1. Aesop was born on Samos.

2. Samos is an island in the Aegean Sea.

3. Aesop began his life in slavery.

4. He was eventually freed by his master.

5. One of his most famous fables is *The Miser.*

Exercise 2
Identify the preposition and its object in each sentence.

1. A miser sold all of his possessions.
2. With the money, he bought gold coins.
3. He had the coins made into a gold bar.
4. He buried the big bar in a field.
5. Every day he went to the field.
6. Someone spotted the miser, guessed his secret, and removed the gold from its hiding place.
7. The next day the miser found a hole without any gold.
8. He was weeping bitterly about his loss.
9. A passerby talked to him and heard his story.
10. The passerby suggested that the miser put a stone into the earth.
11. The passerby said, "The stone will serve the same purpose for you—you didn't use the gold, and you won't use the stone."

Practice Power

Imagine that you are exploring the attic of an old house. What interesting discoveries might you make? Write sentences using six of the following prepositions to describe your discoveries.

above	beside	off	underneath
along	between	onto	until
among	from	out	upon
below	into	over	within
beneath	near	under	without

6.2 *Prepositional Phrases as Adjectives*

A preposition and its object, along with any words that describe the object, form a **prepositional phrase.** A prepositional phrase acts as an adjective or an adverb.

A prepositional phrase used as an adjective is called an adjective phrase. It describes a noun or a pronoun. An **adjective phrase** tells *what kind, which ones, how many,* or *how much* about the word it describes.

> Have you ever heard the story *about Rip Van Winkle?*

The prepositional phrase is *about Rip Van Winkle.* The preposition is *about.* The phrase describes the noun *story.* It tells which story—the story *about Rip Van Winkle.* Therefore this prepositional phrase is an adjective phrase.

Notice how the descriptive adjectives in sentences A and C become adjective phrases when they are rewritten using prepositions and noun objects, as in sentences B and D.

A. The setting is the *colonial* period.
B. The setting is the time *of the colonies.*

C. There are similar *European* stories.
D. There are similar stories *from Europe.*

Exercise 1
Identify the prepositional phrase used as an adjective in each sentence. Tell the noun that it describes.

1. Rip Van Winkle from the Hudson River valley had a messy farm.

2. Lazy Rip never completed the chores on his farm.

3. One day he was resting when he heard the voice of an unfamiliar little man.

4. The stranger and his companions asked directions to a certain mountain.

5. Together they reached a huge cave in the mountain.

6. Rip, the man, and the man's friends spent a long night of merry-making before Rip fell asleep.

7. When he woke, all the other people in the cave had gone.

8. Back home, Rip found that things in the village seemed odd.

9. Many houses in the village had been replaced.

10. He saw a young woman with strange clothing.

11. He asked her questions about the changes.

12. When he told her his name, she exclaimed, "Rip Van Winkle! Why, you've had a nap of one hundred years!"

Exercise 2

Rewrite each sentence. Change the word in italics to an adjective phrase.

Example: I bought a *wooden* carving.
I bought a carving of wood.

1. The *tour* guide described the Catskill Mountains.

2. She pointed out the *stone* statue of Rip Van Winkle.

3. The *Canadian* tourist asked many questions.

4. The *shop* owner showed us many souvenirs.

Practice Power

Use the following groups of words as adjective phrases in sentences of your own.

1. from South America
2. with bright lights
3. across the field
4. at the circus
5. from the museum
6. with big, green spots

6.3 Prepositional Phrases as Adverbs

Prepositional phrases used as adverbs are called adverb phrases. An **adverb phrase** generally describes or tells more about a verb. It answers the question *where, when,* or *how.*

> The teacher discussed Native American tales *during class.*

During class is the prepositional phrase. It acts as an adverb describing the verb *discussed* and answers the question when. Study these sentences.

> We went *to the library.* (describes *went,* tells where)
> We arrived *at noon.* (describes *arrived,* tells when)
> The storyteller read the tale *in a dramatic voice.* (describes *read,* tells how)

Adverbs can be changed into prepositional phrases that act as adverbs.

> **A.** Otter swam *skillfully.*
> **B.** Otter swam *with skill.*
>
> **C.** Otter swam *northward.*
> **D.** Otter swam *to the north.*

Find the prepositional phrases used as adverbs in these sentences.

> We arrived at the lake early.
> By noon we had caught ten fish.

In the first sentence *at the lake* is a prepositional phrase that describes the verb *arrived.* It tells where. In the second sentence *by noon* is a prepositional phrase that describes the verb *had caught.* It tells when. Both are adverb phrases.

Exercise 1
Identify the adverb phrase in each sentence.

1. One day Rabbit was sitting near a lake.

2. Otter was swimming in the water.

3. Otter caught an eel with her mouth.

4. She invited Rabbit to dinner.

5. Otter cooked the eel at her house.

6. She shared the delicious meal with Rabbit.

7. In the morning Rabbit went to fish too.

8. Rabbit jumped into the icy water!

9. Rabbit couldn't swim and soon was sinking in the water.

10. Otter swam to Rabbit.

11. Otter pulled Rabbit from the water.

12. Otter asked, "Why did you jump into the lake?"

13. Rabbit said in a loud voice, "I was fishing."

14. Otter replied, "But you can't swim, so you shouldn't be jumping into deep water."

15. Then Otter caught a fish, and the pair ate dinner on the shore.

Exercise 2

Change each italicized adverb to an adverb phrase.

Example: Rabbit shouted *fearfully.*
Rabbit shouted in fear.

1. Otter *hastily* jumped into the water to save Rabbit.

2. Otter moved *speedily* through the water.

3. Otter spoke *intelligently* to Rabbit.

4. Otter treated Rabbit *patiently.*

5. Otter cooked the dinner *efficiently.*

Practice Power

Use each of the following as an adverb phrase in a sentence.

1. into a backpack

2. onto the boat

3. down the pier

4. under the water

5. out of the lake

6. above the mountains

6.4 *Coordinating Conjunctions*

A **conjunction** is a word that connects words or groups of words. A **coordinating conjunction** connects words or groups of words that are of equal importance in a sentence. The coordinating conjunctions are *and, or,* and *but.*

A coordinating conjunction may connect compound subjects, compound predicates, compound direct objects, or compound subject complements.

> Animals *and* people are characters in some famous African-American folktales. (compound subject)
> Joel Chandler Harris collected *and* recorded the stories more than one hundred years ago. (compound predicate)
> Many people enjoy the antics *and* tricks of Brer Rabbit. (compound direct object)
> Brer Rabbit was smart *and* tricky. (compound subject complement)

Sentences can be connected by a coordinating conjunction. The resulting sentence is called a compound sentence. The conjunction *and* in this example connects two complete sentences.

> Joel Chandler Harris invented a narrator for the stories, *and* they became famous as the Uncle Remus tales.

Exercise 1

Identify the conjunction in each sentence. Tell whether each connects subjects, predicates, direct objects, or subject complements.

1. Miss Meadows often invited Brer Rabbit or Brer Fox over to her house for meals.

2. Her meals were delicious and healthful.

3. One day Brer Fox was whistling and walking in the direction of Miss Meadows's house for lunch.

4. Brer Rabbit sat and devised a plan to get Brer Fox's meal.

5. Brer Rabbit's description of some ripe grapes on a nearby tree got the attention and interest of Brer Fox.

6. Soon Brer Fox spotted the grapevines and ripe fruit on an overhead branch.

7. The grapes and a wasps' nest came down together as Brer Fox tugged on the branch.

8. Brer Fox jumped and yelled as the wasps stung him all over.

9. Soon Brer Rabbit and Miss Meadows were having lunch together.

10. Brer Fox was scratching and moaning as he walked home to get medicine for the stings.

Exercise 2

Identify the conjunctions in these sentences. Tell whether each connects subjects, predicates, direct objects, or sentences.

1. Joel Chandler Harris came from a poor family, and he worked for newspapers most of his life.

2. He recognized and recorded the patterns and rhythms of African-American speech in the Uncle Remus tales.

3. In the tales Brer Rabbit is the weaker animal, but he often outsmarts stronger animals such as Brer Fox.

4. The plots and dialects of the stories were authentic, according to Chandler.

5. People today can read the original versions or various modern adaptations.

Practice Power

Retell a familiar story or fable that has several characters. Underline the conjunctions in your story and tell whether they connect subjects, predicates, direct objects, or sentences.

6.5 *Subordinate Conjunctions*

A **subordinate conjunction** connects a dependent clause to an independent clause in a sentence. An independent clause—also referred to as the main clause—has a subject and a predicate. It can stand alone as a sentence. A dependent clause has a subject and a predicate, but it cannot stand alone as a sentence.

Subordinate conjunctions introduce dependent clauses, such as adverb clauses. An adverb clause can answer the question *when.*

> Laura Ingalls Wilder grew up *when* pioneer life still existed in the Midwest.

In this sentence the subordinate conjunction is *when.* The independent clause is *Laura Ingalls Wilder grew up.* The dependent clause is *when pioneer life still existed in the Midwest.*

Common subordinate conjunctions include *after, as, before, once, since, when, whenever, while,* and *until.*

Can you identify the subordinate conjunction and the dependent clause it introduces in this sentence? Can you identify the independent clause?

> Laura's family moved from Wisconsin after free land was offered to homesteaders.

You are correct if you said that the subordinate conjunction is *after* and that it introduces the dependent clause *after free land was offered to homesteaders.* The independent clause is *Laura's family moved from Wisconsin.*

Exercise 1
Identify the subordinate conjunction in each sentence.

1. Laura Ingalls Wilder didn't write a book about her pioneer experiences until she was in her 60s.

2. She wrote *Little House on the Prairie* after she wrote *Little House in the Big Woods.*

3. *Little House on the Prairie* tells about her experiences when she was five-to-seven years old, in the 1870s.

4. When her family experienced financial problems, they decided to move to Kansas and start a farm.

5. They had many adventures as they were traveling.

6. While they were crossing a big creek, the wagon wheels stopped turning, and the wagon was actually floating.

7. Once they arrived in Kansas, Laura's father built a cabin.

8. While it was still unfinished, a pack of wolves circled the cabin and spent the night howling.

9. Before winter began, her father added a roof, a chimney, a fireplace, and a door to the cabin.

10. Laura and her sister were happy their first Christmas in the cabin when they each received a tin cup, a penny, and some sweets.

Exercise 2

Identify the subordinate conjunction in each sentence. Then identify the independent clause and the dependent clause.

1. Life was hard for Laura as she was growing up.

2. She was only 15 years old when she became a teacher.

3. Whenever the weather was bad, a farmer named Almanzo James Wilder would drive her home from school.

4. After they had dated for two years, they married in 1885 and remained so for 64 years.

5. People have loved her simple but touching stories since they were first published.

Practice Power

Write a paragraph describing the plot of a book you like. Underline the subordinate conjunctions.

6.6 *Interjections*

An **interjection** is a word that expresses a strong or sudden emotion. Interjections are frequently used in greetings and to get the attention of others.

An interjection is usually set off from the rest of the sentence by an exclamation point.

> *Wow!* I didn't know Paul Bunyan was so big.
> I finished my report. *Great!*

Here are some common interjections used to express emotions.

Emotion	Interjection
Joy	Oh! Hooray! Bravo! Yes! Wonderful!
Sorrow	Oh! Ah! Alas!
Caution	Shh! Uh-oh!
Pain	Oh! Ouch!
Wonder	Oh! Ah! My!
Disgust	Ick! Yuck! Ugh! Ha! Yikes! Rats! Good grief!
Surprise	Oh! Well! Aha! Hurrah!
Greeting	Hello! Hi! Goodbye! Aloha!

Exercise 1

Identify the interjections in the sentences. Write what emotion you think each interjection expresses.

1. Well! Paul Bunyan was the biggest baby ever born in the state of Maine.

2. Wow! He weighed 200 pounds at two weeks old.

3. Oh! He had a beard as a baby.

4. Great! He saved a big baby ox from a snowdrift and had a helper for life.

5. Bravo! He became the greatest lumberjack in the entire United States.

6. Oh! He once used bees to scare away the mosquitoes that were bothering his loggers.

7. Ugh! The mosquitoes mated with the bees and produced bee-squitoes, with stingers at both ends.

8. Hooray! Bunyan got rid of the bee-squitoes by luring them to a sugar ship, which took them to a circus.

9. Ah, no one knows for sure where Paul is now—maybe logging near the Arctic Circle.

10. Wonderful! We may hear more tall tales about Paul Bunyan.

Exercise 2

Write an appropriate interjection at the beginning of each sentence. Remember to include an exclamation mark for each interjection.

1. _____ Our class is having a storytelling festival.

2. _____ Luke designed a great flyer for our festival—with illustrations of Pecos Bill and Slewfoot Sue.

3. _____ I really like Sarah's retelling of a tale about Annie Christmas—she uses expressive body movements.

4. _____ I forgot to bring my prop to school—a lasso to use in telling about Pecos Bill.

5. _____ The audience still liked my presentation.

6. _____ Brian brought to class a giant cardboard blue ox as a prop for his presentation on Paul Bunyan.

7. _____ Kendra acted out different scenes while she retold the story of Brer Rabbit.

8. _____ Mandy dressed up like Slewfoot Sue.

9. _____ We all had a lot of fun.

Practice Power

Write five sentences about a tall-tale character, one that you know about or one that you create. Use an interjection in each sentence.

Section 6 Challenge

Read the paragraph and answer the questions.

1. Computers may run the farms of the future. 2. Tractors or robots run by computers will do much of the actual farm work. 3. They will plant and harvest all by themselves! 4. Wheat and corn will also be "grown" by computers. 5. Computers will determine the best time to plant and will control the watering of crops. 6. Farmers will know where all their animals are—without leaving the farmhouse. 7. A tiny computer will be placed on each animal. 8. While they remain sitting in their farmhouses, farmers will check computer screens and see the locations of all the animals. 9. Oh! If the farmers of 100 years ago could see the farms of the future, they might recognize only the cows and the chickens.

1. In sentence 1 find the prepositional phrase.

2. Is the prepositional phrase in sentence 1 used as an adjective or an adverb?

3. In sentence 2 find the conjunction.

4. In sentence 3 does the conjunction join subjects, predicates, or direct objects?

5. In sentence 4 find the words connected by the conjunction and tell how they are used in the sentence.

6. In sentence 5 find the coordinating conjunction. Tell if it connects two subjects, two predicates, or two sentences.

7. In sentence 7 find the prepositional phrase.

8. Tell whether the prepositional phrase in sentence 7 is used as an adjective or an adverb.

9. In sentence 8 find the prepositions.

10. In sentence 8 find the subordinate conjunction. Identify the independent clause and the dependent clause.

11. Find the interjection in the paragraph.

Sentences

7.1   Kinds of Sentences

7.2   Simple Subjects and Simple Predicates

7.3   Complete Subjects and Complete Predicates

7.4   Direct Objects and Indirect Objects

7.5   Subject Complements

7.6   Sentence Order

7.7   Compound Subjects and Compound Predicates

7.8   Compound Direct Objects

7.9   Compound Subject Complements

7.10   Compound Sentences

7.11   Complex Sentences

Sentence Challenge

7.1 Kinds of Sentences

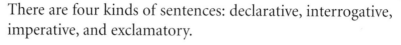

There are four kinds of sentences: declarative, interrogative, imperative, and exclamatory.

A **declarative sentence** makes a statement. It ends with a period.

> The ancient Olympics were part of a festival honoring both Zeus and Pelops.

An **interrogative sentence** asks a question. It ends with a question mark.

> Whom did ancient Greek Olympic games honor?

An **imperative sentence** gives a command or makes a request. It ends with a period.

> Lend me your book on the Olympics.

An **exclamatory sentence** expresses strong emotion. It ends with an exclamation point.

> The Olympic Games date back to 776 BC!

What kind of sentence is each of the following?

> **A.** It is amazing how old the Olympics are!
> **B.** Tell me more about the ancient Olympic games.
> **C.** Where did the ancient Olympics take place?
> **D.** The ancient Olympics took place for almost 12 centuries.

Sentence A is an exclamatory sentence. It shows emotion.
Sentence B is an imperative sentence. It makes a request.
Sentence C is an interrogative sentence. It asks a question.
Sentence D is a declarative sentence. It makes a statement.

Exercise 1

Tell whether each sentence is declarative or interrogative. Add the correct end punctuation.

1. The first ancient Olympic games were held in Greece

2. What were the events in the first Olympics

3. A foot race was probably the first Olympic event

4. There was no Olympic flame at the ancient Olympics

5. When and where did the flame originate

6. It was first used in 1928, at the games in Amsterdam

Exercise 2

Tell whether each sentence is exclamatory or imperative. Add the correct end punctuation.

1. Tell me the distance of the modern marathon

2. Wow, I didn't know it was 26 miles

3. What a long distance that is

4. Name some winners of Olympic marathons

5. What great athletes they were

6. Find out what the marathon commemorates

Exercise 3

Tell whether each sentence is declarative, interrogative, imperative, or exclamatory. Add the correct end punctuation.

1. In 1896 where were the first modern Olympics held

2. Winning athletes in the ancient Olympic games received free food and didn't have to pay taxes

3. When did chariot racing become part of the Olympics

4. What surprising facts this book reveals about the Olympics

5. Tell me the most interesting fact that you learned

6. Give me a brief overview of Olympic history

Practice Power

Write a paragraph of four sentences on the Olympics: one declarative, one interrogative, one imperative, and one exclamatory.

7.2 Simple Subjects and Simple Predicates

The **simple subject** of a sentence is the noun or pronoun that names who or what a sentence is about. To determine the subject, ask *who* or *what* before the verb.

> The *Olympics* occurred every four years for almost twelve centuries.

What occurred? The answer is the noun *Olympics*.

The **simple predicate** is the verb or verb phrase that describes the action or the state of being of the subject.

> Ancient Greeks *participated* in many athletic events.

The subject is *Greeks*. What did the Greeks do? They *participated*. The simple predicate is *participated*.

A simple predicate includes the helping verbs as well as the main verb.

> The Pan-Hellenic Festival at Delphi *has been called* the most prestigious of all the ancient Greek competitions.

The simple predicate is the verb phrase *has been called*.

Identify the simple predicate and the simple subject in each of these sentences.

> **A.** Victors received a wreath made from leaves.
> **B.** In Olympia the wreath was made from olive leaves.

You are correct if you said the following:

A. The simple predicate is *received*. The simple subject is *victors*.

B. The simple predicate is *was made*. The simple subject is *wreath*.

Exercise 1
Identify the simple subject in each sentence.

1. Women participated in an athletic competition in ancient Greece but not in the Olympics.

2. This competition was in honor of Hera, Zeus's wife.

3. Unmarried girls participated in foot races.

4. This women's festival might be as old as the men's.

5. The celebration took place every four years.

Exercise 2

Identify the simple predicate in each sentence.

1. Runners raced at the first Olympics.

2. Later other sports were added.

3. The discus and javelin first appeared in 708 BC.

4. A violent form of boxing permitted kicking and strangle holds, but not biting.

5. Many sports in the modern Olympics have been practiced since ancient times.

Exercise 3

Identify the simple predicate and the simple subject in each sentence.

1. A truce during the Olympic games prohibited fighting in the area of Olympia.

2. Messengers announced the Olympic truce throughout Greece every four years before the start of the next Olympics.

3. The truce protected the athletes and the spectators.

4. The modern Olympics arose from the desire for international cooperation.

5. Athletes from all over the world gather.

Practice Power

Write a brief paragraph about your favorite sport. Underline the simple predicates and circle the simple subjects in your sentences.

7.3 Complete Subjects and Complete Predicates

The simple subject with all the words that describe it is called the **complete subject.**

> *New sports* are added to the Olympics every four years.

In this sentence the complete subject is *new sports.* It includes the simple subject *sports* and the adjective *new.*

The simple predicate with all its objects, complements, and describing words is called the **complete predicate.**

> The pentathlon event *started in ancient Greece.*

In this sentence the complete predicate is *started in ancient Greece.* The simple predicate is *started.* The prepositional phrase *in ancient Greece* acts as an adverb.

Identify the complete subject and the complete predicate in each sentence.

A. Sports at the 1896 Olympics included track and field, gymnastics, tennis, and swimming.
B. Sailing was inaugurated at the 1900 Olympics.

You are correct if you said the following:

A. The complete subject is *sports at the 1896 Olympics.* The complete predicate is *included track and field, gymnastics, tennis, and swimming.* The simple subject is *sports,* and the simple predicate is *included.*

B. The complete subject is *sailing.* The complete predicate is *was inaugurated at the 1900 Olympics.* The simple subject is *sailing;* the simple predicate is *was inaugurated.*

Exercise 1
Identify the complete subject in each sentence.

1. The pentathlon was introduced at the 1912 Olympics.

2. Five events make up the pentathlon.

3. Contestants in the 1912 Olympics participated in the long jump, the javelin, the discus, and two races.

4. Jim Thorpe won the first pentathlon as well as the 10-event decathlon.

5. Many people described Jim Thorpe as the greatest all-around athlete.

Exercise 2

Identify the complete predicate in each sentence.

1. Jim Thorpe's Olympic medals were contested.

2. Thorpe had once received money as an athlete.

3. He played baseball for money.

4. This action made Thorpe a professional athlete, according to the Olympic Committee.

5. All Olympic athletes were supposed to be amateurs at that time.

Exercise 3

Identify the complete subject and the complete predicate in each sentence. Then identify the simple subject and the simple predicate.

1. Olympic management stripped Thorpe of his medals in 1913.

2. The Olympic Committee pardoned Jim Thorpe in 1982.

3. He had died 29 years earlier.

4. Thorpe's medals were returned to his children.

5. The reputation of a great athlete was restored!

Practice Power

Add words to the simple subject and the simple predicate in each sentence. Then name the complete subject and the complete predicate of each.

1. Runners raced.

2. Spectators clapped.

3. Winners waved.

4. Flags flew.

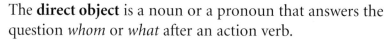

The **direct object** is a noun or a pronoun that answers the question *whom* or *what* after an action verb.

>Some Olympic athletes earned long-lasting *fame.*

In this sentence *fame* is the direct object. *Fame* answers the question *what* after the verb *earned.* What did some Olympic athletes earn? The answer is *fame,* the direct object.

>The book describes Olympic *heroes.*

In this sentence *heroes* is the direct object. *Heroes* answers the question *whom* after the verb *describes.* Whom does the book describe? The answer is *heroes,* the direct object.

Some sentences contain a direct object and an **indirect object.** The indirect object tells *to whom, for whom, to what,* or *for what* an action is done. The indirect object comes before the direct object and after the action verb in a sentence.

>The press gives Olympic *athletes* much attention.

In this sentence *attention* is the direct object. It answers the question *what* after the verb *gives.* What does the press give? It gives *attention,* the direct object. *Athletes* is the indirect object. It answers the question *to whom* the action was done. To whom is much attention given? The indirect object, *athletes,* receives the attention.

Here is a list of some verbs that can take indirect objects.

assign	get	owe	send
bring	give	pay	show
buy	hand	promise	teach
deny	lend	read	tell
forgive	offer	sell	write

Exercise 1
Identify the direct object in each sentence.

1. Fourteen-year-old Nadia Comaneci earned three gold medals in gymnastics at the 1976 Summer Olympics.

2. She established a special record.

3. She earned a score of 10.

4. A 10 represents a perfect mark.

5. Her coach, Bela Karolyi, discovered the young athlete during a visit to a school.

6. The six-year-old was doing cartwheels.

7. The coach invited Nadia to his gymnastics school.

8. According to her coach, Nadia possessed courage.

9. She tried difficult gymnastic moves without fear.

10. She had mental and physical discipline.

Exercise 2
Identify the direct object and the indirect object in each sentence.

1. Bela Karolyi taught young gymnasts moves.

2. He awarded his pupils trophies.

3. He offered Nadia good training.

4. At the Montreal Olympics Nadia showed the world her amazing skills.

5. The judges first gave Nadia a perfect score on the uneven bars for her amazing movements and somersault off the bar.

6. Her three gold medals earned her worldwide fame.

7. Judges awarded Nadia two other medals, a silver and a bronze.

8. She now teaches young people competitive gymnastics.

Practice Power

Use five of the verbs listed on page 442 in sentences of your own. Be sure to include a direct object and an indirect object in each sentence. Circle each direct object and underline each indirect object.

7.5 Subject Complements

A **subject complement** completes the meaning of a linking verb in a sentence. It is part of the predicate. If the subject complement is a noun or a pronoun, it renames the subject. If the subject complement is an adjective, it describes the subject.

Wilma Rudolph was an Olympic *medalist.*

Medalist is a noun subject complement. It renames the subject *Wilma Rudolph.*

Wilma Rudolph was *courageous* in the face of difficulties.

Courageous is an adjective subject complement. It describes the subject *Wilma Rudolph.*

The most common linking verb is the verb *be* in its various forms: *am, is, are, was, were, have been, had been,* and *will have been.*

Identify the complement in each sentence. Tell if it is a noun subject complement or an adjective subject complement.

   A. Wilma Rudolph was an inspiration to many people.
   B. Wilma Rudolph was competitive despite her physical challenges.

A. The subject complement is *inspiration.* It is a noun, and it renames the subject *Wilma Rudolph.*
B. The subject complement is *competitive.* It is an adjective, and it describes the subject *Wilma Rudolph.*

Exercise 1
Identify the subject complement in each sentence. Tell whether it is a noun or an adjective.

1. Wilma Rudolph's family was large.
2. Wilma was the 12th child in a family of 22 children.
3. Her parents were industrious.
4. Wilma was often sick as a child.
5. She was a victim of polio.

6. Her family was diligent in helping with physical therapy.

7. Everyone in the family was supportive of Rudolph.

8. Wilma was a hard worker.

9. She was successful in reaching her goal—to walk again.

10. Soon she was a fast runner.

11. She was a member of the U.S. Olympic team in 1956 and again in 1960.

12. She was the winner of three gold medals in 1960.

13. Her family and all Americans were proud of her.

14. She was a famous athlete of her time.

15. Her accomplishments were truly wonderful.

Exercise 2

Complete each sentence with a noun or an adjective used as a subject complement.

1. A famous athlete is _____.

2. My favorite sport is _____.

3. I was so _____ when we won our first game!

4. My coach is _____.

5. The goalie on our team is _____.

Practice Power

Write six sentences, using each of the following as a subject complement.

1. athlete   3. enthusiastic   5. winter

2. diligent   4. coach   6. team

7.6 *Sentence Order*

A sentence is in **natural order** when the verb follows the subject.

	Subject	Verb	
Rhythmic	*gymnasts*	*twirl*	long ribbons.

A sentence is in **inverted order** when the main verb or a helping verb comes before the subject.

	Verb		Subject
Around the floor gracefully	*dance*	the	*gymnasts.*

Many questions are in inverted order.

Verb		Subject	Verb
What	*do*	rhythmic *gymnasts*	*twirl?*

In the above sentence the helping verb *do* comes before the subject *gymnasts*. Even though the main verb *twirl* follows the subject, the sentence is still in inverted order.

Tell whether each sentence is in natural order or inverted order.

  A. Across the finish line ran the lead runner.
  B. Runners dashed around the track.
  C. Do runners wear special track suits?

You are correct if you said the following:

A. The sentence is in inverted order. The subject *runner* comes after the verb *ran*.

B. The sentence is in natural order. The subject *runners* comes before the verb *dashed.*

C. The sentence is in inverted order. The helping verb *do* comes before the subject *runners.*

Exercise 1
Tell whether each sentence is in natural order or inverted order.

1. Onto the diving board stepped the diver.

2. She jumped up and down.

3. At the edge of the board she paused.

4. Into the water went the diver almost without a splash.

5. On the board flashed her score.

Exercise 2

Rewrite each sentence, putting it in natural order.

1. Around the velodrome track sped the cyclists.

2. Up the hill pedaled the road racer.

3. Across the finish line sped the cyclist.

4. On the podium stood the winner.

Exercise 3

Rewrite each sentence, putting it in inverted order. Write questions where indicated.

1. The horse jumped over the hurdle.

2. The word *equestrian* comes from the Latin word for "horse." (question)

3. The top bar of the hurdle fell down.

4. Points were taken off the rider's score. (question)

Practice Power

Make two sentences from each set of scrambled words. One sentence should be in natural order, and the other should be in inverted order.

1. the cave echoed through our voices

2. waddled to the lake the ducks

3. storm thundered suddenly a valley through the

4. the paint down red the wall dripped

7.7 Compound Subjects and Compound Predicates

A sentence with two or more subjects is said to have a **compound subject.** The connecting word for a compound subject is generally the coordinating conjunction *and* or *or.*

> *Gymnastics* and *ice-skating* attract large TV audiences.

In this sentence the compound subject is *gymnastics* and *ice-skating.* They are the subjects of the verb *attract.*

When *or* is the coordinating conjunction, the verb agrees with the subject closer to the verb.

> The swimmers *or* the coach is featured on the TV show.

Coach is singular; therefore the verb agrees with a singular subject.

Two or more predicates joined by a coordinating conjunction form a **compound predicate.**

> Athletes *develop skill* and *build strength to compete.*

In this sentence the compound predicate is *develop skill* and *build strength to compete. Develop* and *build* tell two things that athletes do.

Exercise 1

Identify the compound simple subjects and the compound simple predicates.

1. Sydney and Athens were sites of recent Olympics.
2. Golf and tug-of-war were once Olympic sports.
3. The bobsled and the luge involve sleds on icy tracks.
4. Olive leaves or pine twigs were used to make crowns for winning athletes at the ancient Olympics.
5. Poems were written and presented at the ancient Olympics.
6. You should research and explain chariot racing.
7. Physical ability and hard work combine to produce an Olympic champion.

Exercise 2

Complete each sentence with a compound subject or a compound predicate. Use nouns, pronouns, or verbs plus other words to complete the sentence.

1. _____ and _____ would be exciting sports to try.

2. Is _____ or _____ your favorite sport?

3. My favorite athletes are _____ and _____.

4. _____ and _____ are team sports at my school.

5. Olympic traditions _____ and _____ the world for decades.

Exercise 3

Combine each pair of sentences into one sentence with a compound subject or a compound predicate. Make certain that the subjects and verbs agree.

1. The Winter Olympic games are exciting to watch.
   The Summer Olympic games are exciting to watch.

2. Jim Thorpe earned an Olympic gold medal.
   Jim Thorpe lost the medal because he had played professional baseball.

3. Athletes take an oath at the games.
   Officials take an oath at the games.

4. Machines determine winners.
   Judges determine winners.

5. Coaches train athletes in the skills of their sports.
   Coaches motivate athletes to do their best.

6. Ice hockey is an Olympic sport.
   Field hockey is an Olympic sport.

Practice Power

Write a paragraph about an activity or sport you do with a friend. Include compound subjects and compound predicates in your sentences.

7.8 Compound Direct Objects

A verb that has two or more direct objects is said to have a **compound direct object.**

> Football players wear *helmets* and *pads.*

To find the direct object, ask *who* or *what* after the verb. In the above sentence the verb is *wear.* Football players wear what? They wear *helmets* and *pads.* The compound direct object is *helmets* and *pads.*

Compound direct objects are usually connected by the coordinating conjunction *and* or *or.*

Exercise 1
Identify the compound direct object in each sentence.

1. Should I bring an umbrella or a rain slicker to the football game?

2. We took scarves and sweaters because of the cold.

3. Bring sandwiches and thermoses of hot chocolate.

4. My dad drove my cousin and me to the game.

5. My dad enjoys soccer and football.

6. We found an old program and some stale candy under the back seat of my dad's car.

7. The vendor handed us programs and pencils.

8. My dad told us the players' names and the basic rules of the game.

9. My dad bought us popcorn and peanuts at halftime.

10. The concession stand sold T-shirts and pennants.

11. We bought souvenirs and photographs of our favorite players.

Exercise 2
Complete each sentence with a compound direct object. Use additional words to complete each direct object if necessary.

1. My friend invited _____ and _____ to a game.

2. Mom gave us _____ and _____ for snacks.

3. We put _____ and _____ into thermoses.

4. We wore _____ and _____.

5. I would like _____ and _____ from the food stand.

6. Spectators see _____ and _____ at a game.

7. Do you like _____ or _____?

8. Do you play _____ or _____ after school?

Exercise 3

Combine each pair of sentence into one sentence with a compound direct object.

1. We saw some good passes from the quarterback.
   We saw some good runs from the quarterback.

2. Greg packed sandwiches for the trip.
   Greg packed snacks for the trip.

3. I bought a team jersey.
   I bought a team photograph.

4. The audience applauded the players.
   The audience applauded the halftime entertainment.

5. We enjoyed the bands.
   We enjoyed the cheerleaders.

6. We brought some autographs home.
   We brought a pennant home.

7. I met the coach after the game.
   I met some players after the game.

Practice Power

Write five sentences about things you enjoy doing or imagine you would enjoy doing at the ocean, a lake, a river, or a pool. Use a compound direct object in each of your sentences.

7.9 Compound Subject Complements

A verb with two or more subject complements is said to have a **compound subject complement.**

> The skater Peggy Fleming was a world *champion* and an Olympic *medalist.*
>
> Peggy Fleming was *graceful* and *athletic.*

In the first sentence *champion* and *medalist* are noun subject complements. They make up a compound subject complement.

In the second sentence *graceful* and *athletic* are adjective subject complements. They form a compound subject complement.

Compound subject complements are usually connected by the coordinating conjunction *and* or *or.*

Identify the subject complements in each sentence. Tell whether they are nouns or adjectives.

> **A.** I am anxious and nervous about skating in my first competition.
> **B.** After the Olympics, Peggy Fleming became a professional skater and a businesswoman.

You are correct if you said the following:

A. The compound complement is *anxious* and *nervous.* The connecting word is *and.* This compound complement is an adjective complement. It describes the subject *I.*

B. The compound complement is *skater* and *businesswoman.* The connecting word is *and.* This compound complement is a noun complement. It renames the subject *Peggy Fleming.*

Exercise 1
Identify the compound subject complement in each sentence. Tell whether it includes nouns or adjectives.

1. Peggy Fleming is an ice-skater and a sports announcer.

2. She has always been stylish and smooth on the ice.

3. Her spins are lovely and amazing.

4. Peggy's childhood loves were baseball and climbing.

5. From the beginning, her first movements on ice skates were effortless and sure.

6. Becoming a good skater was always her dream and goal.

7. In 1968 she was the Olympic champion and gold medal winner in women's figure skating.

8. She was the star of many TV ice specials and the winner of two Emmy awards.

9. She has been famous and respected for decades.

10. She is currently a spokesperson for and supporter of many charitable causes.

11. She is a member of the U.S. Olympic Hall of Fame and the recipient of a *Sports Illustrated* award for special athletes who changed their sport.

Exercise 2

Complete each sentence with a compound complement.

1. My favorite athletes are _____ and _____.

2. My favorite sports are _____ and _____.

3. Are you _____ or _____?

4. We were _____ and _____ when we went to our first skating event.

5. These teams are _____ and _____.

Practice Power

Write a sentence for each pair of adjectives and nouns. Use them as compound subject complements.

1. hockey player, soccer player

2. contestant, winner

3. scared, excited

4. fast, energetic

7.10 Compound Sentences

A **compound sentence** contains two or more independent clauses. An independent clause has a subject and a predicate and can stand alone as a sentence. A compound sentence is formed when two or more independent clauses are connected by the coordinating conjunction *and*, *but*, or *or*.

> The Summer Olympics and the Winter Olympics originally took place during the same year, but now they are held two years apart.

Use a comma before the conjunction when two independent clauses are combined. A semicolon (;) may be used between independent clauses instead of the comma and the coordinating conjunction.

> The Olympic flag has a white background. It has five rings on it. (two separate sentences)
> The Olympic flag has a white background, and it has five rings on it. (compound sentence with a comma and *and*)
> The Olympic flag has a white background; it has five rings on it. (compound sentence with a semicolon)

Because a compound sentence has more than one clause, it must have at least two subjects and two predicates.

Exercise 1

Identify the complete subject and the complete predicate in each independent clause in these compound sentences.

1. The five rings on the Olympic flag are in different colors, and each ring represents an inhabited continent.

2. Athletes from all over the world compete in the games, and the interlocking rings represent international cooperation.

3. The original Olympic flag was presented at the 1914 Olympic Congress, but it was not used until 1920.

4. The flag is lowered at the closing ceremony, and it is presented to the mayor of the next host city.

5. The motto of the Olympic games is *citius, altius, fortius*; this Latin phrase translates as "faster, higher, stronger."

6. Athletes should strive for their best; the achievement of one's best is every athlete's goal.

Exercise 2

Combine each pair of sentences to form compound sentences. First use a comma before the coordinating conjunction *and, but,* or *or.* Then use a semicolon to combine the sentences.

1. The original Olympic flag was retired after the 1984 games. A new flag was flown in 1988 in Seoul, Korea.

2. The Olympic flag is used at ceremonies. It is stored in the host city's town hall until the next games.

3. Ancient Greeks held torch relays. They were not part of the Olympics.

4. The flame of the modern torch is lit at Olympia, Greece. It is then transported by various means to its destination.

5. Runners carry the torch to the host city. Its flame burns there during the games.

6. The Olympic anthem was composed in 1896 for the first modern Olympics. It is now the official Olympics anthem.

7. The head of state of the host country declares the Games open. The Olympic flag is raised.

Practice Power

Write a paragraph about an event at which you were a spectator. Describe what happened and what you saw. Use at least two compound sentences in your writing. Underline the independent clauses.

7.11 *Complex Sentences*

A **complex sentence** contains one independent clause and one dependent clause. An independent clause has a subject and a predicate and can stand on its own as a sentence. A dependent clause has a subject and a predicate, but it cannot stand alone as a sentence. A dependent clause is always used with an independent clause in a sentence.

Dependent clauses that act as adverbs are called **adverb clauses.** An adverb clause can tell *when* something occurred.

> After he had won two world titles in 1988, Dan Jansen was the favorite for a gold medal.

The independent clause is *Dan Jansen was the favorite for a gold medal.* The dependent clause is *after he had won two world titles in 1988.* It is an adverb clause that begins with the subordinate conjunction *after* and answers the question *when.* The dependent clause doesn't make sense by itself. It cannot stand alone as a sentence.

A complex sentence has a subject and a predicate in each of its clauses. In the sentence above, the subject of the dependent clause is *he,* and the verb is *had won.* In the independent clause, the subject is *Dan Jansen,* and the verb is *was.*

Following are some of the subordinate conjunctions used to introduce adverb clauses that indicate time: *after, as, before, since, until, when,* and *while.*

Can you identify the dependent clause, the independent clause, and the subordinate conjunction in this sentence?

> Dan Jansen had won world titles before he raced in the Olympics.

The dependent clause is *before he raced in the Olympics,* and the independent clause is *Dan Jansen had won world titles.* The subordinate conjunction is *before.*

Exercise 1
Tell whether each of the following clauses is dependent or independent.

1. Dan Jansen was born in 1969 in Wisconsin
2. Until he began speed skating
3. Since he was a child
4. After he won sprint championships in 1988
5. When he tried for the eighth time for an Olympic medal

Exercise 2
Identify the adverb clause in each of the complex sentences.

1. Before he competed in the 500-meter speed-skating race in 1988, Dan Jansen learned about the death of his sister from leukemia.
2. While he was rounding a turn, he fell and lost.
3. In 1992 at Albertville Jansen was again the favorite in the 500 after he had won the World Cup championship in that event.
4. He stumbled again as he was racing.
5. After the Olympics were rescheduled for two years later in Norway, Jansen got another chance at a medal.
6. Again he stumbled while he was skating in the 500-meter race.
7. After he had failed at a medal for the seventh time, his last chance was in the 1,000-meter race.
8. When he tried this time, many fans were rooting for him.
9. While he was skating at a world-record pace, he slipped again but still won the race—in world-record time.

Practice Power

Write a paragraph about your favorite Olympic hero. Do research in a library or on the Internet. Use at least three adverb clauses indicating time in your paragraph. Underline the dependent clauses.

Sentence Challenge

Read the selection and answer the questions.

1. Have you ever been to the Statue of Liberty? 2. It stands on Liberty Island in New York harbor; it is a beautiful historic monument. 3. Two spiral staircases lead from the base to the crown. 4. A separate, shorter staircase is then used to reach the torch, which is 305 feet above the base of the statue. 5. The view of New York City from there is magnificent and unique!

6. "Statue of Liberty" is actually a nickname for the huge monument. 7. Its actual name is *Liberty Enlightening the World.* 8. It arrived as a giant birthday present to the United States from France on July 4, 1884. 9. After a French historian had suggested a monument to freedom, the French sculptor Frédéric Bartholdi designed and built the statue. 10. The citizens of France offered the Americans the statue as a gift.

11. In Paris stands a small version of the Statue of Liberty. 12. The large statue in New York harbor and the small one in Paris are reminders of the longtime friendship of the two countries.

1. What kind of sentence is sentence 1? Is it in natural or inverted order?

2. Is sentence 2 a simple or a compound sentence?

3. In sentence 3 find the simple subject and the simple predicate.

4. In sentence 3 find the complete subject and the complete predicate.

5. What kind of sentence is sentence 5?

6. In sentence 6 what is the subject complement? Is it a noun or an adjective?

7. In sentence 10 what are the direct and indirect objects?

8. Find a sentence that has a compound subject.

9. Find a sentence with a compound subject complement.

10. Find the complex sentence with an adverb clause indicating time.

11. Is sentence 11 in natural or inverted order? Rewrite it to reverse the order.

Punctuation and Capitalization

8.1   End Punctuation

8.2   Commas in Series

8.3   Commas with Conjunctions

8.4   Direct Address and *Yes* and *No*

8.5   Apostrophes

8.6   Capital Letters

8.7   Titles

8.8   Other Uses of Capital Letters

8.9   Abbreviations

8.10   Direct Quotations

8.11   Addresses and Letters

Section 8 Challenge

Punctuation marks show how various parts of a sentence relate to each other. They also signal what type a sentence is. Understanding the proper use of punctuation helps in both writing and reading. The end punctuation marks of sentences are periods, question marks, and exclamation points.

Use a **period** at the end of a declarative sentence or an imperative sentence.

- A declarative sentence makes a statement.

    Scientists believe that water once flowed on Mars.

- An imperative sentence gives a command.

    Lend me your book about the planets, please.

Use a **question mark** at the end of an interrogative sentence.

- An interrogative sentence asks a question.

    Was there ever life on Mars?

Use an **exclamation point** at the end of an exclamatory sentence.

- An exclamatory sentence expresses strong emotion.

    What a fascinating question that is!

Exercise 1

Look at the end punctuation of each sentence. Tell what kind of sentence it is and give the rule for end punctuation that applies.

1. Find Olympus Mons, the largest known volcano in our solar system, on the map of Mars.

2. It is three times higher than Mount Everest.

3. That's really huge!

4. The North and South Poles of Mars are covered with ice caps.

5. What are these ice caps made of?

6. Look for the answer on this page.

7. They consist of frozen carbon dioxide and water.

8. What a fascinating planet Mars is!

Exercise 2

Complete the following sentences by adding correct end punctuation.

1. Come over here and look at this model of Mars

2. According to some findings, water must have existed on Mars at some time

3. Will scientists find evidence of past life there

4. Are there fossils of microorganisms to be found in Mars rock

5. What an interesting discovery that would be

6. Read more about current research on Mars

7. What did the rovers on Mars discover

8. How interesting the rovers' photographs are

9. Why has Mars been referred to as the red planet

10. Its reddish soil has rusted iron in it

Practice Power

Write several sentences about one of the planets. Write at least one declarative, one interrogative, one imperative, and one exclamatory sentence. Be sure to use the correct end punctuation.

8.2 Commas in Series

Commas are used to separate three or more words in a series. A comma comes before the coordinating conjunction at the end of the series. Words in a series should be similar in nature and serve the same purpose in the sentence. A series may consist of all nouns, all verbs, all adverbs, all adjectives, or even all phrases.

> *Mercury, Earth, Venus,* and *Mars* are solid planets—or terrestrial planets.
> *Jupiter, Saturn, Uranus, Neptune,* and *Pluto* are gaseous planets.

In each sentence above, the coordinating conjunction is *and*. A comma precedes *and* in both series. Each series functions as the subject of its sentence.

> Scientists *observe, study,* and *chart* the Red Spot, a gigantic whirlwind on Jupiter.

In this sentence commas are used to separate verbs used as simple predicates—*observe, study,* and *chart.*

> The atmosphere of Jupiter includes *hydrogen, helium,* and *ammonia.*
> The teacher assigned *Carl, Fred,* and *Missy* different planets for their reports.
> Several students wrote stories about imaginary trips to *Saturn, Venus, Pluto,* and *Neptune.*

In each sentence above, the series functions as an object. In the first sentence the series is the direct object of *includes.* In the second sentence the series is the indirect object of *assigned,* and in the third sentence the series is the object of the preposition *to.*

> Jupiter is *gigantic, gaseous,* and *stormy.*

In this sentence commas separate adjectives in a series that functions as a subject complement.

Exercise 1
Add commas to these sentences to separate words in series. Then identify the series of words as nouns, verbs, or adjectives.

1. Astronomers view photograph and analyze Jupiter's features.

2. Scientists have used telescopes satellites and space probes to study Jupiter.

3. The inner planets are small rocky and solid.

4. Jupiter is large gaseous and liquid.

5. Storms constantly form swirl and rage on Jupiter.

6. The spots ovals and streaks on Jupiter's cloud tops are weather disturbances.

7. Like Earth, Jupiter tilts spins and orbits the sun.

8. Io Europa Ganymede and Callisto are the four biggest moons of Jupiter.

9. Europa has a shiny icy and cracked surface.

10. Jupiter was studied by the three early scientists Simon Marius Galileo Galilei and Robert Hooke.

11. Important regions of Jupiter include its north polar region south polar region and equatorial zone.

12. Pallas Vesta and Juno are three asteroids that were discovered in the asteroid belt between Jupiter and Mars.

13. Vesta is a large bright and easily visible asteroid.

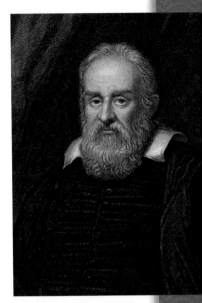

Exercise 2
Use the following series of words in sentences of your own.

1. crowded bustling noisy

2. planetariums aquariums oceanariums

3. question theorize experiment

4. exciting fun interesting

Practice Power

Think about a visit to a park, a mall, or some other place in your neighborhood. What would you see? Write five sentences, each of which contains words in a series. Use commas correctly to punctuate the sentences.

8.3 *Commas with Conjunctions*

A comma is used before the coordinating conjunction *and, but,* or *or* when two independent clauses are joined to form a compound sentence.

> Astronomy is the study of the universe, and it has existed since ancient times.
> Astronomers use large telescopes, but you can study the sky with simple binoculars.
> You can start your study of the solar system with the moon, or you can look for stars in the constellations.

Commas are used in compound sentences but not in compound sentence parts.

> **A.** Comets *and* asteroids fascinate me, *and* I will eventually research *and* submit a report on them.
> **B.** A comet is a solar body of ice *and* dust.
> **C.** Asteroids may contain carbon *or* other materials.

In sentence A a comma is used to separate the independent clauses. Commas are not used, however, in the compound subject *comets and asteroids* in the first clause or in the compound predicate *will research and submit* in the second clause. In sentence B *ice* and *dust,* objects of the preposition *of,* are not separated by a comma. In sentence C a comma does not separate the direct objects *carbon* and *materials.*

Can you explain why a comma is not needed in the following sentence?

> Astronomers observe and map the stars.

The sentence has a compound verb, *observe* and *map,* and compound sentence parts are not separated by commas.

Exercise 1
Rewrite the following sentences, adding commas where needed.

1. You must use your eyes carefully and you will see many new things in the sky.

2. Some people buy telescopes but even binoculars are a good tool for sky watching.

3. Many books show the locations of planets and stars at different times of the year and these books are useful tools.

4. You can view the constellation Orion in the evening in winter or you can look for it during the morning in summer.

5. The stars really are different colors and the star on Orion's shoulder looks red at certain times of year.

Exercise 2

Rewrite the following sentences, adding commas where needed. Not all the sentences need commas.

1. Most cities have a lot of pollution and star watching is difficult in them.

2. Both air pollution and city lights make sky viewing hard in cities.

3. People in cities can usually see only the brighter objects and many stars are faint or hidden.

4. City dwellers should go far from the city and sit in an isolated area under the sky for a good night of sky watching.

5. There is less pollution in isolated areas and a whole new sky will appear before your eyes.

Practice Power

Rewrite the following paragraph. Combine the underlined sentences, using a conjunction and commas where needed.

<u>It was a cold night. We were getting ready to go outside.</u> We wanted to watch the meteor shower that was supposed to begin at midnight. <u>I brought a big thermos of hot chocolate. My dad brought some blankets.</u> We didn't have to wait long. The meteor show was spectacular. We watched meteors shooting across the sky. <u>You can make a wish for every one sighted. I must have made one hundred wishes that night.</u>

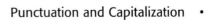

8.4 Direct Address and Yes and No

Commas are used to separate words used in direct address. A noun in direct address names the person spoken to.

When the name of a person addressed is the first word of a sentence, it is followed by a comma.

> Greg, did you know that Mercury is the planet closest to the sun?

When the noun in direct address is the last word of a sentence, a comma is placed before the name.

> Mercury has practically no atmosphere, Alex.

If the name of the person is used within a sentence, one comma is placed before the name and one after the name.

> The planet Mercury, Bob, is quite rocky.

Commas are used after the words *yes* and *no* when either introduces a sentence.

> Yes, the temperature varies greatly on Mercury.
> No, Mercury is not far away from the sun.

Exercise 1
Rewrite the sentences. Add commas for nouns in direct address.

1. A day on Mercury is equal to 58.65 days on Earth Janet.

2. Luis a year on Mercury lasts only eighty-eight Earth days.

3. Mercury orbits the sun Ann faster than any other planet.

4. During a day on Mercury Jae-Hwa the temperature is hotter than any oven.

Exercise 2
Rewrite the sentences. Add a comma after *yes* or *no* when it begins a sentence.

1. Yes a night on Mercury also lasts 58.65 Earth days.

2. Yes the nights on Mercury are colder than any freezer.

3. No there aren't any seasons on Mercury.

4. No Mercury's axis is not tilted.

Exercise 3

Rewrite the sentences. Add commas where needed. Apply all the rules you learned.

1. Yes Mercury was named after a Roman god.

2. Craters on Mercury have names such as Bach Beethoven and Shakespeare.

3. It is the second smallest planet Ellie in our solar system.

4. Yes some scientists George compare Mercury's surface to that of our moon.

5. Mercury shrank over time and its surface wrinkled.

6. No I didn't know Kevin that Mercury is only a little larger than Earth's moon.

Practice Power

Complete each sentence with a noun in direct address. Add commas wherever needed in these sentences.

1. Yes I would love to go stargazing with you tonight _____.

2. No I don't have a telescope _____.

3. Yes it would be great _____ if I could share your telescope.

4. No I can't meet you _____ until about 9:30.

5. Yes I checked with my mom this morning _____.

6. Yes she said I could go _____.

8.5 *Apostrophes*

An **apostrophe** (') is used to show ownership or possession.

To show that one person or thing owns or possesses something, place an apostrophe and an *s* ('*s*) after the singular noun.

> This scientist's research is on the surface of Mars.
> Janis's report will explain the research project.

To show that more than one person or thing owns or possesses something, place an apostrophe after the *s* at the end of a regular plural noun. If a plural noun does not end in -*s*, place an apostrophe and *s* (-'*s*) after the noun.

> The scientists' new telescope is big and powerful.
> The children's telescope is at a window in the attic.

An **apostrophe** is used in a contraction to indicate where a letter or letters have been omitted.

> I *didn't* know that Earth is the third planet from the sun.

In the above sentence *didn't* stands for *did not*. The apostrophe stands for the missing *o* in *not*.

Here is a list of some common contractions.

aren't = are not	it's = it is, it has
can't = cannot	I've = I have
didn't = did not	there's = there is, there has
doesn't = does not	we'll = we will
don't = do not	we've = we have
hasn't = has not	won't = will not
haven't = have not	you're = you are
I'll = I will	you've = you have
isn't = is not	I'm = I am

Exercise 1

Add an apostrophe to show possession where needed in these sentences.

1. Sarahs report had many interesting facts about the moon.

2. The classs interest in the subject goes back to an earlier visit by a NASA scientist.

3. The early Romans name for the moon was *luna.*

4. Explorers trips into space have given us a great deal of information about the moon.

5. Almost a half ton of rock samples from the moon was included in the astronauts cargoes back to Earth.

6. Scientists work on these samples is still going on today.

7. Neil Armstrongs first words on the moon are still quoted.

8. Several astronauts have landed on the moon, and the mens courage has always impressed me.

Exercise 2

Rewrite the following, using one contraction in each sentence.

1. There is no atmosphere on the moon.

2. I have read that the moon may have been part of Earth.

3. Scientists do not know whether a huge object once collided with Earth.

4. We will probably never know whether a piece of Earth broke off and formed the present moon.

5. There is one important effect of the moon on Earth—it causes tides.

6. The moon does not have any light of its own.

7. It is simply reflecting the light of the sun.

8. I am learning more about the moon from this book.

Practice Power

Draw a floor plan of your home or school, showing the location of the things in it. Label your picture to tell what belongs to whom; for example, Bob's desk, Alan's bedroom. Write a paragraph about your drawing. Include at least four contractions.

8.6 *Capital Letters*

The first word of every sentence begins with a capital letter.

> Not all planets in the solar system have moons.

A proper noun begins with a capital letter. A proper noun names a particular person, a particular place, or a particular thing.

Persons: Sally Ride, Copernicus, Aristotle

Places: Mercury, China, New Jersey, Pittsburgh, Lake Erie, Columbia River, the Smithsonian Air and Space Museum, Mars

Organizations: the United Nations, the Red Cross

Streets and avenues: Main Street, Elm Avenue

Holidays: New Year's Day, Hanukhah, Labor Day, Memorial Day, Christmas

Schools: Lakin School, Harvard University

Religious denominations: Catholicism, Methodism, Catholics, Methodists

Members of a political party: Democrats, Republicans

Days of the week: Monday, Tuesday, Sunday

Months of the year: November, May, September

Exercise 1
Rewrite the phrases, adding capital letters where needed.

1. the kennedy space center at cape canaveral in florida

2. independence day on july 4

3. the letter to the johnson space center written by the students of forest park school

4. national aeronautics and space administration on e street in washington, d.c.

5. the first person on the moon on july 16, 1969

Exercise 2

Indicate the sentences in which capital letters are used correctly. Rewrite the sentences with errors in the use of capital letters to correct the errors.

1. The students of Forest school visited a special exhibit at the Johnson Space center in Houston, texas.

2. Our teacher, Mrs. Portman, organized the trip.

3. We went on a tuesday morning in October.

4. we experienced what it is like to be in a weightless environment in a special space capsule.

Exercise 3

Rewrite each sentence, adding capital letters where needed.

1. astronomers have discovered what may be the tenth planet in our solar system.

2. they named it sedna, after an inuit goddess.

3. sedna is believed to be the same size as Pluto.

4. scientists at mount palomar observatory detected sedna.

5. dr. mike brown from the california institute of technology was involved in the observations.

6. brown does not believe that sedna is a real planet.

7. a company with telescopes in arizona and oregon has done follow-up studies on the possible planet.

8. in march 1993 astronomers eugene shoemaker, carolyn shoemaker, and david levy discovered a comet near jupiter.

9. the comet was named comet shoemaker-levy 9.

10. in july 1994 the comet crashed into jupiter.

Practice Power

Write six sentences about a historic event or person. Trade papers with a partner. Proofread each other's work.

8.7 *Titles*

A capital letter is used for the first letter of each important word in the title of a book, movie, TV show, play, poem, song, artwork, sacred book, article, or essay. Articles, prepositions, and conjunctions usually are not capitalized. The first and last words of a title always begin with capital letters.

Title of a book: *The War of the Worlds,* a science fiction classic by H. G. Wells

Title of a play: *Peter Pan* by J. M. Barrie

Title of a poem: "Letter to the Moon" by Jane Yolen

Title of a magazine: *National Geographic*

The first word of every line of most poetry and songs:
A flea and a fly
Flew up in a flue.
Said the flea, "Let us fly!"
Said the fly, "Let us flee!"

Title of a song: "Here Comes the Sun" by George Harrison of the Beatles

Title of a movie: *Star Wars*

Title of an artwork: *Starry Night* by Vincent Van Gogh

Title of a sacred book: Bible, Koran, Torah

Title of an article or an essay: "Is There Life on Mars?"

Titles of books (except sacred books), plays, magazines, movies, and artworks are italicized when typed and underlined when handwritten. Titles of poems, short stories, and magazine articles have quotation marks around them.

Exercise 1
Rewrite the phrases that are capitalized incorrectly to correct them. Use underlining for italicized titles.

1. genesis, the first book of the bible

2. Christina Rossetti's poem, "Who Has Seen the wind?"

3. Frank Sinatra's recording of "Home On The Range"

4. Robert Frost's poem "Stopping by woods on a snowy Evening"

5. Georgia O'keeffe's painting *Evening star*

6. and the rockets red glare, the bombs bursting in air,
   gave proof through the night that our flag was still there
   —"Star Spangled Banner"

7. H. A. Rey's book *The Stars, a new way of seeing them*

8. Madeleine L'Engle's book *A wrinkle in time*

Exercise 2

Rewrite the sentences, adding capital letters where needed. Use underlining for italicized words.

1. Jules Verne's *from the earth to the moon* is an early science-fiction book, with a spaceship shot from a cannon!

2. Janet and Isaac Asimov's *norby chronicles* features robots, people, and travel through time and space.

3. *home on the moon* by Marianne J. Dyson traces humans' interest in the moon.

4. Maura Gouck's book *the solar system* tells readers what they would actually see on a journey among the planets.

5. Ray Bradbury's story "all summer in a day" is about a place where the sun shines for one hour every seven years.

6. Franklyn Branley's *the moon hoax* tells about a newspaper that published made-up stories about life on the moon.

Practice Power

Write five sentences about books, poems, or magazine articles you've read recently, or about movies you've seen. Tell what you liked about each.

8.8 *Other Uses of Capital Letters*

In addition to uses with proper nouns and in titles, capital letters are used for

- the first word in a direct quotation

  NASA officials reported, "The second Mars rover, *Opportunity,* has safely touched down."

- the directions North, South, East, and West, when they refer to specific regions of a country

  On our trip to the South, we watched the launch of the space shuttle from Cape Canaveral.

- the pronoun *I*

  My family and *I* visited the Kennedy Space Center.

- titles that precede a person's name

  When he was elected in 1960, President John F. Kennedy became the country's 35th president.

- initials in a person's name

  H. G. Wells = Herbert George Wells

Exercise 1
Rewrite the phrases, using the correct capitalization.

1. the space centers in the south
2. my sister and i
3. general Omar Bradley
4. a novel by Arthur c. Clarke

Exercise 2
Write each of the following names, using an initial for the italicized words.

1. Sally *Kristen* Ride
2. Captain Neil *Alden* Armstrong
3. John *Fitzgerald* Kennedy
4. Franklyn *Mansfield* Branley

Exercise 3
Rewrite the sentences, adding capital letters where needed.

1. It was January 26, 2004, when my dad exclaimed, "the second rover has landed on Mars!"
2. Brendan wondered if i had seen the first pictures sent back from the Mars rover.
3. Roger exclaimed, "when the rover landed on Mars, i couldn't believe how far it bounced!"
4. Then i inquired, "do you think the pictures from this rover will be better than those from the first Mars rover, *Spirit*?"
5. NASA explained, "we hope to search for evidence that water once flowed on Mars."
6. "could life ever have existed on mars?" i asked.
7. Recently i told Roger, "two asteroids have been named *Spirit* and *Opportunity*."
8. He said sarcastically, "that's better than naming one after you— b. j. catastrophe!"

Practice Power

Select a paragraph in a newspaper article. Rewrite it, removing all the capital letters. Exchange your rewritten article with a partner. Rewrite your partner's article, putting back the capital letters. Compare the paragraph to the original.

8.9 Abbreviations

A period is used after many abbreviations. An **abbreviation** is a shortened form of a word.

Capital letters are used for abbreviations when capital letters would be used if the words were written in full.

Titles

The title Mr. is used in referring to a male and Mrs. or Ms. to a female. Titles are capitalized when they appear before proper names.

Sr. = Senior   Jr. = Junior

Dr. = Doctor   Rev. = Reverend   Gov. = Governor

Time

AD = anno Domini   BC = before Christ

Sun. = Sunday   Fri. = Friday

Jan. = January   Sept. = September

May, June, and July are not abbreviated.

a.m. = before noon   p.m. = after noon

Places

St. = Street   Ave. = Avenue   Rd. = Road

Measurements

in. = inch   ft. = foot   yd. = yard   oz. = ounce

qt.= quart   lb. = pound   gal. = gallon

The abbreviations used in the metric system do not begin with capital letters and are not followed by periods.

m = meter   cm = centimeter   k = kilometer   l = liter

g = gram   mg = milligram   mm = millimeter

The postal abbreviations for the states have two capital letters and are not followed by periods.

NJ = New Jersey   ID = Idaho   PA = Pennsylvania

Exercise 1

Write the abbreviations for each of the following words. Look in a reference book for the state postal abbreviations.

1. February
2. Doctor
3. Vermont
4. liter
5. gram
6. Mister
7. pound
8. California
9. Street
10. Avenue
11. Boulevard
12. August
13. after noon
14. New York
15. December
16. Senior

Exercise 2

Rewrite the sentences to correct any errors in the use of capital letters, abbreviations, and punctuation.

1. I started a diary for my sky watching, and I wrote "mar 5" at the top of the first page

2. The heading for the day that I first saw a meteor shower was "nov 8"

3. I saw them at 11:15 pm

4. Our neighbor, Mr Peterson, has let me use his telescope

5. The instructions with the telescope give these dimensions for the eyepiece: 2 in diameter, 40 mm focal length

6. The diameter of the reflector is 8 in according to the ad

7. The first telescope was probably made in ad 1608

8. The Babylonians discovered the lunar cycle in 750 bc

Practice Power

You need to fill out a card like this to apply for swimming lessons. Copy this card onto a separate sheet of paper. Fill in the information, using abbreviations where possible.

Name:_____
Address: _____
City: _____ State: _____
Date of birth:_____
Height: _____ Weight:_____
Name of parent or guardian:
_____
Desired days and times for lessons:
_____

8.10 *Direct Quotations*

A **direct quotation** is the exact words a person has spoken. A direct quotation is enclosed in quotation marks and is separated from the rest of the sentence by one or more commas. Use a capital letter for the first word of every direct quotation.

When a direct quotation comes at the beginning of a sentence, a comma is placed after the quotation.

> "The planet Saturn is the sixth planet from the sun," explained our teacher.

When a quotation comes at the end of the sentence, a comma is placed before it.

> Mr. Stephens explained, "Its beautiful rings are made mostly of rocks and ice chunks."

When the exact words of a speaker are divided, more than one comma is used to separate the quotation from the rest of the sentence. Use a capital letter for the first word of a quoted sentence, but do not use a capital letter where the quotation continues.

> "The planet," said Gregory, "is visible without the use of a telescope."

When a question mark or exclamation point ends a quotation at the beginning of a sentence, a comma is not needed.

> "Is it the second largest planet in our solar system?" asked Debbie.
> "Saturn has such beautiful rings!" my sister exclaimed.

When a question mark or an exclamation point is part of the direct quotation, as above, it is placed inside the end quotation marks. When the question mark or exclamation point is not part of the quotation, it is outside the quotation marks.

> Did the teacher say, "Choose just one planet to study"?
> I was stunned when I heard Jim say, "I finished my report yesterday"!

Exercise 1

Rewrite the following sentences, adding quotation marks, commas, and end punctuation where they are needed.

1. The planet Saturn is made up almost entirely of liquid gases explained Mr. Valentine

2. Saturn's rings continued Mr. Valentine can only be seen with a telescope

3. Can you see the rings of Saturn without a telescope asked Kevin

4. If Saturn were hollowed out, 764 Earths could fit inside exclaimed Mike

5. Janet asked Did you know that Saturn has winds ten times stronger than a hurricane on Earth

Exercise 2

Rewrite the following sentences, adding quotation marks, commas, end punctuation, and capital letters where they are needed.

1. a day on Saturn equals 11.5 Earth hours explained our teacher

2. how many moons does Saturn have asked Marcia.

3. Saturn has eighteen moons answered Mick and Titan is the largest of them

4. Mr. James asked Did you know that a space probe has recently entered Saturn's orbit in order to study it more closely

5. everyone in our class answered at once no, we didn't

6. we will have more information Mr. Valentine explained as the probes relay it

Practice Power

Interview a friend about why he or she would or would not like to travel into space. Take notes and write down exactly what he or she says. When the interview is over, write a paragraph about the interview. Use direct quotations in your paragraph. Remember to punctuate correctly.

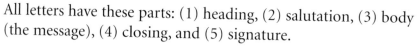

All letters have these parts: (1) heading, (2) salutation, (3) body (the message), (4) closing, and (5) signature.

When writing a personal letter, you need to include only the date in the heading. For business letters include your address.

The inside address of a business letter includes the name and address of the person to whom the letter is being sent.

The salutation is a greeting used at the beginning of a letter. The first word and the name of the person being addressed in the salutation start with capital letters. A comma is used after the salutation in a personal letter. A colon is used in business letters.

> Dear Aunt Jane,   Dear Mr. Wade:

The complimentary close ends a letter. The first word in the complimentary close begins with a capital letter. Use a comma after the complimentary close.

> Sincerely,   Your friend,   Very truly yours,

In the inside address and the address on the envelope, capitalize

- the name of the person addressed
- the name of the street and the city or town
- both letters of a state's postal abbreviation
- abbreviations such as *N.* for *North*, *S.* for *South*, *E.* for *East*, and *W.* for *West*

Use a comma after the name of the city or town.

> Antonia Markham
> 1200 N. Bank Street
> Oakland, IL 60025

Exercise 1
Rewrite the following, adding capital letters and punctuation where needed. Use abbreviations where possible.

1. dear aunt Beatrice

2. very truly yours

3. warmest regards

4. dear mr Andrews

5. sincerely yours

6. beatrice taylor
   1759 niles avenue
   mayfield, ohio 44124

Exercise 2

Read the letter. Add capital letters, punctuation, and abbreviations where needed.

742 jackson avenue
elizabeth new jersey 07201
january 7, 20—

richard vernon
Telescopes to the Universe
173 palm lane drive
oceanside ca 92054

dear mr. vernon

I am very interested in ordering the telescope you advertised in <u>Astronomer</u> magazine.

Can you tell me the dimensions of the telescope? I am interested in a telescope that is easy to pack and move. I plan to use it outdoors, away from the city.

You can respond to the above address or e-mail at <u>alexthomas@city.com.net</u>. You can also call me at home. My phone number is (201) 555-1212.

sincerely yours
Alexander Thomas

Practice Power

Write a letter to a company to ask for information about a product. Also address an envelope to the company. Be sure to use all the parts needed for a business letter and to use capital letters and punctuation correctly.

Section 8 Challenge

Read this story carefully and answer the questions. Paragraphs 1 and 2 have the correct punctuation. Paragraphs 3, 4, 5, 6, and 7 are missing some marks of punctuation and capital letters.

1. Paul woke up on Saturday morning. "Hooray!" he announced to his family. "Today is the day I go ballooning with my friend Nick."

2. Paul dressed, ate, and rode out to Washington State Park with Nick and his family. A pilot, Mr. Jacques A. Charles, met them at the field with a huge yellow and red hot-air balloon. A large brown basket was attached to the bottom. Paul's heart beat faster when the pilot called to them, "Hurry and get in!"

3. how does this work asked nick.

4. the air inside the balloon is heated to make it become lighter than the air outside the balloon, mr charles explained. that is what makes the balloon rise he said.

5. to come down, well have to burn less fuel. Then ill open the rip panel with this cord to deflate the balloon, Mr Charles explained.

6. lets get started cried nick.

7. everyone had a wonderful time that day. when Paul got home, he wrote a letter to Nick. he began, "dear nick." in his letter he thanked Nick for inviting him for the ride. that day Paul decided that hot-air ballooning was an exciting hobby

1. In paragraph 1 why are there quotation marks around "Hooray!" and "Today is the day I go ballooning with my friend Nick"?

2. In paragraph 2 why are there commas after *dressed* and *ate*?

3. In paragraph 2 why is Washington State Park capitalized?

4. In paragraph 2 why are periods used after *Mr* and *A*?

5. In paragraph 2 why does *Paul's* have an apostrophe?

6. Write paragraphs 3, 4, 5, 6, and 7 with the correct punctuation. Add periods, commas, exclamation points, question marks, apostrophes, and quotation marks where needed. Also add capital letters where needed.

Diagramming

9.1 Subjects, Predicates, Direct Objects, Modifiers

9.2 Indirect Objects

9.3 Subject Complements

9.4 Prepositional Phrases

9.5 Interjections

9.6 Compound Subjects and Compound Predicates

9.7 Compound Direct Objects and Indirect Objects

9.8 Compound Subject Complements

9.9 Compound Sentences

9.10 Adverb Clauses

9.11 Diagramming Review

Diagramming Challenge

9.1 *Subjects, Predicates, Direct Objects, Modifiers*

A **diagram** shows how all the words in a sentence fit together. It highlights the most important words in a sentence, and it shows how the other words relate to them.

The most important words in a sentence are the subject and the verb. The subject names the person, place, or thing the sentence is about. The verb is the main word in the predicate; it tells what the subject is or does.

- Start the sentence diagram by drawing a horizontal line.
- Find the verb in the sentence. Write it on the right side of the line.
- Find the subject. Write it in front of the verb.
- Draw a vertical line between the subject and the verb. The vertical line cuts through the horizontal line.

Sentence: Volcanoes erupt.

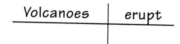

In this sentence the subject is *volcanoes,* and the verb is *erupt.*

Another important word in some sentences is the direct object. The direct object answers the question *whom* or *what* after the verb.

- To diagram a direct object, first position the subject and the verb on the main horizontal line of the diagram.
- Write the direct object on the horizontal line to the right of the verb.
- Draw a vertical line between the verb and the direct object. This line touches the horizontal line but does not cut through it.

Sentence: Volcanoes spout lava.

Words that describe the subject, verb, or direct object are written on slanting lines under those words. Adjectives modify, or describe, nouns, and adverbs modify verbs.

Sentence: The hot lava was flowing slowly.

lava | was flowing
The hot slowly

The article *the* and the adjective *hot* go under the noun *lava*.
The adverb *slowly* goes under the verb *was flowing*.

Exercise 1

Complete the sentence with a direct object of your choice. Add adjectives to describe it if you want. Complete the diagram.

I saw _____.

I | s a w

Exercise 2

Diagram the sentences.

1. Dolphins play.

2. Susie gathered shells.

3. The door squeaks noisily.

4. Koalas eat leaves.

5. Timmy opened the mysterious trunk cautiously.

6. The ancient Greeks built the first theaters.

7. Moira climbed the tall ladder carefully.

8. Christopher Columbus explored Puerto Rico.

9. Sundials tell time.

10. The rain stopped suddenly.

Practice Power

Look at one of the photographs in this book. Write four short sentences about it. Diagram the sentences.

An indirect object tells *to whom, for whom, to what,* or *for what* the action of a verb is done.

Some verbs that can have indirect objects are the following:

assign	hand	promise	teach
bring	lend	read	tell
buy	offer	sell	write
get	owe	send	
give	pay	show	

In a diagram an indirect object is placed on a horizontal line beneath the verb. It is connected to the verb by a slanting line.

Sentence: Dad bought Lila an orange balloon.

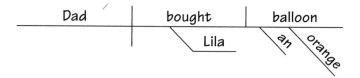

In this sentence *Dad* is the subject, *bought* is the verb, and *balloon* is the direct object. The indirect object is *Lila.* It tells *for whom* the balloon was bought.

Words that describe the indirect object go on a slanting line under the indirect object.

Sentence: Franco sent his grandmother a card.

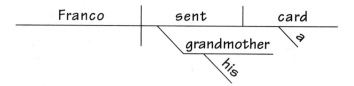

In this sentence *grandmother* is the indirect object. The possessive adjective *his* describes *grandmother* and is placed on a slanting line under *grandmother.*

Exercise 1
Add an indirect object of your choice to this sentence. Complete the diagram.

Kristy gave _____ a present.

| Kristy | gave | present |

Exercise 2
Diagram the sentences.

1. The waiter handed Mom the bill.
2. The visitors brought the patient roses.
3. The magician showed the audience many tricks.
4. My sister lent me her bicycle.
5. An e-pal wrote Ruben a long e-mail.
6. Our grandmother baked us cookies.
7. The principal handed the students diplomas.
8. Food gives people energy.
9. The shop sells customers old records.
10. His sister slowly read Jeff the difficult directions.
11. The ancient Romans gave the months their names.
12. The stand sells fans programs.
13. Our class sent the newspaper a letter.
14. Martha wrote Doug a secret message.
15. The teacher assigned the students a big project.

Practice Power

Write four sentences with indirect objects, each with a different verb from the list on page 486. Diagram them.

9.3 *Subject Complements*

A subject complement follows a linking verb and renames or describes the subject. The most common linking verbs are *be* and its various forms, such as *am, is, are, was, were, have been, has been.* Other common linking verbs are *appear, become, feel, grow, look, remain, seem, sound, stay,* and *taste.* A subject complement can be a noun, a pronoun, or an adjective.

In a diagram a subject complement is written on the main horizontal line after the verb. A line that slants to the left separates the subject complement from the verb. The slanting line touches the horizontal line but does not cut through it.

Sentence: A turtle is a reptile.

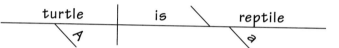

The subject complement *reptile* is a noun that renames the subject *turtle.*

Sentence: Reptiles' skin can be scaly.

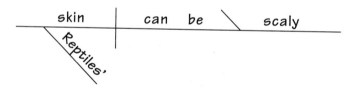

In this sentence the subject complement is the adjective *scaly.* It describes the subject *skin.*

Can you identify the subject complement in this sentence? What part of speech is it?

Sentence: Dinosaurs are extinct reptiles.

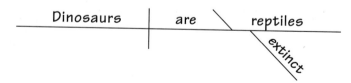

The subject complement *reptiles* is a noun, which renames the subject *dinosaurs.* The adjective *extinct* describes the subject complement.

Exercise 1
Add a subject complement of your choice to this sentence. Copy and complete the diagram.

A snake is _____.

```
  snake    |    is
_____
        \  1 |
```

Exercise 2
Diagram the sentences. Tell if each subject complement is a noun, a pronoun, or an adjective.

1. Breakfast is ready!

2. The gift was a camera.

3. LaToya is a good guitarist.

4. Tundra is frozen land.

5. Those pickles are sour!

6. Dogs are my favorite pets.

7. Is chess difficult?

8. The sunflowers are tall.

9. Asia is vast.

10. Anne of Green Gables is a fictional character.

11. *Apatosaurus* was a large dinosaur.

12. Jason was a Greek hero.

13. The winner was she.

14. Penguins are nonflying birds.

15. My new backpack is purple.

Practice Power

Write and diagram two sentences with subject complements, one with a noun subject complement and one with an adjective subject complement.

9.4 *Prepositional Phrases*

A preposition and its object form a prepositional phrase. The object can be a noun or a pronoun. A prepositional phrase acts as an adjective when it describes a noun or a pronoun. A prepositional phrase acts as an adverb when it describes a verb. A prepositional phrase used as an adverb tells *how, when,* or *where.*

In a diagram a prepositional phrase goes beneath the word it describes.

- The preposition is on a slanting line.
- The object of the preposition is on a horizontal line connected to the slanting line with the preposition.
- Any word that describes the object is positioned beneath the object.

Sentence: We lost a piece of the puzzle.

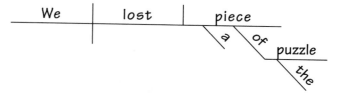

The prepositional phrase *of the puzzle* describes the noun *piece,* so it is an adjective phrase.

Sentence: Susan skated on the thin ice.

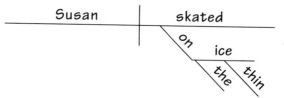

The prepositional phrase *on the thin ice* describes the verb *skated.* It tells where Susan skated. The phrase goes under the verb. The adjectives *the* and *thin* describe the object of the preposition *ice,* and they are positioned on slanting lines beneath that noun.

Exercise 1

Diagram the sentences.

1. The cow jumped over the moon.
2. Native Americans hunted on the prairies.
3. The smell of hot bread filled the kitchen.
4. The hippopotamus is a relative of the pig.
5. The cave is a home for bats.
6. A hammock swung in the breeze.
7. H_2O is the chemical formula for water.
8. The path through the woods is a shortcut.
9. My best friend lives across the street.
10. *Gracias* is the Spanish word for *thank you.*

Exercise 2

Diagram these sentences. Each sentence has more than one prepositional phrase.

1. The trunk in the attic belongs to my grandmother.
2. Motorists in England drive on the left side of the street.
3. The tail of a comet reflects the light of the sun.
4. In the afternoon my sister planted flowers in the garden.
5. The trumpets in an orchestra are located near the trombones.

Practice Power

Write and diagram four sentences with prepositional phrases, two with adjective phrases and two with adverb phrases. Then challenge yourself by writing a sentence that has both an adjective phrase and an adverb phrase and diagramming it.

9.5 Interjections

An interjection is a word that expresses strong or sudden emotion. Interjections may express emotions such as happiness, disgust, pain, agreement, impatience, surprise, and sadness. They include words such as *Ah, Oh, Well, Sh, Hey, Good, Ouch, Oops, Yikes,* and *Wow.* These words or the sentences in which they appear are usually followed by exclamation points.

In a diagram an interjection is placed on a line that is separate from the rest of the sentence. The line is above, at the left of, and parallel to the main horizontal line.

Sentence: Oh! The water is cold.

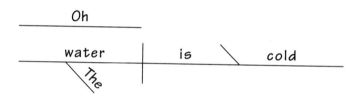

The placement of the interjection remains the same whether the interjection is separated from the rest of the sentence by an exclamation point or by a comma.

Sentence: Oh, that acrobat did an incredible somersault.

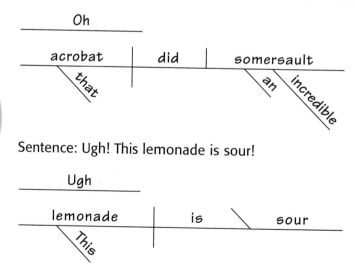

Sentence: Ugh! This lemonade is sour!

Exercise 1

Diagram the sentences.

1. Yuck! You put ketchup on your pizza!

2. Ouch! The sand is hot.

3. Wow! That was an exciting ride.

4. Oh! A brown bear is near that tree.

5. Sh! You should be quiet during the movie.

6. Your song was wonderful! Bravo!

7. Great! I will bring my new sled.

8. No! You are sick on your birthday.

9. Uh-oh, we have another test on Monday!

10. Hooray! Our team scored a goal!

11. This huge box came for me. Great!

12. Ah! The dog has a sore paw.

13. Ouch! I just hit my toe against the refrigerator.

14. Ah, that peacock has lovely feathers.

15. What! You are wearing my sweater!

16. Gee, that is a funny costume.

17. Uh-oh! Do you have the tickets?

18. Sh! Can you hear that strange noise?

19. Ick! A piece of seaweed stuck to my ankle.

20. Ah, this is a peaceful spot for a picnic.

Practice Power

Write and diagram two sentences containing interjections.

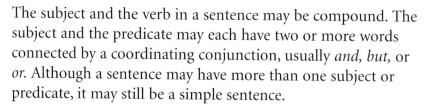
The subject and the verb in a sentence may be compound. The subject and the predicate may each have two or more words connected by a coordinating conjunction, usually *and, but,* or *or.* Although a sentence may have more than one subject or predicate, it may still be a simple sentence.

- Each part of a compound subject or of a compound verb is placed on a separate line. The lines with the compound parts are parallel.

- The coordinating conjunction is placed on a dashed line between the parallel lines.

- The parallel lines are connected to the main horizontal line in the usual position of a subject or a verb.

In this sentence the subject is compound.

Sentence: Todd and Janet went to camp in July.

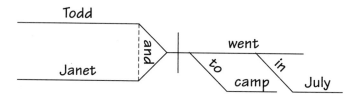

In this sentence the verb is compound.

Sentence: The performers sang and danced.

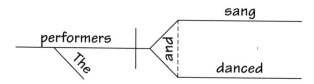

The direct object in this sentence is the object of both verbs.

Sentence: Don mowed and raked the lawn.

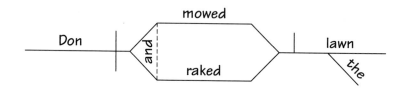

Exercise 1
Diagram the sentences.

1. A giraffe and a zebra approached the camp.
2. Scales or plates cover the bodies of reptiles.
3. The gelatin dessert on the plate wiggled and shimmered.
4. We washed and waxed the cars.
5. The violin and the viola are instruments with strings.
6. I researched butterflies and then wrote my report.
7. Jasmine and Alexis always walk to school together.
8. I held and fed the tiny pig.
9. Peter and Petra are twins.
10. Moos and oinks came from the barnyard.
11. Keesha or Ron speaks Swahili.
12. Paula designed and made her costume.
13. Dictionaries and encyclopedias are good sources of information.
14. That automatic door opens quickly and closes slowly.
15. Chocolate and coffee come from beans.
16. Raisins and carrots are healthful snacks.
17. I sat under the tree and read.
18. California and Florida produce oranges.

Practice Power

Write two sentences with compound subjects and two sentences with compound predicates and then diagram them.

9.7 Compound Direct Objects and Indirect Objects

A sentence may have more than one direct object, each of which answers the question *who* or *what* after the verb. Compound direct objects are usually connected by the conjunction *and* or *or*.

- The parts of a compound direct object are placed on separate parallel lines after the verb.
- The coordinating conjunction is placed on a vertical dashed line between the two parts.
- The compound parts are connected to the main horizontal line in the usual position of a direct object with a vertical line separating the verb and the direct object.

Sentence: The clowns wore baggy clothes and shiny shoes.

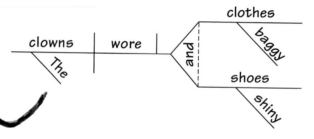

A sentence may have a compound indirect object. An indirect object tells *to whom, for whom, to what,* or *for what* the action of a verb is done.

- The parts of a compound indirect object are placed on separate horizontal lines under the verb.
- The coordinating conjunction is placed on a dashed vertical line between the two parts.
- A slanting line connects the indirect objects to the verb.

Sentence: We sent Helen and Marie invitations to the Halloween party.

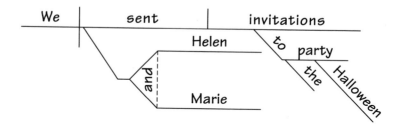

Exercise 1

Diagram the sentences.

1. Paulette studies Spanish and French.

2. The waves tossed seaweed and foam onto the rocks.

3. Skateboarders wear helmets and pads for safety.

4. The Incas made dishes and combs from gold.

5. Some dinosaurs ate fruit and insects.

6. We can choose soup or salad with our meal.

7. Mom bought dishes and skis at the garage sale.

8. We can take ballet or modern dance at this school.

9. Do moose have horns or antlers?

Exercise 2

Diagram the sentences.

1. I offered Sam and Carrie popcorn.

2. The visitors from Brazil taught Katy and Lee Portuguese words.

3. The committee awarded my mother and my father top prize.

4. The sun gives Earth and other planets light.

5. My mother gave my brother and my sister pizza for supper.

6. Our class sent our senator and our representative letters.

7. Jefferson gave Lewis and Clark a difficult mission.

8. Martin wrote Jackson and Milos a message in code.

9. The teacher assigned Uma and Leland the job of cleanup.

Practice Power

Complete the sentences with compound direct objects or indirect objects. Diagram the sentences.

I eat _____ and _____ for breakfast.

I offered _____ and _____ suggestions.

9.8 *Compound Subject Complements*

A sentence may have more than one subject complement. The parts of a compound subject complement are usually connected by the conjunction *and* or *or*. A subject complement comes after a linking verb and renames or describes the subject.

- The parts of a compound subject complement are placed on separate parallel lines after the verb.
- The coordinating conjunction is placed on a dashed vertical line between the parts.
- The parallel lines are connected to the main horizontal line and separated from the verb by a line that slants toward the subject.

This sentence has nouns as a compound subject complement.

Sentence: The best pitchers on the team are Rosalyn and Lillian.

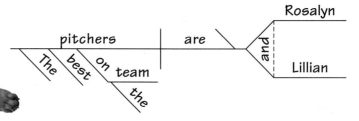

This sentence has adjectives as a compound subject complement.

Sentence: Our dog is friendly and smart.

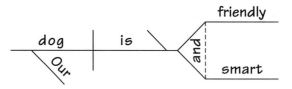

Can you tell whether this compound subject complement consists of nouns or adjectives?

Sentence: The steps to the attic are steep and narrow.

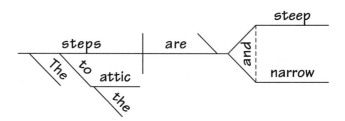

Exercise 1

Diagram the sentences.

1. The bread was hard and moldy.
2. Two forms of water are steam and ice.
3. The violin is old and priceless.
4. The words from the parrot were loud and shrill.
5. Two young fictional detectives are Encyclopedia Brown and Nancy Drew.
6. These young detectives are clever and inquisitive.
7. The name of my new turtle will be Swifty or Shelly.
8. Mercury is a metal but a liquid.
9. Tea can be green or black.
10. The stars of the play are Bianca and Brody.
11. Homegrown tomatoes are tasty and juicy.
12. Rain forests are warm and humid.
13. My breakfast was cereal and a banana.
14. Big Ben is a famous clock and a symbol of Great Britain.
15. Shakespeare was an actor and a playwright.
16. Most piglets are tiny and cute.

Practice Power

Complete the sentences with compound subject complements. Diagram the sentences. Tell whether each subject complement consists of nouns or adjectives.

My lunch is usually _____.

The weather in spring is _____.

My favorite sports are _____.

My favorite fictional characters are _____.

9.9 *Compound Sentences*

A compound sentence contains two or more independent clauses connected by the coordinating conjunction *and, but,* or *or.* An independent clause has a subject and a predicate and expresses a complete thought.

- The clauses are placed on parallel horizontal lines.
- Each independent clause is diagrammed as a separate sentence, on its own horizontal line—with its own subject, verb, and complements or objects.
- The coordinating conjunction is placed on a dashed vertical line that connects the left edge of the horizontal lines.

Sentence: My skateboard is yellow, and Gwen's skateboard is blue.

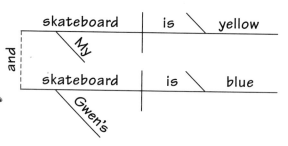

In each clause the subject is *skateboard* and the verb is *is.* The coordinating conjunction *and* connects the left edge of the horizontal lines.

Sentence: I studied my lines for the play, but I forgot them during rehearsal.

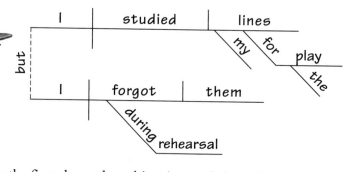

In the first clause the subject is *I,* and the verb is *studied.* In the second clause the subject is *I,* and the verb is *forgot.* The coordinating conjunction *but* connects the left edge of the horizontal lines.

Exercise 1

Diagram the sentences.

1. Iran is a country with a rich history, and its former name is Persia.

2. The store opened its doors for the sale, and the crowds rushed inside.

3. The circus of P. T. Barnum began its tours in the 1800s, and traveling circuses are still popular.

4. You should read the recipe carefully, or you might forget an ingredient.

5. The project on solar power won first prize at school, and the school entered it in the statewide competition.

6. My little brother will be a pumpkin in the Thanksgiving play, and I will be a Pilgrim.

7. In Greek mythology, Helios rode a fiery chariot across the sky, and this ride warmed the earth with sunlight.

8. George Washington Carver studied peanuts and soybeans, and he found many new uses for them.

9. The moon determines the months of the Chinese calendar, and the first day of each month is also the darkest day.

10. My sister got the ingredients, and we made s'mores over the campfire.

11. We often water the orchids, but we rarely water the cacti.

12. I did well in the spelling contest, but I missed *spelunker.*

13. People sometimes take wild animals into their homes, but wild animals are usually poor choices for pets.

Practice Power

Add an independent clause to each of the following. Diagram each resulting compound sentence.

The parade started   **The glass fell**
The playground was empty   **We searched the Web**

9.10 *Adverb Clauses*

A dependent clause has a subject and a verb, but it does not express a complete thought and it cannot stand alone. In a sentence a dependent clause always accompanies an independent clause.

An adverb clause is a dependent clause that describes a verb and tells *when* about a verb in the independent clause. A subordinate conjunction connects an adverb clause to an independent clause. Some common subordinate conjunctions are *after, as, before, once, since, when, whenever, while,* and *until.*

- The adverb clause—with its subject, verb, and any complements or objects—is placed on a horizontal line under the line for the independent clause and parallel to it.
- The subordinate conjunction is placed on a slanting dashed line that connects the verb in the adverb clause to the word in the independent clause that the adverb clause describes. It usually goes to the verb.

Sentence: Whenever I have a chance, I eat chocolate.

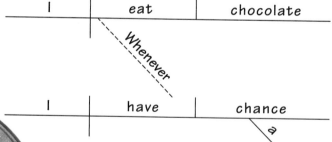

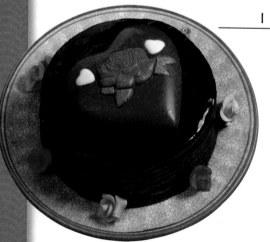

The subject of the independent clause is *I*, and the verb is *eat*. The subject of the dependent clause is *I*, and the verb is *have*. The clauses are connected by the subordinate conjunction *whenever*.

Sentence: I always break a granola bar into pieces before I eat it.

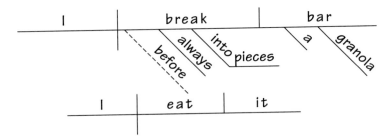

In the independent clause the subject is *I,* and the verb is *break.*
In the dependent clause the subject is *I,* and the verb is *eat.* The
subordinate conjunction *before* connects the two clauses.

Exercise 1
Diagram the sentences.

1. You can taste the brownies after they cool.

2. When I returned the lost cat, the owner gave me a reward.

3. The ground shook violently when the earthquake struck.

4. Gold ore is dull when it in the ground.

5. The performance artist was motionless for a long time as
   a large crowd gathered around her.

6. After Kyle opened the door, the dog ran outside.

7. Sherry's experiment was going well until she dropped the beaker.

8. Catherine and Susan take a volleyball whenever they go to the park.

9. When Atalanta stopped for the golden apples, she lost the race.

10. Rodney took the message after he answered the phone.

11. My dog barks and jumps when I arrive at the door.

Practice Power

Add independent clauses to these adverb clauses to form
sentences. Diagram the sentences.

When the bell rang   **After we went on the field trip**

9.11 *Diagramming Review*

Can you identify the main elements in these sentences?

Sentence: Oranges contain vitamin C.

Sentence: The tongues of anteaters are long.

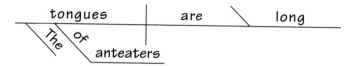

Both sentences have subjects and verbs. The first sentence has a direct object (*vitamin C*), and the second sentence has a subject complement (*long*).

Can you identify all the adjectives, adverbs, adjective phrases, and adverb phrases in this sentence?

Sentence: Colorful animals and useful plants survive together in the damp, dense tropical forests of South America.

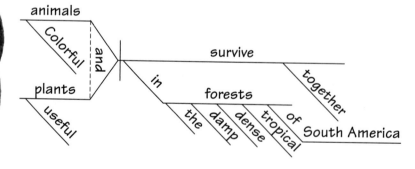

Can you identify the compound part in this sentence? How does it function in the sentence?

Sentence: Alaska produces lumber and oil.

A compound sentence and a sentence with an adverb clause have separate horizontal lines. Which kind of sentence is this?

Sentence: When the curtain rose, I was alone on stage.

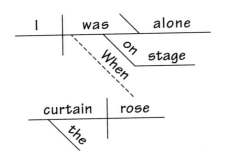

Exercise 1
Diagram the sentences.

1. A group of geese is a gaggle.

2. My grandmother raises chickens.

3. Mount Vernon was the home of George Washington.

4. Scouts wear caps and neckerchiefs with their uniforms.

5. Congress granted Native Americans citizenship in 1924.

6. Libya and Algeria are in North Africa.

7. Susan B. Anthony died before women got the vote.

8. Hawks are birds of prey, and they are characterized by strong claws.

9. Maya Angelou is a novelist and a poet.

10. We arrived late after our bus had a flat tire.

11. Drums boomed as the parade passed.

12. I studied hard after the teacher announced the math contest.

Practice Power

Write five sentences, incorporating as many sentence elements as possible. Exchange sentences with a partner. Diagram each other's sentences.

Diagramming Challenge

Study the diagram and answer the questions.

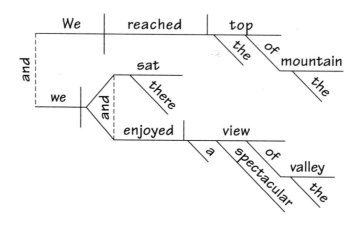

1. Is the sentence simple or compound?

2. What is the coordinating conjunction connecting the clauses?

3. Identify the subject and the verb in each clause in the sentence.

4. What is the compound sentence part? What is the coordinating conjunction?

5. Identify the adjectives and the adverb in the sentence.

6. Identify the prepositional phrases. What kind is each?

7. Write out the sentence.

Grammar and Mechanics Handbook

Grammar

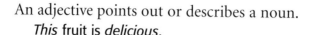

ADJECTIVES

An adjective points out or describes a noun.
> *This* fruit is *delicious.*

Adjectives That Compare

Most adjectives have three degrees of comparison: positive, comparative, and superlative.

The positive degree of an adjective shows a quality of a noun.
> The meerkat is *cute.*
> The giraffe is *tall.*

The comparative degree of an adjective is used to compare two items or two sets of items. It is often used with *than.* To form the comparative degree, *-er* is often added to an adjective.
> The meerkat is *cuter* than the wart hog.
> The giraffe is *taller* than the okapi.

The superlative degree of an adjective is used to compare three or more items or sets of items. To form the superlative degree, *-est* is often added to an adjective.
> The meerkat is the *cutest* animal in the zoo.
> The giraffe is the *tallest* animal in Africa.

Some adjectives that compare have special forms.
> Vanilla ice cream is *good.*
> Strawberry ice cream is *better* than vanilla.
> Chocolate ice cream is the *best* flavor of all.

> The baby isn't feeling *well* today.
> She felt *worse* yesterday.
> She felt *worst* of all on Sunday.

> We had a *bad* storm yesterday.
> It was a *worse* storm than the one last week.
> The *worst* storm we had was in December.

Some adjectives that compare use *more, most, less,* and *least. More, most, less,* and *least* are used with adjectives of three or more syllables and with some adjectives of two syllables.
> Carla is a *more careful* worker than Luis.
> Lindsey is *less careful* than Carla.

Marta is the *most intelligent* student in class.
She is also the *least gullible* student.

The comparison adjectives *fewer* and *fewest* are used with plural count nouns. The comparison adjectives *less* and *least* are used with noncount nouns.

I have *fewer* pencils than Jody does.
I have *less* paper too.
Mark has the *fewest* pens.
Carmen has the *least* chalk.

Adjectives That Tell How Many

Some adjectives tell how many or about how many.

Only *six* members came to the meeting.
A *few* members were sick.

Some adjectives tell numerical order.

I finished reading the *sixth* chapter.

Articles

Articles point out nouns. *The, a,* and *an* are articles. *The* is the definite article. It points out a specific person, place, or thing. *A* and *an* are indefinite articles. They point out any one of a class of people, places, or things. Use *a* before a consonant sound and *an* before a vowel sound.

The man ate *a* peach and *an* apple.

When two or more nouns joined by *and* refer to different people, places, or things, use an article before each noun. When two or more nouns joined by *and* refer to the same person, place, or thing, use an article before the first noun only.

The coach and *the* players celebrated their win.
The teacher and coach is Mr. Simmons.

Demonstrative Adjectives

Demonstrative adjectives point out a specific person, place, or thing. The demonstrative adjectives are *this, that, these,* and *those.*

Singular	Plural
this flower	*these* bushes
that flower	*those* bushes

This and *these* point out things or persons that are near. *That* and *those* point out things or persons that are farther away.

This flower is red. (singular and near)
Those bushes are tall. (plural and far)

Descriptive Adjectives

A descriptive adjective tells more about a noun. It can tell how something looks, tastes, sounds, feels, or smells. It can tell about size, number, color, shape, or weight.

A descriptive adjective often comes before the noun it describes.

A *tall* tree stood near the *red* barn.

A descriptive adjective can follow a linking verb as a subject complement. It describes the subject of the sentence.

The tree near the red barn was *tall*.

Interrogative Adjectives

An interrogative adjective is used to ask a question. The interrogative adjectives are *what, which,* and *whose.* An interrogative adjective comes before a noun.

What movie did you see?
Which theater did you go to?
Whose car did you take?

Possessive Adjectives

A possessive adjective shows who or what owns something. A possessive adjective is used before a noun. The possessive adjectives are *my, your, his, her, its, our,* and *their.*

I have *my* camera, and Lucy has *her* phone.

Proper Adjectives

Proper adjectives are formed from proper nouns. A proper adjective always begins with a capital letter.

When we went to China, I ate *Chinese* food.

ADVERBS

An adverb tells more about a verb. Many adverbs end in *-ly.*

An adverb of time tells when or how often something happens.

I went to the mall *yesterday.*
I *sometimes* go to the toy store.

An adverb of place tells where something happens.

I went *outside* after dinner.
I played *there* until it was dark.

An adverb of manner tells how something happens.

> My new skateboard goes *fast*.
>
> I ride it *gracefully*.

Adverbs That Compare

An adverb can compare the actions of two or more person or things. To compare the actions of two persons or things, *-er* is often added to an adverb. To compare the actions of three or more persons or things, *-est* is often added to an adverb.

> Sam went to bed *later* than Henry.
>
> Luke went to bed *latest* of us all.

Some adverbs that compare use *more* and *most*. Use *more* and *most* with adverbs ending in *-ly* and with adverbs of three or more syllables.

> Sam answered *more sleepily* than Henry.
>
> Luke answered *most sleepily* of us all.

Negatives

Some adverbs form negative ideas. Use *not, n't* for *not* in a contraction, or *never* to express a negative idea. Do not use more than one negative word in a sentence.

> He will *not* be ready on time.
>
> He *can't* find his sneakers.
>
> He *never* remembers where he left them.

ANTECEDENTS

The noun to which a pronoun refers is its antecedent. A pronoun must agree with its antecedent in person and number. The pronouns *he, him,* and *his* refer to male antecedents. The pronouns *she, her,* and *hers* refer to female antecedents. The pronouns *it* and *its* refer to animals or things. See NUMBER, PERSON.

CLAUSES

A clause is a group of words that has a subject and a predicate.

Adverb Clauses

An adverb clause is a dependent clause used as an adverb. An adverb clause can tell when.

> *As soon as I get home*, I'll do my homework.
>
> I'll play video games *after we eat dinner*.

Dependent Clauses

A dependent clause cannot stand alone as a sentence.

While I was at the mall, my cell phone rang.

Independent Clauses

An independent clause, or main clause, can stand alone as a sentence.

I put on my helmet before I got on my bike.

CONJUNCTIONS

A conjunction is a word used to join two words or groups of words in a sentence.

Coordinating Conjunctions

A coordinating conjunction joins two words or groups of words that are similar. The words *and, but,* and *or* are coordinating conjunctions.

My dad *and* I went to the pool.
I can swim *but* not dive.
The pool is never too hot *or* crowded.

Subordinate Conjunctions

A subordinate conjunction connects a dependent clause to an independent clause in a sentence.

After we drive to the pool, we'll change clothes.
We'll swim *until* it is time to go home for dinner.

CONTRACTIONS

A contraction is a short way to write some words. An apostrophe (') is used to show where one or more letters have been left out of the words.

Many contractions are formed with the word *not.*

do not = don't	was not = wasn't
cannot = can't	will not = won't

Many contractions are formed with personal pronouns.

I am = I'm	he is = he's
you are = you're	we have = we've

DIRECT OBJECTS

The direct object in a sentence is the noun or pronoun that receives the action of the verb. The direct object tells whom or what after the verb. Two or more direct objects joined by *and* or *or* form a compound direct object.

> My mom made *pasta* and *salad.*
> I helped *her.*

INDIRECT OBJECTS

An indirect object is the noun or pronoun that tells to whom, for whom, to what, or for what an action is done. A sentence cannot have an indirect object unless it has a direct object. The indirect object comes after the verb and before the direct object.

> The reporter asked *the mayor* a question.
> The mayor gave *her* a long answer.

INTERJECTIONS

An interjection is a word that expresses a strong or sudden emotion. An interjection is set off from the rest of the sentence by an exclamation point.

> *Wow!* That was a great game.
> You kicked the winning goal. *Great!*

NOUNS

A noun is a word that names a person, a place, or a thing. See NUMBER.

Collective Nouns
A collective noun names a group of people, places, animals, or things that are considered as a unit.

> The science *club* raised a *swarm* of bees.

Common Nouns
A common noun names any one member of a group of persons, places, or things.

> My *cousin* saw a *dog* run down the *street.*

Count Nouns

Count nouns name things that exist as individual units. You can count them. A count noun has a singular and a plural form.

The *players* wore *mitts* and *helmets*.

Noncount Nouns

Noncount nouns name things that cannot be counted. A noncount noun has only a singular form.

His *advice* was to add more *salt*.

Nouns in Direct Address

A noun in direct address names the person spoken to. A noun used in direct address is set off from the rest of the sentence by a comma or commas.

Peter, are you coming with us?

Bring your skateboard, *Carla*, and wear your helmet.

Plural Nouns

A plural noun names more than one person, place, or thing. Most plurals are formed by adding -*s* or -*es* to the singular form. Some nouns have irregular plural forms. Some nouns have the same form in the singular and plural.

The *children* have some *turtles* and some *fish*.

Possessive Nouns

The possessive form of a noun shows possession or ownership.

A singular possessive noun shows that one person owns something. To form the singular possessive, add an apostrophe (') and the letter *s* to a singular noun.

baby	baby's bottle
Tess	Tess's soccer ball
woman	woman's purse

A plural possessive noun shows that more than one person owns something. To form the plural possessive of most nouns, add an apostrophe (') after the plural form of the noun.

| babies | babies' bottles |
| the Smiths | the Smiths' house |

To form the plural possessive of an irregular noun, add an apostrophe and *s* ('*s*) after the plural form.

| women | women's purses |
| mice | mice's cheese |

Proper Nouns

A proper noun begins with a capital letter and names a particular person, place, or thing.

Meg saw *Shadow* run down *Pine Street.*

Singular Nouns

A singular noun names one person, place, or thing.

The *girl* has a *kite* and a *skateboard.*

NUMBER

The number of a noun or pronoun indicates whether it refers to one person, place, or thing (singular) or more than one person, place, or thing (plural).

PERSON

Personal pronouns and possessive adjectives change form according to person—whether they refer to the person speaking (first person), the person spoken to (second person), or the person, place, or thing spoken about (third person).

PHRASES

A phrase is a group of words that is used as a single part of speech.

Adjective Phrases

An adjective phrase is a phrase used as an adjective.

The woman *in the red hat* is my aunt.

Adverb Phrases

An adverb phrase is a phrase used as an adverb.

The man sat *on the park bench.*

Prepositional Phrases

A prepositional phrase is made up of a preposition, the object of the preposition, and any modifiers of the object. See PREPOSITIONS.

Verb Phrases

A verb phrase is a group of words that does the work of a single verb. A verb phrase contains a main verb and one or more helping verbs such as *is, are, have, can,* and *do.*

They *are studying.*

They *will be studying* until dinnertime.

In some questions and statements the parts of a verb phrase may be separated.

> *Did* they *finish* their projects?
> Dolores *has* not *finished* hers.

PREDICATES

The predicate of a sentence tells what the subject is or does.

Complete Predicates
The complete predicate of a sentence is the simple predicate and any words that go with it.

> Tom *rode his new bike.*

Compound Predicates
Two predicates joined by *and, but,* or *or* form a compound predicate.

> Karen *got a glass* and *poured some milk.*

Simple Predicates
The simple predicate of a sentence is a verb, a word or words that express an action or a state of being.

> The boys *ran* noisily down the street.
> They *were* happy.

PREPOSITIONS

A preposition is a word that shows a relationship between a noun or pronoun and another word in a sentence.

> We put the doghouse *under* the tree.
> The dog *with* the red collar is Karen's.

Object of the Preposition
The noun or pronoun that follows a preposition is the object of the preposition.

> We put the doghouse under *it.*
> The dog with the red *collar* is Karen's.

Prepositional Phrases
A prepositional phrase is a preposition, the object of the preposition, and any words that describe the object. A prepositional phrase can be used as an adjective or an adverb.

> We put the doghouse *under the tall green tree.*
> The dog *with the shiny, new red collar* is Karen's.

PRONOUNS

A pronoun is a word that takes the place of a noun. See ANTECEDENTS, NUMBER, PERSON.

Demonstrative Pronouns

A demonstrative pronoun is used to point out a person, place, or thing. The demonstrative pronouns are *this, that, these,* and *those.*

Singular	Plural
this	these
that	those

This and *these* point out things or persons that are near. *That* and *those* point out things or persons that are farther away.

> *This* is my favorite book. (singular and near)
> *Those* are my cousin's old comic books. (plural and far)

Intensive Pronouns

An intensive pronoun is used to emphasize a noun that comes before it. The intensive pronouns are *myself, yourself, himself, herself, itself, ourselves, yourselves,* and *themselves.*

> Corrine *herself* didn't know she had won.
> They created the prizes *themselves.*

Interrogative Pronouns

An interrogative pronoun is used to ask a question. The interrogative pronouns are *who, whom, what,* and *whose.*

> *Who* broke the window?
> *What* happened when it started to rain?
> *Whose* is the ruined book?
> *Whom* did you call about the problem?

Personal Pronouns

A personal pronoun refers to the person speaking or to the person or thing that is spoken to or about. In this sentence *I* is the person speaking, *you* is the person spoken to, and *them* are the people spoken about. See PERSON, NUMBER.

> *I* heard *you* calling *them.*

Object Pronouns

An object pronoun can be the direct or indirect object of a sentence or the object of a preposition. The object pronouns are *me, you, him, her, it, us,* and *them.* Two or more object pronouns can be joined by *and* or *or* to form a compound object.

Karen will help *them*.
Chris will help *her* and *me*.
Karen and Chris will come with *us*.
We will tell *him* the plan later.

Plural Pronouns

A plural pronoun refers to more than one person, place, or thing.
They are helping *us*.

Possessive Pronouns

A possessive pronoun shows ownership or possession. A possessive pronoun takes the place of a noun. It takes the place of the owner and the thing that is owned. The possessive pronouns are *mine, yours, his, hers, its, ours,* and *theirs*.
My cap is here, and your cap is over there.
Mine is here, and *yours* is over there.

Reflexive Pronouns

A reflexive pronoun is used as the direct or indirect object of a verb or the object of a preposition. The reflexive pronouns are *myself, yourself, himself, herself, itself, ourselves, yourselves,* and *themselves*.
Paul cut *himself* when he sliced the tomato.
Carla made *herself* a jelly sandwich.
The children made lunch for *themselves*.

Singular Pronouns

A singular pronoun refers to one person, place, or thing.
I gave *it* to *her*.

Subject Pronouns

A subject pronoun can be used as the subject or the subject complement of a sentence. The subject pronouns are *I, you, he, she, it, we,* and *they*. Two or more subject pronouns can be joined by *and* or *or* to form a compound subject or subject complement.
She is a great tennis player.
She and *I* play tennis often.
The winner of our matches is usually *she*.

SENTENCES

A sentence is a group of words that expresses a complete thought. Every sentence has a subject and a predicate.

Complex Sentences

A complex sentence contains one independent clause and one or more dependent clauses. The clauses are joined by subordinate conjunctions. See CLAUSES, CONJUNCTIONS.

> Before I go to school, I eat a good breakfast.
> I watch TV while I am eating.

Compound Sentences

Two sentences, or independent clauses, joined by a comma and *and, but,* or *or* form a compound sentence.

> Ming is eating, but Lili is sleeping.

Declarative Sentences

A declarative sentence makes a statement. It tells something. A statement ends with a period (.).

> Your jacket is in the closet.

Exclamatory Sentences

An exclamatory sentence expresses strong or sudden emotion. It ends with an exclamation point (!).

> How cold it is today!

Imperative Sentences

An imperative sentence gives a command or makes a request. The subject of an imperative sentence is generally *you,* which is often not stated. A command ends with a period (.).

> Please wear your jacket.

Interrogative Sentences

An interrogative sentence asks a question. It ends with a question mark (?).

> Are you ready?
> Where is your jacket?

Inverted Order

A sentence is in inverted order when the main verb or a helping verb comes before the subject.

> There *are shoes* everywhere.
> Piled on the desk *is* her *homework.*
> *Does she* ever clean up her room?

Natural Order

A sentence is in natural order when the verb follows the subject.

> *Ophelia leaves* her things everywhere.

SUBJECT COMPLEMENTS

A subject complement follows a linking verb in a sentence. It is a noun or pronoun that renames the subject or an adjective that describes the subject. Two or more subject complements joined by *and, but,* or *or* form a compound subject complement.

That firefighter is a *hero.*
Her actions were *brave* and *skillful.*
The officer who received the medal was *she.*

SUBJECTS

The subject of a sentence is who or what the sentence is about. The subject can be a noun or a pronoun.

Complete Subjects

The complete subject is the simple subject and the words that describe it or give more information about it.

The *little gray kitten* is playing.

Compound Subjects

Two or more subjects joined by *and* or *or* form a compound subject.

Bob, Carl, and *Lisa* went to the movies.
Norman or *I* will sweep the floor.

Simple Subject

The simple subject is the noun or pronoun that a sentence tells about.

His little *dog* likes to chase balls.
It runs very fast.

SUBJECT-VERB AGREEMENT

A subject and verb must agree, whether the verb is a main verb or a helping verb. If a compound subject is joined by *or,* the verb agrees with the subject closest to it.

I *like* chocolate ice cream.
My brother *likes* peach ice cream.
Our parents *like* strawberry ice cream.

I *am building* a birdhouse.
The boys or she *is going to help.*
They *are building* a garage.

A collective noun is generally considered singular even though it means more than one person or thing, and its verb must agree with the singular form.

Our *class is entering* the contest.

When a sentence starts with *there is, there are, there was,* or *there were,* the subject follows the verb. The verb must agree with the subject.

There *is* a *book* on the desk.
There *were* some *pencils* in the drawer.

TENSE

The tense of a verb shows when the action takes place.

Future Tense
The future tense tells about something that will happen in the future.

One way to form the future tense is with a form of the helping verb *be* plus *going to* plus the present form of a verb.

I *am going to make* toast.
Dad *is going to butter* it.
They *are going to eat* it.

Another way to form the future tense is with the helping verb *will* and the present form of a verb.

Our class *will go* to the museum.
The guide *will explain* the exhibits.

Future Perfect Tense
The perfect future tense tells about an action that will have been completed by some time in the future. The future perfect tense is formed with *will* plus *have* plus the past participle of a verb.

I *will have finished* my homework by dinnertime.
I *will have made* a salad by that time too.

Future Progressive Tense
The future progressive tense tells about something that will be happening in the future. The future progressive tense is formed with *will* and the present participle or with a form of *be* plus *going to* and the present participle.

I *will be doing* my homework this evening.
My cousins *are going to be helping* me.

Past Perfect Tense

The past perfect tense tells about an action that was finished before another action in the past. The past perfect tense is formed with *had* and the past participle of a verb.

> She *had come* straight home after school.
> She *had finished* her homework before dinner.

Past Progressive Tense

The past progressive tense tells what was happening in the past. The past progressive tense is formed with *was* or *were* and the present participle of a verb.

> I *was feeding* the cat.
> My parents *were reading*.

Present Perfect Tense

The present perfect tense tells about an action that happened at some indefinite time in the past or about an action that started in the past and continues into the present. The present perfect tense is formed with a form of *have* and the past participle of a verb.

> He *has finished* his homework.
> They *have lived* in that house for three years.

Present Progressive Tense

The present progressive tense tells what is happening now. The present progressive tense is formed with *am, is,* or *are* and the present participle of a verb.

> We *are watching* TV.
> I *am eating* popcorn.
> My sister *is drinking* juice.

Simple Past Tense

The simple past tense tells about something that happened in the past. The simple past tense of regular verbs is formed by adding *-d* or *-ed* to the present form of a verb.

> We *cooked* breakfast this morning.
> Mom *fried* the eggs.

Simple Present Tense

The simple present tense tells about something that is always true or something that happens again and again. The present part of a verb is used for the present tense. If the subject is a singular noun or *he, she,* or *it, -s* or *-es* must be added to the verb.

> Prairie dogs *live* where it's dry.
> A prairie dog *digs* a burrow to live in.

VERBS

A verb shows action or state of being. See TENSE.

Action Verbs

An action verb tells what someone or something does.

> The boy *is running.*
> Seals *bark.*

Being Verbs

A being verb shows what someone or something is. Being verbs do not express action.

> The boy *is* tired.
> The seal *was* hungry.

Helping Verbs

A verb can have more than one word. A helping verb is a verb added before the main verb that helps make the meaning clear.

> We *will* go to the movie.
> We *might* buy some popcorn.

Irregular Verbs

The past and the past participle of irregular verbs are not formed by adding *-d* or *-ed.*

Present	Past	Past Participle
sing	sang	sung
send	sent	sent
write	wrote	written

Linking Verbs

A linking verb joins the subject of a sentence to a subject complement. Being verbs can be linking verbs.

> My aunt *is* a professional writer.
> She *has become* famous.
> The winner of the writing award *was* she.

Principal Parts

A verb has four principal parts: present, present participle, past, and past participle. The present participle is formed by adding *-ing* to the present. The past and the past participle of regular verbs are formed by adding *-d* or *-ed* to the present.

Present	Present Participle	Past	Past Participle
walk	walking	walked	walked
wave	waving	waved	waved

The past and the past participle of irregular verbs are not formed by adding *-d* or *-ed* to the present.

Present	Present Participle	Past	Past Participle
do	doing	did	done
fly	flying	flew	flown
put	putting	put	put

The present participle is often used with forms of the verb *be*.
We *are walking* to school.
I *was doing* my homework.

The past participle is often used with forms of the verb *have*.
We *have walked* this way before.
He *has done* his homework.

Regular Verbs

The past and the past participle of regular verbs are formed by adding *-d* or *-ed* to the present.

Present	Past	Past Participle
jump	jumped	jumped
paste	pasted	pasted

Verb Phrases

A verb phrase is made up of one or more helping verbs and a main verb.
I *should have shown* you my drawings.
I *am entering* them in the art contest.
You *can see* them there.

In questions and some statements, the parts of a verb phrase may be separated.
Did Caroline *bring* the potato salad?
Marcus *has* not *arrived* yet.

Mechanics

CAPITAL LETTERS

Use a capital letter to begin the first word in a sentence.
> Tomorrow is my birthday.

Use a capital letter to begin the first word in a direct quotation.
> Patrick Henry said, "Give me liberty or give me death."

Use a capital letter to begin a proper noun. A proper noun names a particular person, place, or thing.
> Jesse Owens competed in the Olympics in Berlin.
> John F. Kennedy attended Harvard University.
> This year Easter falls on Sunday, March 27.
> The White House is on Pennsylvania Avenue.
> Some Catholics are Democrats, and some are Republicans.
> The head of the local Red Cross is Cora Smith.

Use a capital letter to begin a proper adjective.
> I love to eat Chinese food.

Use a capital letter to begin a title that precedes a person's name.
> Mrs. Novak
> Dr. Ramirez
> Governor Charles Ryan

Use a capital letter for initials in a person's name.
> M. L. King = Martin Luther King
> George W. Bush = George Walker Bush

Use a capital letter for abbreviations when a capital letter would be used if the word were written in full.
> Sun. = Sunday   Oct. = October

Use a capital letter to begin the directions North, South, East, and West when they refer to specific regions of the country.
> On our trip to the West, we saw the Painted Desert.

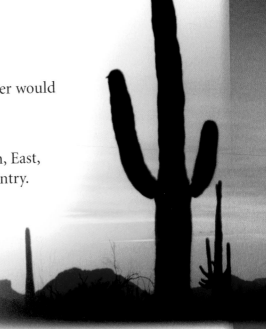

Use a capital letter to begin the important words in the title of a book, movie, TV show, play, poem, song, artwork, sacred book, article, or essay. The first and last words of a title are always capitalized. Articles, prepositions, and conjunctions are usually not capitalized unless they are the first or last word of the title.

> *The Secret Garden*
> "Sing a Song of Cities"
> *The Lion King*

Use a capital letter to begin every line of most poems and songs.

> My country, 'tis of thee,
> Sweet land of liberty,
> Of thee I sing.

The personal pronoun *I* is always a capital letter.

PUNCTUATION

Apostrophes

Use an apostrophe to form possessive nouns.

> Keisha's skateboard
> the children's lunches
> the horses' stalls

Use an apostrophe to replace the letters left out in a contraction.

> didn't   can't   wasn't

Commas

Use a comma to separate the words in a series.

> Mark, Anton, and Cara made the scenery.
> They hammered, sawed, and nailed.

Use a comma or commas to separate a name in direct address.

> Carl, will you help me?
> Do you think, Keshawn, that we will finish today?

Use a comma before the coordinating conjunction when two short sentences are combined in a compound sentence.

> Dad will heat the soup, and I will make the salad.
> Dad likes noodle soup, but I like bean soup.

Use a comma to separate the names of a city and state.

> She comes from Philadelphia, Pennsylvania.

Use a comma or commas to separate a direct quotation from the rest of the sentence. When a question mark or exclamation point ends a quotation at the beginning of a sentence, the comma is not needed.

"Hey," called Mario, "where are you going?"
"I'm going to the movies," Juana answered.
"Hurry up!" Paco yelled.

Use a comma after the word *yes* or *no* that introduces a sentence.

No, I can't go to the movies tonight.

Use a comma after the closing of a letter and after the salutation of a personal letter.

Exclamation Point
Use an exclamation point after an exclamatory sentence.

We won the game!

Use an exclamation point after an interjection.

Wow! The ice cream looks delicious.

When an exclamation point is part of a direct quotation, it is placed inside the quotation marks. When the exclamation point is not part of the quotation, it is placed outside the quotation marks.

Tom yelled, "I quit!"
I was shocked when she said, "I'll do it"!

Periods
Use a period after a declarative or an imperative sentence.

The cat is hungry.
Please feed it.

Use a period after most abbreviations.

| Sun. | Sept. | ft. | yd. | a.m. |
| Ave. | St. | gal. | oz. | p.m. |

Periods are not used after abbreviations for metric measures.

km   cm

Use a period after a personal title.

Mr. Frank Cummings   Dr. Hilda Doolittle
Mrs. Joanna Clark   Sgt. Barry Lindon

Use a period after an initial.

    John F. Kennedy   U.S.A.

    J. K. Rowling   B.S.A.

Question Marks

Use a question mark after an interrogative sentence.

    Where are you going?

When a question mark is part of a direct quotation, it is placed inside the quotation marks. When the question mark is not part of the quotation, it is placed outside the quotation marks.

    The teacher asked, "Where is Nepal?"

    Did the teacher say, "Nepal is in Asia"?

Quotation Marks

Use quotation marks to show the exact words a person says in a direct quotation.

    Carla said, "I can't find my markers."

    "Where," asked her mother, "did you leave them?"

Use quotation marks around the titles of poems, stories, or magazine articles. Titles of books, plays, movies, magazines, and artworks are italicized when they are typed and underlined when they are handwritten. Titles of sacred books are not italicized or underlined.

    "Paul Revere's Ride"

    "Snow White and the Seven Dwarfs"

    Harry Potter and the Half-Blood Prince

    <u>Mona Lisa</u>

    the Bible

Index

A

Abbreviations, 476–77, 525, 527
Action verbs, 386–87, 523
Addresses, 84, 85, 480–81, 526
Adjective phrases, 424–25, 490–91, 515
Adjectives, 361–84
  comparison with, 376–77, 378–79, 380–81, 508–09
  definition of, 362, 484, 508
  demonstrative, 358–59, 517
  descriptive, 362–63, 510
  diagramming, 484–85
  expanding sentences with, 244, 245, 246
  interrogative, 382–83, 510
  possessive, 350–51, 510
  prepositional phrases as, 424–25, 490–91, 515
  proper, 364–65, 510
  as subject complements, 374–75, 444–45, 488, 520
  suffixes for, 134–35
  that tell how many, 372–73, 509
  using exact, 24–25
  words used as nouns and, 334–35
  See also Adjective phrases
Adverb clauses, 418–19, 456, 457, 502–3, 511
Adverb phrases, 426–27, 490–91, 515
Adverbs, 409–20
  comparison with, 412–13, 511
  definition of, 410–11, 484, 510–11
  dependent clauses as, 418–19, 456, 457, 502–3, 511
  diagramming, 484–85
  expanding sentences with, 244, 245, 246
  prepositional phrases as, 426–27, 490–91, 515
  suffixes for, 136–37
  troublesome, 414–15
  See also Adverb phrases

Almanacs, 292, 293
Antecedents, 354–55, 511
Antonyms, 248–51
Apostrophes, 320, 356, 468–69, 512, 514, 526
Articles, definite and indefinite, 366–67, 368–69, 509
Atlases, 291, 292
Audience
  descriptions, 122, 123
  how-to articles, 46, 47
  how-to talks, 66
  oral book reports, 180, 181
  oral descriptions, 142
  oral personal narratives, 28
  oral research reports, 294
  personal narratives, 10
  persuasive speeches, 256
  persuasive writing, 242
  storytellers' contests, 218

B

Being verbs, 386–87, 523
Body
  book reports, 164, 165
  business letters, 84, 85, 90–91, 480, 481
  how-to articles, 48
  oral personal narratives, 28
  personal narratives, 12
  persuasive speeches, 256
  persuasive writing, 236
  research reports, 276, 277
Body language, 144, 145, 219, 257
Book reports, 158–95
  body, 164, 165
  characters, 160, 162
  conclusions, 164, 165
  content editing, 188–89
  copyediting, 192–93
  drafting, 186–87
  facts and opinions in, 162, 163, 166–67, 176–79
  introductions, 164, 165, 167
  oral, 180–83
  planning, 166

  plot summaries, 160–61, 163, 166
  prewriting, 184–85
  proofreading, 193
  publishing, 194–95
  purpose of, 164
  revising, 190–91
  settings, 160, 162, 166
  themes, 162, 163, 166
Books
  citation of, 280, 281
  in libraries, 252–55
  titles of, 472–73, 526, 528
Business letters. *See* Letters, business
Business telephone calls, 104–7

C

Capitalization, 470–82
  abbreviations, 476–77, 525
  direct quotations, 478, 479, 525
  titles of works, 472–73, 526
  uses of, 470–71, 474–75, 525–26
Catalogs, library, 254–55
Checklists
  business telephone calls, 106
  content editor's, 36, 74, 112, 150, 188, 226, 264, 302
  copyeditor's, 40, 78, 116, 154, 192, 230, 268, 306
  Internet research, 62
  proofreader's, 41, 79, 117, 155, 193, 231, 269, 307
Chronological order, 126–27, 143
Clauses, 418, 511. *See also* Adverb clauses; Dependent clauses; Independent clauses
Collective nouns, 322–23, 513, 521
Commas
  after *yes* and *no*, 466–67, 527
  in compound sentences, 96, 97, 454, 455, 464–65, 526
  in direct address, 330, 331, 466–67, 526

with direct quotations, 478, 479, 527

in a series, 462–63, 526

uses of, 526–27

Common nouns, 314–15, 513

Comparative degree, 376–77, 378–79, 380–81, 412–13, 508

Complex sentences, 456–57, 519

Compound sentences

commas in, 96, 97, 454, 455, 464–65, 526

coordinating conjunctions with, 96, 97, 428–29

definition of, 454–55, 500, 519

diagramming, 500–501

Compound words, 286–89

Conclusions

book reports, 164, 165

how-to articles, 48, 49

oral personal narratives, 28

oral research reports, 296, 297

personal narratives, 12, 13

persuasive speeches, 257, 259

persuasive writing, 238

research reports, 276, 277

Conjunctions, 428, 512. *See also* Coordinating conjunctions; Subordinate conjunctions

Content editing, 36–37, 74–75, 112–13, 150–51, 188–89, 226–27, 264–65, 302–3

Contractions, 356–57, 468–69, 512, 526

Coordinating conjunctions

commas with, 454–55, 464–65, 526

with compound sentence parts, 98–99, 428–29, 448

with compound sentences, 96–97, 428–29, 454–55

definition of, 428–29, 512

diagramming, 500

Copyediting, 40, 78, 116, 154, 192–93, 230–31, 268–69, 306–7

Count nouns, 322–23, 380–81, 514

Creative writing. *See* Tall tales

D

Declarative sentences, 436–37, 460, 461, 519, 527

Demonstrative adjectives, 370–71, 509–10

Demonstrative pronouns, 358–59, 517

Dependent clauses

as adverbs, 418–19, 456, 457, 511

definition of, 418, 430, 431, 456, 502, 512

Descriptions, 120–57

audience, 122, 123

chronological order, 126–27

content editing, 150–51

copyediting, 154

drafting, 148–49

graphic organizers for, 130–33, 147

oral, 142–45

prewriting, 146–47

proofreading, 155

publishing, 156–57

revising, 152–53

sensory details in, 122, 124–25, 142, 149

spatial order in, 126–27

visualizing, 122, 123

Descriptive adjectives, 362–63, 510

Diagramming, 483–506

adjectives, 484–85

adverb clauses, 502–3

adverbs, 484–85

basics of, 484–85

compound direct objects, 496–97

compound indirect objects, 496–97

compound predicates, 494–95

compound sentences, 500–501

compound subject complements, 498–99

compound subjects, 494–95

direct objects, 484–85, 496–97

indirect objects, 486–87, 496–97

interjections, 492–93

predicates, 484–85, 494–95

prepositional phrases, 490–91

subject complements, 488–89

subjects, 484–85, 494–95

Dialog, 225

Dictionaries, 138–41

Direct address, 330–31, 466–67, 514, 526

Direct objects

compound, 98, 99, 450–51, 496–97, 513

definition of, 326, 344–45, 442–43, 484, 513

diagramming, 484–85, 496–97

nouns as, 326–27, 329

pronouns as, 344–45

Direct quotations, 474, 475, 478–79, 525, 527, 528

Drafting, 34–35, 72–73, 110–11, 148–49, 186–87, 224–25, 262–63, 300–301

E

Encyclopedias, 280, 281, 290, 291, 292

End punctuation, 460–61. *See also* Exclamation points; Periods; Question marks

Exaggeration, 206, 207

Exclamation points

after exclamatory sentences, 436, 437, 460–61, 519, 527

after interjections, 432, 433, 513, 527

Exclamatory sentences, 436–37, 460, 461, 519, 527

F

Facts and opinions, 162, 163, 166–67, 176–79, 242, 243
Fewer/less, 380–81
Fiction books, 242, 243
Figurative language, 206–9
Flowcharts, for how-to articles, 71
Forms, filling out, 100–103
Future tenses
    definition of, 521
    perfect, 404–5, 521
    progressive, 398–99, 521
    simple, 396–97

G

Good/well, 414, 415
Graphic organizers
    flowcharts, 71
    Venn diagrams, 132–33
    word webs, 130–31, 147, 283

H

Helping verbs, 388, 389, 523
Homophones, 210–13
How-to articles, 44–81
    audience, 46, 47
    body, 48
    conclusions, 48, 49
    content editing, 74–75
    copyediting, 78
    drafting, 72–73
    flowcharts for, 71
    introductions, 48, 49
    point of view, 46, 47
    prewriting, 70–71
    proofreading, 79
    publishing, 80–81
    revising, 76–77
    step-by-step order in, 50–53, 54–57
    topics, 46, 47
    transition words in, 54–57
    See also How-to talks
How-to talks, 66–69

I

Imperative sentences, 436–37, 460, 461, 519, 527
Independent clauses (main clauses), 418, 430, 431, 454, 456, 512
Indirect objects
    definition of, 328, 346, 442–43, 486, 496–97, 513
    diagramming, 486–87, 496–97
    nouns as, 328–29
    pronouns as, 346–47, 517
Intensive pronouns, 352–53, 517
Interjections, 432–33, 492–93, 513, 527
Internet. *See* Web sites
Interrogative adjectives, 382–83, 510
Interrogative pronouns, 358–59, 517
Interrogative sentences, 436–37, 460, 461, 519, 528
Introductions
    book reports, 164, 165, 167
    how-to articles, 48, 49
    oral personal narratives, 28
    oral research reports, 296, 297
    personal narratives, 12, 13, 14
    persuasive speeches, 256
    persuasive writing, 236, 238
    research reports, 276

L

Language
    figurative, 206–9
    formal, 86–87, 111
Less/fewer, 380–81
Less/least, 378–79, 380–81, 509
Letters, business, 82–119
    addresses, inside, 84, 85, 480, 481
    body, 84, 85, 90–91, 480, 481
    closings, 84, 85, 480–81
    content editing, 112–13
    copyediting, 116
    drafting, 110–11
    headings, 84, 85, 480, 481
    language of, 86–87, 111
    prewriting, 108–9
    proofreading, 117
    publishing, 118–19
    purposes of, 88, 89
    revising, 114–15
    salutations, 84, 85, 480, 481
    signatures, 84, 85, 480, 481
    types of, 88, 89
Libraries, 252–55
Linking verbs, 374, 406–7, 444, 488, 523
Listening tips, 31, 69, 106, 107, 144, 183, 221, 259, 297

M

Magazines (periodicals), 292, 293, 472–73
Metaphors, 208, 209
Meter, in poetry, 216, 217
More/most, 378–79, 509, 511

N

Negative words, 414, 415, 511
Noncount nouns, 322–23, 380–81, 514
Nonfiction books, 242, 243
Nonsense verse, 214–17
Note cards, 30, 258, 259, 278–79, 280
Note taking, 278–79
Nouns, 313–36
    collective, 322–23, 513, 521
    common, 314–15, 513
    count and noncount, 322–23, 380–81, 514
    definition of, 314–15, 513
    in direct address, 330–31, 514
    as objects, 326–27, 328–29
    proper, 314–15, 364–65, 470, 515

as subject complements, 324–25, 444–45, 488, 520
as subjects, 324–25
suffixes for, 134–35
using exact, 24, 25
words used as adjectives and, 334–35
words used as verbs and, 332–33
See also Plural nouns; Singular nouns

O

Object pronouns, 344–45, 346–47, 348–49, 517–18
Objects of prepositions, 326–27, 344–45, 422–23, 516
Opinions, 162, 163, 166–67, 176–79, 242, 243
Oral book reports, 180–83
Oral descriptions, 142–45
Oral personal narratives, 28–31
Oral research reports, 294–97
Order
  chronological, 126–27, 143
  spatial, 126–27
  step-by-step, 50–53, 54–57
  time, 14, 15
Organizing
  descriptions, 126–29, 143
  how-to talks, 66
  oral book reports, 180
  oral research reports, 294
  persuasive speeches, 258, 259
Outlines, 282–85

P

Past participle, 390–91, 392–93, 394–95, 523, 524
Past tenses
  irregular verbs, 392–93, 394–95, 523, 524
  perfect, 402–3, 522

progressive, 398–99, 522
regular verbs, 390–91, 524
simple, 396–97, 522
Perfect tenses, 400–401, 402–3, 404–5, 521, 522
Periodicals (magazines), 292, 293, 472–73
Periods, 436, 437, 460–61, 476, 519, 527
Personal narratives, 6–43
  audience, 10
  body, 12
  conclusions, 12, 13
  content editing, 36–37
  copyediting, 40
  details in, 8, 9
  drafting, 34–35
  introductions, 12, 13, 14
  oral, 28–31
  point of view, 8
  prewriting, 32–33
  proofreading, 41
  publishing, 42–43
  revising, 38–39
  time order, 14, 15
  tone of voice, 10, 11
  topics, 8, 9
Personal pronouns, 338–39, 340–41, 517. *See also* Pronouns
Persuasive speaking, 256–59
Persuasive writing, 234–71
  audience, 242
  body, 236
  conclusions, 238
  content editing, 264–65
  copyediting, 268–69
  drafting, 262–63
  introductions, 236, 238
  opinions and facts in, 242, 243
  positions on topics, 236, 237, 238, 239
  prewriting, 260–61
  proofreading, 269
  publishing, 270–71
  revising, 266–67
  tone of voice, 240, 241, 243, 263
  See also Persuasive speaking

Phrases, 515. *See also* Adjective phrases; Adverb phrases; Prepositional phrases; Verb phrases
Plural nouns
  definition of, 316–17, 318–19
  possessive, 320–21, 468–69, 514
Plural pronouns, 338–39, 518
Poetry
  nonsense verse, 214–17
  titles of, 472–73, 526, 528
Point of view, 8, 46, 47
Positions, for persuasive writing and speaking, 236, 237, 238, 239, 256
Positive degree, 376, 412, 508
Possessive adjectives, 350–51, 510
Possessive nouns
  apostrophes with, 468–69, 526
  definition of, 320–21, 514
Possessive pronouns, 350–51, 518
Practicing speeches, 30, 68, 69, 144, 145, 182, 220, 221, 258, 296, 297
Predicates
  complete, 440–41, 516
  compound, 98, 99, 494–95, 516
  definition of, 438, 484, 516
  diagramming, 484–85, 494–95
  simple, 438–39, 516
Prefixes, 172–75
Preparing speeches, 68, 69, 182, 220, 296
Prepositional phrases
  as adjectives, 424–25, 490–91, 515
  as adverbs, 426–27, 490–91, 515
  definition of, 326, 424, 515
  expanding sentences with, 246, 247
Prepositions, 422–23, 516. *See also* Objects of prepositions

Presenting speeches, 30, 181
Present participle, 390–91, 394–95, 524
Present tenses
    irregular verbs, 392–93, 394–95, 523, 524
    perfect, 400–401, 522
    progressive, 398–99, 522
    regular verbs, 390–91, 524
    simple, 396–97, 523
Prewriting, 32–33, 70–71, 108–9, 146–47, 184–85, 222–23, 260–61, 298–99
Progressive tenses, 398–99, 521, 522
Pronouns, 337–60
    antecedents and, 354–55, 511
    contractions that contain, 356–57, 512
    definition of, 338, 517
    demonstrative, 358–59, 517
    intensive, 352–53, 517
    interrogative, 382–83, 510
    object, 344–45, 346–47, 348–49, 517–18
    personal, 338–39, 340–41, 517
    possessive, 350–51, 518
    reflexive, 352–53, 518
    singular and plural, 338–39, 518
    subject, 342–43, 348–49, 518
Proofreading, 41, 79, 117, 155, 193, 231, 269, 307
Proper adjectives, 364–65, 510
Proper nouns, 314–15, 364–65, 470, 515
Publishing, 42–43, 80–81, 118–19, 156–57, 194–95, 232–33, 270–71, 308–9
Punctuation, 459–82, 526–28. *See also individual marks*

Q

Question marks, 436, 437, 460–61, 519, 528
Quotation marks, 225, 280, 478, 479, 528

Quotations, direct, 474, 475, 478–79, 525, 527, 528

R

Real/very, 414, 415
Reference books, 243, 290–92
Reflexive pronouns, 352–53, 518
Research reports, 272–309
    body, 276
    conclusions, 276
    content editing, 302–3
    copyediting, 306–7
    drafting, 300–301
    introductions, 276
    note taking, 278–79
    oral, 294–97
    outlines for, 282–85
    prewriting, 298–99
    proofreading, 307
    publishing, 308–9
    reference materials for, 290–93
    researching, 275
    revising, 304–5
    topics, 274, 275
    topic sentences, 276, 277
    Works Cited page, 280–81
Revising, 38–39, 76–77, 114–15, 152–53, 190–91, 228–29, 266–67, 304–5
Rhyme scheme, 216, 217
Roots, 92–95
Run-on sentences, 170–71

S

Semicolons, 454, 455
Sensory details, 122, 124–25, 142, 149
Sentences, 435–58
    combining parts of, 98–99
    complex, 456–57, 519
    declarative, 436–37, 460, 461, 519, 527
    definition of, 518
    exclamatory, 436–37, 460, 461, 519, 527

    expanding, 244–47
    imperative, 436–37, 460, 461, 519, 527
    interrogative, 436–37, 460, 461, 519, 528
    inverted order of, 446–47, 519
    natural order of, 446–47, 519
    revising, 168–71
    run-on, 170–71
    simple, combining, 96–97
    variety in, 16–19, 168, 244
    See also Compound sentences
Series, commas in, 462–63, 526
Similes, 206, 207, 208, 209
Simple sentences, combining, 96–97
Simple tenses, 396–97, 522, 523
Singular nouns
    definition of, 316–17, 318–19, 515
    possessive, 320–21, 468–69, 514
Singular pronouns, 338–39, 518
Spatial order, 126–27
Speeches
    how-to talks, 66–69
    oral book reports, 180–83
    oral descriptions, 142–45
    oral personal narratives, 28–31
    oral research reports, 294–97
    persuasive, 256–59
    storytellers' contests, 218–21
Step-by-step order, 50–53, 54–57
Storyteller's contests, 218–21
Subject complements
    adjectives as, 374–75, 444–45, 488, 520
    compound, 452–53, 498–99, 520
    definition of, 444, 488
    diagramming, 488–89, 498–99

linking verbs and, 406–7

nouns as, 324–25, 444–45, 488, 520

Subject pronouns, 342–43, 348–49, 518

Subjects

agreement with verbs, 520–21

complete, 440–41, 520

compound, 98, 99, 448–49, 494–95, 520

definition of, 438, 484, 520

diagramming, 484–85, 494–95

nouns as, 324–25

pronouns as, 342–43, 348–49, 518

simple, 438–39, 520

Subordinate conjunctions, 430–31, 456, 457, 502, 512

Suffixes, 134–37

Superlative degree, 376–77, 378–79, 380–81, 412–13, 508

Synonyms, 58–61

T

Tall tales, 196–233

content editing, 226–27

copyediting, 230–31

dialog in, 225

drafting, 224–25

heroes of, 198, 199, 200, 201, 202, 203

language of, 199, 204, 206

prewriting, 222–23

problems and solutions in, 198, 204, 205

proofreading, 231

publishing, 232–33

revising, 228–29

storyteller's contests, 218–21

Telephone calls, business, 104–7

Tenses, verb, 396, 521–23. *See also* Future tenses; Past tenses; Perfect tenses; Present tenses; Progressive tenses; Simple tenses

There is/there are, 416–17, 521

Thesaurus, 20–23

Time order, 14, 15

Titles of works

capitalization of, 472–73, 526

citation of, 280–81

punctuation of, 280, 528

Tone of voice

business telephone calls, 104

oral book reports, 181

oral descriptions, 144, 145

oral personal narratives, 29

personal narratives, 10, 11

persuasive speaking, 257

persuasive writing, 240, 241, 243, 263

storytellers' contests, 219

Topics

how-to articles, 46, 47

how-to talks, 66, 67

oral personal narratives, 28

personal narratives, 8, 9

research reports, 274, 275

Topic sentences, 276

Transition words, 54–57

V

Venn diagrams, 132–33

Verb phrases, 388–89, 515–16, 524

Verbs, 385–408

action, 386–87, 523

agreement with subjects, 520–21

being, 386–87, 523

definition of, 386, 523

diagramming, 484–85, 494–95

helping, 388, 389, 523

irregular, 392–93, 394–95, 523, 524

linking, 374, 406–7, 444, 488, 523

principal parts of (*see* Past participle; Past tenses; Present participle; Present tenses)

regular, 390–91, 524

suffixes for, 136–37

tenses, 396, 521–23 (*see also* Future tenses; Past tenses; Perfect tenses; Present tenses; Progressive tenses; Simple tenses)

using exact, 26–27

words used as nouns and, 332–33

See also Verb phrases

Verse, nonsense, 214–17

Very/real, 414, 415

Visual aids, 68, 181, 295

W

Web sites

citation of, 281

filling out forms on, 100, 103

as resources, 62–65

Well/good, 414, 415

Words, using exact, 24–27, **187**

Word webs, 130–31, 147, 283

Works Cited page, 280–81

Writer's Workshops

book reports, 184–95

business letters, 108–19

descriptions, 146–57

how-to articles, 70–81

personal narratives, 32–43

persuasive writing, 260–71

research reports, 298–309

tall tales, 222–33

Acknowledgments

Literature

Excerpt from *Sarah, Plain and Tall* by Patricia MacLachlan. Copyright © 1985 by Patricia MacLachlan. Used by permission of HarperCollins Publishers.

"A Foolish Cow" and "The Otter and the Ocelot" from *It's Raining Pigs & Noodles* by Jack Prelutsky. Text copyright © 2000 by Jack Prelutsky. Used by permission of HarperCollins Publishers.

"Nonsense!" by Jack Prelutsky. *The Random House Book of Poetry for Children*. Copyright © 1983. Published by Random House Books for Young Readers.

"Eletelephony" by Laura Richards. *Tirra Lirra: Rhymes Old and New*. Copyright © 1955. Published by Little, Brown and Company.

Excerpt from *American Tall Tales* by Adrien Stoutenburg. Copyright © 1966 by Adrien Stoutenburg. Published by Puffin Books, Penguin (USA) Inc.

Excerpt from *Little House in the Big Woods* by Laura Ingalls Wilder. Text copyright © 1932 by Laura Ingalls Wilder. Copyright renewed 1960 by Roger L. MacBride. Published by HarperCollins Publishers.

Cover from *Frindle* by Andrew Clements. Text copyright © 1996 by Andrew Clements. Illustrations copyright © 1996 by Brian Selznick. Published by Aladdin Paperbacks, an imprint of Simon & Schuster Children's Publishing Division.

Cover from *A Week in the Woods* by Andrew Clements. Copyright © 2002 by Andrew Clements. Published by Aladdin Paperbacks, an imprint of Simon & Schuster Children's Publishing Division.

Cover from *James and the Giant Peach* by Roald Dahl. Illustrations copyright © 1996 by Lane Smith. Published by Puffin Books, Penguin Books USA Inc.

Cover from *United Tates of America* by Paula Danziger. Copyright © 2002 by Paula Danziger. Book design by Steve Scott. Published by Scholastic Inc.

Cover from *Skylark* by Patricia MacLachlan. Copyright © 1994 by Patricia MacLachlan. Published by HarperCollins Children's Books.

Illustration

Doron Ben-Ami: Illustrations: 7, 13, 47, 50, 52(b), 61, 85, 91, 97, 99, 104, 121, 123, 132, 140, 149, 151(b), 155, 157, 170, 173, 174, 187, 204, 205, 211, 215, 235, 237, 245, 249, 252, 263, 265, 281, 287, 289

Photography

Alamy: 374, 389, 437, 441, 454, 463, 465, 467, 469, 470, 501

Corbis: 137, 146, 147, 151(t & b), 153, 157, 197, 199, 217(t), 273, 324, 325, 329, 338, 343, 345, 349, 351, 360, 371, 430

Getty: 11, 89, 120, 125, 129, 131, 144, 158, 162, 175, 182, 216, 234, 243, 246(t), 250, 255, 258, 272, 275, 280(t), 284(b), 288, 291, 299, 300, 308 342, 408, 420, 443, 444, 452, 457

Phil Martin Photography: 8, 15, 16, 19, 21, 24, 28, 30, 35, 40, 49, 51, 54, 55, 59, 64, 66, 68, 73, 75, 79, 86(b), 93, 95, 100, 101, 103, 107, 108, 111, 112, 114-115, 116, 117, 134, 138, 142, 150, 155, 160, 161, 163, 165, 166, 167, 172, 176, 180, 181, 183, 187, 188, 189, 191, 195, 198, 202, 204, 207, 218, 219, 220(br), 221, 226, 233, 240, 242(tl), 251(b), 253, 256, 257, 259, 261, 271, 274, 279, 285, 290, 294, 295, 296, 297, 298, 303, 306, 307, 344, 348, 350, 356, 383(b)

Northwind Picture Archive: 10, 12, 23, 26, 31, 86(t), 98(t), 196, 203(t), 206, 213, 220(t), 276, 277

Stock Montage: 6, 44, 48, 52(t), 60, 65, 69, 82, 88, 92, 102, 106, 141, 164, 168, 179, 239, 282, 292

Loyola Press has made every effort to locate the copyright holders for the cited works used in this publication and to make full acknowledgment for their use. In the case of any omissions, the Publisher will be pleased to make suitable acknowledgments in future editions.